P9-BYQ-866

HTML 4

FOR THE WORLD WIDE WEB

VISUAL QUICKSTART GUIDE FOURTH EDITION

 **Peachpit Press**

by Elizabeth Castro

HTML 4 for the World Wide Web, Fourth Edition:
Visual QuickStart Guide
by Elizabeth Castro

Peachpit Press
1249 Eighth Street
Berkeley, CA 94710
(510) 524-2178
(510) 524-2221 (fax)

Find us on the World Wide Web at: http://www.peachpit.com
Or check out Liz's Web site at http://www.cookwood.com/
Or contact Liz directly at html@cookwood.com

Peachpit Press is a division of Addison Wesley Longman

Copyright © 2000 by Elizabeth Castro
All images (except photographs of wild animals)
are copyright © 1997–2000 by Elizabeth Castro

Cover design: The Visual Group

Notice of rights

All rights reserved. No part of this book may be reproduced or transmitted in any form or by any means, electronic, mechanical, photocopying, recording, or otherwise, without prior written permission of the publisher. For more information on getting permission for reprints and excerpts, contact Gary-Paul Prince at Peachpit Press.

Notice of liability

The information in this book is distributed on an "As is" basis, without warranty. While every precaution has been taken in the preparation of this book, neither the author nor Peachpit Press shall have any liability to any person or entity with respect to any loss or damage caused or alleged to be caused directly or indirectly by the instructions contained in this book or by the computer software and hardware products described herein.

Trademarks

Visual QuickStart Guide is a registered trademark of Peachpit Press, a division of Addison Wesley Longman. Many of the designations used by manufacturers and sellers to distinguish their products are claimed as trademarks. Where those designations appear in this book, and Peachpit Press was aware of a trademark claim, the designations appear as requested by the owner of the trademark. All other product names and services identified throughout this book are used in editorial fashion only and for the benefit of such companies. No such use, or the use of any trade name, is intended to convey endorsement or other affiliation with this book.

ISBN: 0-201-35493-4

0 9 8 7 6 5 4

Printed in the United States of America

For my parents
(all four of them!)
who didn't always agree,
but who supported me anyway.

Special thanks to:

Nancy Davis, *at Peachpit Press, who I'm happy to report is not only my awesome editor, but also my friend.*

Kate Reber, *at Peachpit Press, for her help getting this book printed.*

Nolan Hester, *formerly of Peachpit Press, who edited the first and second editions of this book, and who tech-edited this one.*

Andreu Cabré, *for his feedback, for his great Photoshop tips, and for sharing his life with me.*

Llumi *and* **Xixo**, *for chasing cherry tomatoes and each other around my office and for helping me think up examples of HTML documents.*

And all the readers *of earlier versions of this book, who took the time to write me (html@cookwood.com) with accolades, questions, and suggestions.*

Table of Contents

Table of Contents

Introduction

Using the latest versions!

This book explains how to create Web pages using HTML 4 and Cascading Style Sheets, Level 2, which are currently the latest versions of each.

The World Wide Web is the Gutenberg press of our time. Just about anyone can create their own Web site and then present it to the Internet public. Some Web pages belong to businesses with services to sell, others to individuals with information to share. You get to decide what your page will be like.

All Web pages are written with HTML. HTML lets you format text, add graphics, sound, and video, and save it all in a Text Only or ASCII file that any computer can read. (Of course, to project video or play sounds, the computer must have the necessary hardware.) The key to HTML is in the *tags*, keywords enclosed in less than (<) and greater than (>) signs, that indicate what kind of content is coming up.

While there are many software programs that will create HTML code for you *(see page 350)*, learning HTML yourself means you'll never be limited to a particular program's features. Instead you'll be able to add whatever you need without having to struggle with confusing software or wait for software updates.

In this book, you'll find clear, easy-to-follow instructions that will take you through the process of creating Web pages step-by-step. It is ideal for the beginner, with no knowledge of HTML, who wants to begin to create Web pages.

If you're already familiar with HTML, this book is a perfect reference guide. You can look up topics in the hefty index and consult just those subjects about which you need more information.

The Internet, the Web, and HTML

Sure, you've heard of the Internet, but what is it exactly? Simply put, the Internet is a collection of computers that are all connected to each other. Some people, typically at universities and large companies, have 24-hour connections, while others use a modem to link their home computers during a certain amount of time each day. Regardless of the type of connection, once you're on, you and your computer become a part of the Internet and are linked to every other computer that's also connected at that moment.

The World Wide Web, for its part, is much more ethereal. It is an ever-changing, kaleidoscopic collection of hundreds of millions of documents, all of which reside someplace on the Internet and are written in HTML.

HTML, or *HyperText Markup Language*, has two essential features—hypertext and universality. Hypertext means you can create a link in a Web page that leads the visitor to any other Web page or to practically anything else on the Internet. It means that the information on the Web can be accessed from many different directions. Tim Berners-Lee, the creator of the Web, wanted it to work more like a person's brain and less like a static source of data, such as a book.

Universality means that because HTML documents are saved as ASCII or Text Only files, virtually any computer can read a Web page. It doesn't matter if your visitors have Macintosh or Windows machines, or whether they're on a Unix box or even a hand-held device like a Palm. The Web is open to all.

Figure i.1 *Many pages, like the one shown, look almost the same on Internet Explorer for Windows 5 (top) and Netscape Communicator 4 for Macintosh. (You'll learn how to create layouts like these in Chapter 9, Tables.)*

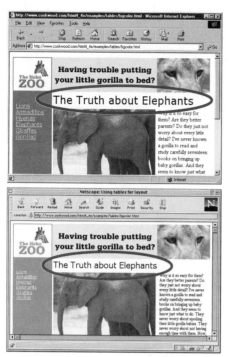

Figure i.2 *Take a closer look. In Explorer for Windows (top), all of the text—especially the header— is much larger than in Netscape for Macintosh. Images generally change little from browser to browser and platform to platform.*

Open but Not Equal

However, while HTML is available to all, that doesn't mean that everyone experiences it the same way. It's something like Central Park in New York City. You and I can both go take a walk there. However, if you live in a penthouse apartment on Fifth Avenue and I sleep on a bench, our view of the park will be quite different.

So it is with HTML. While practically any computer can display Web pages, what those pages actually look like depends on the type of computer, the monitor, the speed of the Internet connection, and lastly, the software used to view the page: the *browser*. The most popular browsers today are Internet Explorer and Netscape Communicator. There are versions of each for both Windows and Mac. Unfortunately none of these displays a Web page exactly like the next **(Figure i.2)**. So, in other words, it's not enough to design a beautiful park, you've also got to worry about your visitor's accommodations.

But as you worry, remember that your control is limited. While the New York City Tourist Board would like to ensure that everyone has a good time in their town, they're not handing out free vouchers for rooms at the Park Plaza Hotel. You can't either. You can only be aware that folks are viewing your pages with different setups and then create your pages accordingly—so that the largest number of visitors can view your page as close to the way you want them to as is possible. This book will show you how.

The Browser Wars

Now imagine what would happen if each hotel and apartment building on Fifth Avenue staked out a bit of Central Park and put a fence around it, limiting access to its own residents. It's bad enough that those of us on park benches can only glimpse in to "exclusive" areas. But, there's also the problem that folks from one hotel can't get to the piece of park that belongs to the other hotel. Instead of a rich, public resource, teeming with rollerbladers, hot dog carts, and strolling elders, the park is divided into small, sterile, isolated lots. This is what is happening on the Web.

In 1994, Netscape put up the first fences on the Web in the so-called browser wars. In order to attract users, they threw universality to the wind and created a set of extensions to HTML that only Netscape could handle. For example, Web surfers using Netscape could view pages with different size and color text, photographs (in JPEG format), background color and images, and in later versions, multiple pages in a single window, called frames. Surfers with any other browser would get errors and funny looking results. Or nothing at all.

But people liked those extensions so much that they flocked to Netscape's "hotel". By June of 1996, it had become the most popular computer program in the world with 38 million users.

Microsoft soon joined in and started fencing in its own chunk of the Web. Again, to attract users they added non-standard extensions to HTML that only Internet Explorer, Microsoft's browser, could recognize.

So who do you design for? Netscape users or Explorer users? It's a designer's nightmare. And the Web is suffering because of it.

The Push for Standards

The Web's United Nations is an organization called the World Wide Web Consortium (*www.w3.org*), often abbreviated as W3C, and directed by the Web's inventor, Tim Berners-Lee. Their aim is to convince the Web community of the importance of universality while attempting to satisfy its thirst for beautiful looking pages. They want to take down the fences.

Both Netscape Communications (now a part of America Online) and Microsoft are members of the W3C, as are other important Web-related companies, including Adobe and Macromedia (makers of some of the more important Web tools), and many others. The idea is that these companies come together and agree on the standards and then try to differentiate their products with speed, ease of use, price, or other features that don't turn the Web back into the tower of Babel.

Unfortunately, the W3C can not completely control the efforts of its members, it can only suggest compliance. And its members continue to strive for the biggest, baddest piece of software on the Web—and then to sell lots of copies of it.

According to The Web Standards Project (*www.webstandards.org*), founded by a coalition of top-flight designers disgusted with the increasing fragmentation of the Web, Web designers waste an incredible 25% of their time devising workarounds for proprietary tags, writing multiple versions of pages to satisfy each browser, and simply educating their clients about the impossibility of creating certain effects for all browsers.

The Push for Standards

The Current Battlegrounds

While support for the HTML 4 specification recommended by the W3C is almost complete, there continue to be skirmishes around several other key issues.

Cascading Style Sheets

One of the W3C's major efforts at peacekeeping was to develop Cascading Style Sheets (CSS), a system that separates the content of a page (written in HTML) from the format (written in CSS) and in so doing allows for more complete control over the design of a Web page while keeping the page universal. In addition, CSS can be applied to several pages at once, helping the designer save time by storing all the formatting in one file.

That was the theory, anyway. In practice, neither Microsoft nor Netscape, despite having participated in the development of CSS, has gotten around to fully implementing it in their browsers. In fact, the browser that best supports CSS is a newcomer to the battle: Opera, developed in Norway by a company whose chief technical officer is Håkon Lie, one of the major forces behind CSS at the W3C.

The lack of universal support for CSS has not discouraged designers from using it, however. CSS's powerful formatting and layout capabilities have attracted designers in much the same way that Netscape's extensions did in their day. With much the same problems: pages that work only on some browsers and that completely break down in others.

For a compatibility chart and complete set of tester pages—so that you can have an up-to-date reference of which browsers support which features of CSS and HTML 4—check out *www.cookwood.com/browser_tests/*.

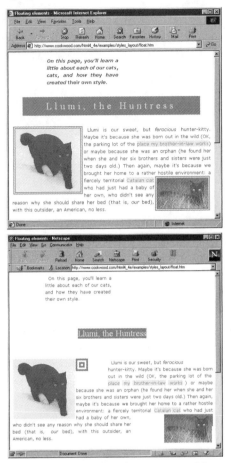

Figure i.3 *Netscape Communicator 4's woefully inadequate support for Cascading Style Sheets (bottom) in comparison to Internet Explorer 5 (top) is one of the major factors leading to its loss in popularity on the Web. It also makes designing cross-browser pages something of a nightmare. (Both illustrations are from Windows machines.)*

JavaScript, DOM, and DHTML

Advanced Web designers often use a scripting language called JavaScript and a system of naming the parts of the Web page—the Document Object Model, or DOM—together with HTML and CSS to create dynamic content on a page. These effects are sometimes called Dynamic HTML or DHTML.

While JavaScript has been standardized as ECMAScript, *(www.ecma.ch/stand/ECMA-262.htm)*, the major browsers have not come to an agreement about the DOM, despite the fact that the W3C has already issued a recommendation *(www.w3.org/DOM/)* about what it should look like.

The Current Battlegrounds

What To Do?

The Web Standards Project *(see page 15)* is demanding that each browser support CSS1, the DOM, and ECMAScript before slapping on any additional proprietary features. Until that happens, however, each Web designer will have to think about what kind of browser and computer their public is likely to use and then design their pages accordingly.

For example, if your desired audience is a group of cutting-edge Web designers, you can probably get away with using fewer standard tags and proprietary extensions—those folks probably have the latest version of Explorer or Netscape. On the other hand, if you want to reach the widest public possible, you may want to design for the lowest common denominator, eschewing CSS and DHTML altogether, and making your pages sharp, fast, and above all else, universal.

In addition, you might want to take a look at Statmark's site *(http://www.statmark.com)*, which offers statistics that reveal how many folks are using which browsers, on which platforms, with what kind of monitors, on which days of the week, and at what time of day (really!) You can use this incredibly rich source of data to help ensure that your pages are well designed for the majority of Web surfers.

This book explains all the standard HTML tags as well as the few non-standard extensions that are still supported only by Netscape or only by Explorer (which are marked with an appropriate icon). It also describes Cascading Style Sheets Level 2 in detail. Note that some versions and platforms of some browsers do not completely support the HTML 4 or CSS specifications.

Figure i.4 *In this book, non-standard HTML code that is only recognized by Netscape is marked with the N only icon (left). Non-standard code that is only recognized when viewed with Internet Explorer is marked with the IE only icon (right).*

The Future: XML

One of the problems with the Web is that there is so much information, it's sometimes hard to find what you're looking for. Even the search indexes like AltaVista and Yahoo have a hard time keeping track of all of the pages. At present, the best search engine has catalogued less than 15% of the Web.

Part of the W3C's answer to this problem is XML, *Extensible Markup Language*. XML, a sort of cousin to HTML, has two important features. First, it allows Web page creators to create their own tags according to their needs: A Wall Street broker's page might have <stockname> and <openbid> tags, while a Llama farm's page might have <sire> and <cria> tags.

Second, XML completely separates content from formatting through the use of style sheets. That means that there is no data in an XML document contained in tags that only give formatting instructions. Rather, all the data is identified by the XML tags in which it is enclosed. Pages written in XML will be much easier for computers to read and to catalog, making search engines more powerful and the Web a more useful tool.

The problems? First, at present, only Internet Explorer 5 can read XML files directly. Older browsers need XML to be converted to HTML before viewing. Second, and more importantly, XML is nowhere near as forgiving as HTML. In fact, it's downright persnickety. It fusses about upper- and lowercase letters, quotation marks, and closing tags, among other things. Since many Web designers won't directly feel the benefits of XML's advanced features, XML's pickiness may mean that most regular folks will stick with HTML—which should be fine. Browsers will continue to support HTML for years to come.

The Future: XML

The HTML VQS Web Site

With the Web constantly changing, it seemed most appropriate to add a dynamic element to this book: the HTML VQS Web site. In fact, there are two.

At *www.peachpit.com/vqs/html4* you can find the full table of contents, all of the example files, an excerpt from the book, and a list (hopefully short) of errata.

At *www.cookwood.com*, you'll find a gallery of pages created by folks who have read this and earlier versions of this book, links to reviews and comments, updates, and all of the example files.

You'll also find a lively Question and Answer board *(www.cookwood.com/html4_4e/qanda)* where you can post your most vexing questions—and easy ones too. I hang out there regularly and will do my best to answer. If you're so inclined, feel free to step in and answer questions yourself. Your help will be greatly appreciated.

Finally, because cross-browser testing is such an important and ever-changing issue these days, you'll also be able to find an up-to-date compatibility chart and complete set of tester pages for both HTML 4 and CSS on my Web site *(www.cookwood.com/browser_tests/)*.

And you can always write me directly at html@cookwood.com with any questions, suggestions, or even complaints that you may have.

See you on the Web!

HTML Building Blocks

Writing HTML

You can create an HTML document with any word processor or text editor, including the very basic TeachText or SimpleText on the Mac and Notepad or WordPad for Windows, both of which come free with the corresponding system software.

You can also buy a Web page editor, like PageMill or Dreamweaver, and then use the information in this book to tweak the page until it's exactly the way you want it. Web page editors are discussed in more detail in Appendix A, *HTML Tools*, starting on page 349.

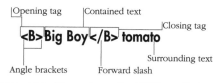

Figure 1.1 *The anatomy of an HTML tag. Notice there are no extra spaces between the contained text and the angle brackets (greater than and less than signs). Also, the surrounding text, in this example, the word* tomato, *is unaffected by the tag.*

HTML Tags

HTML tags are commands written between less than (<) and greater than (>) signs, also known as *angle brackets*, that indicate how the browser should display the text **(Figure 1.1)**. There are opening and closing versions for many (but not all) tags, and the affected text is *contained* within the two tags. Both the opening and closing tags use the same command word but the closing tag carries an initial extra forward slash symbol /.

Attributes

Many tags have special *attributes* that offer a variety of options for the contained text. The attribute is entered between the command word and the final greater than symbol **(Figure 1.2)**. Often, you can use a series of attributes in a single tag. Simply write one after the other—in any order—with a space between each one.

Figure 1.2 *Some tags can take optional attributes that further define the formatting desired.*

HTML Tags

Values

Attributes in turn often have *values*. In some cases, you must pick a value from a small group of choices. For example, the CLEAR attribute for the BR tag can take values of *left, right,* or *all.* Any other value given will be ignored **(Figure 1.3)**.

Other attributes are more strict about the *type* of values they accept. For example, the HSPACE attribute of the IMG tag will accept only integers as its value, and the SRC attribute of the IMG tag will only accept URLs for its value **(Figure 1.4)**.

Quotation marks

Generally speaking, values should be enclosed in straight quotation marks "" (NOT curly ones ""). However, you can omit the quote marks if the value only contains letters (A–Z, a–z), digits (0–9), a hyphen (-), or a period (.). I usually use quotes around URLs to ensure that they're not misinterpreted by the server.

Upper- and lowercase letters

I display the HTML code in this book in all uppercase letters for one simple reason—to help you distinguish it from the rest of the text. There is no reason you have to follow that example, unless it's more comfortable for you to do so. Browsers will recognize HTML code whether you type it in all caps or in small letters or in a mixture of both.

Do note, however, that XHTML, which is the same thing as HTML but in "XMLese" *(see page 19)* is indeed case sensitive. Still, you only have to worry about it if you're creating XML documents.

Value for CLEAR

<BR CLEAR=left>

Figure 1.3 *Some tags, like BR shown here, take attributes with given values, of which you can choose only one. You don't need to enclose one word values in quotation marks.*

SRC is an attribute of IMG
Value for SRC

<IMG SRC="image.gif" HSPACE=5>

HSPACE is also an attribute of IMG
Value for HSPACE

Figure 1.4 *Some tags, like IMG shown here, can take more than one attribute, each with its own values. Notice that while file names like* image.gif *are generally enclosed in double quotes, one word or numeric values like 5 without special symbols need not be.*

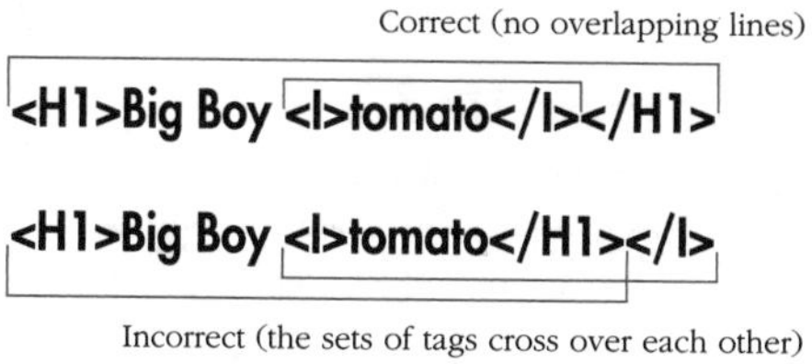

Correct (no overlapping lines)

<H1>Big Boy <I>tomato</I></H1>

<H1>Big Boy <I>tomato</H1></I>

Incorrect (the sets of tags cross over each other)

Figure 1.5 *To make sure your tags are correctly nested, connect each set with a line. None of your sets of tags should overlap any other set; each interior set should be completely enclosed within the next larger set.*

Nesting Tags

In some cases, you may want to modify your page contents with more than one tag. For example, you may want to add italic formatting to a word inside a header. There are two things to keep in mind here. First, not all tags can contain all other kinds of tags. As a general rule, those tags that affect entire paragraphs (the W3C calls this *block-level*) can contain tags that affect individual words or letters (*inline*), but not vice versa.

Second, order is everything. Whenever you use a closing tag it should correspond to the last unclosed opening tag. In other words, first A then B, then /B, and then /A **(Figure 1.5)**.

Nesting Tags

Spacing

HTML browsers will ignore any extra spaces that exist between the tags in your HTML document. You can use this to your advantage by adding spaces and returns to help view the elements in your HTML document more clearly while you're writing and designing your page **(Figure 1.6)**.

On the other hand, you won't be able to count on returns or spaces to format your document. A return at the end of a paragraph in your HTML document will not appear in the browsed page. Instead, you'll use a P tag *(see page 39)* to begin each new paragraph **(Figure 1.7)**.

However, you can't repeat several P tags to add space between paragraphs. The extra tags are simply ignored. Instead, you can use styles to specify precisely how much space should go between elements in your Web page *(see page 280)*. There are also several less-standard methods for controlling spacing *(see pages 39, 102, 106, and 109)*.

Tags with automatic line breaks

Block-level tags generally include automatic, logical line breaks. For example, you don't need to use a new paragraph tag after a header, since a header automatically includes a line break. In fact, you only need to insert a new paragraph tag if you're using the tag to apply styles *(see page 248)*. Some common block-level tags are P, H1, BR, UL, and TABLE.

Inline tags that affect only a few letters or words do not automatically begin on a new line. Some common inline tags are EM, B, and IMG.

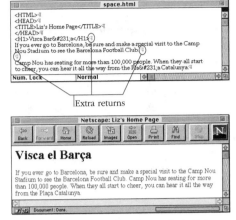

Extra returns

Figure 1.6 *Extra returns and spaces help distinguish the different parts of the HTML document in the text editor but are completely ignored by the browser.*

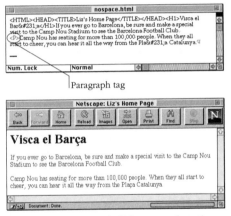

Paragraph tag

Figure 1.7 *I've removed all the returns from the document in Figure 1.6, but added a single <P> tag. The only difference in the final result is from the new tag.*

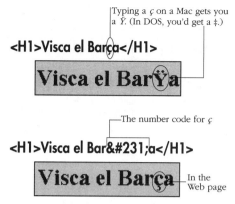

Typing a ç on a Mac gets you a Ÿ. (In DOS, you'd get a ‡.)

`<H1>Visca el Barça</H1>`

The number code for ç

`<H1>Visca el Bar&#231;a</H1>`

In the Web page

Figure 1.8 *To display a ç properly, you must use either its number or its name. It looks awful in your HTML document, but on the Web page, where it counts, it's beautiful—on any platform.*

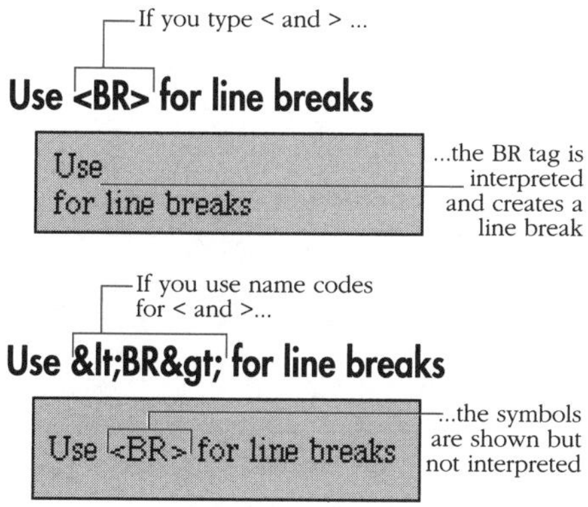

If you type < and > ...

Use `<BR>` for line breaks

...the BR tag is interpreted and creates a line break

If you use name codes for < and >...

Use `&lt;BR&gt;` for line breaks

...the symbols are shown but not interpreted

Figure 1.9 *You must use name or number codes to show the symbols <, >, ", and & on your Web page. See Special Symbols on page 353 for details.*

Special Symbols

The standard ASCII set contains 128 characters and can be used perfectly well for English documents. However, accents, curly quotes, and many commonly used symbols unfortunately cannot be found in this group. Luckily, HTML can contain any character in the full ISO Latin-1 character set (also known as ISO 8859-1). In Windows and Unix systems, just enter the character in the usual way and it will display properly in the browser.

Watch out! Even though you can type special characters, accents and so on in your Macintosh and DOS based PC, these systems do not use the standard ISO Latin-1 character set for the characters numbered 129-255 and will not display them correctly in the Web page. You must enter these special characters with either *name* or *number codes* **(Figure 1.8)**.

Name codes are more descriptive (and are case sensitive), like *é* for *é* and *Ñ* for *Ñ*. However, not every character has a name code. In that case, you will need to use a number code, which is composed of an ampersand, number symbol, the character number in the Latin-1 character set and a semicolon. The number code for *é* is *é* and for *Ñ* is *Ñ*. See *Special Symbols* on page 353 for a complete listing and more instructions.

There are four symbols that have special meanings in HTML documents. These are the greater than (>), less than (<), straight double quotation marks ("), and the ampersand (&). If you simply type them in your HTML document, the browser may attempt to interpret them **(Figure 1.9)**. To show the symbols themselves, use a name or number code.

File Names

A Web page is nothing more than a text document written with HTML tags. Like any other text document, Web pages have a file name that identifies the documents to you, your visitors, and to your visitors' Web browser. There are a couple tips to keep in mind when assigning file names to your Web pages that will help you organize your files, make it easier for your visitors to find and access your pages, and ensure that their browsers view the page correctly.

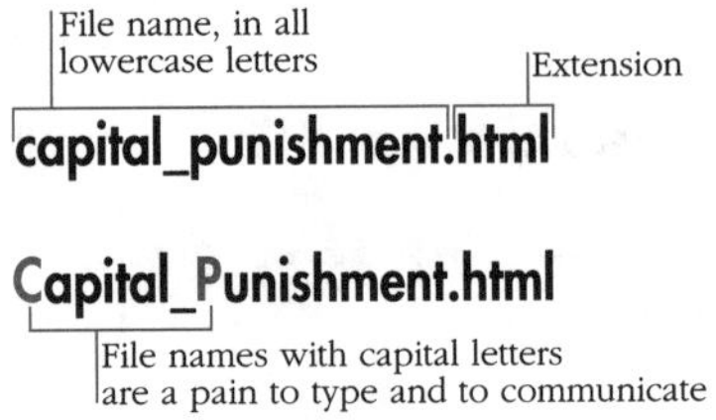

Use lowercase file names

Since the file name you choose for your Web page determines the address *(see page 27)* that your visitors will have to type to get to your page, you can save your visitors from inadvertent typos (and headaches) by using only lowercase letters in your file names. It's also a big help when you go to create links between your pages yourself. If all your file names have only small letters, it's just one less thing you'll have to worry about.

Use the proper extension

The principal way a browser knows that it should read a text document as a Web page is by looking at its extension: .htm or .html. If the page has some other extension, like say ".txt", the browser will treat it as text, and show all your nice HTML code to the visitor.

- Macintosh users—unless you're on a Mac server and *all* your visitors use Macs— this goes for you too.

- Windows folks, be aware that Windows doesn't always reveal a document's real extension. Save your Web pages within double quotes to be sure *(see page 34)*.

- Only folks on Windows 3.1 are limited to .htm. Practically everyone else can use either .htm or .html without problem. Just be consistent to avoid headaches.

File name, in all lowercase letters   Extension

capital_punishment.html

Capital_Punishment.html

File names with capital letters are a pain to type and to communicate

Figure 1.10 *Remember to use all lowercase letters for your file names and to add either the .htm or .html extension. Mixing upper and lowercase letters makes it harder for your visitors to type the proper address and find your page.*

http://www.yoursite.com/WebPages/ TORTURE/Capital_Punishment.html

Figure 1.11 *Don't forget to use all lowercase letters for your directories and folders as well. The key is consistency. If you don't use uppercase letters, your visitors (and you) don't have to waste time wondering, "Now, was that a capital C or a small one?"*

Figure 1.12 *Your basic URL contains a scheme, server name, path, and file name.*

Figure 1.13 *A URL with a trailing forward slash and no file name points to the default file in the last directory named (in this case the* liz *directory). Some common default file names are* index.html *and* default.htm.

Figure 1.14 *When the user clicks this URL, the browser will begin an FTP transfer of the file* prog.exe.

Figure 1.15 *A URL for a newsgroup looks a bit different. There are no forward slashes after the scheme and colon, and generally, there is no file name. (Although you could add the message number or ID, a message's extremely short lifespan limits its usefulness as a link.)*

Figure 1.16 *A URL for an e-mail address is similar in design to a newsgroup URL (Figure 1.15); it includes the* mailto *scheme followed by a colon but no forward slashes, and then the e-mail address itself.*

Figure 1.17 *To reference a file on your hard disk, use the* file *scheme. If you're on a Windows machine, specify your hard disk by letter and follow it with a vertical bar:* file:///c|/path/filename.

URLs

Uniform resource locator, or URL, is a fancy name for *address*. It contains information about where a file is and what a browser should do with it. Each file on the Internet has a unique URL.

The first part of the URL is called the *scheme*. It tells the browser how to deal with the file that it is about to open. One of the most common schemes you will see is HTTP, or Hypertext Transfer Protocol. It is used to access Web pages **(Figure 1.12)**.

The second part of the URL is the name of the server where the file is located, followed by the path that leads to the file and the file's name itself *(see page 26)*. Sometimes, a URL ends in a trailing forward slash with no file name given **(Figure 1.13)**. In this case the URL refers to the default file in the last directory in the path (which generally corresponds to the home page).

Other common schemes are HTTPS, for secure Web pages; FTP (File Transfer Protocol) for downloading files from the Net **(Figure 1.14)**; Gopher, for searching for information; News, for sending and reading messages posted to a Usenet newsgroup **(Figure 1.15)**; Mailto, for sending electronic mail **(Figure 1.16)**; and File, for accessing files on a local hard disk **(Figure 1.17)**.

A scheme is generally followed by a colon and two forward slashes. Mailto and News are exceptions; these take only a colon.

Notice that the File scheme uses three slashes. That's because the host, which in other schemes goes between the second and third slashes, is assumed to be the local computer. Always type schemes in lowercase letters.

Absolute URLs

URLs can be either absolute or relative. An *absolute URL* shows the entire path to the file, including the scheme, server name, the complete path, and the file name itself *(see page 26)*. An absolute URL is analogous to a complete street address, including name, street and number, city, state, zip code, and country. No matter where a letter is sent from, the post office will be able to find the recipient. In terms of URLs, this means that the location of the absolute URL itself has no bearing on the location of the actual file referenced—whether it is in a Web page on your server or on mine, an absolute URL will look exactly the same.

When you're referencing a file from someone else's server, you'll always use an absolute URL. You'll also need to use absolute URLs for FTP and Gopher sites and for newsgroups and e-mail addresses—in short, any kind of URL that doesn't use an HTTP protocol.

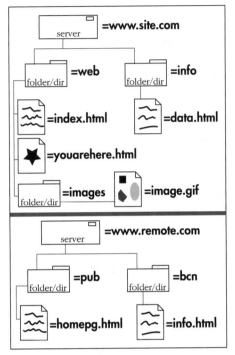

Figure 1.18 *Here is a typical, but simple representation of two servers (or hard disks), and the files that each contains. The table below shows the relative URLs for each file that you would use when writing the* youarehere.html *file. The absolute URLs shown would work in any file.*

File name	Absolute URL (anywhere)	Relative URL (in *youarehere.html*)
index.html	www.site.com/web/index.html	index.html
image.gif	www.site.com/web/images/image.gif	images/image.gif
data.html	www.site.com/info/data.html	../info/data.html
homepg.html	www.remote.com/pub/homepg.html	*(none: use absolute)*
info.html	www.remote.com/bcn/info.html	*(none: use absolute)*

Absolute URLs vs. Relative URLs

URLs

Inside the current folder, there's a
file called *index.html*

"index.html"

Figure 1.19 *The relative URL for a file in the same folder (see Figure 1.18) as the file that contains the link is just the file's name and extension.*

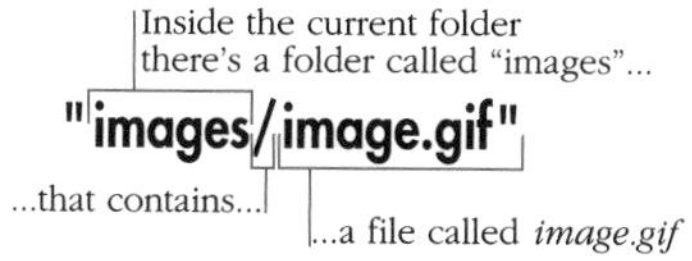

Inside the current folder
there's a folder called "images"...

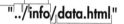
"images/image.gif"

...that contains...
...a file called *image.gif*

Figure 1.20 *For a file that is within a folder inside the current folder (see Figure 1.18), add the folder's name and a forward slash in front of the file name.*

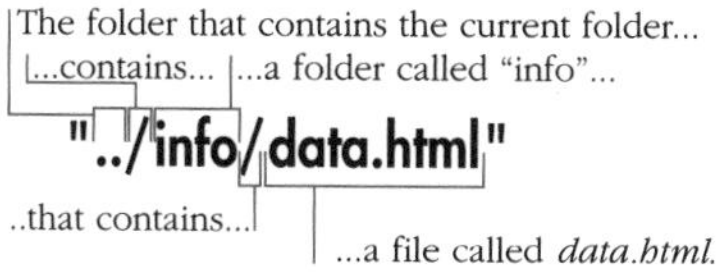

The folder that contains the current folder...
...contains... ...a folder called "info"...

"../info/data.html"

..that contains...
...a file called *data.html.*

Figure 1.21 *This file, as you can see in Figure 1.18, is in a folder that is inside the folder that contains the current folder (whew!). In that case, you use two periods and a slash to go up a level, and then note the subdirectory, followed by a forward slash, followed by the file name.*

Relative URLs

To give you directions to my neighbor's house, instead of giving her complete address, I might just say "it's three doors down on the right". This is a *relative* address—where it points to depends on where the information is given from. With the same information in a different city, you'd never find my neighbor.

In the same way, a *relative URL* describes the location of the desired file with reference to the location of the file that contains the URL itself. So, you might have the URL say something like "show the xyz image that's in the same directory as the current file".

Thus, the relative URL for a file that is in the same directory as the current file (that is, the one containing the URL in question) is simply the file name and extension **(Figure 1.19)**. You create the URL for a file in a subdirectory of the current directory with the name of the subdirectory followed by a forward slash and then the name and extension of the desired file **(Figure 1.20)**.

To reference a file in a directory at a *higher* level of the file hierarchy, use two periods and a forward slash **(Figure 1.21)**. You can combine and repeat the two periods and forward slash to reference any file on the same hard disk as the current file.

Generally, you should always use relative URLs. They're much easier to type and they make it easy to move your pages from a local system to a server—as long as the relative position of each file remains constant, the links will work correctly.

One added advantage of relative URLs is that you don't have to type the scheme—as long as it's HTTP.

Starting Your Web Page

This chapter explains how to design and organize your site, how to give your page a little structure, how to begin to write the contents of your page, and then how to save and look at what you've created.

Designing Your Site

Although you can just jump in and start writing HTML pages right away *(see page 34)*, it's a good idea to first think about and design your site. That way, you'll give yourself direction and save reorganizing later.

To design your site:

1. Figure out why you're creating this page. What do you want to convey?

2. Think about your audience. How can you tailor your content to appeal to this audience? For example, should you add lots of graphics or is it more important that your page download quickly?

3. How many pages will you need? What sort of structure would you like it to have? Do you want visitors to go through your site in a particular direction, or do you want to make it easy for them to explore in any direction?

4. Sketch out your site on paper.

5. Devise a simple, consistent naming system for your pages, images, and other external files *(see page 26)*.

✔ Tips

■ On the other hand, don't overdo the design phase of your site. At some point, you've got to dig in and start writing.

■ If you're not very familiar with the Web, do some surfing first to get an idea of the possibilities. You might start with Yahoo's Cool Links: *http://www.yahoo.com/ Entertainment/Cool_Links/*.

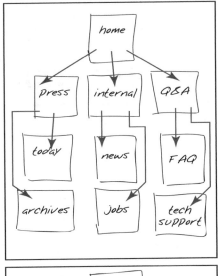

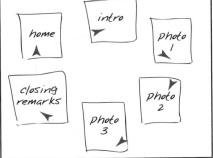

Figure 2.1 *Sketching out your site and thinking about what it might contain can help you decide what sort of structure it needs: a centralized, hierarchical model (top), a circular model that leads the visitor from one page to the next (above), or some other system.*

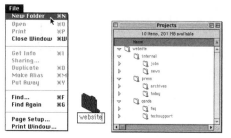

Figure 2.2 *On a Mac, select New Folder, and then give the folder a name. Then create a separate folder for each section of your site.*

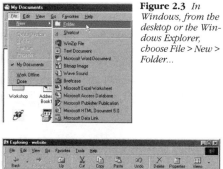

Figure 2.3 *In Windows, from the desktop or the Windows Explorer, choose File > New > Folder...*

Figure 2.4 *...and give the folder a name. Then divide it into additional folders if needed. You can use the Windows Explorer (as shown here) to display the complete hierarchy of your site.*

Organizing Files

Before you start to create your files, it's a good idea to figure out where you're going to put them.

To organize your files:

1. Create a central folder or directory to hold all the material that will be available at your Web site. On the Mac, choose File > New Folder in the Finder **(Figure 2.2)**. In Windows, from the Active Desktop, choose File > New > Folder **(Figure 2.3)**.

2. Divide the central folder in a way that reflects the organization of your Web site. You may decide to create a separate folder for HTML documents, one for images, and one for other external files. If you have a large site with many pages, you may wish to divide the site into categories or chapters, placing the images in the individual folders.

✔ Tip

■ Use simple, one-word names without symbols or punctuation for your files *and* folders. Use all lowercase letters so that your URLs are easier to type and thus your pages are easier to reach. For more details on how to create good file names, consult *File Names* on page 26.

Organizing Files

Creating a New Web Page

You don't need any special tools to create a Web page. You can use *any* word processor, even WordPad or SimpleText, which are included with the basic Windows and Macintosh system software.

To create a new Web page:

1. Open any text editor or word processor.

2. Choose File > New to create a new, blank document **(Figure 2.5)**.

3. Create the HTML content as explained in the rest of this book, starting on page 35.

4. Be sure to save your file as directed on page 40.

✔ Tips

■ If you like Microsoft Word, you can use it for writing HTML too. Just be sure to save the file correctly (as Text Only and with the .htm or .html extension). For more details, consult *Saving Your Web Page* on page 40.

■ If you use PageMill, FrontPage, or some other Web page editor to start your pages, you can still tweak their HTML code. Just choose File > Open from your text editor of choice and open the file. Then use the rest of this book to add your own HTML tags by hand and create the HTML page *you* want.

■ Well, you *can* use SimpleEdit or Word-Pad, but if you want to get fancy, try BBEdit for Mac or HomeSite for Windows. Both have powerful search and replace function, automatic HTML tags in color, syntax checkers for debugging problematic pages, and assorted other helpful features. For more details, consult *HTML Editors* on page 350.

Figure 2.5 *Open your text editor or word processor and choose File > New. (Shown are Simple-Text for Macintosh at far left and WordPad for Windows.)*

Figure 2.6 *This is SimpleText's document window where you'll write the HTML code for your Web page (that you'll learn from this book). There's not much to it.*

Figure 2.7 *This is WordPad's document window where Windows users can create HTML pages.*

Creating a New Web Page

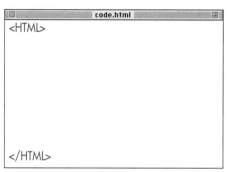

Figure 2.8 *The HTML tags identify the contents of your document as HTML code.*

Figure 2.9 *An empty HTML document doesn't look very exciting in the browser.*

Starting Your Web Page

The very first thing that you should type on your page is the HTML tag. It identifies the contents of your text document as HTML code.

To start your Web page:

1. Type **<HTML>**.

2. Leave a few spaces for creating the rest of your page (using the rest of this book).

3. Type **</HTML>**.

✔ Tips

- Perhaps even more important than the HTML tag—which is optional, after all—is the file extension *(see page 26)*. Of course, we humans also benefit from the HTML tag, since it indicates what the rest of the document holds.

- Create a template with the HTML tags already typed in as a starting point for all your pages.

- Earlier editions of this book recommended using the !DOCTYPE tag to tell the browser which version of HTML was used for the page. The truth is, however, that although the W3C would like you to use the !DOCTYPE tag, I haven't found a single browser that cares one way or the other. On the other hand, I do get buckets of e-mail from people confused about it. So, I've changed my mind. If you're concerned about following the W3C's specifications to the letter, check out *www.w3.org/TR/REC-html40/struct/global.html#h-7.2.* Otherwise, just forget about the !DOCTYPE tag.

Creating the Foundation

Most Web pages are divided into two sections: the HEAD and the BODY. The HEAD section is where you define the title of your page, include information about your page for search engines like AltaVista, set the location of your page, add advanced formatting information, and write scripts. Except for the title *(see page 37)*, the contents of the HEAD section are not readily visible to the visitor.

To create the HEAD section:

1. Directly after the HTML tag *(see page 35)*, type **<HEAD>**.

2. Leave a few spaces for the contents of the HEAD section.

3. Type **</HEAD>**.

The BODY of your HTML document encloses the content of your Web page, the part that your visitors will see, including the text and graphics.

To create the BODY:

1. After the final </HEAD> tag, type **<BODY>**.

2. Leave a few spaces for the contents of your Web page (which you'll create with the help of the rest of this book).

3. Type **</BODY>**.

✔ Tips

- Although the HEAD and BODY tags are optional, I do recommend that you use them since they help the browser tell where the HEAD and BODY *sections* (which are not optional) begin and end.

- Another reason not to omit the HEAD and BODY tags is to control when a particular script will run *(see page 292)*.

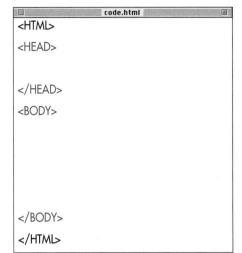

Figure 2.10 *Every HTML document should be divided into a HEAD and a BODY.*

Figure 2.11 *There's still no content for the browser to display.*

```
█                code.html                █
<HTML><HEAD>

<TITLE>Barcelona, Capital of Catalunya
</TITLE>

</HEAD><BODY>




</BODY></HTML>
```

Figure 2.12 *The TITLE tag is the only element in the HEAD section that is readily visible to the user. It is a required element.*

Figure 2.13 *The title of a Web page is generally shown in the title bar of the window.*

Figure 2.14 *The title also appears in your visitor's History window (this is Explorer)...*

Figure 2.15 *...and in your visitor's Favorites and Bookmarks menus (this is Netscape).*

Creating a Title

Each HTML page must have a title. A title should be short and descriptive. In most browsers, the title appears in the title bar of the window. Perhaps even more importantly, the title is used by search indexes like Yahoo and AltaVista as well as in your visitors' browsers' history lists and bookmarks.

To create a title:

1. Place the cursor between the opening and closing HEAD tags *(see page 36)*.

2. Type **<TITLE>**.

3. Enter the title of your web page.

4. Type **</TITLE>**.

✔ Tips

■ The TITLE tag is required.

■ A title cannot contain any formatting, images, or links to other pages.

■ A page's title directly reflects its ranking in most search engines. The closer a title is to the exact words that a potential visitor types—without any extra words—the higher up it will appear in the listings.

■ You should choose the title carefully. It is used in History lists, Favorite lists, and Bookmarks menus to identify your page **(Figures 2.14 and 2.15)**.

■ Don't use colons or backslashes in your titles. Since these symbols cannot be used by some operating systems for file names, they'll have to be removed manually before saving the file.

■ If your title has special characters like accents or foreign letters, you'll have to format these characters with their name or number codes. Consult *Special Symbols* on page 353 for more information.

Organizing the Page

HTML provides for up to six levels of headers in your Web page for dividing your page into manageable chunks. You will seldom have to use more than three.

To organize your Web page with headers:

1. In the BODY section of your HTML document, type **<Hn**, where *n* is a number from 1 to 6, depending on the level of header that you want to create.

2. If desired, to align the header, type **ALIGN=direction**, where *direction* is left, right, or center.

3. Type **>**.

4. Type the contents of the header.

5. Type **</Hn>** where *n* is the same number used in step 1.

✔ Tips

■ Think of your headers as hierarchical dividers. Use them consistently.

■ The only official rule about headers is that the higher the level (the smaller the number), the more prominently they should be displayed. Nevertheless, the major browsers currently display them all the same: in Times New Roman, boldface, at 24, 18, 14, 12, 10 and 8 points (9 points on the Mac), respectively.

■ You can use styles to format headers with a particular font, size, or color (or whatever). For details, see Chapter 13, *An Introduction to Cascading Style Sheets.*

■ Add a named anchor to your headers so that you can create links directly to that header from a different web page *(see page 120).*

```
code.html
<HTML><HEAD><TITLE>Barcelona, Capital of
Catalunya</TITLE></HEAD>

<BODY>

<H1>Home of the 1992 Summer
Olympics</H1>




</BODY></HTML>
```

Figure 2.16 *Don't repeat the information from your title in the header. The header should help organize the information on the page in sections while the title summarizes that information.*

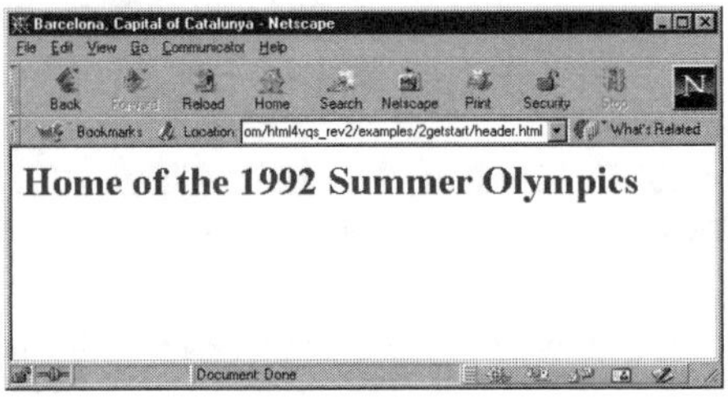

Figure 2.17 *First level headers are most often displayed in 24 point, Times New Roman, in boldface.*

```
┌──────────────── code.html ────────────────┐
<HEAD>

<TITLE>Barcelona, Capital of Catalunya</TITLE>

</HEAD>

<BODY>

<H1>Home of the 1992 Summer
Olympics</H1>

Although Barcelona was transformed by the
renovation and construction projects undertaken
in preparation for the 1992 Summer Olympics,
the city maintained its cosmopolitan but friendly
personality that has enchanted visitors for more
than one thousand years.

<P>Mayor Pasqual Maragall gave the inaugural
address at the Opening Ceremonies by offering
a welcome in the four official languages of the
Summer Olympics: Catalan, Spanish, English
and French.

</BODY></HTML>
```

Figure 2.18 *Since headers include automatic line breaks (and this page does not use styles), there is no pressing need to include a <P> before the first paragraph. You do need to insert a <P> before the second paragraph.*

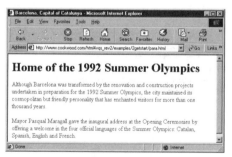

Figure 2.19 *The amount of space inserted with a <P> tag depends on the size of the text surrounding it.*

Starting a New Paragraph

HTML does not recognize the returns that you enter in your text editor. To start a new paragraph in your Web page, you use the P tag.

To begin a new paragraph:

1. Type **<P**.

2. If desired, to align the text in the paragraph, type **ALIGN=direction**, where *direction* is left, right, or center.

3. Type **>**.

4. Type the contents of the new paragraph.

5. If desired, you may type **</P>** to end the paragraph, but it is not required.

✔ Tips

- All block-level elements, like Hn and HR *(see page 24)*, include automatic carriage returns. That means you don't need to add a <P> to start a new paragraph after using such an element **(Figure 2.18)**.

- If you are using styles to format paragraphs, you must mark every paragraph with opening *and* closing P tags. Any text that is not tagged will not be formatted.

- You can use styles to format paragraphs with a particular font, size, or color (or whatever). For details, see Chapter 13, *An Introduction to Cascading Style Sheets.*

- The amount of space between each paragraph depends on the size of the text surrounding it. For more control, consult *Setting the Line Height* on page 263 and *Controlling Spacing* on page 267.

- One quick and dirty trick for adding extra space between paragraphs is to type ** ** (a non-breaking space) between each additional P tag.

Saving Your Web Page

If you're using a simple text editor to create your Web pages, you shouldn't have any trouble saving a Web page. But if you're using a fancy word processor, you have to insist that you don't want all of the extra information that the program will package with the file. Instead, you save the file as *Text Only*: pure letters, numbers, and a few special characters here and there. That way, any computer will be able to open your Web page. Then, to ensure that any browser will know what to do with the file once it's open, it's essential to use the proper file extension.

To save your Web page:

1. Once you've created your Web page, choose File > Save As from your text editor or your word processor **(Fig. 2.20)**.

2. In the dialog box that appears, choose Text Only, Text Document, ASCII (or however your program words it) for the format. (SimpleText for Mac always saves in Text Only so you don't have to worry.)

3. Give the document the .htm or .html extension. (This is very important!)

4. Choose the folder in which to save the Web page *(see page 33)*.

5. Click Save.

✔ **Tips**

■ Only Windows 3.1 users are limited to the three letter extension, .htm. Practically everyone else—Windows 95/98, Unix, and Macintosh—can choose what they like best. Just be consistent.

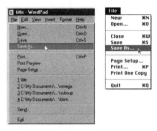
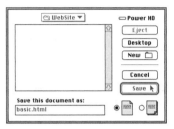

Figure 2.20 *Choose File > Save As from your word processor or text editor. (WordPad is on the left, SimpleText on the right.)*

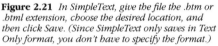

Figure 2.21 *In SimpleText, give the file the .htm or .html extension, choose the desired location, and then click Save. (Since SimpleText only saves in Text Only format, you don't have to specify the format.)*

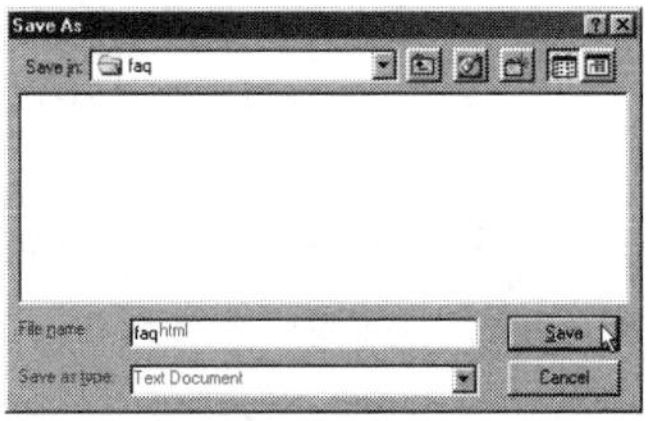

Figure 2.22 *In WordPad, give the file the .htm or .html extension, choose Text Document under Save as type, choose the desired location, and then click Save.*

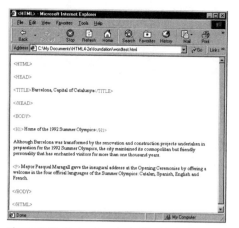

Figure 2.23 *If your page looks like this in the browser, with all of your HTML tags visible to the naked eye, you probably used Word's confusing Save as HTML command. Instead, choose Save As and then select the Text Only format and add the .htm or .html extension by hand.*

Figure 2.24 *If you're using a heavy-duty word processor with lots of features—like Microsoft Word, shown here—be sure not to select the Save as HTML command. It'll "code your code". Instead, choose Save As and then choose your format and extension manually.*

■ Although you Mac users can get away with not using extensions on your own machines, you have to think about your audience. If you want the other 90% (or so) of the Web public to be able to view your page properly, add that extension.

■ Some word processors (like Microsoft Word and Corel WordPerfect to name a few) offer a "Save as HTML" option. *Don't touch it!* That option is for folks who want to create a Web page from a word processing document without learning HTML. But, if you write your own HTML code by following the instructions in this book and then choose that option, the word processor will, as one reader wrote me, "code your code" and the result is a disaster **(Figure 2.23)**. Instead, just choose Save As and then choose Text Only for the format **(Figure 2.24)**.

■ If you're on a Windows machine and find that some other extension is getting added on to your filename without your consent, try enclosing the file name in double quotation marks when you go to save it. That tells Windows to leave the name alone.

■ Name your page "index.html" (or sometimes "default.htm", depending on your server—ask your ISP!) to designate that page as the default page for its directory. Then, whenever a visitor types the URL for that directory, that default page will be displayed.

■ If you don't have such a default page in each directory, most servers will show a list of the directory's contents (which you may or may not want to reveal to your visitors). To keep those prying eyes out, create a default page for every directory on your server.

Saving Your Web Page

Viewing Your Page in a Browser

Once you've created a page, you'll want to see what it looks like in a browser. In fact, since you don't know which browser your visitors will be using, it's a good idea to look at the page in *several* browsers *(see page 13)*.

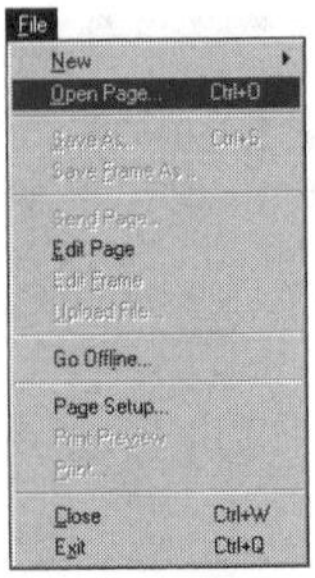

To look at your page in a browser:

1. Open your browser software (Communicator, Explorer, etc.)

2. Choose File > Open, Open File, or Open Page (just *not* Open Location), depending on the browser **(Figure 2.25)**.

3. In the dialog box that appears, either type the location of the page on your hard disk, or click Browse (IE) or Choose File (Netscape) to find it **(Figure 2.26)**.

4. If you've clicked Browse or Choose File in step 3, in the new dialog box that appears, navigate to the folder on your hard disk that contains the desired Web page and click Open **(Figure 2.27)**.

5. Click Open in the Open Page dialog box. The page is displayed in the browser just as it will appear when you actually publish it on the server *(see page 329)*.

✔ Tips

■ If your Web page does not appear in the Open dialog box, make sure that you have saved it as Text Only and given it the .htm or .html extension *(see page 40)*.

■ You don't have to close the document in the text editor before you view it with a browser. This makes editing much faster—you can switch to the editor, make your changes, and then come back to the browser and click Reload to view the changes.

■ It is not necessary to publish your pages on the server before you view them.

Figure 2.25 *From the desired browser (this is Communicator for Windows), choose File > Open Page. In Explorer for Windows, it's called File > Open. In Explorer for Mac, it's File > Open File.*

Figure 2.26 *On Windows machines, you'll get an intermediary box asking if you want to type the path in by hand. If you don't (!), click the Choose File button (in IE4, it's Browse). You'll get the dialog box shown in Figure 2.27.*

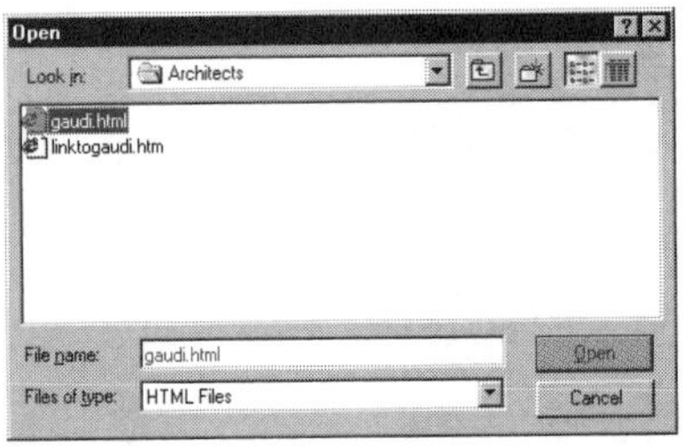

Figure 2.27 *Choose the file that you want to open and click the Open button.*

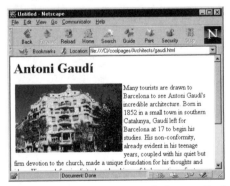

Figure 2.28 *The page appears in the browser. Check it over well to see if it's coming out the way you planned.*

Text Formatting

If you're used to choosing your favorite font, size, and color from a set of familiar menus, formatting text in your Web page may seem a bit clumsy, even archaic. Instead of simply selecting the text and then the appropriate menu command, you'll enclose the desired text in tags that indicate the formatting style you wish to apply. Before you get too annoyed, remember that the beauty of HTML is that all the formatting is contained in text, and thus your pages can be read by any computer.

There are two methods for formatting text. The first, and more basic, method, described in detail in this chapter, uses regular HTML tags and attributes to format distinct pieces of text individually. Although the W3C has deprecated many of these tags—which means that they are still valid but that it hopes to remove them from the official specifications at some point in the future—they are still the easiest and most widely used formatting tools in HTML.

However, if your formatting is complex or your documents are long and numerous, hand formatting your pages can become very tedious. Style sheets, which let you assign an entire group of characteristics to a bit of text in one fell swoop, are the solution. You'll learn how to use them starting with Chapter 13, *An Introduction to Cascading Style Sheets.*

About Deprecated Tags

As you read through this chapter, you may notice that many of the tags have been deprecated. That means that the World Wide Web Consortium—the organizational body that publishes the standard HTML specifications—doesn't want you to use them. They'd prefer you use CSS to format your documents *(see page 239)*. While deprecated tags are still currently "proper HTML" the W3C says it plans to drop those tags at some point in the future. Why, you might ask, would I devote an entire chapter to tags that are on their way out?

Why indeed. There are several reasons actually. First and foremost, HTML is much simpler than CSS. I firmly believe that the Web would still be a forgotten project on someone's desk if folks had had to learn style sheets in order to create a page. Frankly, style sheets are often overkill. To format a couple of words on a page, an HTML tag is a lot less work.

The second reason to explain these tags is that most people still use them and browsers still support them. Whether the W3C eliminates them or not from the official HTML specifications will not change that. There is no browser manufacturer that will ever stop supporting them. How could they do such a thing and risk not being able to view a huge piece of the Web?

Finally, and perhaps most importantly, styles are not universally supported by browsers. In contrast, while most of the tags in this chapter have been deprecated, they still work correctly in *both* Explorer and Netscape. Until Cascading Style Sheets are better supported, using styles may mean leaving out part of your audience.

```
┌──────────── code.html ─────────────┐
<HTML><HEAD><TITLE>Using different
fonts</TITLE></HEAD><BODY>

<FONT FACE="Lithos Black, Chicago">You can
change the font face</FONT> of just a few
letters.

<P><FONT FACE="New Century, Futura
ExtraBold">Or you can change the font face for
an entire sentence or paragraph</FONT>.

<P>If the user's browser doesn't have the first
font, it looks for the second. <FONT
FACE="Springfield, Extra Bold">If the browser
can't find any of the fonts listed, it uses the font
specified in the user's preferences</FONT>.

</BODY></HTML>
└─────────────────────────────────────┘
```

Figure 3.1 *You may list as many fonts as you wish in each FONT tag in order of preference. Separate each choice with a comma and a space. Don't forget to add the desired style (Bold, Condensed, etc.).*

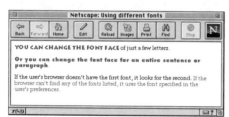

Figure 3.2 *Fonts give your page more personality. Note that only Lithos, in the first paragraph, and Futura ExtraBold—but not New Century—in the second paragraph, were available on this system. The last paragraph is displayed in the default font since neither of the special fonts chosen was available on the system.*

Changing the Font

In order to make Web pages more universal, early versions of HTML did not allow the designer to specify a particular font. Since version 3.2, however, you can choose exactly what fonts you'd *prefer* to use. Of course, if the visitor does not have the desired fonts installed on their system, the text is rendered in the default font.

To change the font:

1. Before the text to be changed, type **<FONT FACE="fontname1**, where *fontname1* is your first choice of fonts. Type the complete name of the desired font, including the style.

2. If desired, type **, fontname2**, where *fontname2* is your second choice of fonts, should the user not have the first font installed on his system. Each successive font should be separated from the previous one by a comma.

3. Repeat step 2 for each additional font choice.

4. Type **">** to complete the FONT tag.

5. Type the text that should be displayed with the given font.

6. Type **</FONT>**.

✔ Tips

- The FONT tag is also used to change the size *(see page 48)* and the color *(see page 50)* of the text. You can combine all attributes in the same tag, e.g., **<FONT SIZE=4 FACE="Garamond Bold" COLOR="#121212">**.

- While FONT is deprecated in HTML 4 *(see page 43)*, it is still a perfectly valid tag. For information on using style sheets to control font usage (and to download fonts for your visitors), see page 258.

Changing the Font

Making Text Bold or Italic

One way to make text stand out is to format it in bold face or italics.

To make text bold:

1. Type **<B>**.

2. Type the text that you want to make bold.

3. Type **</B>**.

To make text italic:

1. Type **<I>** (that's *i* as in *italic*).

2. Type the text that you want to make italic.

3. Type **</I>**.

✔ Tips

■ You can also use the less common EM and STRONG tags to format text. These are *logical* formatting tags for "emphasizing" text or marking it as "strong". In most browsers, EM is displayed in italics and STRONG in bold. Both require opening (<EM>, <STRONG>) and closing tags (</EM>, </STRONG>).

■ You may use CITE (the logical tag for marking citations) to make text italic, although it is less widely recognized and less widely used than the I tag.

■ For more control over bold and italics, try style sheets. For details, consult *Creating Italics* on page 260 and *Applying Bold Formatting* on page 261.

■ The ADDRESS tag—old-fashioned but still legal HTML—is another logical tag for making text italic. It's usually only used to format the Web page designer's e-mail address.

```
code.html

<HTML><HEAD><TITLE>Bold and Italic
text</TITLE></HEAD>

<BODY>

<H1>Barcelona Night Life</H1>

<P>Barcelona is such a great place to live.
People there really put a premium on
<B>socializing</B>. Imagine it being more
important to go out with your friends than to get
that big promotion. Even when you're, gasp,
<I>pushing 30</I>. They say there are more
bars in Barcelona than in the rest of the European
community <I>combined</I>.

</BODY></HTML>
```

Figure 3.3 *You may use bold or italic formatting anywhere in your HTML document, except in the TITLE.*

Figure 3.4 *Bold and italic formatting are the simplest and most effective ways to make your text stand out.*

```
code.html
<HTML><HEAD><TITLE>Changing the default
size for text</TITLE></HEAD><BODY>

<BASEFONT SIZE="5">

<H1>Barcelona Night Life - The Large Print
Edition</H1>

<P>Barcelona is such a great place to live.
People there really put a premium on
<B>socializing</B>. Imagine it being more
important to go out with your friends than to get
that big promotion. Even when you're, gasp,
<I>pushing 30</I>. They say there are more
bars in Barcelona than in the rest of the European
community <I>combined</I>.

</BODY></HTML>
```

Figure 3.5 *The BASEFONT tag goes at the top of your document, just after the BODY tag. It affects all of the text in the document, except the headers.*

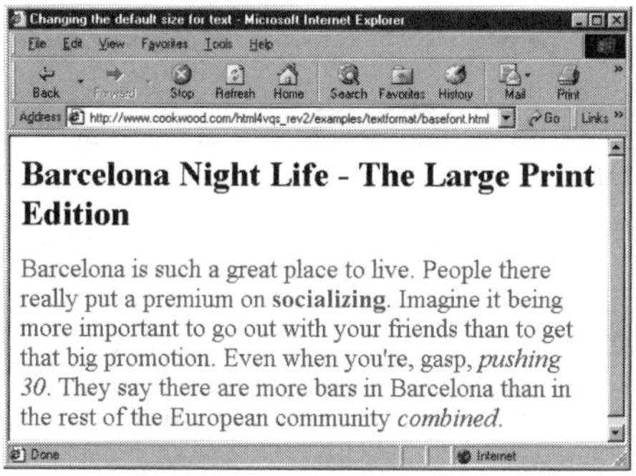

Figure 3.6 *You should have a good reason to change the default size for text. Remember that your visitors may have already chosen how they prefer to view text.*

Choosing a Default Size for Text

You can select a size for all of the body text on your page with the BASEFONT tag. Then change individual sections or words with either the FONT tag *(see page 48)* or the BIG and SMALL tags *(see page 49)*.

To choose a default size for body text:

1. Type <BASEFONT.

2. Type SIZE="n">, where n is a number from 1 to 7. The default is 3.

✔ Tips

- The value you choose for BASEFONT is always relative to the default size set in the visitor's browser. A value of 3 will display text at the same size as the browser's default size. So, if the browser's default size is 12 points (which is the norm), values 1 to 7 for BASEFONT correspond to 8, 10, 12, 14, 18, 24, and 36 points respectively. If the browser's default size is 14, the point sizes jump up accordingly.

- Windows machines tend to display text larger than Macs. If you use Windows, be aware that the text will probably appear smaller on a Mac (and vice-versa).

- Only use one BASEFONT tag in each HTML document. To change individual characters, use FONT *(see page 48)*.

- BASEFONT is deprecated in HTML 4. To set the size of your text with style sheets, consult *Setting the Font Size* on page 262.

- Some browsers (IE4 and IE5, for example) support setting the default font and color with the BASEFONT tag. Use the FACE and COLOR attributes as described on page 45 and page 51, respectively.

- BASEFONT does not affect headers.

Changing the Text Size

When you need to change the size of a bit of your text, you can do it in one of two ways, either by selecting a specific size or by specifying that the selection be bigger or smaller than the surrounding text. Either way, the results also depend on the preferences set by your visitors *(see first tip on page 47)*.

To set the specific size of one or more characters:

1. Type **<FONT**.

2. Type **SIZE="n">**, where *n* is a number from 1 to 7.

3. Type the text whose size you wish to change.

4. Type **</FONT>**.

✔ Tips

■ A value of 3 represents the browser's default size for text—usually Times 12 point. The tricky part is that every visitor can change their own browser's default text by tweaking the preferences.

■ Use the FONT tag to change the size of just a few characters or words. Use BASE-FONT *(see page 47)* to change the default size for all the text on the page. The FONT tag overrides the BASEFONT tag (unless you use a relative value—see page 49).

■ The FONT tag can also be used to change the color *(see page 51)* and typeface *(see page 45)* of individual letters.

■ The FONT tag has been deprecated in HTML 4. For more information on changing the size of text with style sheets, consult *Setting the Font Size* on page 262.

```
code.html
<HTML><HEAD><TITLE>Changing the size of
just a bit of the text</TITLE></HEAD>
<BODY>
<H1>Barcelona Night Life</H1>
<P><FONT SIZE="6">B</FONT>arcelona is
such a great place to live. People there really put
a premium on <B>socializing</B>. Imagine it
being more important to go out with your friends
than to get that big promotion. Even when
you're, gasp, <I>pushing 30</I>. They say there
are more bars in Barcelona than in the rest of the
European community <I>combined</I>.
</BODY></HTML>
```

Figure 3.7 *The big differences between FONT and BASEFONT are that FONT can use relative values and depend on the BASEFONT value, and that it affects individual characters, instead of the entire page.*

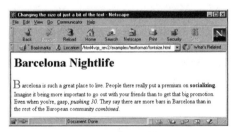

Figure 3.8 *You can use the FONT tag to increase the size of the initial capital letter in each paragraph.*

Changing the Text Size

```
code.html
<HTML><HEAD><TITLE>Changing the relative
size of text</TITLE></HEAD><BODY>

<H1>Barcelona Night Life</H1>

<P><FONT SIZE="6">B</FONT>arcelona is
such a great place to live. People there really put
a premium on <B>socializing</B>. Imagine it
being more important to go out with your friends
than to get that big promotion. Even when
you're, gasp, <I>pushing 30</I>. They say there
are more bars in Barcelona than in the rest of the
European community <I>combined</I>.
<BIG>Don't get me wrong,</BIG> I don't mean
that everyone gets drunk all the time--bars are
for hanging out and talking or for having a cup
of coffee (espresso, of course).

<P><SMALL>The opinions expressed on this
page are mine and mine alone. </SMALL>

</BODY></HTML>
```

Figure 3.9 *The BIG and SMALL tags continue to form part of the standard HTML specifications.*

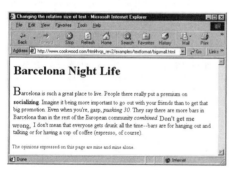

Figure 3.10 *In this example, the main text is displayed at the default size and the bigger and smaller text stand out nicely.*

The BIG and SMALL tags change the relative size of a given word or phrase with respect to the surrounding text.

To make the text bigger or smaller than the surrounding text:

1. Type **<BIG>** or **<SMALL>** before the text that you wish to make bigger or smaller, respectively.

2. Type the text that should be bigger or smaller.

3. Type **</BIG>** or **</SMALL>** according to the tag used in step 1.

One more way to change the size of text with respect to surrounding text:

1. Type **<FONT SIZE=**.

2. Type **+n** or **-n** to specify how much bigger or smaller than the surrounding text you want the affected text to be.

3. Type **>**.

4. Type the text that should be bigger or smaller.

5. Type **</FONT>**.

✔ Tips

■ Although the BIG and SMALL tags have not been deprecated in HTML 4, you may still want to use style sheets in order to have more control over the size of the text. For more information, consult *Setting the Font Size* on page 262.

■ Both the BIG and SMALL tags as well as the FONT tag (with relative values) have a cumulative effect if used more than once. So **<SMALL><SMALL>teensy text </SMALL></SMALL>** would be *two* sizes smaller than surrounding text.

■ The FONT tag has been deprecated; BIG and SMALL have not.

Changing the Text Size

Choosing a Default Color for Text

The TEXT attribute for the BODY tag lets you specify a default color for all of the text on the page. You can then change the color of individual words or paragraphs with the FONT tag *(see page 51)*.

To choose a default color for text:

1. Inside the BODY tag, type **TEXT**.

2. Type **="#rrggbb"**, where *rrggbb* is the hexadecimal representation of the color.

   Or type **="color"**, where *color* is one of the 16 predefined colors.

✔ Tips

■ The TEXT attribute lets you choose one color for all of the text. The FONT tag with the COLOR attribute *(see page 51)* lets you choose a color for individual letters or words, and overrides the TEXT attribute.

■ See Appendix C and the inside back cover for a listing of hexadecimal values and common color representations.

■ You can also specify the color of the background *(see page 98)* and of links *(see page 133)*. Make sure all the colors work well together.

■ You might want to check your page on a monochrome monitor before distributing it. What looks good in color may be impossible to read in grays.

■ The TEXT attribute is deprecated in HTML 4. For details on changing text color with styles, see page 265.

■ Both major browsers allow the visitor to override the colors that you might specify for the Web page **(Figure 3.13)**.

```
code.html
<HTML><HEAD><TITLE>Changing the default
color for text</TITLE></HEAD>

<BODY TEXT="#FF0000">

<H1>Barcelona Night Life</H1>

<P><FONT SIZE="6">B</FONT>arcelona is
such a great place to live. People there really put
a premium on <B>socializing</B>. Imagine it
being more important to go out with your friends
than to get that big promotion. Even when
```

Figure 3.11 *Remember to select a text color that works well with your background color. (If you don't specify the background color, it will either be gray, by default, or the color the visitor has chosen for their browser.)*

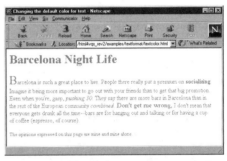

Figure 3.12 *Although this example is pretty basic, you can see that changing the color of your text can give your Web pages an immediate impact. You can see this page on the Web (see page 20).*

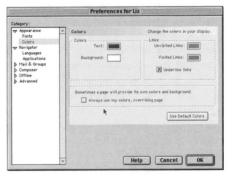

Figure 3.13 *Don't forget that your control is limited. Your visitors can override your color choices by adjusting the preferences in their browser (this is Netscape but IE's dialog box is quite similar). The trick is to not make your pages so dependent on color that they break if the visitor gets involved.*

```
                code.html
<HTML><HEAD><TITLE>Changing the color of
just a bit of the text</TITLE></HEAD>

<BODY TEXT="#FF0000">

<H1><FONT COLOR="blue">Barcelona Night
Life</FONT></H1>

<P><FONT SIZE="6">B</FONT>arcelona is
such a great place to live. People there really put
a premium on <B>socializing</B>. Imagine it
being more important to go out with your friends
than to get that big promotion. Even when
you're, gasp, <I>pushing 30</I>. They say there
are more bars in Barcelona than in the rest of the
European community <I>combined</I>.
<BIG>Don't get me wrong,</BIG> I don't mean
that everyone gets drunk all the time--bars are
for hanging out and talking or for having a cup
of coffee (espresso, of course).

<P><SMALL>The opinions expressed on this
page are mine and mine alone. </SMALL>

</BODY></HTML>
```

Figure 3.14 *Color names are not case sensitive. In addition, note that there's no problem with using names sometimes (as for the header) and hexadecimal values elsewhere (as for the body text).*

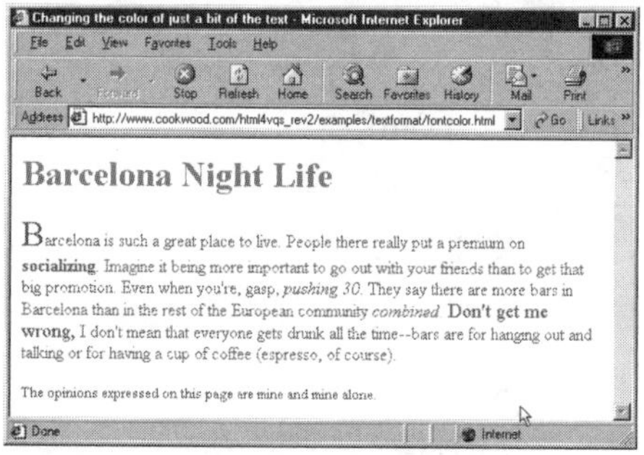

Figure 3.15 *Remember the body text is already red (see page 50). Now I've made the header blue (honest, check it out on the Web!—see page 20).*

Changing the Text Color

A great way to make part of your page stand out is with color. You can change some of the text to one color and leave the rest in black. Or you can create a rainbow effect and really distract your readers.

To change the text color:

1. In front of the text whose color you wish to change, type **<FONT COLOR**.

2. Type **="#rrggbb"**, where *rrggbb* is the hexadecimal representation of the desired color *(see Appendix C)*.

   Or type **="color"**, where *color* is one of the 16 predefined colors *(see Appendix C)*.

3. Type the final **>** of the FONT tag.

4. Type the text that you wish to color.

5. Type **</FONT>**.

✔ Tips

■ See Appendix C and the inside back cover for a listing of hexadecimal values and common colors.

■ Besides color, the FONT tag is also used to change the size *(see page 48)* and font *(see page 45)* of the text. You can change all three attributes at the same time: **<FONT SIZE=5 FACE= "Garamond" COLOR="red">**.

■ To change the color of all of the body text at once, use the TEXT attribute in the BODY tag *(see page 50)* or use style sheets *(see page 265)*.

■ The FONT/COLOR tag overrides colors set with BODY/TEXT *(see page 50)*.

■ FONT is deprecated in HTML 4. For more on changing color with styles, consult *Setting the Text Color* on page 265.

Changing the Text Color

Creating Superscripts and Subscripts

Letters or numbers that are raised or lowered slightly relative to the main body text are called superscripts and subscripts, respectively. HTML 4 includes tags for defining both kinds of offset text.

To create superscripts or subscripts:

1. Type **<SUB>** to create a subscript or **<SUP>** to create a superscript.

2. Type the characters or symbols that you wish to offset relative to the main text.

3. Type **</SUB>** or **</SUP>**, depending on what you used in step 1, to complete the offset text.

✔ Tips

- Most browsers automatically reduce the font size of a sub- or superscripted character by a few points.

- Superscripts are the ideal way to format certain foreign language abbreviations like Mlle for *Mademoiselle* in French or 3^a for *Tercera* in Spanish.

- Subscripts are perfect for writing out chemical molecules like H_2O.

- Superscripts are also handy for creating footnotes. You can combine superscripts and links to make active footnotes (the visitor jumps to the footnote when they click the number or asterisk). For more information, see Chapter 7, *Links*.

- Super- and subscripted characters gently spoil the even spacing between lines. You can remedy the situation **(Fig. 3.18)** by reducing the size of the superscript one additional point: **<FONT SIZE=-1> ^{superscripted text}</FONT>**. For more details, see page 49.

```
code.html
<HTML><HEAD><TITLE>Using superscripts and
subscripts</TITLE></HEAD><BODY>

<H1>Famous Catalans</H1>

<P><FONT SIZE="+3">W</FONT>hen I was in
the sixth grade, I played the cello. There was a
teacher at school who always used to ask me if I
knew who "Pablo Casals" was. I didn't at the
time (although I had met Rostropovich once at a
concert). Actually, Pablo Casals' real name was
<I>Pau</I> Casals, Pau being the Catalan
equivalent of Pablo<SUP>1</SUP>.

<P>In addition to being an amazing cellist, Pau
Casals is remembered in this country for his
empassioned speech against nuclear
proliferation at the United Nations<SUP>2
</SUP> which he began by saying "I am a
Catalan. Catalonia is an oppressed nation."

<P><SUP>1</SUP>It means Paul in English.

<BR><SUP>2</SUP>In 1963, I believe.

</BODY></HTML>
```

Figure 3.16 *The opening SUP or SUB tag precedes the text to be affected.*

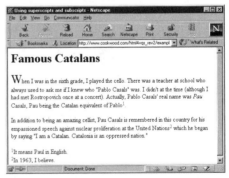

Figure 3.17 *Notice that there is more space between lines 3 and 4 of the first paragraph and lines 1 and 2 of the second than between the other lines.*

Figure 3.18 *If you use the FONT tag (SIZE="-1") with the SUP tag, the lines remain properly spaced.*

```
code.html
<HTML><HEAD><TITLE>Underlining and
striking out text</TITLE></HEAD><BODY>

<H1>Famous Catalans</H1>

<P><FONT SIZE="+3">W</FONT>hen I was in
the sixth grade, I played the cello. There was a
teacher at school who always used to ask me if I
knew who "Pablo Casals" was. I didn't <U>at the
time</U> <STRIKE>(although I had met
Rostropovich once at a concert) </STRIKE>.
Actually, Pablo Casals' real name was
<I>Pau</I> Casals, Pau being the Catalan
equivalent of Pablo<SUP>1</SUP>.

<P>In addition to being an amazing cellist, Pau
Casals is remembered in this country for his
empassioned speech against nuclear
proliferation at the United
Nations<SUP>2</SUP> which he began by
saying "I am a Catalan. Catalonia is an
oppressed nation."

<P><SUP>1</SUP>It means Paul in English.
<BR><SUP>2</SUP>In 1963, I believe.
```

Figure 3.19 *Although the U and STRIKE tags are both deprecated, they're still well supported.*

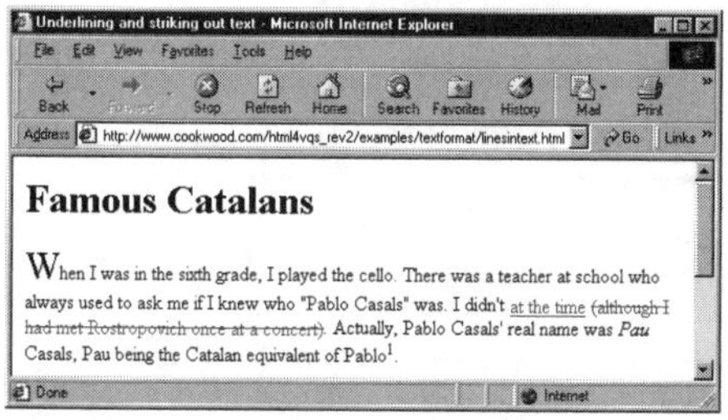

Figure 3.20 *Underlined text can be confusing since visitors generally associate it with a link.*

Striking Out or Underlining Text

Most browsers can display lines either through or under text. Strike out text is most useful to show revisions to text. Underlining is another way of emphasizing text, especially newly added text.

To strike out or underline text:

1. Type **<STRIKE>** or **<U>** for strike out text and underlining, respectively.

2. Type the text that should appear with a line through or under it.

3. Type **</STRIKE>** or **</U>**.

✔ Tips

■ Both the STRIKE and U tags have been deprecated in HTML 4. There is also a shorthand S tag for STRIKE that has also been deprecated.

■ There are two new tags in the official HTML 4 specifications that are designed to strike out and underline text: DEL (for deleted) and INS (for inserted) respectively. At press time, however, only Explorer displays them correctly.

■ Although fonts and colors let designers indicate links in new ways, most Web sites continue to use underlining to show links to other Web pages *(see page 117)*. You may confuse visitors by underlining text that does not bring them to a new page.

■ Lynx displays EM and STRONG text with an underline. Users may be confused by further underlining.

■ You can apply underlining, strike out, and even overlining with styles. For more details, consult *Underlining Text* on page 270.

Using a Monospaced Font

Every visitor to your page has two fonts specified in their browser's preferences: one regular, proportionally spaced one and the other monospaced, like a typewriter's text. By default these are Times and Courier, respectively. If you are displaying computer codes, URLs, or other information that you wish to offset from the main text, you might want to format the text with the monospaced font.

To format text with a monospaced font:

1. Type **<CODE>**, **<KBD>**, **<SAMP>**, or **<TT>**.

2. Type the text that you want to display in a monospaced font.

3. Type **</CODE>**, **</KBD>**, **</SAMP>**, or **</TT>**. Use the tag that matches the code you chose in step 1.

✔ Tips

- TT (which stands for *typewriter text)* is the monospaced font tag that is used most often. CODE is for formatting computer *code* in languages like C or Perl. KBD is for formatting *keyboard* instructions. And SAMP is for displaying *sample* text. None of these tags is used very often. The truth is monospaced text is kind of ugly.

- Remember that the monospaced font tags will not have a very dramatic effect in browsers that display all their text in monospaced fonts (like Lynx).

- You can also format several lines of monospaced text with the PRE tag *(see page 113).*

```
<HTML><HEAD><TITLE>Using monospaced
fonts</TITLE></HEAD><BODY>

<H2>Perl Tutorial, Lesson 1</H2>

<P>If you're on a UNIX server, every Perl script
should start with a shebang line that describes
the path to the Perl interpreter on your server. The
shebang line might look like this:

<P><CODE>#!/usr/local/bin/perl</CODE>

</BODY></HTML>
```

Figure 3.21 *CODE not only formats its contents with a monospaced font but also indicates that the contents are computer code. It's a logical tag.*

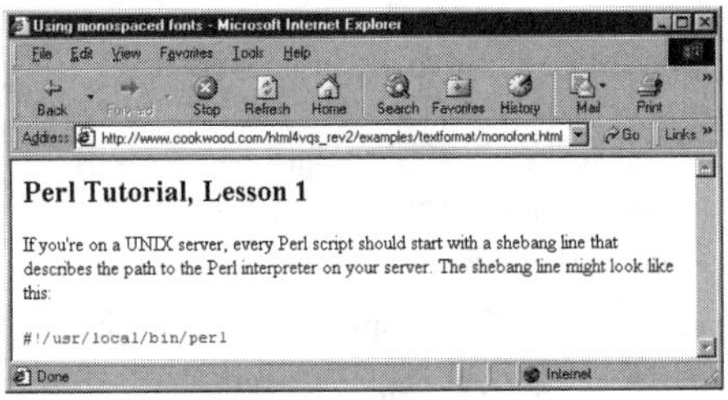

Figure 3.22 *Monospaced text is perfect for URLs and computer code and anything else that should look kind of geeky.*

Figure 3.23 *Any text tagged with CODE, KBD, SAMP, or TT will be displayed in the font that your visitors have chosen for monospaced text for their browser. The dialog box shown here is the Windows Fonts box. It appears when you choose Tools > Internet Options from Explorer and then click the Fonts button in the General tab.*

Using a Monospaced Font

```
┌─────────────────────────────┐
│ ▓▓▓▓▓    code.html    ▓▓▓▓▓ ▣│
├─────────────────────────────┤
<HTML><HEAD><TITLE>Using blinking text
</TITLE></HEAD><BODY>

<H1>Famous Catalans</H1>

<P><FONT SIZE="+3">E</FONT>ver heard of
Montserrat Caball&eacute;, Josep Carreras, and
Vict&ograve;ria dels &Agrave;ngels? (You may
know these last two by their Spanish names:
Jos&eacute; Carreras and Victoria de los
&Aacute;ngeles.) Did you know they were
<BLINK>all Catalans</BLINK>? The things you
learn!

</BODY></HTML>
```

Figure 3.24 *Although you can include an image in your blinking definition, so to speak, only the text will blink.*

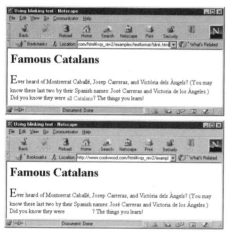

Figure 3.25 *Blinking text appears normal (top), then disappears (bottom), then reappears.*

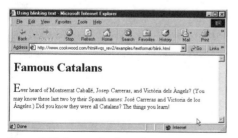

Figure 3.26 *Internet Explorer does not now and probably never will recognize the blink tag.*

Making Text Blink

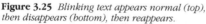 Another way to make text stand out is to make it blink. You can apply the BLINK tag to anchors, links, or any important text that you have on the page.

To make text blink:

1. Type **<BLINK>**.

2. Type the text that you want to blink.

3. Type **</BLINK>**.

✔ Tips

■ Blinking text—and other high contrast images on your page—can provoke seizures in folks with epilepsy. It's also considered a bit gauche in the sophisticated world of Web design. You might want to be careful where and how much you use it.

■ You can include an image in your blinking definition, but it won't blink.

■ You may not use blinking text in the TITLE.

■ Internet Explorer does not recognize the BLINK tag and probably never will. Could it be because the BLINK tag was one of the driving factors behind arch rival Netscape's rise to fame?

■ You can use styles to create blinking text. For more information, consult *Making Text Blink* on page 271.

Hiding Text (Adding Comments)

One diagnostic tool available to every HTML author is the addition of comments to your HTML documents to remind you (or future editors) what you were trying to achieve with your HTML tags.

These comments appear only in the HTML document when opened with a text or HTML editor. They will be completely invisible to visitors in the browser.

To add comments to your HTML page:

1. In your HTML document, where you wish to insert comments, type **<!--**.

2. Type the comments.

3. Type **-->** to complete the commented text.

✔ Tips

■ Comments are particularly useful for describing why you used a particular tag and what effect you were hoping to achieve.

■ Another good use for comments is to remind yourself (or future editors) to include, remove, or update certain sections.

■ You should view your commented page with a browser before publishing (see Chapter 21, *Publishing Your Page on the Web*) to avoid sharing your (possibly) private comments with your public.

■ Beware, however, of comments that are *too* private. While invisible in the browser, they cheerfully reappear when the user saves the page as HTML code (source). For more information on saving a page's code, consult *The Inspiration of Others* on page 310.

```
code.html
<HTML><HEAD><TITLE>Barcelona, Capital of
Catalunya</TITLE></HEAD><BODY>

<H1>Home of the 1992 Summer Olympics</H1>

<!--A little flowery, but I guess it will do.-->
Although Barcelona was transformed by the
renovation and construction projects undertaken
in preparation for the 1992 Summer Olympics,
the city maintained its cosmopolitan but friendly
personality that has enchanted visitors for more
than one thousand years.

<P>Mayor Pasqual Maragall gave the inaugural
address at the Opening Ceremonies by offering
a welcome in the four official languages of the
Summer Olympics: Catalan, Spanish, English
and French. He said:

<P>Benvingut als Jocs Ol&#237;mpics de 1992

<BR>Bienvenido a los Juegos Ol&#237;mpicos
de 1992

<BR>Welcome to the 1992 Olympic Games

<!--Find out if this is the correct French
translation-->

<BR>Bienvenu aux Jeux Olympiques de 1992

<P>And the crowd went wild. In lots more than
four languages.

</BODY></HTML>
```

Figure 3.27 *Comments are a great way to add reminders to your text. You can also use them to keep track of revisions.*

Figure 3.28 *The comments are completely invisible to the user when the page is viewed in a browser— unless she decides to download the source HTML.*

Creating Web Images

What Program to Use?

In this chapter, I use Adobe Photoshop to work with images. It is the best all-around image editing program and is available for both Macintosh and Windows. The techniques in this chapter work with version 3 and up.

If you don't have Adobe Photoshop, I recommend trying Paint Shop Pro for Windows or GraphicConverter for Macintosh.

Creating images for the Web is a bit different from creating images for output on paper. Although the basic characteristics of Web images and printable images are the same, five main factors distinguish them: format, color, transparency, speed, and animation. This chapter will explain the important aspects of each of these five factors and how to use that knowledge to create the most effective images for your Web site.

Please note, however, that this chapter is no substitute for your image editing program's documentation. Nor is it meant to be a manual for learning about design. Instead, use this chapter to learn about the particular *components and features* that distinguish Web images. Then combine that knowledge with your computing and design expertise to create awesome images for your page.

Now let's look at those five factors that you should keep in mind as you create Web images.

Format

People who print images on paper don't have to worry about what their readers will use to look at the images. You do. The Web is accessed every day by millions of Macs, Windows-based PCs, Unix, and other kinds of computers. The graphics you use in your Web page should be in a format that each of these operating systems can recognize. Presently, the two most widely used formats on the Web are GIF and JPEG, with PNG gaining in popularity. Current versions of Explorer and Netscape can view all three image formats.

Color

Unlike printed images, Web images are usually viewed on a computer monitor. You knew that. But did you know that some monitors (called 8 bit) are limited to displaying 256 colors? Further, the system software and browsers reserve up to 40 colors for their own use. When displaying images on these monitors, browsers use a particular set of 216 colors (256 minus 40), often called the *browser safe palette*. If the images on your page contain more than 216 colors, or if they contain colors other than the 216 in the browser safe palette, the browser will try to combine existing colors to reproduce the missing ones (called *dithering*). The results are not always pretty **(Figure 4.1)**.

If all your visitors have 24-bit monitors, you don't have a problem. According to Statmark *(www.statmark.com)*, 35% of the general Web public have a 24-bit or better monitor. Some 55% have 16-bit monitors (called "Thousands" on a Mac), and only 10% are still on 256-color monitors. Still, if you want to make sure that images don't look fuzzy to these last folks, you should restrict at least the large areas of your images to colors that belong to the browser safe palette. For details on creating images with the browser safe palette, see page 66.

Transparency

Transparency is important for two reasons. First, you can use it to create complex layouts by making one image move behind another. Second, you can take advantage of transparency to give an image a non-rectangular outline, adding visual interest to your pages **(Figure 4.2)**. Both GIF and PNG allow transparency; JPEG does not.

Figure 4.1 *Both of these images have exactly 18 colors and look about the same on high-end monitors. But notice how the* dither *image is full of noise and patterning (called dithering) while the* safe *image is clean and sharp. That's because the* safe *image uses browser safe colors and the* dither *image doesn't.*

Creating Web Images

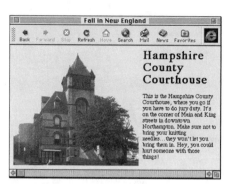

Figure 4.2 *The courthouse image's transparent background helps the image blend into the page, no matter what background color the visitor has chosen to view Web pages against. Real transparency is only available for GIF and PNG images.*

Speed

The fourth principal difference between Web images and printed images is that your visitors have to wait for Web images to download. (Imagine waiting for pictures to appear in your morning paper!)

How can you keep download time to a minimum? The easiest way is to use small images. The larger an image's physical size, the longer it takes to appear before your visitors' eyes. For tips on reducing your image's physical size, see page 62.

The second way to speed up download time is by compressing the image. There are three popular compression methods (that correspond to the three major formats): LZW (for GIF images), JPEG, and PNG. LZW is particularly effective for computer-generated art like logos, rendered text, and other images that have large areas of a single color. In fact, if you can reduce the number of colors in an image, LZW can often (but not always) compress the image even more. For more details on reducing colors, see page 69.

JPEG, on the other hand, is better at compressing photographs and other images that have many different colors. In fact, if you blur an image, thereby creating even more colors, JPEG compression is often more effective *(see page 77)*.

Of course, each method has its drawbacks. Because LZW is patented, developers have to pay royalties on software that uses it. This is one of the principal reasons the PNG format was created. Further, GIF images are limited to 256 colors. JPEG also has two disadvantages. First, it is *lossy* compression—deciding that the eye cannot distinguish as many colors as are in your original image, it may eliminate them permanently to save space. Uncompressing the image will not restore the lost data. Second, its compression information takes up a lot of space and is simply not worth it for smaller images. For details on compressing images with JPEG, see pages 76–77.

PNG compresses better than LZW without losing information like JPEG. Its major drawback is that Microsoft and Netscape have been slow to adopt it. For details on creating PNG images, see page 79.

Another way to keep your visitors happy while they're waiting is to offer a sneak preview of what the image will look like. All three major formats offer some form of progressive display, often called *interlacing*. For details on progressively rendering images, consult pages 73, 76, and 79.

Animation

One thing you won't be seeing on paper anytime soon are moving images. On the Web, they're everywhere. For information on creating animated images, see page 74. GIF (and not JPEG) images can be animated. You can also create animation with Flash *(see page 351)*.

Figure 4.3 *Logotypes and other computer-generated images or images with few colors are compressed efficiently with LZW and thus could be saved in GIF format. Even better at compressing images of this type is PNG format, though fewer browsers can view PNG images inline.*

Figure 4.4 *Full-color photographs and other naturally created images, or images with more than 256 colors should be saved in JPEG format.*

Creating Web Images

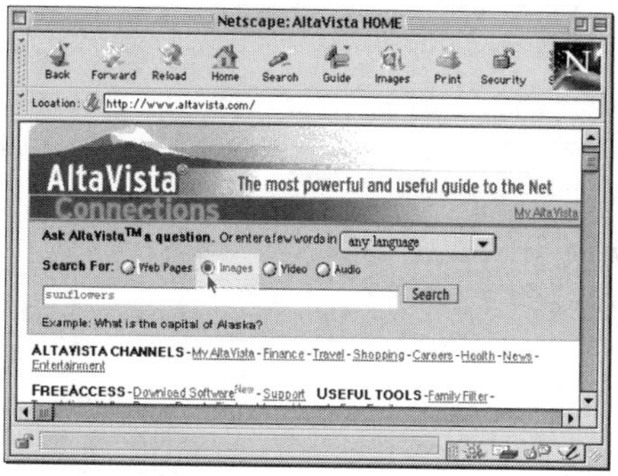

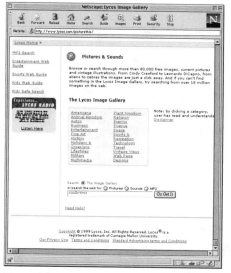

Figure 4.5 *Click the Images button at AltaVista to search for images that match the criteria you've typed.*

Figure 4.6 *Lycos' Image Gallery is a great place to get images for personal use, but be sure to read the disclaimer: you can't use the images on commercial sites nor alter them in any way except size.*

Getting Images

So how do you get an image that you can use for your Web page? There are three principal ways. You either buy or download ready-made images, digitize your photographs or handdrawn images with a scanner, or draw images from scratch in an image editing program like Photoshop. Once you've got them in your computer, you can adapt them to the Web, if necessary, with the rest of the techniques in this chapter.

To get images:

- You can use AltaVista *(www.altavista.com)* to find images on the Web. Click the Images button next to the Search box, and enter your criteria as usual **(Figure 4.5)**. Or go to *www.lycos.com/picturethis/* for Lycos' Image Gallery **(Figure 4.6)**.

- Many companies—like Adobe and others—sell stock photography and images on CD. Such disks often have several versions of each image for different purposes. Look for the Web or Multimedia version.

- Generally, the free images you find on the Web are for personal use only and cannot be modified. Images you buy can usually be used for any purpose (except for reselling the images themselves). Read any disclaimers or licenses carefully.

- Kodak and other companies will develop a roll of film directly onto a CD.

- Scanners and digital cameras have gotten incredibly cheap. If you want to put a lot of your own photos (or paper-bound images) on your page, one of these might be your best bet.

- If you create your own images, save them at 72 dpi in GIF, JPEG, or PNG. Don't save them as BMP—only Explorer for Windows users will be able to see them.

Getting Images

Making Images Smaller

Perhaps one of the most important improvements you can make to your page is to reduce the physical size of the images. This makes the images load more quickly and also helps visitors focus on what's really important.

To make images smaller by cropping:

1. Select the crop tool **(Figure 4.7)**. (You may have to click the Selection tool to find it—or just press the letter C.)

2. Use the crop tool to outline the important area of your image **(Figure 4.8)**.

3. If desired, adjust the area to be cropped by dragging the boxes around the selection border.

4. Double click in the center of the selection. The area around the selection disappears and all that's left is a lean, focused image **(Figure 4.9)**.

✔ Tip

■ Cropping does not change the proportions of the image. It simply gets rid of the parts of the image that you (or your visitors) don't need.

Figure 4.7 *Choose the crop tool in the upper-left box of the tool palette. It may be necessary to click and hold a selection tool and then choose the crop tool from the pop-up menu.*

Figure 4.8 *Use the crop tool to select the area of the image that you want to keep. Then double click in the center of the selection.*

Figure 4.9 *This image is less than one third the size of the larger image and thus will load more than three times faster. In addition, it focuses the visitor's attention on what's important.*

Making Images Smaller

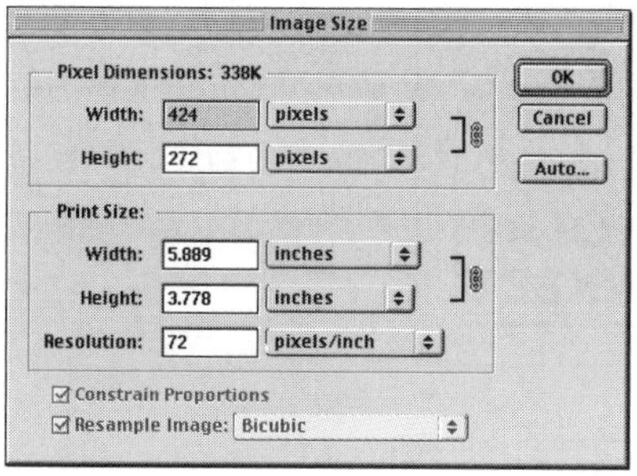

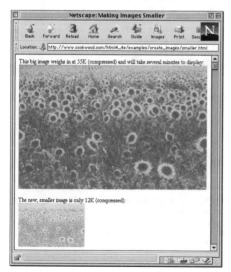

Figure 4.10 *Make sure both Constrain Proportions and Resample Image are checked. Notice the original file size was 338K (uncompressed)!*

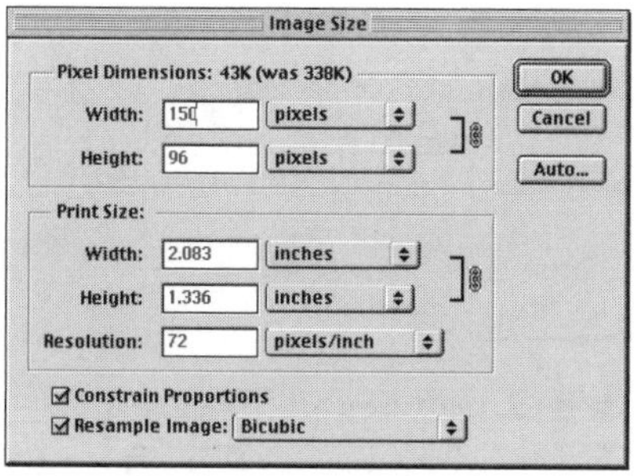

Figure 4.11 *Change the resolution to 72 and the width to 400 or less. The new file size is 43K (uncompressed), which is much better.*

Figure 4.12 *The original oversized image is shown at the top of this window. The new reduced image is shown below.*

To make images smaller by changing the image size:

1. Choose Image > Image Size.

2. In the Image Size dialog box that appears, make sure the Constrain Proportions and Resample Image options are both checked **(Figure 4.10)**.

3. Make sure the resolution is set to 72 **(Figure 4.11)**.

4. Enter the desired final dimensions for the image.

5. Click OK. The image is resized.

✔ Tips

■ Adjusting the resolution automatically adjusts the width. If you want to create an image of a given width, adjust the resolution first and then type in the desired width.

■ Use these techniques to create icons or miniatures that point to oversized or external images *(see page 86)*. Just remember to save the icon with a different name so as not to replace the full-size image **(Figure 4.12)**.

Making Images Smaller

Exporting GIF Images from Photoshop

Use the GIF format for logos, banners, and other computer-generated images. GIF images are limited to 256 colors or fewer.

To export GIF images from Photoshop:

1. Create an RGB image at 72 dpi **(Figure 4.13)**.

2. Choose File > Export > GIF89a Export **(Figure 4.14)**. The GIF 89a Export dialog box appears **(Figure 4.15)**.

3. If desired, click the Transparency Index Color box to choose how transparency will be displayed in your image. For details on creating transparency itself, see page 70.

4. If desired, choose an option in the Palette submenu or load a custom palette. For details, consult *Reducing the Number of Colors* on page 69.

5. If desired, click the Preview button to see how the image will appear given the palette and number of colors chosen in the previous step.

6. If desired, click the Interlaced option in the bottom-left corner. For more information, consult *Interlacing GIF Images* on page 73.

7. Click OK.

8. In the dialog box that appears, give the image a short name with the .gif extension **(Figure 4.16)**.

9. Click Save.

Figure 4.13 *Create an RGB image at 72 dpi. Since most monitors can't view images at higher resolutions, any higher value is just wasting bandwidth—and your visitors' time. And yes, that is a quarter moon.*

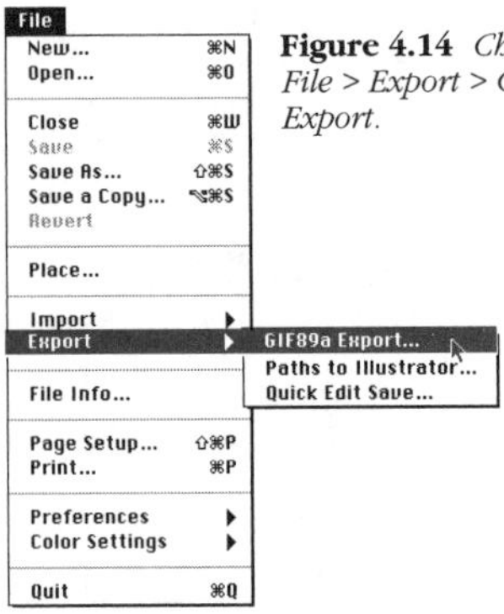

Figure 4.14 *Choose File > Export > GIF89a Export.*

Figure 4.15 *Choose the desired options in the GIF89a Export dialog box for transparency, color reduction, and interlacing.*

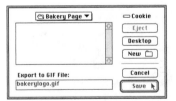

Figure 4.16 *Once you click OK in the GIF89a Export dialog box (Figure 4.15), the Save dialog box appears. Photoshop automatically appends the .gif extension to the name. If necessary, change the name and/or folder. Then click Save.*

Figure 4.17 *If you have several layers in your document and only want to include some of them in the exported GIF, simply hide the unwanted ones before exporting. In this example, I've hidden the background to export just the main portion of the logo.*

Figure 4.18 *To export a caption with your GIF image, first choose File Info in the File menu.*

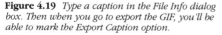

Figure 4.19 *Type a caption in the File Info dialog box. Then when you go to export the GIF, you'll be able to mark the Export Caption option.*

✔ Tips

■ Windows users: These techniques work just as well in Photoshop for Windows.

■ Only the visible layers are exported. Hide any layers that you don't want to include in the GIF image **(Figure 4.17)**.

■ If GIF89a Export doesn't appear in your Export submenu, it's because you have an old version of Photoshop. You can download the GIF89a plug-in from Adobe *(www.adobe.com)*. Or you can create GIF images by converting the document to Indexed-color, Grayscale, or Bitmap mode, and then saving the document in CompuServe GIF format.

■ By using the Export plug-in, you maintain the original (RGB) image as well as the new GIF image. You can return to the RGB image, modify it, and then export new GIFs as desired.

■ If your image is on a transparent layer, transparent areas are automatically converted to transparency in the GIF image. For more information, consult *Creating Transparency* on pages 70–71.

■ The fewer colors in your final image, the smaller it will be and the faster it will load. For details, consult *Reducing the Number of Colors* on page 69.

■ On the Mac, check the Export Caption option in the Save box if you've added a caption to the File Info dialog box (using File > File Info) and you want to include that information with the GIF file for use with Fetch or other image cataloging software **(Figures 4.18 and 4.19)**.

■ Since icons add to the size of your file, choose Never (under Image Previews) in the Preferences dialog box.

Using (Mostly) Browser Safe Colors

When browsers on an 8-bit monitor encounter images on a page with more than 216 colors, they automatically use a special set of colors called the *browser safe palette* to approximate the rest. The results are often less than stellar. On the other hand, if you limit yourself to 216 colors, it's hard to create soft, anti-aliased edges—which are crucial for text. A compromise is in order: browser safe colors for big areas, other colors for edges.

In order to pick browser safe colors for large areas, you'll have to load them into your Swatches palette.

To load the browser safe palette:

1. Locate the Web Safe Colors palette in the Photoshop 5 folder.

   Or, if you have an earlier version of Photoshop, download the browser safe palette from my Web site *(see page 20)*.

2. Choose Window > Show Swatches to display the Swatches palette **(Figure 4.20)**. The Swatches palette appears **(Figure 4.21)**.

3. Choose Replace Swatches in the Swatches palette menu **(Figure 4.22)**.

4. In the dialog box that appears, select the palette you located or downloaded in step 1 and click Open **(Figure 4.23)**. The browser safe colors appear in the Swatches palette **(Figure 4.24)**.

✔ Tip

■ Choose Load Swatches in step 3 above if you prefer to *add* the browser safe colors without eliminating the existing colors in your palette.

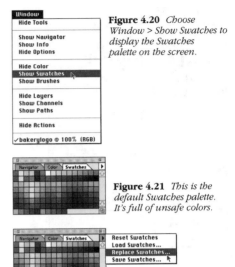

Figure 4.20 *Choose Window > Show Swatches to display the Swatches palette on the screen.*

Figure 4.21 *This is the default Swatches palette. It's full of unsafe colors.*

Figure 4.22 *Choose Replace Swatches from the submenu that comes off of that little arrow at the top-right corner of the Swatches palette.*

Figure 4.23 *Choose a browser safe palette and click Open. In Photoshop 5 you'll find the Web Safe Colors palette in the Color Palettes folder, in the Goodies folder, in the Adobe Photoshop 5 folder. If you have an earlier version of Photoshop, you can download the Browser Safe Palette from this book's Web site— see page 20.*

Figure 4.24 *The full set of 216 browser safe colors is displayed in the Swatches palette. You can choose any of these for the large areas of your Web images.*

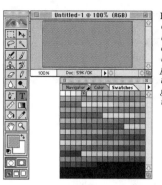

Figure 4.25 *Choose the background color from the browser safe palette and fill the background with it.*

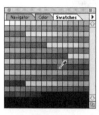

Figure 4.26 *Choose a foreground color for the text from the browser safe palette.*

Figure 4.27 *Choose the font, size, and other characteristics, type the desired text, and make sure you check the Anti-Aliased option.*

Figure 4.28 *Even though the edges are anti-aliased (and thus not browser safe) the text does not dither. It'd be perfect for a header if I cropped it a little better and wrote something useful.*

Although the example I show here is about text, you can use this technique to create any Web image. It'll look as good as possible on 8-bit monitors because most of the color is browser safe. And it'll look great on 24-bit monitors because the edges are smooth and anti-aliased.

To use (mostly) browser safe colors to create text:

1. Load the browser safe palette as described on the preceding page.

2. Create a new document in RGB mode.

3. If desired, choose a background color from the Swatches palette and fill the background with it **(Figure 4.25)**.

4. Choose a foreground color from the Swatches palette **(Figure 4.26)**.

5. Choose the type tool and click in the image where you wish to create the text. The Type Tool box appears.

6. Type the desired text and check the Anti-Aliased option **(Figure 4.27)**.

7. Click OK. The text appears in the image. Note that the body of the text (and of the background) is Web safe, while the colors used to create the smooth, anti-aliased edges are probably not **(Figure 4.28)**.

8. Export the image to GIF as described on page 64.

✔ Tips

- Really want to stick to Web safe colors? Don't use any anti-aliased tools, like Text, Selection, Feathering, etc.

- Use this technique to create professional looking headlines with unusual fonts.

Using (Mostly) Browser Safe Colors

Converting to Browser Safe Colors

If you've already created all your images and want to make sure that they only use browser safe colors, you can load a browser safe palette and have Photoshop map the unsafe colors to the safe ones as best it sees fit.

To convert to browser safe colors:

1. Choose File > Open to open an existing image.

2. If the image is not already in RGB mode, choose Image > Mode > RGB.

3. Choose Image > Mode > Indexed Color **(Figure 4.30)**. The Indexed Color dialog box appears **(Figure 4.31)**.

4. In the Palette pop-up menu, choose Web. A value of 216 is automatically entered for the number of colors.

5. Click OK.

✔ Tips

■ Remember that the goal is for the visitor to see a clear, crisp image—not that the image use one set of colors or another. With that in mind, note that Photoshop may have to dither the browser safe colors to create the original ones. You may be better off just leaving the image the way it is—or creating it from scratch with browser safe colors.

■ You generally should not use this technique on photographs. Instead, use the Adaptive palette, or save them as JPEG images *(see page 76)*.

Figure 4.29 *This is the original image, created with non browser safe colors.*

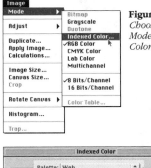

Figure 4.30 *Choose Image > Mode > Indexed Color.*

Figure 4.31 *In the Indexed Color dialog box, choose Web in the Palette menu. The Colors option will be set to 216 automatically.*

Figure 4.32 *The quality of the results depends on the colors you originally chose for the image. If Photoshop has to heavily dither browser safe colors to simulate the original ones, you may be better off not changing the colors at all.*

Figure 4.33 *Choose Adaptive for Palette and then enter the desired number of colors in the Colors box. Finally, click the Preview button to see how the illustration will look on the page.*

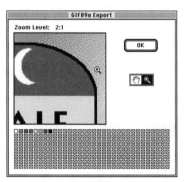

Figure 4.34 *With only eight colors, the dithering is very obvious. Click OK to go back to the GIF89a Export dialog box and try another value.*

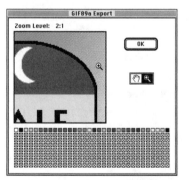

Figure 4.35 *A value of 32 considerably reduces the amount of colors—with minimal dithering.*

Reducing the Number of Colors

Whether or not you've decided to keep to browser safe colors, you can make compression more efficient by reducing the number of colors in your GIF images. And better compression means faster loading.

To reduce the number of colors in an image:

1. Open an RGB image with Photoshop.

2. Choose File > Export > GIF89a Export.

3. In the GIF 89a Export dialog box, choose Adaptive in the Palette pop-up menu **(Figure 4.33)**.

4. Enter the desired number of colors in the Colors box.

5. Click Preview to see how the image will look with this number of colors **(Figures 4.34 and 4.35)**. Use the magnifying glass and the hand to examine the image carefully. Click OK to return to the main dialog box.

6. Repeat steps 4–5 until you find the least number of colors you can live with.

7. Click OK and save the document.

✔ Tips

■ If the image is already in indexed color and you wish to reduce the colors further, you have two choices. Either convert the document to RGB mode and then follow the steps above, or convert the image to RGB mode and then choose Image > Mode > Indexed Color and enter a smaller number of colors in the Colors box of the dialog box that appears.

■ If you're going to save the image as JPEG, reducing the number of colors results in *larger* files *(see page 77)*.

Creating Transparency

With Photoshop's GIF89a Export command, you can make any part of a GIF image transparent so that it blends almost seamlessly with the page. You can create your image on a transparent layer, make one or more colors transparent, or you can create an extra channel and make *it* transparent.

To make a layer transparent:

1. Open an RGB image in Photoshop.

2. Select the part of the image that you wish to export **(Figure 4.36)**.

3. Choose Edit > Copy. Then choose Edit > Paste **(Figure 4.37)**. (In Photoshop 4, choose Edit > Paste Layer.)

4. Hide or eliminate all layers except the transparent one **(Figure 4.38)**.

5. Continue from step 2 on page 64.

To make certain colors transparent:

1. Create or open an indexed-color image in Photoshop.

2. Choose File > Export > GIF89a Export.

3. In the dialog box that appears, choose the eyedropper and click the color(s) in the image that you want to make transparent **(Figure 4.39)**. You can also click colors in the color table below the image. Hold down Option (Mac) or Alt (Windows) as you click to restore colors to their original state.

4. The transparent areas of the image are displayed in the color shown in the Transparency Index Color box. Click in the box to change the color.

5. Click OK and give the file a name.

Figure 4.36 *Select the part of the image that you wish to export as a GIF image.*

Figure 4.37 *Choose Edit > Copy (left). Then choose Edit > Paste (right).*

Figure 4.38 *Hide all the layers except the transparent one by clicking on the eye icon to the left of the layer name. Note that transparency in Photoshop is displayed with a checkerboard (left).*

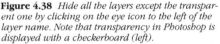

Figure 4.39 *If you export an indexed-color image, you can choose which colors should be transparent by clicking them with the eyedropper. Hold down Option (Mac) or Alt (Windows) to restore colors to their original state. (Note that the moon, because it is white like the background, is also made transparent.)*

Figure 4.40 *Select the part of the image that you want to make transparent. In this example, the white background is selected but the white moon is not.*

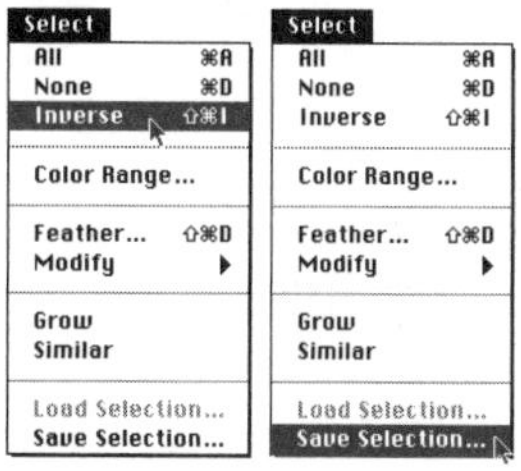

Figure 4.41 *Choose Select > Inverse (left). Then choose Select > Save Selection.*

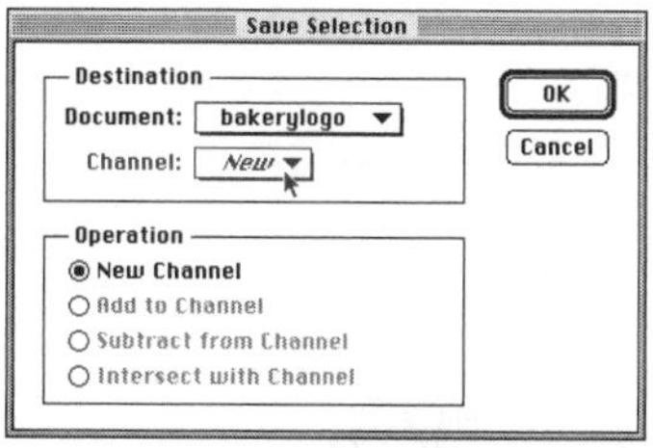

Figure 4.42 *In the Save Selection dialog box, choose New in the Channel menu and click OK.*

Figure 4.43 *Choose the desired channel in the Transparency From submenu. The transparent areas will be shown with the color chosen in the Transparency Index Color box. Notice that the moon will not be transparent, even though it is the same color as the rest of the transparent area (the background).*

Photoshop also lets you make certain areas transparent, regardless of their color. This is ideal for creating a transparent background without knocking out similar colors in the body of the image.

To make a selection transparent:

1. Create or open an indexed-color image in Photoshop.

2. Select the part of the image that you want to make transparent **(Fig. 4.40)**.

3. Choose Select > Inverse **(Fig. 4.41)**.

4. Choose Select > Save Selection **(Figure 4.41)**.

5. In the Save Selection dialog box that appears, choose New from the Channel menu and click OK **(Figure 4.42)**.

6. Deselect everything.

7. Choose File > Export > GIF89a Export.

8. In the dialog box that appears, choose the channel number in the Transparency From submenu **(Figure 4.43)**. Press Option (Mac) or Alt (Windows) if you want to invert the selection.

9. Click OK and give the file a name.

✔ Tips

■ Any part of an image that you mark as transparent is replaced by the color specified in the Transparency Index Color box. This is one reason it's better to use the Export option and leave the original image intact.

■ To ensure that anti-aliased edges look good, make sure the image's original background color (now transparent) matches the *page's* background color *(see page 98)*.

Creating Transparency

Creating Fake Transparency

Fake transparency means making the image's background the same color as the background of your page so that the image blends in as if the background were transparent.

To fake transparency by making the background a solid color:

1. Open the image in Photoshop, or another image editing program.

2. Use the lasso and other selection tools to select everything except the background **(Figure 4.44)**.

3. Choose Select > Inverse to select only the background **(Figure 4.45)**.

4. Click the Background color control box to set it to the desired color.

5. Press Delete to change the color of the selected area (the background) to the current background color **(Figure 4.46)**.

6. Save the image.

✔ Tips

■ It's probably a good idea to choose a browser safe color for the background. Otherwise, it will dither on 256 color monitors. For more details, consult *Using (Mostly) Browser Safe Colors* on page 66.

■ You can also use this method to simulate transparency in JPEG images.

■ This is also a good way to prepare images for programs that only allow you to make one color transparent.

■ Of course, if your visitors override the background color, the effect is lost.

Figure 4.44 *Select the image itself, using the lasso or other selection tools.*

Figure 4.45 *Choose Select > Inverse to select everything but the image, that is, to select the background.*

Background color control

Figure 4.46 *Once you've inverted the selection, click the Background color control, choose the desired background color, and then press the Delete key to change the background to one solid color, in this case, white.*

Figure 4.47 *If you are exporting a GIF image from RGB mode, the Interlaced option will appear in the bottom-left corner of the GIF89a Export dialog box.*

Figure 4.48 *If the image was in indexed color, the Interlace option appears at the right in the center of the dialog box.*

Interlacing GIF Images

Interlacing an image prepares it so that a browser can show it at gradually increasing resolutions. Although the initial image is blurry, the visitor does not have to wait for the finished image to appear. Instead, the visitor can scroll around the page and then return when the image is complete.

To interlace an image:

1. Open the image in Photoshop.

2. Choose File > Export > GIF89a Export.

3. Check the Interlaced option in the dialog box that appears. The box is slightly different for RGB **(Figure 4.47)** vs. indexed-color images **(Figure 4.48)**, but the effect is the same.

4. Click OK.

5. Enter a short name and extension in the dialog box that appears.

✔ Tip

■ For information on creating JPEG images that appear gradually, similar to the interlacing effect in GIF images, consult *Creating JPEG Images* on page 76.

Figure 4.49 *A browser will show the interlaced image gradually, allowing the visitor to move around the page and read the text while the image comes into full view.*

Interlacing GIF Images

Creating Animated GIFs

The GIF89a format can contain several images at once which are displayed one after another. You can use this feature to create slide shows or approximate moving images. The most popular shareware tool for creating animated GIFs on Windows machines is GIF Construction Set by Alchemy Mindworks. On the Mac, try GIFBuilder, a freeware program developed by Yves Piguet.

To create an animated GIF with GIF Construction Set for Windows:

1. Create the series of images that will form the animated GIF. The images can be in GIF, JPEG, or even BMP format.

2. Open GIF Construction Set.

3. Choose File > Animation Wizard **(Figure 4.50)**. A series of dialog boxes appear.

4. Mark the appropriate options in each of the Wizard's panels. You'll have a chance to select the GIF files from step 1 that you want to use for the animated GIF **(Figure 4.51)**.

5. When the Animation Wizard has finished, it'll display the complete set of files. Click the eyeglasses in the toolbar to see a preview of your animation **(Figure 4.52)**.

✔ Tips

- GIF Construction Set can do much more than just assemble pre-fabricated GIF files, as I've shown you here.

- Download GIF Construction Set from *www.mindworkshop.com/alchemy/gifcon.html*. It's shareware and costs $20.

- You insert an animated GIF on your page just like any other image *(see page 82)*.

Figure 4.50 *Choose File > Animation Wizard to create a simple animated GIF from a series of files with GIF Construction Set.*

Figure 4.51 *The Animation Wizard will ask you a series of questions, including which files it should create the animated GIF from, as shown here.*

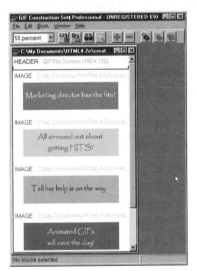

Figure 4.52 *When the Animation Wizard has finished compiling the animated GIF it displays the file. You can make additional changes or go ahead and save it. (You can view this pseudo-BurmaShave animated GIF in action on my Web site: www.cookwood.com/html4_4e/examples.)*

Creating Animated GIFs

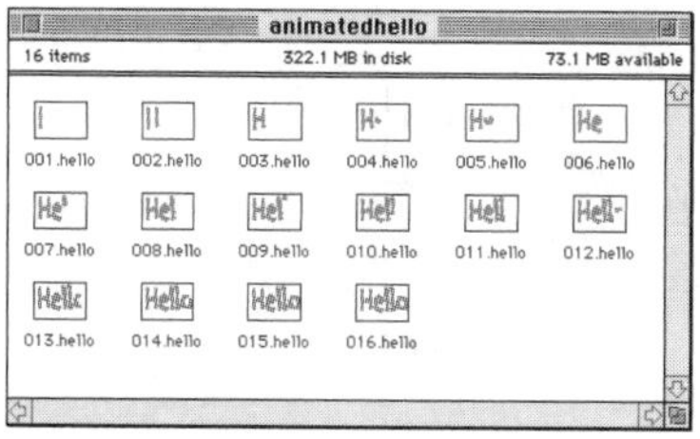

Figure 4.53 *Create the individual files in Photoshop, PICT, or GIF format. If you number them sequentially, they'll appear in order automatically in GIFBuilder.*

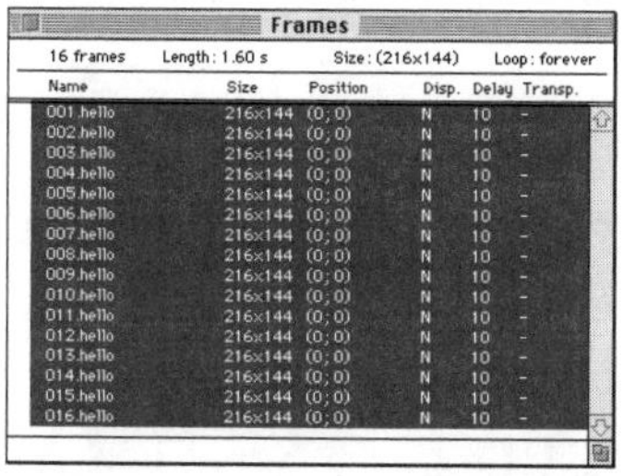

Figure 4.54 *Once you drag the files to the GIF-Builder Frames window, they'll appear in alphabetical order. Reorder them as needed.*

Figure 4.55 *Choose Animation > Start to test the animated GIF. The image appears in the Animation window. It's kind of hard to show in a book... (but you can see it at www.cookwood.com/ html4_4e/examples/).*

Figure 4.56 *When you're satisfied with the animated GIF, choose Save in the File menu and then, in the Save dialog box, give the file a name, with the .gif extension. Click Save.*

Figure 4.57 *The resulting GIF image looks normal in the Finder, but it dances on any browser that recognizes the GIF89a format.*

To create an animated GIF with GIFBuilder for Macintosh:

1. Create the series of images that will form the animated GIF **(Figure 4.53)**. The images can be in Photoshop, PICT, or GIF format, among others.

2. Open GIFBuilder.

3. Select all the images and drag them to the appropriate window. The images will appear in alphabetical order, by default **(Figure 4.54)**. You can reorder them as necessary.

4. If desired, choose Animation > Start to see a preview of your animated GIF **(Figure 4.55)**.

5. If desired, choose Loop in the Options menu to determine if the animation should play once, more than once, or continuously (Forever).

6. Add new images by choosing File > Add Frame.

7. Once you are satisfied with your animated GIF, choose File > Save.

8. In the Save dialog box, give the animated GIF a name, ending with the .gif extension, and click Save **(Figure 4.56)**. The new conglomerated file looks just like a regular GIF **(Figure 4.57)**.

✔ Tip

■ You can find GIFBuilder's home page at *iawww.epfl.ch/Staff/Yves.Piguet/clip2gif-home/GifBuilder.html* (that hyphen is part of the address), but he suggests you download the program (if you're in the United States) from *www.download.com*.

Creating JPEG Images

Use JPEG compression for photographs and for images with more than 256 colors.

To save an image with JPEG compression:

1. Open the image with Photoshop, or the desired image editing program.

2. Choose Image > Mode > RGB Color, if it's not already selected **(Figure 4.58)**.

3. Choose File > Save As.

4. In the Save As dialog box that appears, choose JPEG in the Format pop-up menu **(Figure 4.59)**.

5. Give the file a name and the .jpg or .jpeg extension (it doesn't matter which), and then click Save.

6. In the JPEG Options dialog box that appears, choose the desired quality **(Figure 4.60)**.

7. If desired, choose Progressive to have the image appear gradually in the browser. You can also specify how many scans or passes it will take to display the full image.

8. Click OK.

✔ Tips

■ Because I've found that the Progressive option creates smaller images than the other options, I always choose that option when saving JPEG images—even when I don't care about progressive display.

■ You may want to experiment with different compression values until you get an image with sufficient quality at a file size you (and your visitors) can live with.

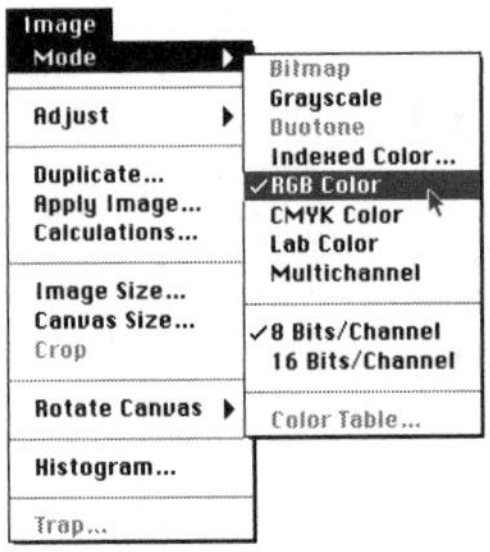

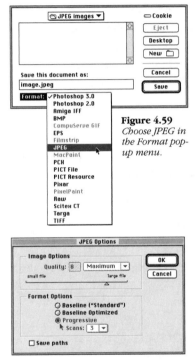

Figure 4.58 *In Photoshop, a JPEG image may be in either RGB Color or CMYK Color. However, since Web images are generally viewed on a monitor, you should use RGB mode.*

Figure 4.59 *Choose JPEG in the Format pop-up menu.*

Figure 4.60 *Choose a compression quality (higher compression means less quality) and then a format option. I recommend always choosing Progressive since it always seems to result in a smaller file.*

Figure 4.61 *This is the original image. It has a file size of some 69K.*

Figure 4.62 *Choose Filter > Blur > Blur to lessen the differences in the image from one area to another thereby making the compression more efficient.*

Figure 4.63 *Your visitors probably won't complain about the loss in sharpness (can you tell?) but they'll appreciate the fact that the image is now only 60K. (The image size given in the status area is the uncompressed size.)*

Blurring Images to Aid JPEG Compression

Because of the way JPEG works, the softer the transition from color to color, the more efficiently the image can be compressed. So, if you blur the image slightly, you may be able to reduce the file size—and thus the load time—even further.

To blur images to aid JPEG compression:

1. Create or open the RGB image.

2. Choose Filter > Blur > Blur **(Fig. 4.62)**. The image is blurred slightly.

3. Save the image as JPEG as described on page 76.

✔ **Tips**

■ This is one of those cases in which a little goes a long way. You don't need to blur the image beyond recognition to get file size savings. Don't forget: you want your visitors to be able to recognize what's in the picture.

■ You have to decide if the slight loss of detail is worth faster download times and less waiting for your visitors. If all your visitors use 14K modems on 256-bit monitors, this technique may be very useful. Visitors with T1 lines on high-end systems, on the other hand, may not benefit enough from the speed improvement to make sacrificing image sharpness worthwhile.

■ Since Photoshop always displays the uncompressed size in the status bar **(Figure 4.63)**, you have to check the size of the image file from the Desktop, or, even better, after it has been uploaded to the server.

Creating Low Resolution Images

If you have a lot of large images on your page, you can make life more pleasant for your visitor by creating a low resolution image that the browser can show immediately while it takes its time loading the higher resolution image.

To create a low resolution version of your image:

1. Open your image in Photoshop, or other image editing program.

2. Choose Image > Image Size **(Figure 4.64)**.

3. Check Constrain Proportions and Resample Image at the bottom of the Image Size dialog box. **(Figure 4.65)**.

4. Change the value of Resolution to 18 dpi and click OK **(Figure 4.66)**.

5. Choose File > Save As and give the low resolution image a new name.

6. Click Save.

✔ Tips

- There is no difference between creating a low resolution image and changing the size of the image using the Width and Height fields *(see page 63)*. Changing an image's size by changing its resolution is just an easy way to reduce it evenly to half or a quarter of its original size.

- When you insert a low resolution image on your page, you must use the WIDTH and HEIGHT attributes to specify the dimensions of *the original image* or else both the versions will appear in miniature. For more details, see page 87.

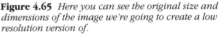

Figure 4.64 *Choose Image > Image Size.*

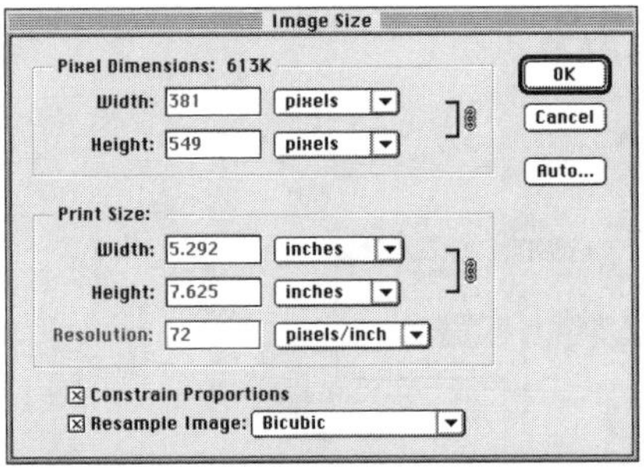

Figure 4.65 *Here you can see the original size and dimensions of the image we're going to create a low resolution version of.*

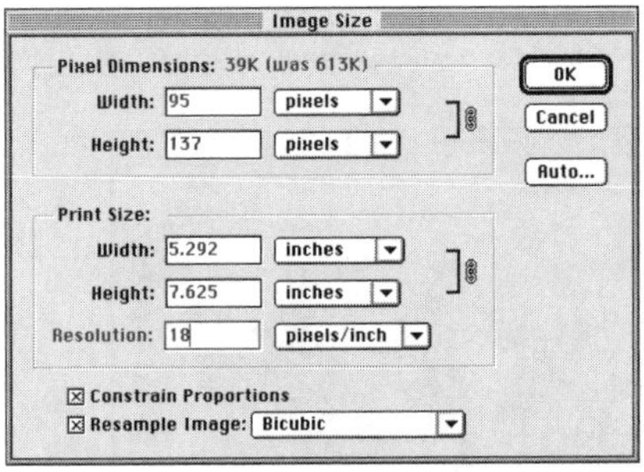

Figure 4.66 *With Constrain Proportions and Resample Image checked at the bottom of the dialog box, change the Resolution to 18. Notice that the file size shrinks to 39K but that the print dimensions remain the same.*

Creating Low Resolution Images

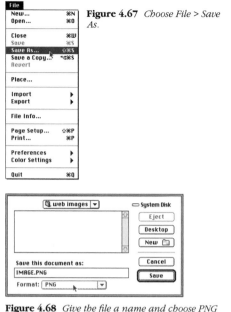

Figure 4.67 *Choose File > Save As.*

Figure 4.68 *Give the file a name and choose PNG in the Format pop-up menu. Then click Save.*

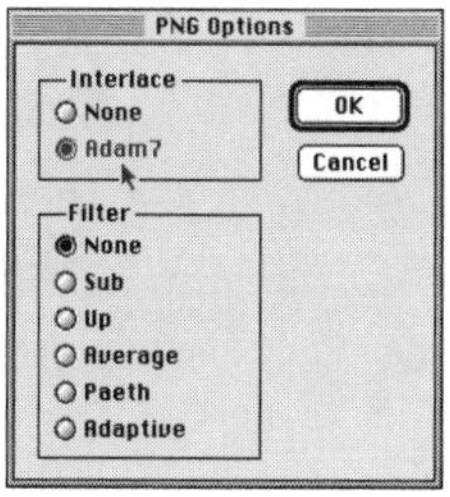

Figure 4.69 *Choose Adam7 under Interlace to have the PNG appear gradually in your visitors' browsers.*

Creating PNG Files

Although GIF is the most popular image format on the Web today, the W3C hopes that tomorrow everyone will be inserting PNG images on their pages. PNG (pronounced *ping*) has many advantages over GIF, not least among them the fact that its compression scheme is not patented and thus software developers can implement it for free. It also compresses more effectively than GIF, is not lossy, and allows partial transparency. Its major disadvantage is that it is relatively unknown and the major browsers have taken a while to support it. In fact, while current versions of both Explorer and Communicator view PNG images inline, they still don't support all its features.

To create a PNG image:

1. Create an RGB image.

2. Choose File > Save As **(Figure 4.67)**.

3. In the dialog box that appears, choose PNG in the Format pop-up menu and click Save **(Figure 4.68)**. The PNG Options dialog box appears.

4. If desired, choose Adam7 to create an interlaced image **(Figure 4.69)**.

5. Click OK.

✔ Tips

■ Unfortunately, Adobe has not made available information about the filters offered in Photoshop's PNG Options dialog box. They are for choosing different compression methods.

■ You can get more information about the PNG format on the PNG home page: *www.cdrom.com/pub/png/png.html*.

Creating PNG Files

Using Images

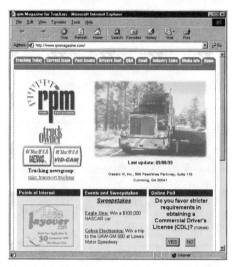

Once you've created the fastest-loading, hottest-looking images you can—perhaps with the techniques in the previous chapter—you're ready to get back to HTML and get those images on your page.

Figure 5.1 *This page, nicely designed by Brian Foster, uses images well. Notice that much of the text in the upper row of buttons is made with GIF images. (Only real text is shown in black here.)*

Inserting Images on a Page

You can place all kinds of images on your Web page, from logos to photographs. Images placed as described here appear automatically when the visitor jumps to your page, as long as the browser is set up to view them.

To insert an image on a page:

1. Place the cursor where you want the image to appear.

2. Type **<IMG SRC="image.ext"** where *image.ext* indicates the location of the image file on the server.

3. If desired, type **BORDER=n**, where *n* is the thickness of the border in pixels.

4. Type the final **>**.

✔ Tips

■ Add a <P> or <BR> before an image definition to start it on its own line.

■ For information on creating images especially for Web pages, consult Chapter 4, *Creating Web Images*.

■ Use this technique to place GIF, JPEG, PNG, or any other kind of images that the browser recognizes.

■ Don't expect your visitors to wait more than 30 seconds to load and view your page (about 30K total with a 14.4 Kbps modem connection). To get by this limit, create miniatures *(see page 63)* of large images and let visitors choose to view the larger images *(see page 86)* only if desired.

■ You can't change the border color.

■ Images used in a link *(see page 128)* automatically have a thin, blue border. Use BORDER=0 to eliminate it.

```
code.html
<HTML><HEAD><TITLE>Inserting an Inline
Image</TITLE></HEAD>

<BODY>

<H1>Cookie and Woody</H1>

<P>Generally considered the sweetest and yet
most independent cats in the Pioneer Valley,
Cookie and Woody are consistently
underestimated by their humble humans.

Here's Cookie and Woody, exhausted after
helping us pack the last time we moved:

<P><IMG SRC="catsonbox.gif">

</BODY></HTML>
```

Figure 5.2 *It's a good idea to enclose the name of the image file within quotation marks, although, if the name contains only letters and numbers and one period, it's not officially required.*

Figure 5.3 *Images are aligned to the left side of the page, by default. To wrap text around an image, use the ALIGN attribute (see pages 88 and 89).*

```
code.html
<HTML><HEAD><TITLE>Providing alternate
text</TITLE></HEAD><BODY>

<H1>Cookie and Woody</H1>

<P>Generally considered the sweetest and yet
most independent cats in the Pioneer Valley,
Cookie and Woody are consistently
underestimated by their humble humans.

Here's Cookie and Woody, exhausted after
helping us pack the last time we moved:

<P><IMG SRC="catsonbox.gif" ALT="Image of
Cookie and Woody sleeping on a box">

</BODY></HTML>
```

Figure 5.4 *If your alternate text contains one or more spaces, you must enclose it in quotation marks.*

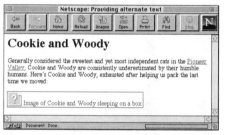

Figure 5.5 *The alternate text appears if the image can't be found, if the visitor has deselected Autoload images, or if the browser doesn't support images.*

Figure 5.6 *On Windows machines, when the visitor points at an image with alternate text, the alternate text appears in a tool tip. This is a great way to give your visitors extra information about an image.*

Offering Alternate Text

Some browsers do not support images at all. Other browsers support them but the visitor may have such a slow connection that they choose not to view the images, or to load them in manually. You can create text that will appear if the image, for whatever reason, does not.

To offer alternate text when images don't appear:

1. Place the cursor where you want the image (or alternate text) to appear.

2. Type **<IMG SRC="image.ext"**, where *image.ext* is the location of the image on the server.

3. Type **ALT="**.

4. Type the text that should appear if, for some reason, the image itself does not.

5. Type **">**.

✔ Tips

- On Windows, the text specified with the ALT tag is also used as a *tool tip*. In other words, when the visitor points at the image with the pointer, the ALT text appears **(Figure 5.6)**.

- HTML 4 considers ALT a *required* attribute. Nevertheless, if you do forget ALT once or twice, you will not be struck with lightning. I don't think.

- If the image is just for formatting, like a horizontal line or a bullet image, the W3C suggests you use **ALT=""**.

- Some browsers, like Lynx, that do not support images, are used by the blind because they can read the contents of the ALT tag out loud. This is just one more reason to add alternate text to your images.

Specifying Size for Speedier Viewing

When a browser gets to the HTML code for an image, it must load the image to see how big it is and how much space must be reserved for it. If you specify the image's dimensions, the browser can fill in the text around the image as the image loads, so that your visitors have something to read while waiting for the images.

There are several ways to get the exact dimensions of your images. If you've downloaded the images off the Web, you can use Netscape or Explorer to tell you how big the image is. (If you've created the image yourself, your image editing program should also be able to tell you how big the image is.)

To figure out the size of your image with Netscape:

Open the image by itself in Netscape. The image's dimensions are displayed in the browser's title bar **(Figure 5.7)**.

To figure out the size of your image with Explorer:

1. Open the image by itself in Explorer.

2. Right click the image and choose Properties **(Figure 5.8)**. The Properties box appears. The dimensions are displayed near the bottom **(Figure 5.9)**.

To figure out the size of your image with Photoshop:

1. Open the image in Photoshop.

2. Choose Image > Image Size.

3. Choose pixels for the unit of measure in both the Width and Height pop-up menus. The dimensions are displayed.

Figure 5.7 *If you open an image by itself in Netscape, the image's dimensions are displayed in the title bar.*

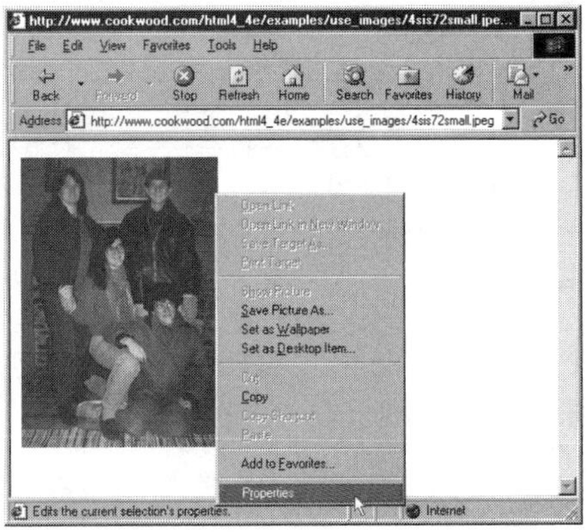

Figure 5.8 *Right click an image in Explorer and choose Properties in the pop-up menu.*

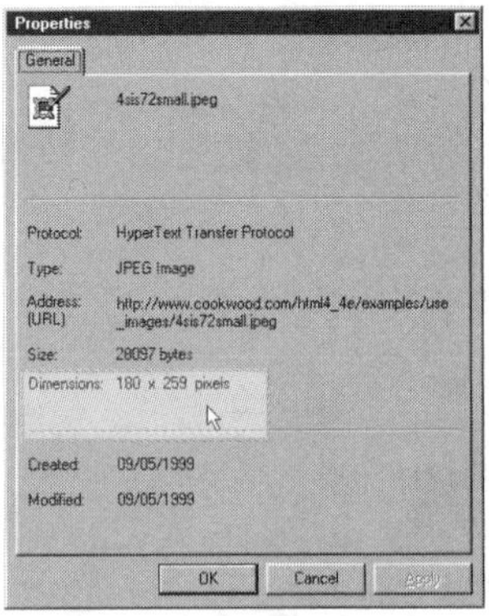

Figure 5.9 *The dimensions in pixels of the image are displayed in the lower area of the Properties box.*

```
code.html
<H1>The Four Sisters</H1>

<P>The Four Sisters Corporaton was begun by
the previously unknown four sisters. Here's a rare
photo:

<P><IMG SRC="4sis72small.jpeg" WIDTH=180
HEIGHT=259 ALT="The Four Sisters">

<P>Beatrice, the oldest sister, shown here on the
left, is the Art Director for TFS . She joined the
corporation in 1960 and has been one of its
most ardent supporters. Jocelyn, shown here
kneeling is the corporation's Director of
Education and Training. She oversees the
training courses for all of TFS' employees and
dependents. Eugenia, the third sister, shown
sitting in this picture, is the new Human
Resources Director. She is in charge of recruiting
new members of the TFS family. Last but not least
is Kimberly, Head of Research and Development.
```

Figure 5.10 *If you specify the exact height and width values in pixels, the browser won't have to spend time doing it and will display the image more quickly.*

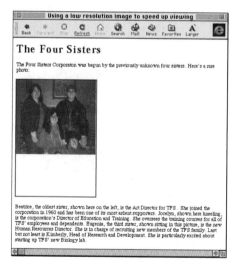

Figure 5.11 *Notice that the second paragraph of text is displayed even though the image has not finished loading. This means your visitors will have something to do while they're waiting.*

To specify the size of your image for speedier viewing:

1. Figure out the size of your image using one of the techniques described on page 84.

2. In your HTML document where you wish the image to appear, type **<IMG SRC="image.location"**, where *image.location* is the location of the image on the server.

3. Type **WIDTH=x HEIGHT=y**, using the values you jotted down in step 1 to specify the values for *x* and *y* (the width and height of your image) in pixels. For more information on using WIDTH and HEIGHT to scale images consult *Scaling an Image* on page 92.

4. Add other image attributes as desired and then type the final **>**.

Specifying Size for Speedier Viewing

Linking Icons to External Images

If you have a particularly large image, you can create a miniature version or icon of it *(see page 63)* that displays quickly on the page and then add a link that leads the visitor to the full size image.

To link a small icon to your larger image:

1. Place the cursor in your HTML page where you wish the icon to be placed.

2. Type **<A HREF="image.location">**, where *image.location* is the location of the full sized image on your server.

3. Type **<IMG SRC="icon.location"**, where *icon.location* is the location of your icon on the server.

4. If desired, type **ALT="alternate text"**, where *alternate text* is the text that should appear if, for some reason, the icon does not.

5. Type the final **>** of the icon definition.

6. Type the label text that you wish to accompany the icon. It's a good idea to include the actual size in K of the full sized image so the visitor knows what they're getting into by clicking it.

7. Type **</A>** to complete the link to the full sized image.

✔ Tips

■ Using miniatures is an ideal way to get a lot of graphic information on a page without making your visitors wait too long to see it. Then they can view the images that they are most interested in at their leisure.

■ For more on links, see page 117.

```
                    code.html
<HTML><HEAD><TITLE>Using an icon linked to
a larger image</TITLE></HEAD><BODY>

<H1>Cookie and Woody</H1>

<P>Generally considered the sweetest and yet
most independent cats in the Pioneer Valley,
Cookie and Woody are consistently
underestimated by their humble humans.

Here's Cookie and Woody, exhausted after
helping us pack the last time we moved:

<P><A HREF="catsonbox.gif">
<IMG SRC="catsonbox.icon.gif"
ALT="Image of Cookie and Woody sleeping on
a box">The full image is 56K.</A>

</BODY></HTML>
```

Figure 5.12 *Remember to use the full size image in the link and the icon in the image definition.*

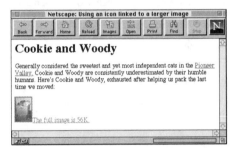

Figure 5.13 *In this example, the icon is 2K and takes 2 seconds to load. The visitor can choose to view the larger image (by clicking the icon) or to continue reading the page.*

Figure 5.14 *If the visitor clicks the icon, the browser opens a new window with the full size image.*

```
code.html
<HTML><HEAD><TITLE>Using a low resolution
image to speed up viewing</TITLE>

</HEAD><BODY>

<H1>The Four Sisters</H1>

<P>The Four Sisters Corporaton was begun by
the previously unknown four sisters. Here's a rare
photo:

<P><IMG SRC="4sis72.jpeg"
LOWSRC="4sis18.jpeg" WIDTH=381
HEIGHT=549 ALT="The Four Sisters">

</BODY></HTML>
```

Figure 5.15 *The HEIGHT and WIDTH attributes are discussed on page 53. They are necessary here to show both images at the proper size.*

Figure 5.16 *The low resolution image is replaced gradually by the higher resolution image. The callout line marks the division between the two. The status information in the lower-left corner shows how much more time it will take to finish loading the high resolution image. Without the lower resolution image, the visitor would have to wait all that time before seeing anything.*

Using Low Resolution Images

You can reference both high and low resolution versions of your image so that the low resolution image loads quickly and keeps the visitor's interest while the high resolution version wows your visitors, once it loads in.

To use a low resolution version of an image:

1. Create a low resolution version of your image *(see page 78)*.

2. Place the cursor where you want the full resolution image to appear.

3. Type **<IMG SRC="image.gif"**, where *image.gif* is the location on the server of the high resolution image.

4. Type **LOWSRC="imagelow.gif"**, where *imagelow.gif* is the location on the server of the low resolution image.

5. Type **HEIGHT=x WIDTH=y**, where x and y are the height and width in pixels, respectively of the original image. If you do not specify these values, browsers use the size of the low resolution image for both images.

6. If desired, type **ALT="substitute text"**, where *substitute text* is the text that will appear if the visitor can't view images with their browser.

7. Type the final **>**.

✔ Tips

- LOWSRC is not standard HTML, but both major browsers recognize it.

- There's no law that says LOWSRC has to be the same image as SRC. You can set it to some other image for a special semi-animated effect.

Using Low Resolution Images

Wrapping Text around Images

You can use the ALIGN attribute (with the *left* and *right* variables only) to wrap text around an image.

To wrap text around one side of an image:

1. Type **<IMG SRC="image.location"** where *image.location* indicates the location of the image on the server.

2. *Either* type **ALIGN=left** to align the image to the left of the screen while the text flows to the right *or* type **ALIGN=right** to align the image to the right edge of the screen while the text flows on the left side of the image.

3. Add other image attributes, as described in other parts of this chapter, if desired.

4. Type the final **>**.

5. Type the text that should flow next to the image.

✔ Tips

- Don't get confused about right and left. When you choose **ALIGN=right**, it's the *image* that goes to the right (while the text goes to the left). When you choose **ALIGN=left**, again, the image will be on the left side with the text flowing around the right side.

- The ALIGN attribute is deprecated in HTML 4. For details on using styles to wrap text, consult *Wrapping Text around Elements* on page 283.

- Why use ALIGN for wrapping text? I don't know. Personally, I'd prefer a WRAP attribute, but it doesn't exist. For more on ALIGN, see page 93.

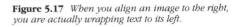

```
<BODY>

<IMG SRC="house.gif" ALIGN=right>

<H1>The Pioneer Valley: Northampton</H1>

This triplex on South Street is a good [snip]

</BODY></HTML>
```

Figure 5.17 *When you align an image to the right, you are actually wrapping text to its left.*

Figure 5.18 *The image is aligned to the right and the text wraps around it.*

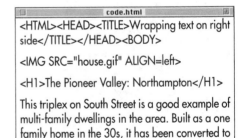

```
<HTML><HEAD><TITLE>Wrapping text on right side</TITLE></HEAD><BODY>

<IMG SRC="house.gif" ALIGN=left>

<H1>The Pioneer Valley: Northampton</H1>

This triplex on South Street is a good example of multi-family dwellings in the area. Built as a one family home in the 30s, it has been converted to
```

Figure 5.19 *To make the image appear on the left with the text wrapped around the right side, use ALIGN=left.*

Figure 5.20 *With the image on the left, the text wraps around on the right side.*

Wrapping Text around Images

```
code.html
<HTML><HEAD><TITLE>Wrapping text around
more than one
image</TITLE></HEAD><BODY>

<IMG SRC="courthouse.gif" ALIGN=right>

<H1>The Pioneer Valley: Northampton</H1>

This building, that some might say looks like a
church, is actually the Hampshire County
Courthouse. If you ever get called to be on a
grand jury, or a traverse jury for that matter, this
is where you should report. The venerable [snip]

<IMG SRC="house.gif" ALIGN=left>

<BR>This triplex on South Street is a good
example of multi-family dwellings in the area.
Built as a one family home in the 30s, it has been
converted to a three family with separate
entrances, heating and electricity. Thanks to the
area colleges--Smith, Amherst, UMass, Mt.
```

Figure 5.21 *The image always precedes the text that should flow around it.*

Figure 5.22 *The first image is aligned to the right and the text flows to its left. The next image appears after the last line of text in the preceding paragraph and pushes the following paragraph to the right.*

To wrap text between two images:

1. Type **<IMG SRC="right.image" ALIGN=right>** where *right.image* indicates the location on the server of the image that should appear on the right side of the screen.

2. Type the text that should flow around the first image.

3. Type **<IMG SRC="left.image" ALIGN=left>** where *left.image* indicates the location on the server of the image that should appear on the left side of the screen.

4. If desired, type **<P>** to begin a new paragraph, that will be aligned with the image placed in step 3.

5. Type the text that should flow around the second image.

✔ Tips

- The key is to place each image *directly before* the text it should "disrupt."

- Each image will continue to push the text to one side until it either encounters a break *(see page 90)* or until there is no more text.

- Notice that in this example one of the images has a transparent background and one doesn't. You can mix all types of images on a page. For more information on creating transparency, see page 70.

- The ALIGN attribute is deprecated in HTML 4 in favor of style sheets. Styles let you control text wrap in all your images with just one step. For more information, consult *Wrapping Text around Elements* on page 283.

Wrapping Text around Images

Stopping Text Wrap

A wrapped image affects all the text that follows it, unless you insert a special line break. The CLEAR attribute added to the regular BR tag indicates that the text should not begin until the specified margin is clear (that is, at the end of the image or images).

To stop the text from wrapping:

1. Create your image and the text *(see pages 88 and 89)*.

2. Place the cursor where you want to stop wrapping text to the side of the image.

3. *Either* type **<BR CLEAR=left>** to stop flowing text until there are no more images aligned to the left margin.

   Or type **<BR CLEAR=right>** to stop flowing text until there are no more images aligned to the right margin.

   Or type **<BR CLEAR=all>** to stop flowing text until there are no more images on either margin.

✔ Tip

- The CLEAR attribute is deprecated in HTML 4 in favor of style sheets. For information on using styles to control the text flow, consult *Stopping Text Wrap* on page 284.

```
code.html
<IMG SRC="house.gif" ALIGN=right>
<H1>The Pioneer Valley: Northampton</H1>
<IMG SRC="wraplogo2.gif" ALIGN=left>
<BR CLEAR=left>
This triplex on South Street is a good example of
```

Figure 5.23 *Notice the order: first comes the house, then the header, then the logo, then the text.*

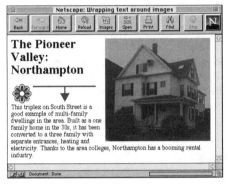

Figure 5.24 *The CLEAR=left attribute makes the text stop flowing until it reaches an empty left margin (that is, below the bottom of the left-aligned flower).*

```
code.html
<IMG SRC="house.gif" ALIGN=right>
<H1>The Pioneer Valley: Northampton</H1>
<IMG SRC="wraplogo2.gif" ALIGN=left>
<BR CLEAR=all>
```

Figure 5.25 *The order is the same as in the last example; only the CLEAR attribute has changed.*

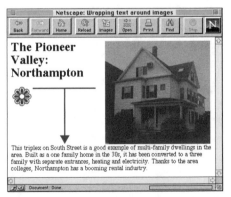

Figure 5.26 *The CLEAR=all code stops the flow of text until all images have been passed.*

Figure 5.27 *Both Netscape and Internet Explorer have the bad habit of cramming text right up next to images. Netscape (shown) leaves no space above or below an image. Internet Explorer leaves hardly any space to either side of the image.*

```
code.html
<P><IMG SRC="house.gif" ALIGN=right
VSPACE=15>

<H1>The Pioneer Valley: Northampton</H1>

<P><BR CLEAR=right><IMG
SRC="wraplogo2.gif" ALIGN=left HSPACE=6>

This triplex on South Street is a good example of
multi-family dwellings in the area. Built as a one
```

Figure 5.28 *You can add either HSPACE or VSPACE, or both, to your images.*

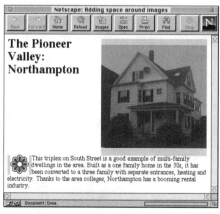

Figure 5.29 *One of the unfortunate side effects of VSPACE is that it adds space both to the top and to the bottom of an image. Although the lower paragraph is no longer jammed against the house, the words* The Pioneer *are no longer aligned with the top of the image.*

Adding Space around an Image

Look carefully at the image in Figure 5.27. If you don't want your text butting right up to the image, you can use the VSPACE and HSPACE attributes to add a buffer around your image.

To add space around an image:

1. Type **<IMG SRC="image.location"** where *image.location* indicates the location on the server of your image.

2. Type **HSPACE=x** where *x* is the number of pixels of space to add on *both* the right and left sides of the image.

3. Type **VSPACE=x** where *x* is the number of pixels of space to add on *both* the top and bottom of the image.

4. Add other image attributes as desired and type the final **>**.

✔ Tips

- You don't have to add both HSPACE and VSPACE at the same time.

- If you just want to add space to one side of the image, use Photoshop to add blank space to that side, and skip HSPACE and VSPACE altogether. Then, make the blank space transparent *(see page 70)*.

- Both HSPACE and VSPACE are deprecated in HTML 4 in favor of style sheets. For more information about using styles to control the space around your images, consult *Adding Padding Around an Element* on page 280 and *Setting the Margins around an Element* on page 281.

- Explorer leaves 4 pixels to the right of the image (but not the left), by default.

Adding Space around an Image

Scaling an Image

You can change the size of an image just by specifying a new height and width in pixels. This is an easy way to have large images on your page without long loading times. Beware, though, if you enlarge your pictures too much, they'll be grainy and ugly.

To scale an image:

1. Type **<IMG SRC="image.location"**, where *image.location* is the location on the server of the image.

2. Type **WIDTH=x HEIGHT=y** where *x* and *y* are the desired width and height, respectively, in pixels, of your image.

3. Add any other image attributes as desired and then type the final **>**.

✔ Tips

■ Don't use the WIDTH and HEIGHT extensions to *reduce* the image size. Instead, create a smaller image. It will load faster and look better.

■ You can also use styles to control the width and height of elements. For more information, consult *Setting the Height or Width for an Element* on page 278.

Figure 5.30 *The image's original size is revealed in Photoshop by holding down the Option key and clicking in the lower-left corner of the window.*

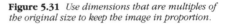

<HTML><HEAD><TITLE>Scaling an inline image</TITLE></HEAD><BODY>

<IMG SRC="gazebo.gif" WIDTH=206 HEIGHT=290 ALIGN=right HSPACE=20>

<H1>The Berkshires</H1>

<P>Home to Tanglewood and Jacob's Pillow, The Berkshires welcome thousands of tourists from as

Figure 5.31 *Use dimensions that are multiples of the original size to keep the image in proportion.*

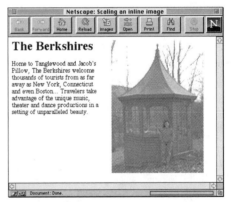

Figure 5.32 *The image quality is not great, but it loads twice as fast as it would if it were really twice as big.*

<HTML><HEAD><TITLE>Scaling an inline image</TITLE></HEAD><BODY>

<IMG SRC="gazebo.gif" WIDTH=256 HEIGHT=235 ALIGN=right HSPACE=20>

<H1>The Berkshires</H1>

<P>Home to Tanglewood and Jacob's Pillow, The Berkshires welcome thousands of tourists from as

Figure 5.33 *Distort images by using non-proportional values for WIDTH and HEIGHT.*

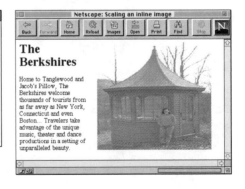

Scaling an Image

```
                  code.html
<HTML><HEAD><TITLE>Aligning an image
</TITLE></HEAD><BODY>

<IMG SRC="A.gif">lign <IMG SRC="star.gif"
ALIGN="texttop"> star with texttop<P>

<IMG SRC="A.gif">lign <IMG SRC="star.gif"
ALIGN="top"> star with top<P>

<IMG SRC="A.gif">lign <IMG SRC="star.gif"
ALIGN="middle"> star with middle <P>

<IMG SRC="A.gif">lign <IMG SRC="star.gif"
ALIGN="absmiddle"> star with absmiddle<P>

<IMG SRC="A.gif" ALIGN="texttop">lign <IMG
```

Figure 5.34 *It's important to note that the letter A is an image, not an actual letter. It is aligned (by default) with the bottom of the text in the top four examples, and with the top of the text in the last two examples.*

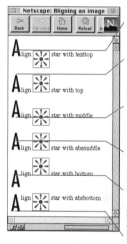

Texttop aligns the image with the highest text in the line

Top aligns the image with the highest element in the line

Middle aligns the middle of the image with the baseline

Absmiddle aligns the middle of the image with the middle of the largest item

Bottom aligns the bottom of the image with the bottom of the text

Absbottom aligns the bottom of the image with the bottom of the largest item

Figure 5.35 *There are four elements on each line: an image of the letter A, some text, a star, and some more text. The six possible alignment positions are illustrated with the star.*

Aligning Images

Perhaps, the more expected use of the ALIGN attribute is for aligning images with text. You can align an image in various ways to a single line in a paragraph. However, be careful with multiple images on the same line—different ALIGN options have different effects depending on which image is taller and which appears first.

To align an image with text:

1. Type **<IMG SRC="image.location"** where *image.location* indicates the location on the server of the image.

2. Type **ALIGN=direction** where *direction* is one of the attributes described in Figure 5.35: *texttop, top, middle, absmiddle, bottom, or absbottom.*

3. Add other attributes as desired and then type the final **>**.

4. Type the text with which you wish to align the image. (This text may also precede the image.)

✔ Tips

- You may not align an image and wrap text around it at the same time.

- Internet Explorer has trouble with aligning more than one image on a line. The results are erratic. In addition, it treats *texttop* as *top, absmiddle* as *middle* and *absbottom* as *bottom.*

- The ALIGN attribute is deprecated in HTML 4. That means the W3C recommends you start using style sheets to control how elements are aligned on your page *(see page 282).*

Aligning Images

Using a Banner

Having a newspaper-like banner at the top of every Web page is a good way to link your pages together visually.

To place a banner at the top of each page:

1. Create an image that measures approximately 450 x 100 pixels. You can make it narrower and shorter, but you shouldn't make it much wider. Otherwise it won't fit easily on most screens **(Figure 5.36)**.

2. After converting it to indexed color, using the smallest bits/pixel ratio you can stand, save it as a GIF image *(see page 64)*.

3. Use this exact same image at the top of each of your Web pages, by typing **<IMG SRC="image.name">**, where *image.name* is the location on the server of the banner.

✔ Tips

■ You can count on most folks having a 600 pixel wide browser screen.

■ By using the same image on each Web page, you create the illusion of a static banner. At the same time, since the image is saved in the cache after it is loaded the first time, it will load almost immediately onto each new page your visitor jumps to.

■ A better but slightly more complicated way to make a banner is to divide your page into two frames and place the banner in the upper frame *(see page 171)*.

■ Readers of earlier editions requested a "Created with Liz Castro's HTML 4 VQS Guide" banner to put on their sites. You can now download such a banner from *www.cookwood.com/html4_4e/banner/*. And if you do, thanks!

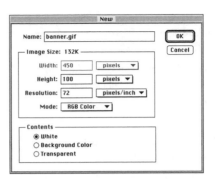

Figure 5.36 *When you create your image (here in Photoshop) make sure it is 450 pixels wide, or less.*

```
code.html
<HTML><HEAD><TITLE>Using a
banner</TITLE></HEAD>
<BODY>
<IMG SRC="banner.gif" ALT="SE banner">
<H1>New products</H1>
<UL>
<LI>AstroFinder 3
<LI>Pleiades Expander
<LI>Southern Cross
</UL> </BODY></HTML>
```

Figure 5.37 *The only thing special about a banner is that it is the first element in the BODY section.*

Figure 5.38 *The banner appears at the top of the page.*

```
code.html
<HTML><HEAD><TITLE>Using horizontal
rules</TITLE></HEAD>

<BODY>

<IMG SRC="banner.gif" ALT="SE banner">

<H1>New products</H1>

<UL>

<LI>AstroFinder 3

<LI>Pleiades Expander

<LI>Southern Cross

</UL>

<HR SIZE="10" WIDTH="80%" ALIGN="center"
NOSHADE>

</BODY></HTML>
```

Figure 5.39 *The HR tag includes an automatic line break both before and after the rule.*

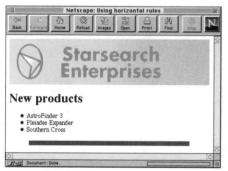

Figure 5.40 *Horizontal rules are helpful for dividing sections on your page.*

Adding Horizontal Rules

One graphic element that is completely supported by the majority of the browsers is the horizontal rule. There are several attributes you can use to jazz up horizontal rules, although they've all been deprecated in HTML 4 in favor of styles.

To insert a horizontal rule:

1. Type **<HR** where you want the rule to appear. The text that follows will appear in a new paragraph below the new rule.

2. If desired, type **SIZE=n**, where n is the rule's height in pixels.

3. If desired, type **WIDTH=w**, where w is the width of the rule in pixels, or as a percentage of the document's width.

4. If desired, type **ALIGN=direction**, where *direction* refers to the way a rule should be aligned on the page; either *left, right,* or *center.* The ALIGN attribute is only effective if you have made the rule narrower than the document.

5. If desired, type **NOSHADE** to create a solid bar, with no shading.

6. Type the final **>** to complete the horizontal rule definition.

✔ Tip

■ All of the attributes for HR (but not the HR tag itself) have been deprecated in HTML 4. The W3C recommends using styles to decorate your horizontal rules. For more information, consult Chapter 16, *Layout with Styles.*

Adding Horizontal Rules

Page Layout

There are several HTML tags that apply to an entire page, instead of being limited to just a few words or paragraphs. I call these elements *page layout* features and restrict them to this chapter.

Included among these features are setting margins and columns, controlling the spacing between the elements on a page, changing the background color for the entire page, dividing a page into logical sections, positioning elements in layers, and determining when line breaks should, and shouldn't, occur.

Using Background Color

Tired of basic gray? The BGCOLOR tag lets you set the background color of each Web page you create.

To set the background color:

1. In the BODY tag, after the word BODY but before the final >, type **BGCOLOR="#rrggbb"**, where *rrggbb* is the hexadecimal representation of the desired color.

   Or type **BGCOLOR=color**, where *color* is one of the 16 predefined colors.

2. Add other attributes to the BODY (like link and text colors) as desired.

✔ Tips

- See Appendix C and the inside back cover for a complete listing of hexadecimal values and common color representations. Appendix C also includes a list of the 16 predefined colors.

- For more information on setting the link colors, consult *Changing the Color of Links* on page 133. For more information on setting the text color, consult *Choosing a Default Color for Text* on page 50 or *Changing the Text Color* on page 51.

- To use an image for the background, consult *Using Background Images* on page 99.

- Most browsers let your visitors override any background color set by you, the page designer **(Figure 6.3)**.

- The BGCOLOR attribute has been deprecated in HTML 4. The W3C recommends using styles to control the background *(see page 286)*.

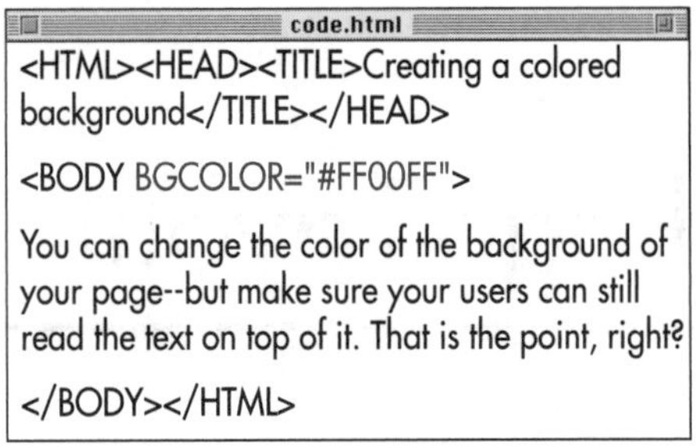

```
code.html
<HTML><HEAD><TITLE>Creating a colored
background</TITLE></HEAD>
<BODY BGCOLOR="#FF00FF">
You can change the color of the background of
your page--but make sure your users can still
read the text on top of it. That is the point, right?
</BODY></HTML>
```

Figure 6.1 *Add the BGCOLOR attribute to the BODY tag to set the background color for the page.*

Figure 6.2 *Changing the background color is an easy way to give your pages a distinctive flavor. Beware though of visitors who view pages with their own colors (see Figure 6.3 below)—especially if the color of your text depends on your background color.*

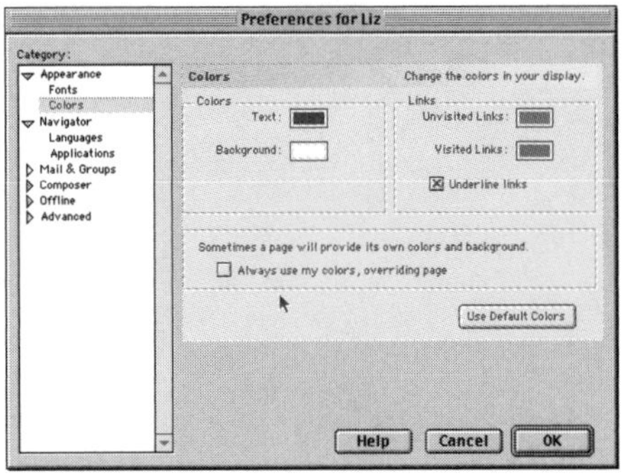

Figure 6.3 *This is Netscape's preferences dialog box in which your visitors can choose not to use the colors that you, the designer, have specified for a page. (Explorer has a similar option.)*

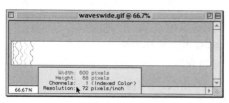

Figure 6.4 *In this example, I've created a background image that is 68 pixels high and 600 pixels wide. It compresses beautifully to less than 2K, but since browsers automatically tile images smaller than the window, it will fill the background as completely as any bigger image.*

```
code.html
<TITLE>Using an image as a background
</TITLE></HEAD>

<BODY BACKGROUND="waveswide.gif">

<TABLE CELLSPACING="2" CELLPADDING="1">

<TR>

<TD WIDTH=80 VALIGN=TOP> </TD>

<TD VALIGN=TOP><H2>The Mardi Gras Home
Page</H2>

Mardi Gras is gearing up to be the best ever this
year. Come down to New Orleans and see how
we throw a party!
```

Figure 6.5 *To keep text from overlapping my background image along the left side, I've placed the text in a table with two columns, and left the first column empty. For more information about tables, consult Chapter 9, Tables. Notice you can't add extra image attributes (like LOWSRC) to the BODY tag.*

Figure 6.6 *Because the image is so wide, it does not repeat horizontally (and leaves room for text that is easy to read).*

Using Background Images

You can use one image as the backdrop for your entire page. *Backdrop* is the operative word here. A background image should not detract from the readability of your page, but instead make it more attractive.

To use a background image:

1. In the BODY tag at the beginning of your page, type **BACKGROUND=**.

2. Type **"bgimage.gif"**, where *bgimage.gif* is the location on the server of the image you want to use.

3. If desired, type **BGPROPERTIES= fixed** to make the image a stationary watermark.

✔ Tips

- Take advantage of the fact that browsers automatically tile smaller images when creating your background **(Figure 6.6)**.

- With an image editing program, try increasing the brightness and lowering the contrast to soften the background image so it doesn't distract from your page's content.

- Save your visitor loading time by using the same background image on a series of pages. After the image has been loaded for the first page, each subsequent page uses a cached version which loads much more quickly.

- The BACKGROUND attribute is deprecated in HTML 4. For details on using styles to create a background image, see page 286.

Centering Elements on a Page

In Chapter 2, *Starting Your Web Page*, you learned how to align paragraphs and headers. There is, however, a more general centering tag that can be used with virtually any element on your page: the CENTER tag.

To center elements on a page:

1. Type **<CENTER>**.

2. Create the element that you wish to center.

3. Type **</CENTER>**.

✔ Tips

- You can use the CENTER tag with almost every kind of HTML element, including paragraphs, headers, images, and forms, even if there is another method for centering that element.

- For more details on aligning paragraphs, consult *Starting a New Paragraph* on page 39. For more information on aligning headers, consult *Organizing the Page* on page 38.

- For information on aligning images with text, consult *Aligning Images* on page 93.

- For details on dividing your document into sections that you can then align, consult *Creating Custom HTML Tags* on page 251.

- For information on using styles to center text, consult *Aligning Text* on page 269.

```
code.html
<HTML><HEAD><TITLE>Centering
text</TITLE></HEAD>
<BODY>
<H2 ALIGN=CENTER>The Earth's Core</H2>
<CENTER>At the center of the earth, more than
6000 kilometers from the surface, the
temperature is a toasty 6500 degrees Kelvin.
</CENTER>
<P>Not bad for a little planet.
</BODY></HTML>
```

Figure 6.7 *Note that the header,* The Earth's Core, *is centered by the method described on page 38.*

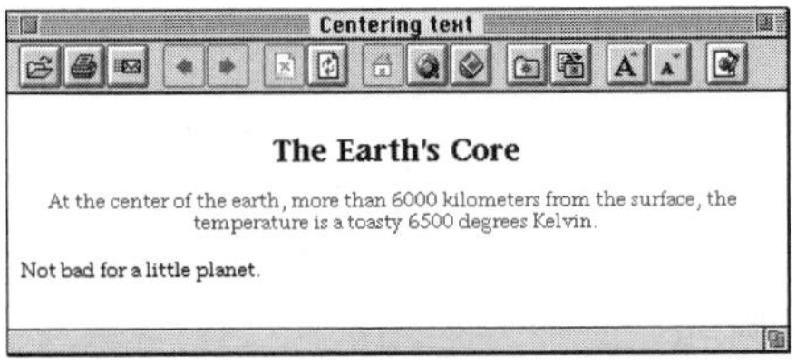

The Earth's Core

At the center of the earth, more than 6000 kilometers from the surface, the temperature is a toasty 6500 degrees Kelvin.

Not bad for a little planet.

Figure 6.8 *Centering a bit of text is a good way to call attention to it. The CENTER tag is supported by practically all browsers (despite having been deprecated by the W3C).*

Centering Elements on a Page

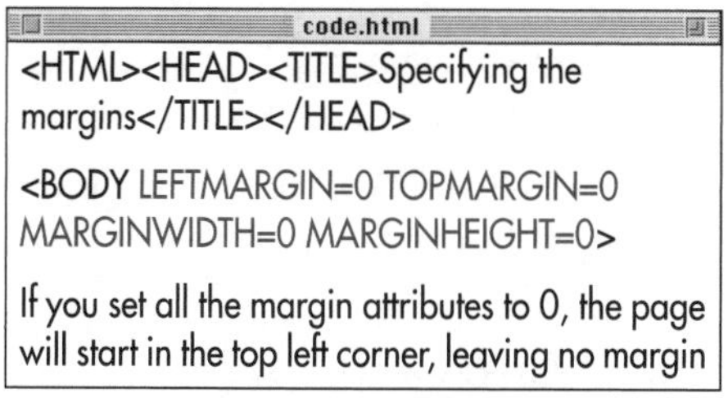

```
          code.html
<HTML><HEAD><TITLE>Specifying the
margins</TITLE></HEAD>

<BODY LEFTMARGIN=0 TOPMARGIN=0
MARGINWIDTH=0 MARGINHEIGHT=0>
```
If you set all the margin attributes to 0, the page
will start in the top left corner, leaving no margin

Figure 6.9 *Inside the BODY tag, set values for both
Netscape's and Explorer's attributes.*

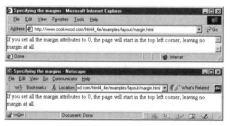

Figure 6.10 *Each browser ignores the other one's
particular attributes so you have to use all four to
have the browsers display the margins correctly.*

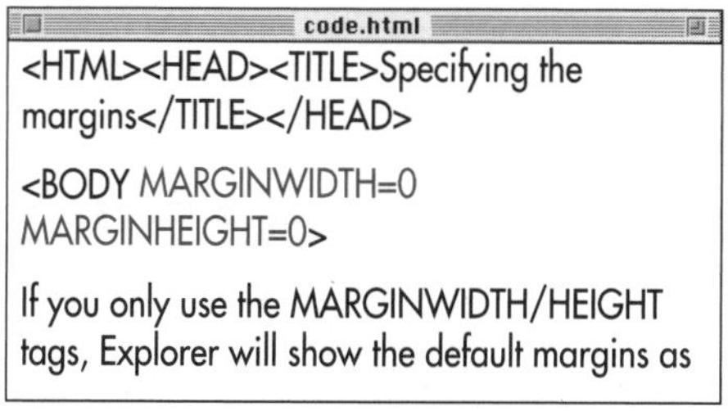

```
          code.html
<HTML><HEAD><TITLE>Specifying the
margins</TITLE></HEAD>

<BODY MARGINWIDTH=0
MARGINHEIGHT=0>
```
If you only use the MARGINWIDTH/HEIGHT
tags, Explorer will show the default margins as

Figure 6.11 *If you only use say, the attributes that
Netscape recognizes (MARGINWIDTH and MARGIN-
HEIGHT), then Netscape will display the margins
properly but Explorer will not.*

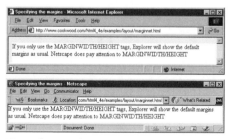

Figure 6.12 *Explorer goes back to displaying
default margins (top) while Netscape is still happy
with just the MARGINWIDTH and MARGINHEIGHT
attributes.*

Specifying the Margins

Both Netscape and Internet Explorer add a
certain amount of space, by default, between
the contents of a page and the edges of the
window. And both let you specify how much
space you want there to be. Unfortunately,
since they don't understand each other's
methods, you'll have to use both.

To specify the margins:

1. For your Explorer users, in the
    BODY tag, after the word BODY
    but before the final >, type **LEFT-
    MARGIN=x TOPMARGIN=y**, where *x* is
    the width in pixels of the space between
    the left border of the window and the
    contents of the page and *y* is the height
    in pixels between the top border of the
    window and the contents of the page.

2. For Netscape folks, in the BODY
    tag, after the word BODY but
    before the final >, type **MARGIN-
    WIDTH=x, MARGINHEIGHT=y**, where *x*
    and *y* are the same values as in step 1.

✔ Tips

■   The LEFTMARGIN and TOPMARGIN tags
    were developed by Microsoft and do not
    belong to HTML 4 (or any earlier version).

■   The attributes MARGINWIDTH and
    MARGINHEIGHT are part of the standard
    HTML 4 specifications when used with
    FRAME *(see page 175)*, but not with
    BODY. (But they still work fine.)

■   The official way to change margins is
    with styles, though neither browser sup-
    ports those specifications perfectly either.
    For more details, consult *Setting the Mar-
    gins around an Element* on page 281.

■   You can set only the left or only the top
    margin if you wish.

Creating a Line Break

When you start a new paragraph with the P tag *(see page 39)*, most browsers insert a large amount of space. To begin a new line without so much space, use a line break.

The BR tag is perfect for poems or other short lines of text that should appear one after another without a lot of space in between.

To insert a line break:

Type **
** where the line break should occur. There is no closing BR tag.

✔ Tips

- You can use multiple BR tags to create extra space between lines or paragraphs.

- Although you can now control spacing with much more precision thanks to style sheets *(see page 273)*, there are also some Netscape extensions for controlling the space between lines. For more information, consult *Creating Indents* on page 106. You can also use a transparent image to create the proper amount of space between lines. For more information on this technique, consult *Using Pixel Shims* on page 109.

- You can use special values with the BR tag for creating line breaks with text that is wrapped around images. For more information, consult *Stopping Text Wrap* on page 90.

```
code.html
<HTML><HEAD><TITLE>Creating line
breaks</TITLE></HEAD><BODY>

<H1>The Worldwide Conference on Keeping It
Together</H1>

<P>Opening Hymn:

<P>We have to keep it together
<BR>Never come apart,
<BR>Birds of a feather,
<BR>Close to our heart.

<P><EM>12 December 1996. London.
</EM>The Worldwide Conference on Keeping It
Together met today for the first time as a group.
They had originally met separately in their
respective states. Discussed today was whether
or not the group should vote on a charter
together or whether each sovereign state should
vote separately. They couldn't quite keep it
together.

</BODY></HTML>
```

Figure 6.13 *I've used a P tag to start the first line to set the group off from the remaining text. Then, each line of the "hymn" is separated with a line break.*

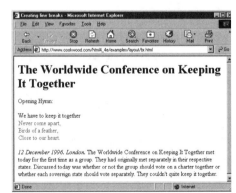

Figure 6.14 *No matter how wide this window is, there will always be a line break between each of the lines in the "Opening Hymn". There is less space between lines with a BR tag than with a P tag.*

```
code.html
<HTML><HEAD><TITLE>Creating line breaks
</TITLE></HEAD><BODY>

<H1><NOBR>The Worldwide Conference on
Keeping It Together</NOBR></H1>

<P>Opening Hymn:

<P>We have to keep it together
<BR>Never come apart,
<BR>Birds of a feather,
<BR>Close to our heart.

<P><EM>12 December 1996. London.
</EM>The Worldwide Conference on Keeping It
Together met today for the first time as a group.
They had originally met separately in their
```

Figure 6.15 *I have placed <NOBR> tags around the header text to ensure that the entire sentence is displayed on one line in the browser.*

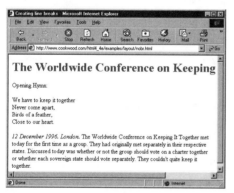

Figure 6.16 *With the NOBR tags, the headline is kept on one line, even when it extends past the width of a visitor's browser window.*

Keeping Lines Together

You may have certain phrases in your document that you don't want separated. Or you may want to keep a word and an image together, no matter what.

To keep elements on one line:

1. Type **<NOBR>**.

2. Create the text or elements that should appear all on one line.

3. Type **</NOBR>**.

✔ Tips

- Elements within NOBR tags will not be separated, unless there is a WBR tag *(see page 104)*, even if the size of the window causes them to be displayed off the screen, and thus invisible to the user **(Figure 6.16)**.

- Unlike the NOWRAP attribute used in tables to keep a cell's contents on a single line *(see page 165)*, the NOBR tag must have an opening and closing tag and only affects the text contained within the two.

- NOBR is not standard HTML. Nevertheless, both Netscape and Internet Explorer support it.

- You can also insert a non-breaking space (type ** **) between words that should not be separated.

Creating Discretionary Line Breaks

Regular line breaks *(see page 102)* are permanent. No matter how big the visitor makes her window, the poem will never be displayed on one line. However, there are many situations in which you'd like to control where a line breaks—if the break is necessary—but keep the line altogether if the break is not necessary. This kind of line break is called *discretionary*.

To create discretionary line breaks:

1. Enclose the text in NOBR tags as described on page 103.

2. Type **<WBR>** where you'd like the line to break, if a break is necessary.

✔ Tips

- It doesn't make sense to use the WBR tag without the NOBR tags.

- Line breaks created with WBR only appear if the window is small enough to warrant them. Otherwise, the elements will not be separated.

- The WBR tag is not part of the standard HTML 4 specifications. Just the same, both Netscape and Explorer support it.

```
<HTML><HEAD><TITLE>Creating line
breaks</TITLE></HEAD><BODY>

<H1><NOBR>The Worldwide Conference on
<WBR>Keeping It Together</NOBR></H1>

<P>Opening Hymn:
<P>We have to keep it together
<BR>Never come apart,
<BR>Birds of a feather,
<BR>Close to our heart.
```

Figure 6.17 *The NOBR tag keeps all the enclosed elements on the same line. The WBR tag allows a line break—if necessary—depending on window size.*

Figure 6.18 *When the visitor makes the window too narrow for the entire header to fit, the line is divided where you inserted the WBR tag.*

Figure 6.19 *If the visitor expands the window so that the entire line can fit, the line break is not used.*

```
                    code.html
<HTML><HEAD><TITLE>Creating space
between paragraphs</TITLE></HEAD>

<BODY>

<SPACER TYPE=horizontal SIZE=36>Spacers
are an ideal substitute for tabs, which don't exist
in HTML. Instead, use a spacer for indenting your
paragraphs.

<SPACER TYPE=vertical SIZE=24>

<SPACER TYPE=horizontal SIZE=36> Personally,
I've never been very fond of indented
paragraphs, myself, preferring the rather square
block text. Sigh.

</BODY></HTML>
```

Figure 6.20 *Make sure you take out any P tags when using vertical spacers. Otherwise, the paragraphs will have extra space between them.*

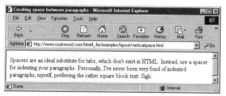

Figure 6.21 *Since we haven't used a P tag, the two paragraphs run together in Internet Explorer, which doesn't understand the SPACER tag.*

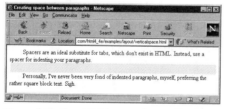

Figure 6.22 *On a 72 dpi screen, there will be exactly 1/3 inch of white space between the two paragraphs—as long as they're viewed in Netscape. Compare this example with the one shown in Figure 6.25.*

Specifying the Space Between Paragraphs

The amount of space between paragraphs, when you use the P or BR tags, is determined by the size of the surrounding text. Larger text has larger spaces. Smaller text has smaller spaces. Netscape's SPACER tag lets you specify exactly how much space should appear between one line and another.

To specify the space between paragraphs:

1. Place the cursor between the two lines to be separated.

2. Type **<SPACER**.

3. Type **TYPE=vertical**.

4. Type **SIZE=n**, where n is the amount of space, in pixels, that should appear between the two lines.

5. Type the final **>**.

✔ Tips

■ The space between lines is usually specified in points, not pixels. Thanks to Steve Jobs, on most Macintosh monitors one point is almost exactly equal to one pixel. So if you want 10 points of space, use a value of 10 in step 4. Windows monitors tend to have a slightly lower resolution, and thus slightly bigger pixels. For 10 points, use 8 or 9 pixels.

■ The SPACER tag with a value of *vertical* for the TYPE attribute creates an automatic line break. You do not need to use the P tag—it will create the same amount of space it always has, in *addition* to the SPACER's space.

Specifying the Space Between Paragraphs

Creating Indents

You can't type a tab, or specify a tab stop in HTML documents. However, there are a number of ways to create indents for your paragraphs for Netscape browsers.

To create indents:

1. Place the cursor where you want the space to appear.

2. Type **<SPACER**.

3. Type **TYPE=horizontal**.

4. Type **SIZE=n**, where *n* is the desired indent size, in pixels.

5. Type the final **>** tag.

6. Type the text of the indented paragraph.

✔ Tips

■ You can use horizontal spaces anywhere you want, not just at the beginning of a text paragraph.

■ How much is a pixel? It all depends on the resolution of your users' screens, which is typically, but not always, 72 dpi. In this case, 36 pixels is 1/2 inch, 18 pixels is 1/4 inch. Your best bet is to be consistent on your page and/or test the result on more than one screen.

■ You can also use pixel shims *(see page 109)* or styles *(see page 267)* to create indented paragraphs.

■ Internet Explorer 5 still doesn't understand Netscape's SPACER tag. It probably never will.

■ For information on controlling vertical spacing, consult *Specifying the Space Between Paragraphs* on page 105.

```
code.html
<HTML><HEAD><TITLE>Using
spacers</TITLE></HEAD>

<BODY>

<SPACER TYPE=horizontal SIZE=36>Spacers
are an ideal substitute for tabs, which don't exist
in HTML. Instead, use a spacer for indenting your
paragraphs.

<P>

<SPACER TYPE=horizontal SIZE=36> Personally,
I've never been very fond of indented
paragraphs, myself, preferring the rather square
block text. Sigh.
```

Figure 6.23 *Use horizontal spacers for indenting paragraphs, or any place you need to add an invisible, horizontal block of space.*

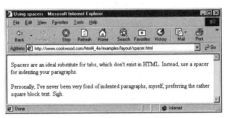

Figure 6.24 *Internet Explorer ignores horizontal spacers completely, aligning all text to the left. To indent text for Explorer, use pixel shims (see page 109) or styles (see page 267).*

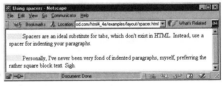

Figure 6.25 *Horizontal spacers are effective when viewed with Netscape.*

```
┌─────────────────────────────────┐
│ ▣          code.html          ▣ │
├─────────────────────────────────┤
│ <HTML><HEAD><TITLE>Indents with │
│ lists</TITLE></HEAD><BODY>      │
│                                 │
│ <H2>Sneaky ways to create       │
│ indents</H2>                    │
│                                 │
│ Using lists to create indents is│
│ not exactly legal but it does   │
│ work--in any browser. The W3    │
│ Consortium would prefer that you│
│ use styles. But until you do,   │
│ list indents will come in handy.│
│                                 │
│ <UL>The basic technique is to   │
│ create a list for each section  │
│ that you want to indent. Don't  │
│ create any list items--since    │
│ they are always marked with a   │
│ bullet. Oh, and there's no way  │
│ to make hanging indents or      │
│ first-line indents. If you want │
│ to get fancy, use styles.</UL>  │
│                                 │
│ </BODY></HTML>                  │
└─────────────────────────────────┘
```

Figure 6.26 *You can use lists (without the LI tag) to create indented paragraphs.*

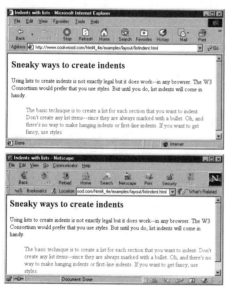

Figure 6.27 *List indents work on most browsers but they have two disadvantages: the W3C wishes you wouldn't use them and they don't offer much flexibility in the way of hanging or first-line indents.*

Creating Indents (with Lists)

When Netscape Gold was released, its Web page editor had one nifty feature: you could create paragraph indents that worked on most any browser. Looking at the code revealed the secret: the indents were created with lists.

To create indents with lists:

1. Place the cursor where you'd like to create indented text.

2. Type **<UL>**.

3. Type the contents of the indented text. You can type as many paragraphs as you want.

4. Type **</UL>**.

✔ Tips

■ This method won't work for hanging indents or first-line indents.

■ For real indents using style sheets, consult *Controlling Spacing* on page 267.

Creating Blocks of Space

 Netscape's SPACER tag is also useful for creating blocks of space that you can wrap text around.

To create blocks of space:

1. Place the cursor where the space should appear, before any text that will wrap around it.

2. Type **<SPACER**.

3. Type **TYPE="block"**.

4. Type **WIDTH=w HEIGHT=h**, where *w* and *h* are the width and height, respectively, of the block, in pixels.

5. To wrap text around the block, type **ALIGN=left** or **ALIGN=right**, depending on which side of the block you want the text.

    To align the block next to the text, without wrapping the text around it, type **ALIGN=direction**, where *direction* is top, middle, or bottom.

6. Type the final **>**.

✔ Tips

- For more information on wrapping text, consult *Wrapping Text around Images* on page 88. For more information on the alignment options, consult *Aligning Images* on page 93.

- Internet Explorer does not understand Netscape's SPACER tag—and probably never will.

- To create a *colored* block of space, use a pixel shim *(see page 109)*.

```
code.html
<HTML><HEAD><TITLE>Creating blocks of
space</TITLE></HEAD><BODY>

<SPACER TYPE="block" WIDTH=100
HEIGHT=100 ALIGN=left>If you like to create
big margins around your text, spacers are ideal
for the job.

<P>Just use the spacer tag as if it were an
invisible image. And wrap the text right around
it as usual.

</BODY></HTML>
```

Figure 6.28 *When creating a block-shaped space, you have to specify the width and the height, along with an alignment, to determine where the space will appear.*

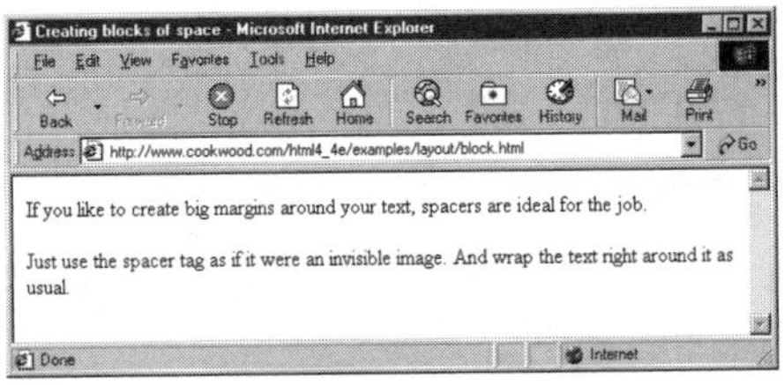

Figure 6.29 *Don't forget: the SPACER tag has absolutely no effect in Internet Explorer (shown here). It only works with Netscape browsers.*

Figure 6.30 *Block shaped spaces are ideal for setting large, invisible margins—in Netscape. (I've colored the space to illustrate it in this book, but it's really invisible.)*

Creating Blocks of Space

```
┌─────────────── code.html ──────────────┐
<HTML><HEAD><TITLE>Using pixel shims
</TITLE></HEAD><BODY>

<IMG SRC="pixelshim.gif"  WIDTH=100
HEIGHT=150 HSPACE=3 ALIGN=left>

<P><B>Or, perhaps better yet, use a pixel shim.
It has the advantage of being recognized by most
browsers, and you can make it any color you
want.</B>

</BODY></HTML>
```

Figure 6.31 *A pixel shim is nothing more than a one pixel by one pixel image, of any color you like, expanded to the desired size, and aligned as necessary.*

Figure 6.32 *The principal advantage of pixel shims is that they work in almost any browser. In addition, they are small and load quickly and they can be made any color you need. Notice, however, that Explorer (top) leaves slightly more space to the right of the image than Netscape.*

Using Pixel Shims

A shim in the physical world is a little piece of wood (or sometimes paper) that you stick under one of the legs of your table (for example) to make it stop wobbling. A *pixel shim* is a wedge of pixels, sometimes in color, that you insert between elements on a page to shore up the balance and alignment.

To use a pixel shim:

1. Create a 1 pixel by 1 pixel GIF image in the desired color *(see page 64)*.

2. In your HTML document, type **<IMG SRC="pixelshim.gif"**, where *pixelshim.gif* is the name of the image created in step 1.

3. Type **WIDTH=w HEIGHT=h**, where *w* and *h* are the desired (not the actual) width and height, in pixels, of the desired space.

4. To wrap text around the shim, type **ALIGN=left** or **ALIGN=right** *(see page 88)*.

   Or you can align the shim next to the text (and not around it) by typing **ALIGN=direction**, where *direction* is top, middle, or bottom *(see page 93)*.

5. Add other image attributes, as desired.

6. Type the final **>**.

✔ Tips

- Pixel shims are recognized by most browsers since they're just images, forced to work in a new way.

- In addition, pixel shims are tiny (and thus, load quickly) and can be made any color you want—or transparent.

- You can download pixel shims from my site: *http://www.cookwood.com/*.

Using Block Quotes

You can use block quotes to set off a section of your text—like a quotation by a famous author—from the surrounding text. As usual, different browsers display block quotes in different ways. Some center the text in an indented paragraph in the middle of the page, while others simply italicize the special text.

To create a block quote:

1. Type **<BLOCKQUOTE>**.

2. Type the desired HTML formatting for the text, like **<P>**, for example.

3. Type the text that you wish to appear set off from the preceding and following text.

4. Complete the HTML tag begun in step 2, if necessary.

5. Type **</BLOCKQUOTE>**.

✔ Tips

■ Text should not be placed directly between the opening and closing BLOCKQUOTE tags, but rather between other HTML tags within the BLOCK-QUOTE tags. (However, many browsers will display a block quote correctly even if you ignore this rule.)

■ Block quotes can contain additional text formatting like B or I.

■ Earlier versions of Explorer did not add a line break before the block quote. Version 5 does **(Figure 6.34)**.

■ You can also use styles to indent text on both sides. For more information, consult *Setting the Margins around an Element* on page 281.

---

code.html

`<HTML><HEAD><TITLE>`Creating a block quote`</TITLE></HEAD><BODY>`

Sometimes I get to the point where I'm not sure anything matters at all. Then I read something like this and I am inspired:

`<BLOCKQUOTE>`

`<P>`It's not hard to figure out what's good for kids, but amid the noise of an increasingly antichild political climate, it can be hard to remember just to go ahead and do it: for example, to vote to raise your school district's budget, even though you'll pay higher taxes. (If you're earning enough to pay taxes at all, I promise, the school needs those few bucks more than you do.) To support legislators who care more about afterschool programs, affordable health care, and libraries than about military budges and the Dow Jones industrial average. To volunteer time and skills at your neighborhood school and also the school across town. To decide to notice, rather than ignore it, when a neighbor is losing it with her kids, and offer to babysit twice a week. This is not interference. Getting between a ball player and a ball is interference. The ball is inanimate.

`</BLOCKQUOTE>`

Figure 6.33 *A block quote can be as short or as long as you need. You can even divide it into various paragraphs by adding P tags as necessary.*

Figure 6.34 *Block quotes are generally indented from both sides.*

```
code.html
<HTML><HEAD><TITLE>Quoting shorter
passages</TITLE></HEAD>

<BODY>

<P>So I said <Q LANG=en>What's going on
here?</Q>

<P>I ella em va dir <Q lang=ca>Qu&egrave;
passa? Que no veus que li estic intentant
ajudar?</Q>

</BODY></HTML>
```

Figure 6.35 *The Q tag is for marking shorter, inline passages of text. The language code specified determines the type of quotation marks that will be used.*

```
Quoting shorter passages
Back  Forward  Stop  Refresh  Home  Search  Mail  News  Favorites  Larger

So I said What's going on here?

I ella em va dir Què passa? Que no veus que li estic intentant ajudar?
```

Figure 6.36 *The Q tag is not yet supported by either Explorer (shown here) or Netscape, despite being part of the standard HTML 4 specifications.*

Quoting Short Passages of Text

Block quotes, as described on the preceding page, are block-level elements, that is, they always start on a new line. HTML 4 includes a new tag for marking shorter, inline passages. Although neither Netscape nor Explorer currently supports this new tag, it may be useful for future versions.

To quote short passages of text:

1. Type **<Q**.

2. If desired, type **LANG=xx**, where *xx* is the two letter code for the language the quote will be in. This code determines the type of quote marks that will be used ("" for English, «» for many European languages, etc.).

3. Type **>**.

4. Type the text to be quoted.

5. Type **</Q>**.

✔ Tips

■ Although the Q tag is part of the standard HTML 4 specifications, neither Explorer nor Communicator (version 4) supports it yet.

■ Once it's supported, use Q for phrases within a larger paragraph and use BLOCKQUOTE *(see page 110)* for entire paragraphs.

■ Point your browser at *www.sil.org/sgml/iso639a.html* to find a complete list of language codes.

Quoting Short Passages of Text

Creating Columns

You can divide your page into columns with a special extension that only Netscape recognizes. The extension is still pretty limited, however. First, all columns must be the same width. Second, if you make the columns too narrow, they will overlap and look horrible.

To create columns:

1. In your HTML document, type **<MULTICOL**.

2. Type **COLS=n**, where *n* is the number of columns desired. Each column will be the same size.

3. If desired, type **GUTTER=n**, where *n* is the width of the space between the columns, in pixels or as a percentage.

4. If desired, type **WIDTH=n**, where *n* is the width of the entire column set, including the gutter, in pixels or as a percentage of window size.

5. Type the final **>** to finish the column definition.

6. Create the elements (text or images) that will go into the columns.

7. Type **</MULTICOL>**.

✔ Tips

■ If you omit the WIDTH attribute, the columns will expand to fit whatever size window the user has created.

■ You can nest one set of columns with another. Simply repeat steps 1–7 when you reach step 6 of the outer set.

■ If you don't use the GUTTER attribute, Netscape automatically leaves 10 pixels between columns.

```
code.html

<FONT SIZE=-1>

<MULTICOL COLS=2 GUTTER=30
WIDTH=85%>

A multicolumn layout is typical of newspaper articles. You start
reading down the first column and when you read the bottom,
the text starts up again at the top of the next column. Of course,
it all depends on how tall your window is. And how is that
controlled? By the width of the columns. Netscape will try to
divide the text evenly among the columns you've defined,
making them as long as necessary, but as even as possible.

<P>Use page breaks wherever necessary to start a new line.
Or use a line break instead. Or insert images, or whatever.

<P>Hey, the headline's a joke, get it?

</MULTICOL>

After the final multicol tag, you can go back to one column text.
Or create another set of columns, with as many columns as you
like.

</FONT></BODY></HTML>
```

Figure 6.37 *The only required attribute in the MULTICOL tag is COLS: you must determine how many columns you want. (I've reduced the size of the text in this illustration to better fit on the page.)*

Figure 6.38 *Columns are perfect for newspaper style articles. These take up 85% of the screen, as defined in the HTML document. In addition, I've made the text one size smaller so as to better fit in the columns.*

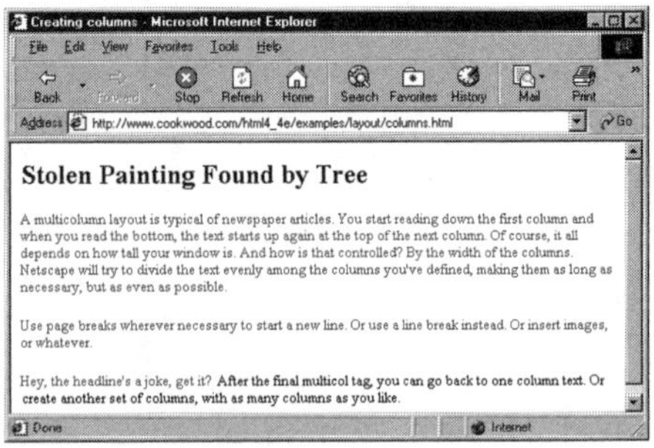

Figure 6.39 *Internet Explorer does not recognize the MULTICOL tag. The last paragraph runs into the column text, since there was no P tag.*

```
code.html
<HTML><HEAD><TITLE>Using preformatted
text</TITLE></HEAD><BODY>

<P>Here's a table that can be read with
<STRONG>ANY</STRONG> browser:

<PRE>
              Black Bears          Grizzlies
        Babies Adults Total   Babies Adults Total
Northampton  2      4     6      0      1      1
Becket       5     22    27      0      0      0
Worthington  7      5    12      2      1      3
</PRE></BODY></HTML>
```

Figure 6.40 *By using a monospaced font when writing your HTML code, you can see pretty much how the preformatted text will appear.*

Figure 6.41 *Preformatted text is always displayed with a monospaced font.*

```
code.html
<P>Here's a table that can be read with
<STRONG>ANY</STRONG> browser:
<PRE>
            <STRONG>Black Bears</STRONG>
<STRONG>Grizzlies</STRONG>
        Babies Adults Total   Babies Adults Total
Northampton  2      4     6      0      1      1
Becket       5     22    27      0      0      0
Worthington  7      5    12      2      1      3
</PRE></BODY></HTML>
```

Figure 6.42 *Adding formatting throws the alignment off in the HTML code but shouldn't affect the output in the browser.*

Figure 6.43 *Although the headers looked badly aligned in the HTML document (Figure 6.42), they look fine in the browser when the tags disappear.*

Using Preformatted Text

Usually, each browser decides where to divide each line of text, depending mostly on the window size, and eliminates extra spaces and returns. Preformatted text lets you maintain the original line breaks and spacing that you've inserted in the text. It is ideal for home-made tables and ASCII art.

To use preformatted text:

1. Type **<PRE>**.

2. Type the text that you wish to preformat, with all the necessary spaces, returns, and line breaks.

3. Type **</PRE>**.

✔ Tips

- Preformatted text is generally displayed with a monospaced font like Courier.

- Use a monospaced font in your text or HTML editor when composing the pre-formatted text so that you can see what it will look like in the browser.

- You can insert additional formatting (like STRONG, for example) within preformatted text **(Figures 6.42 and 6.43)**. However, you should do it *after* you set up your text, since the tags take up space in the HTML document, but not in the page.

- You can make homemade tables with preformatted text just by controlling the spaces between column entries. These tables will be readable by *all* browsers, not just the ones that currently support official tables.

Using Preformatted Text

Positioning Elements with Layers

Positioning Elements with Layers

Although they had already promised to work towards a universal standard for HTML, Netscape developed a set of proprietary tags for positioning HTML elements in early 1997. Because Netscape has yet to completely support the official method for positioning elements *(see pages 274–277)*, you may be forced to rely on layers (and perhaps a JavaScript program that determines which browser is being used) to position objects in Netscape browsers.

To position elements with layers:

1. Type **<LAYER**.

2. If desired, type **ID=name**, where *name* identifies the layer to JavaScript programs.

3. Type **TOP=m**, where *m* is the number of pixels the layer's contents should be offset from the top edge of the browser window.

4. Type **LEFT=n**, where *n* is the number of pixels the layer's contents should be offset from the left edge of the browser window.

5. If desired, type **WIDTH=w**, where *w* is the width of the layer in pixels.

6. If desired, type **HEIGHT=h**, where *h* is the height of the layer in pixels.

7. If desired, type **SRC="source.html"**, where *source.html* is the initial HTML content that should appear in the layer **(Figure 6.47)**.

8. If desired, type **CLIP="t,l,r,b"** where *t, l, r,* and *b* are the offsets in pixels from the top, left, right, and bottom.

---

code.html

<HTML><HEAD><TITLE>Positioning elements with layers</TITLE></HEAD><BODY>

<LAYER ID=layer1 TOP=10 LEFT=50 WIDTH=100 HEIGHT=100 BGCOLOR=yellow Z-INDEX=1>

This is the very bottom layer. It's yellow. </LAYER>

<LAYER ID=layer2 TOP=20 LEFT=60 WIDTH=160 HEIGHT=80 BGCOLOR=orange Z-INDEX=2>

This is the second layer from the bottom. It's orange.</LAYER>

<LAYER ID=layer3 TOP=40 LEFT=80 WIDTH=40 HEIGHT=40 BGCOLOR=black Z-INDEX=3>

<FONT COLOR=white>This is layer 3. It's black.</FONT></LAYER>

<LAYER ID=layer4 TOP=70 LEFT=200 WIDTH=100 HEIGHT=100 BGCOLOR=red Z-INDEX=1>

This layer is at the same level as the first one, that is, the bottom.</LAYER>

<NOLAYER>

This page contains elements positioned with layers. It only works in Netscape Communicator 4.</NOLAYER>

</BODY></HTML>

Figure 6.44 *Each layer is defined separately with its own coordinates. I've just entered plain text as the contents of each layer, but you can add any other HTML tags you like, except frames.*

Figure 6.45 *There are four layers in this example. Layers become really useful when combined with JavaScript.*

Figure 6.46 *Explorer makes a total mess of layers with content—despite the NOLAYER option.*

```
code.html
<HTML><HEAD><TITLE>Positioning elements
with layers</TITLE></HEAD><BODY>

<LAYER ID=layer1 TOP=10 LEFT=300
WIDTH=50 HEIGHT=60 BGCOLOR=aqua
Z-INDEX=1 SRC="layer1.html"></LAYER>

<LAYER ID=layer2 TOP=50 LEFT=30
WIDTH=300 HEIGHT=80 BGCOLOR=magenta
Z-INDEX=2 SRC="layer2.html"></LAYER>

<NOLAYER>This page contains elements
positioned with layers. It only works in Netscape
Communicator 4.</NOLAYER>

</BODY></HTML>
```

Figure 6.47 *If you know Explorer users are going to try and view your page, you should use the SRC attribute in the LAYER tags to insert content and then the NOLAYER tags to alert Explorer users to the fact that they won't see the effect.*

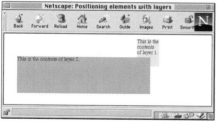

Figure 6.48 *Communicator displays the contents from the files in the SRC attribute.*

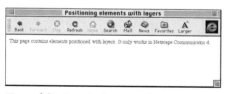

Figure 6.49 *Since Explorer completely ignores LAYER tags, it won't try to insert the content of layers defined by the SRC attribute. Instead, it simply and cleanly displays the contents of the NOLAYER tags.*

9. If desired, type **Z-INDEX=z**, where *z* is a number indicating the layer's level if it overlaps other layers. The higher the value of z, the higher the layer.

10. If desired, type **BGCOLOR=color**, where *color* is one of the predefined colors listed on page 357.

11. If desired, type **BACKGROUND= "image.gif"**, where *image.gif* is the image that you'd like to use for the background of the layer.

12. Type **>**.

13. Create the contents of the layer.

14. Type **</LAYER>**.

✔ **Tips**

- Layers are designed to be combined with JavaScript to create dynamic pages. For more information, check out *http:// developer.netscape.com/docs/manuals/ communicator/dynhtml/layers3.htm.* My basic examples don't quite do it justice.

- You can create content for browsers (like Explorer) that don't recognize the LAYER tags. Simply enclose it in opening and closing NOLAYER tags **(Figure 6.49)**.

- To create relatively positioned elements (that is, elements that are offset with respect to their natural position in the flow), use opening and closing ILAYER tags instead of LAYER tags.

- The official way to position elements precisely is with styles *(see Chapter 16, Layout with Styles)*, not this non-standard LAYER tag. However, since Netscape doesn't support the standard method completely, you may wish to use both techniques simultaneously.

Links

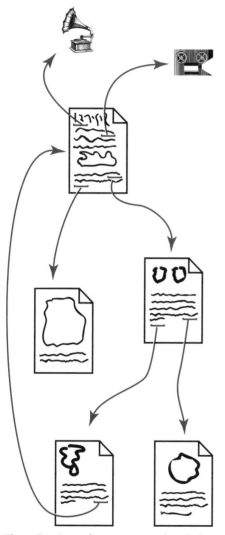

Links

Links are the distinguishing feature of the World Wide Web. They let you skip from one page to another, call up a movie or a recording of The Nields (or *your* favorite band), and download files with FTP.

A link has three parts: a destination, a label, and a target. The first part, the *destination*, is arguably the most important. You use it to specify what will happen when the visitor clicks the link. You can create links that show an image, play a sound or movie, download files, open a newsgroup, send an e-mail message, run a CGI program, and more. The most common links, however, connect to other Web pages, and sometimes to specific locations on other Web pages called *anchors*. All destinations are defined by writing a URL *(see page 27)* and are generally only visible to the visitor in the status area of the browser.

The second part of the link is the *label*, the part the visitor sees and clicks on to reach the destination. It can be text, an image, or both. Label text is often, but not always, shown underlined. The more appealing, enticing, and attractive the label, the more likely a visitor will click on it. In fact, eliciting Web visitors' clicks is an art.

The last part of the link, the *target*, is often ignored or left up to the browser. The target determines where the destination will be displayed. The target might be a particular named window or frame, or a *new* window or frame.

Figure 7.1 *Some of your pages may have links to many other pages. Other pages may have only one link. And still others may have no links at all.*

Creating a Link to Another Web Page

If you have more than one Web page, you will probably want to create links from one page to the next (and back again). You can also create connections to Web pages designed by other people on other servers.

To create a link to another Web page:

1. Type **<A HREF="page.html">** where *page.html* is the URL of the destination Web page.

2. Type the label text, that is, the text that will be underlined or highlighted in blue, and that when clicked upon will take the user to the URL referenced in step 1.

3. Type **</A>** to complete the definition of the link.

✔ **Tips**

- As a general rule, use relative URLs for links to Web pages on your site and absolute URLs for links to Web pages on other sites. For more details, consult *URLs* on page 27.

- So, a link to a page at another site might look like: **<A HREF="http://www.site.com/directory/page.html"> Label text</A>** **(Figures 7.5, 7.6, and 7.7)**.

- You can often create a link to a site's home page by using *http://www.site.com/* or *http://www.site.com/directory/*. The trailing forward slash tells the browser to search for the default file, usually called *index.html*, in the last directory mentioned (or in the root directory, if none has been mentioned).

- It's a good idea to use all lowercase letters for your URLs to avoid problems on the many servers that are case sensitive.

```
code.html

<HTML><HEAD><TITLE>Creating a Simple
Link</TITLE></HEAD>

<H1>Cookie and Woody</H1>

<P>Generally considered the sweetest and
yet most independent cats in the <A
HREF="pionerval.html">Pioneer Valley,</A>
Cookie and Woody are consistently
underestimated by their humble humans.

</BODY></HTML>
```

Figure 7.2 *Only the text within the link definition (in this case the words* Pioneer Valley*) will be clickable.*

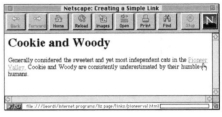

Figure 7.3 *When a visitor points at a link (generally displayed in blue underlined text), the destination URL is shown in the status area. If they actually click on a link…*

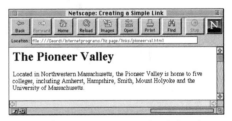

Figure 7.4 *…the page associated with that destination URL is displayed in their browser.*

Creating a Link to Another Web Page

```
code.html
<H1>Cookie and Woody</H1>
<P>Generally considered the sweetest and yet
most independent cats in the <A
HREF="pioneerval.html"> Pioneer Valley,</A>
Cookie and Woody are consistently
underestimated by their humble humans.

<H1>Pixel</H1>

<P>If you'd like to meet a JavaCat, check out
<A
HREF="http://www.chalcedony.com/pixel/">
Pixel</A> at Tom Negrino and Dori Smith's
great site about their <A HREF= "http://
www.chalcedony.com/javascript/"><EM>
JavaScript for the World Wide Web: Visual
```

Figure 7.5 *If you're creating links to someone else's Web site, you'll have to use an absolute URL, with the http://, server, full path, and file name.*

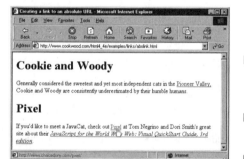

Figure 7.6 *Links to absolute URLs look and work the same as relative URLs.*

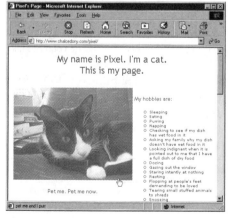

Figure 7.7 *A click on the link brings you to this page on the other server.*

■ There seems to be some question in the Web community about whether it's OK to link to any page on a site besides the home page. A direct "deep" link, as they're sometimes called, helps your visitor arrive promptly at their destination. However, they may miss important information or advertising that the site's creators left on the home page. One possible compromise is to give the direct connection as well as a connection to the site's home page. You may want to create a link to *your* home page from every other page on your site in case other sites create deep links to your inner pages.

■ Don't make the link's label too long. If the label is part of a sentence, keep only the key words within the link definition, with the rest of the sentence before and after the less than and greater than signs.

■ Try not to use "Click here" for a label. Instead use the key words that already exist in your text to identify the link.

■ You may apply text formatting (or styles) to the label.

■ You can also use an image as a label. For more details, consult *Using Images to Label Links* on page 128.

■ To create a link to a particular location on a Web page, use an anchor. For more details, see pages 120–121.

■ You can make the link appear in a given window or frame. For more information, consult *Targeting Links to Specific Windows* on page 122.

■ You can create keyboard shortcuts for links. For more details, see page 126.

■ You can determine the tab order for visitors who use their keyboards to navigate your page. For more details, consult *Setting the Tab Order for Links* on page 127.

Creating Anchors

Generally, a click on a link brings the user to the *top* of the appropriate Web page. If you want to have the user jump to a specific section of the Web page, you have to create an *anchor* and then reference that anchor in the link.

To create an anchor:

1. Place the cursor in the part of the Web page that you wish the user to jump to.

2. Type **<A NAME="anchor name">**, where *anchor name* is the text you will use internally to identify that section of the Web page.

3. Add the words or images that you wish to be referenced.

4. Type **</A>** to complete the definition of the anchor.

✔ Tips

- You are only *required* to add quotation marks around the anchor name when it is more than one word.

- In a long document, create an anchor for each section and link it to the corresponding item in the table of contents.

- Be aware that Netscape uses the term *targets* or *named anchors* when they mean anchors, although targets are something completely different *(see page 122)*.

```
<HTML><HEAD><TITLE>Creating an anchor to
make a dynamic table of contents</TITLE>
<HEAD> <BODY>

<H1>Table of Contents</H1>

<OL><LI><A HREF="#intro">Introduction</A>
<LI><A HREF="#descrip">Description of the Main
Characters</A>
<LI><A HREF="#devel">Development</A>
<LI><A HREF="#climax">Climax</A>
<LI><A HREF="#denoue">Denouement</A>
</OL>

<H1><A NAME="intro">Introduction</A></H1>

This is the intro. If I could think of enough things to
write about, it could span a few pages, giving all
the introductory information that an introduction
should introduce.

<H1><A NAME="descrip">Description of the
Main Characters</A></H1>

Frankie and Johnny are the main characters. She's
jealous, and seems to have a reason to be. He's a
sleaze, and will pay the price.

<H1><A NAME="devel">Development</A> </H1>

This is where everything starts happening. Johnny
goes out, without Frankie, without even tellin' her
where he's going. She's not crazy about it, but she
lets him go. A while later, she gets thirsty and de-
cides to go down to the corner bar for some beer.
Chatting with the bartender, she learns that Johnny
has been there with no other than Nellie Bly. Furi-
ous, she catches the cross town bus to find him.

<H1><A NAME="climax">Climax</A></H1>

When Frankie gets to Nellie's house, she looks up
and sees them kissing on the balcony. With tears
in her eyes, she picks up her shot gun and kills her
Johnny. He falls to the ground.

<H1><A NAME="denoue">Denouement</A></H1>

Frankie feels bad but it's kind of late now, and
Johnny <EM>was</EM> a lech. But the police
come and cart her off anyway.

</BODY></HTML>
```

Figure 7.8 *A long document like this one can be greatly helped by a dynamic table of contents. In this example, each section has its own anchor name so that a click on the corresponding item in the table of contents at the top of the page brings the visitor directly to the section they're interested in. (See Figure 7.9 and Figure 7.10 on page 121.)*

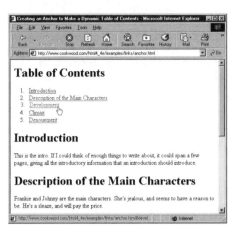

Figure 7.9 *When the visitor points at a link with an anchor, the URL and the anchor name appear in the status bar (in the lower-left corner of the window).*

Figure 7.10 *Once the visitor clicks the link, the particular part of the page that the anchor references is displayed at the top of the browser window.*

Linking to a Specific Anchor

Once you have created an anchor you can define a link so that a user's click will bring them directly to the section of the document that contains the anchor, not just the top of that document.

To create a link to an anchor:

1. Type **<A HREF="#**.

2. Type **anchor name**, where *anchor name* is the NAME of the destination section *(step 2 on page 120)*.

3. Type **">**.

4. Type the label text, that is, the text that will be underlined or highlighted in blue, and that when clicked upon will take the user to the section referenced in step 2.

5. Type **</A>** to complete the definition of the link.

✔ **Tips**

■ If the anchor is in a separate document, use **<A HREF="page.html#anchorname">** to reference the section. (There should be no space between the URL and the #.) If the anchor is on a page on a different server, you'll have to type **<A HREF= "http://www.site.com/path/page .html#anchorname">**.

■ While you obviously can't add anchors to other people's pages, you can take advantage of the ones that they have already created. View the source code of their documents to see which anchor names correspond to which sections. (For help viewing source code, consult *The Inspiration of Others* on page 310.)

■ If the anchor is at the bottom of the page, it may not display at the top of the window, but rather towards the middle.

Linking to a Specific Anchor

Targeting Links to Specific Windows

Targets let you open a link in a particular window, or even in a new window created especially for that link. This way, the page that contains the link stays open, enabling the user to go back and forth between the page of links and the information from each of those links.

To target links:

Within the link definition, type **TARGET="title"**, where *title* is the name of the window where the corresponding page should be displayed.

✔ Tips

■ Target names are case sensitive! You can leave off the quotes if you keep the target name to just one word.

■ Open a link in a completely new window by using **TARGET=_blank**.

■ If you target several links to the same window (e.g., using the same name), the links will all open in that same window.

■ If a named window is not already open, the browser opens a new window and uses it for all future links to that window.

■ Targets are most effective for opening Web pages (or even FTP links) in particular windows or frames. They don't make sense for e-mail or news links which open in different kinds of windows.

■ For more information on targeting frames, consult *Targeting Links to Particular Frames* on page 181.

■ You can use targeted windows as a simpler kind of frames. For more information, consult Chapter 10, *Frames*.

```
                    code.html
<H1>Nathaniel Hawthorne</H1>
Nathaniel Hawthorne was one of the most
important writers of 19th century America. His
most famous character is <A HREF="hester.html"
TARGET=characters>Hester Prynne</A>, a woman
living in Puritan New England. Another famous
object of Hawthorne's writing was <A HREF="http:
//www.ripon.edu/dept/pogo/presidency/Pierce/"
TARGET=characters>Franklin Pierce</A>, the 14th
president of the United States.
<P>Besides <A HREF="scarlet.html" TARGET=books>
<EM>The Scarlet Letter</EM></A>, Hawthorne
wrote <A HREF="gables.html" TARGET=books>
<EM>The House of Seven Gables</EM>, <A HREF=
"blithedale.html" TARGET=books><EM>The
Blithedale Romance</EM></A>, <A HREF=
"faun.html" TARGET=books><EM>The Marble
Faun</EM></A>, and many others.
</BODY></HTML>
```

Figure 7.11 *In this example, some links will appear in the* characters *window and others will appear in the* books *window.*

Figure 7.12 *When the visitor clicks a link with a target...*

Figure 7.13 *...the corresponding page is shown in the targeted window. In this example, it's the* characters *window.*

```
code.html
<HTML><HEAD><TITLE>American Writers of the
19th Century</TITLE>
<BASE TARGET=characters>
</HEAD><BODY>
<H1>Nathaniel Hawthorne</H1>
Nathaniel Hawthorne was one of the most
important writers of 19th century America. His most
famous character is <A HREF="hester.html">Hester
Prynne</A>, a woman living in Puritan New
England. Another famous object of Hawthorne's
writing was <A HREF="http://www.ripon.edu/dept/
pogo/presidency/Pierce/"> Franklin Pierce</A>,
the 14th president of the United States.
<P>Besides <A HREF="scarlet.html"
TARGET=books> <EM>The Scarlet Letter</EM>
</A>, Hawthorne wrote <A HREF="gables.html"
TARGET=books><EM>The House of Seven Gables
</EM>,  <A HREF="blithedale.html"
TARGET=books> <EM>The Blithedale Romance
</EM></A>, <A HREF="faun.html" TARGET=
books> <EM>The Marble Faun</EM></A>, and
many others.
</BODY></HTML>
```

Figure 7.14 *Use the BASE tag to set the default target (in this case the* characters *window) in order to save typing. Notice that I no longer have to specify the target for the links in the first paragraph. This document is equivalent to the one shown in Figure 7.11.*

Setting the Default Target

A link, by default, opens in the same window or frame that contains the link. You can choose another target for each link individually, as described on page 122, or specify a default target for all the links on a page.

To set a default target for a page:

1. In the HEAD section of your Web page, type **<BASE**.

2. Type **TARGET="title"**, where *title* is the name of the window or frame in which all the links on the page should open, by default.

3. Type **>** to complete the BASE tag.

✔ Tips

■ Target names are case sensitive! You can leave off the quotes if you keep the target name to just one word.

■ You can override the default target specified in the BASE tag by adding a target to an individual link as described on page 122.

■ The BASE tag is optional. If you do not use it, the default target will be the window that is currently displaying the page with the link.

■ You can also use the BASE tag to set the base URL for constructing relative URLs. This can be particularly useful when a Perl CGI script, located off in the cgi-bin directory, is generating the HTML page, and you want to reference a bunch of images or links in the main part of your server. Use **<BASE HREF="base.url">** where *base.url* is the URL that all relative links should be constructed from, or put another way, the *virtual* location of the generated HTML page.

Creating Other Kinds of Links

You are not limited to creating links to other Web pages. You can create a link to any URL—FTP sites, files that you want visitors to be able to download, newsgroups, and messages. You can even create a link to an e-mail address.

To create other kinds of links:

1. Type **<A HREF="**.

2. Type the URL:

   - For a link to any file on the Web, including movies, sounds, programs, Excel spreadsheets, or whatever, type **http://www.site.com/path/file.ext**, where *www.site.com* is the name of the server and *path/file.ext* is the path to the desired file, including its extension.

   - For a link to an FTP site, type **ftp://ftp.site.com/path**, where *ftp.site.com* is the server and *path* is the path to the desired directory or file.

   - For a newsgroup, type **news:newsgroup**, where *newsgroup* is the name of the desired newsgroup. For a particular message, type **news:article**, where *article* is the number (as shown in the header) of the individual article.

   - For a link to an e-mail address, type **mailto:name@site.com**, where *name@site.com* is the e-mail address.

   - For a link to a telnet site (like a library catalog), type **telnet://site**, where *site* is the name of the server you want to open the telnet connection to.

3. Type **">**.

```
┌─────────────────────────────────────────┐
│■               code.html               ■│
├─────────────────────────────────────────┤
<H1>Getaway Destinations</H1>

<P>There are lots of different kinds of links that you
can create on a Web page.

<P>You might want to create a link to a directory on
<A HREF="ftp://ftp2.netscape.com/pub/
communicator/">Netscape's FTP site</A> to help
visitors download the latest version of Netscape
Communicator. Or you can point them to a specific
file like the <A HREF="ftp://ftp2.netscape.com/pub/
communicator/english/4.61/mac/complete_install
/Comm4.61_Complete_EX.bin">Mac PowerPC
version of Communicator 4.61</A> so they don't
have to navigate the FTP site.

<P>To allow access to a <A HREF="ftp://name:
password@ftp.site.com/directory">private FTP
site</A>, you have to preface the server name with
the user name and password.

<P>A link to an e-mail address is a great way to
elicit comments about your Web page.
Unfortunately, spammers are great at snatching up
e-mail addresses from Web pages and filling your
mailbox with non-solicited junk. Don't think so? <A
HREF="mailto:liz@cookwood.com"> Tell me</A>
about it.

<P>Links to newsgroups help visitors find other people
interested in the same topic. For example, check out
the <A HREF="news:rec.pets.cats"> newsgroup for
cat lovers</A>. Can you believe there's no special
section for Woody and Cookie?  If you write a
particularly scintillating message, you could create
a <A HREF="news:34F243FF.887441BD@innet.com">
link to it</A> (although messages expire really
quickly and the link will die when it does).

<P>Many libraries let you <A HREF="telnet://
208.133.228.1">log into their system</A> from
home with telnet to see if a particular book is
available or checked out. Most browsers don't view
telnet connections inline, but instead open a helper
application like NCSA Telnet.

<P>Hey, what if you just want to let your visitors
download a file that's on your server in the same
directory as your Web pages? No problem. The link
will look like any other Web link. Here, download
the Windows version of the <A HREF="http://
www.cookwood.com/html4_4e/examples/links/
linkexamples.zip"> examples</A> from this
chapter.
```

Figure 7.15 *You can create a link to all different kinds of URLs.*

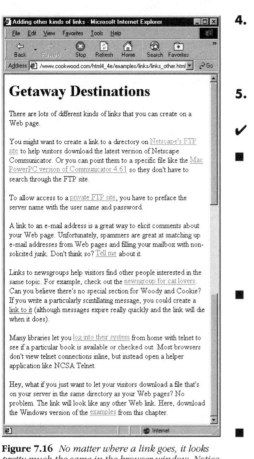

Figure 7.16 *No matter where a link goes, it looks pretty much the same in the browser window. Notice that I've tried to create labels that flow with the body of the text—instead of a lot of "click me's". These are all real links (OK, except the private FTP site). You can see where they lead by opening this page in your own browser—http://www.cookwood.com/html4_4e/examples/links/links_other.html*

4. Type the label for the link, that is, the text that will be underlined or highlighted, and that when clicked upon will take the visitor to the URL referenced in step 2.

5. Type **</A>**.

✔ Tips

■ If you create a link to a file that a browser doesn't know what to do with (like an Excel file, for example), the browser will either try to open a helper program to view the file or will try to download it to the visitor's hard disk. For more information, consult *Helper Applications and Plug-ins* on page 218.

■ It's a good idea to compress files that you want visitors to download. This makes them faster to download and it also protects them from being corrupted as they go from one system to another. Aladdin Systems *(www.aladdinsys.com)* has some good compression tools for both Macs and Windows machines.

■ You can also create links to less common destinations (like Gopher and WAIS servers). Just enter the URL in step 2.

■ You can preface an FTP URL with **name:password@** to access a private FTP site. Beware that browsers keep track of where you've been, however, including your password. (For example, in Netscape, type about:global.)

■ If you want to create an FTP link to a particular directory on the FTP site (as opposed to an individual file), simply use *ftp://ftp.site.com/directory.* You don't need to use the trailing forward slash. When you don't specify a specific file to download, the browser automatically displays the contents of the last directory in the path.

Creating Other Kinds of Links

Creating Keyboard Shortcuts for Links

One great new feature of HTML 4 is the ability to add keyboard shortcuts to different parts of your page, including links.

To add a keyboard shortcut to a link:

1. Inside the link's tag, type **ACCESSKEY="**.

2. Type the keyboard shortcut (any letter or number).

3. Type the final **"**.

4. If desired, add information about the keyboard shortcut to the text so that the visitor knows that it exists.

✔ Tips

■ Typing a keyboard shortcut selects the link, but the visitor has to press Return to follow it.

■ On Windows systems, to invoke the keyboard shortcut, visitors use the Alt key plus the letter you've assigned.

■ Keyboard shortcuts don't yet work on Macs. If and when they do, visitors will presumably use the Command key.

■ Keyboard shortcuts don't work in Netscape or with frames, unless the visitor selects the frame—which kind of defeats the purpose.

■ Keyboard shortcuts that you choose may override the browser's shortcuts. If you assign a popular shortcut used in a browser to some part of your form (like S for Save), you may annoy your visitors. Keep in mind though, that at least on Windows machines, the "important" browser keyboard shortcuts go with the Ctrl key, not Alt.

```
                    code.html
<HTML><HEAD><TITLE>Adding keyboard
shortcuts to links</TITLE><BASE TARGET=cats>
</HEAD><BODY>

<H1>Our Cats</H1>

Each of our cats has their own home page. Click
on the corresponding link or use the keyboard
shortcut to see each one.

<BR><A HREF="woody.html" ACCESSKEY=w>
Woody</A> (Alt-W)

<BR><A HREF="cookie.html" ACCESSKEY=c>
Cookie</A> (Alt-C)

<BR><A HREF="xixona.html" ACCESSKEY=x>
Xixona</A> (Alt-X)

<BR><A HREF="llumeta.html" ACCESSKEY=l>
Llumeta</A> (Alt-L)
```

Figure 7.17 *Create a keyboard shortcut for a link by adding the ACCESSKEY attribute to its tag. The explanatory text (Alt-W, etc.) is optional but helpful.*

Figure 7.18 *There's no way to tell a link has a keyboard shortcut unless you've labeled it as such.*

Figure 7.19 *When the keyboard shortcut is used, the link is immediately accessed (and the corresponding page is shown).*

```
code.html
<HTML><HEAD><TITLE>Adding keyboard
shortcuts to links</TITLE>
<BASE TARGET=cats></HEAD><BODY>

<TABLE BORDER=1 CELLPADDING=4
WIDTH=80% ALIGN=center>

<TR ALIGN=center><TD><A HREF="toc.html"
TABINDEX=2 TARGET=info>Contents</A>

<TD><A HREF="search.html" TABINDEX=2
TARGET=info>Search</A>

<TD><A HREF="company.html" TABINDEX=2
TARGET=info>About Us</A></TABLE>

<H1>Our Cats</H1>

Each of our cats has their own home page. Click
on the corresponding link or use the keyboard
shortcut to see each one.

<BR><A HREF="woody.html" ACCESSKEY=w
TABINDEX=1>Woody</A> (Alt-W)

<BR><A HREF="cookie.html" ACCESSKEY=c
TABINDEX=1>Cookie</A> (Alt-C)

<BR><A HREF="xixona.html" ACCESSKEY=x
TABINDEX=1>Xixona</A> (Alt-X)

<BR><A HREF="llumeta.html" ACCESSKEY=l
TABINDEX=1>Llumeta</A> (Alt-L)
```

Figure 7.20 *This page begins with a table of links, which, while useful, don't have anything to do with this particular page. So that the first tab selects the first "real" link, I've assigned it the lowest tab index.*

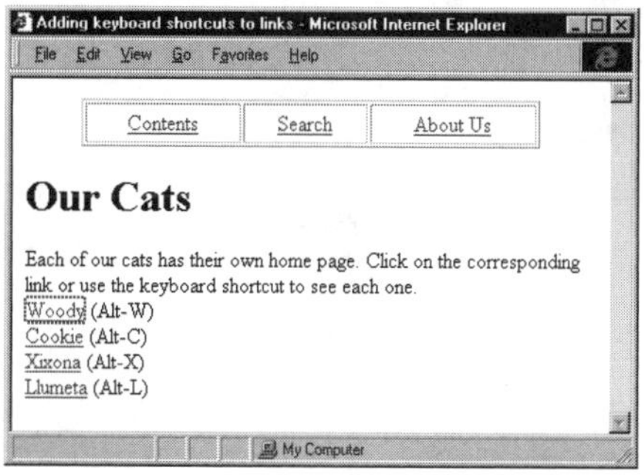

Figure 7.21 *When the visitor hits Tab the first time (OK, the second time, see the second to last tip), the Woody link is selected. If they hit Tab again, Cookie will be selected, and so on until Llumeta. At that point, a tab will bring them up to the Contents link.*

Setting the Tab Order for Links

Many browsers let users navigate through the links, image maps, and form elements with the Tab key. You can determine a custom tab order, to emphasize certain elements.

To set the tab order:

In the link's tag, type **TABINDEX=n**, where *n* is the number that sets the tab order.

✔ Tips

- To *activate* a link the visitor must tab to it and then press Enter.

- The value for TABINDEX can be any number between 0 and 32767. Use a negative value to take a link out of the tab sequence altogether.

- By default, the tab order depends on the order of the elements in the HTML code. When you change the tab order, the lower numbered elements are activated first, followed by higher numbered ones.

- Elements with the same tab index value are accessed in the order in which they appear in the HTML page.

- You can also assign tab order to client-side image maps and form elements. For more information, consult *Creating a Client-Side Image Map* on page 130 or *Setting the Tab Order* on page 213, respectively.

- Actually, when the visitor hits Tab for the first time, the page's URL is selected (in the Address/Location bar, even if it's hidden). The *second* time they hit Tab, the link with the lowest tab index on the page will be selected.

- In a page with frames, the visitor has to select the frame before they can tab through the links it contains.

Using Images to Label Links

In this age of graphical interfaces, people are used to clicking on images and icons to make things happen. Adding an image to a link creates a navigational button that the visitor can click to access the referenced URL. (For more information about images, see Chapter 4, *Creating Web Images*, and Chapter 5, *Using Images*.)

To use images to label links:

1. Type **<A HREF="destination.html">**, where *destination.html* is the URL of the page that the user will jump to when they click the button.

2. Type **<IMG SRC="image.location"** where *image.location* gives the location of the image file on the server.

3. If desired, type **BORDER=n**, where *n* is the width in pixels of the border. Use a value of 0 to omit the border.

4. Add other image attributes as desired and then type the final **>**.

5. If desired, type the label text, that is, the text that will be underlined or highlighted in blue, that when clicked upon will take the user to the URL referenced in step 1.

6. Type **</A>** to complete the link.

✔ Tips

- If you invert steps 5 and 6, only a click on the *image* will produce the desired jump. A click on the text has no effect. (You can also leave the text out altogether.)

- Use small images.

- Clickable images are surrounded by a border with the same color as the active links (generally blue). For no border, use a value of 0 in step 3.

```
code.html
<HTML><HEAD><TITLE>Creating a Button
(Using an Image in a Link)</TITLE></HEAD>
<BODY>

<H1>Cookie and Woody</H1>

<P>Generally considered the sweetest and yet
most independent cats in the <A
HREF=pioneerval.html>Pioneer Valley,</A>
Cookie and Woody are consistently
underestimated by their humble humans.

<P><A HREF="prevpage.html"><IMG
SRC=pointleft.gif ALT="Previous page"></A>

<A HREF="nextpage.html"><IMG
SRC=pointright.gif ALT="Next page"></A>

<P><A HREF="mailto:lcastro@crocker.com">
<IMG SRC=writeletter.gif ALT="Send mail"
ALIGN=center> Send me comments</A> on this
page!
```

Figure 7.22 *There is no text in the first two button links. The final </A> comes right after the image tag.*

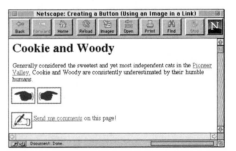

Figure 7.23 *If you do add text to the link, make sure you insert a space between the text and the image (or use HSPACE or styles to space the text, see page 91).*

Figure 7.24 *This is the original pointright.gif image. It does not have a border. Borders are automatically added in the browser to all images used to label links. You can adjust the border with the BORDER attribute in the IMG tag.*

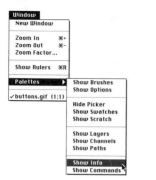

Figure 7.25 *In Photoshop, choose Show Info in the Palettes submenu in the Window menu.*

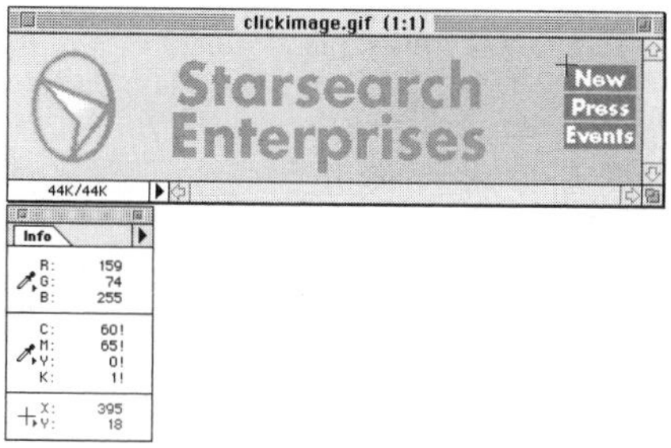

Figure 7.26 *Place the cursor in the left-hand corner of the rectangle and jot down the x and y coordinates shown in Photoshop's Info palette. (In this example, x=395 and y=18.)*

Dividing an Image into Clickable Regions

A clickable image is like a collection of buttons combined together in one image. A click in one part of the image brings the user to one destination. A click in another area brings the user to a different destination.

There are two important steps to implementing a clickable image: First you must map out the different regions of your image, and second you must define which destinations correspond to which areas of the image.

To divide an image into clickable regions:

1. Create a GIF image, consulting Chapter 4, *Creating Web Images*, as necessary.

2. Open the GIF image in Photoshop or other image editing program.

3. Choose Window > Palettes > Show Info **(Figure 7.25)**.

4. Point the cursor over the top-left corner of the region you wish to define.

5. Using the Info window, jot down the *x* and *y* coordinates for that corner **(Figure 7.26)**.

6. Repeat steps 4–5 for the bottom-right corner of a rectangle, or for each point of a polygon.

✔ Tip

■ For more information on a few tools that can help you divide your image into clickable regions, consult *Image Map Tools* on page 352.

Dividing an Image into Clickable Regions

Creating a Client-Side Image Map

Image maps link the areas of an image with a series of URLs so that a click in each area brings the user to a different page. There are two kinds of image maps, *client-side* and *server side (see page 132)*. Client-side image maps run more quickly because they are interpreted in your visitors' browsers and don't have to consult the server for each click. In addition, since they do not require a CGI script, they are simpler to create, and you don't need to consult your Internet service provider, nor get their permission. Only very old browsers may not understand them.

To create a client-side image map:

1. In the HTML document that contains the image, type **<MAP**.

2. Type **NAME="label">**, where *label* is the name of the map.

3. Type **<AREA** to define the first clickable area.

4. Type **SHAPE="type"**, where *type* represents the area's shape. Use *rect* for a rectangle, *circle* for a circle, and *poly* for an irregular shape.

5. For a rectangle, type **COORDS="x1, y1, x2, y2"**, where *x1, y1, x2,* and *y2* represent the upper-left and lower-right corners of the rectangle, as obtained on page 129, and shown in Figure 7.26.

   For a circle, type **COORDS="x, y, r"** where *x* and *y* represent the center of the circle and *r* is the radius.

   For a polygon, type **COORDS="x1, y1, x2, y2, x3, y3"** (and so on), giving the x and y coordinates of each point on the polygon.

```
code.html
<HTML><HEAD><TITLE>Creating a client-side
image map</TITLE></HEAD><BODY><P>

<MAP NAME="banner">

 <AREA SHAPE="rect" COORDS="395, 18,
445, 35" HREF="newinfo.html">

 <AREA SHAPE="rect" COORDS="395, 38,
445, 55" HREF="pressrelease.html">

 <AREA SHAPE="rect" COORDS="395, 58,
445, 75" HREF="events.html">

 </MAP>
```

Figure 7.27 *You can put the map anywhere you like in your HTML document. Each clickable area is defined by its own set of coordinates, and has an individual URL.*

```
code.html
</MAP>

<IMG SRC="clickimage.gif" ALT="SE banner"
USEMAP="#banner" WIDTH=

"450" HEIGHT="100" ALIGN="BOTTOM"
ISMAP>

<H1>Starsearch Enterprises</H1>
```

Figure 7.28 *Type the image definition in the desired place in your HTML document. The most important piece is the USEMAP=#label attribute. Don't forget the number sign (#).*

```
code.html
<H1>Starsearch Enterprises</H1>

<UL>

<LI><A HREF="http://www.castro.com/
lcastro/newinfo.html">New programs</A>

 <LI><A HREF="http://www.castro.com/
lcastro/pressrelease.html">Press releases</A>

<LI><A HREF="http://www.castro.com/
lcastro/events.html">Upcoming events</A>

<LI><A HREF="http://www.castro.com/
lcastro/infoSE.html">About Starsearch
Enterprises</A>
```

Figure 7.29 *It's a good idea to repeat the links in text form below the image for those users who can't or don't want to view images. Otherwise, those users won't be able to navigate to your other pages.*

Figure 7.30 *When your users point at one of the defined areas, the destination URL appears in the status bar at the bottom of the window.*

Events

(Under Construction) This page is for upcoming events.

Figure 7.31 *And if a user clicks the link, the browser will immediately display the corresponding page.*

6. Type **HREF="url.html"**, where *url.html* is the address of the page that should appear when the user clicks in this area.

Or type **NOHREF** if a click in this area should have no result.

7. If desired, type **TARGET="windowname"**, where *windowname* is the name of the window where the page should appear. For more information, see page 122.

8. If desired, add a keyboard shortcut by typing **ACCESSKEY=x** *(see page 126)*.

9. Type **>** to complete the definition of the clickable area.

10. Repeat steps 3–9 for each area.

11. Type **</MAP>** to complete the map.

12. Type **<IMG SRC="image.gif"**, where *image.gif* is the name of the image to be used as an image map.

13. Add any other image attributes.

14. Type **USEMAP="#label"**, where *label* is the map name defined in step 2.

15. Type the final **>** for the image.

✔ Tips

■ Usually, maps are in the same HTML document as the image that uses them. Internet Explorer, however, can use maps that are in an external HTML file. Simply add the full URL of that file in front of the label name: **USEMAP="map.html#label"**.

■ With overlapping areas, most browsers use the URL of the first area defined.

■ For information on using server-side image maps, see page 132.

Creating a Client-Side Image Map

Using a Server-Side Image Map

To use a server-side image map, you have to have the *imagemap* program on your NCSA HTTPd server or *htimage* on your CERN server. The program should be located in the cgi-bin directory. Ask your server administrator for help, if necessary.

To use a server-side image map:

1. In your HTML document type **<A HREF="http://www.yoursite.com/cgi-bin/imagemap**, where *imagemap* is the name of the program that interprets your set of coordinates.

2. Type **/path/coords"** (adding no spaces after step 1) indicating the path to the text file that contains the coordinates (the map) for the image.

3. Type the final **>** of the link definition.

4. Type **<IMG SRC="clickimage.gif"** where *clickimage.gif* is the image that you want your readers to click.

5. Type **ISMAP** to indicate a clickable image for a server-side map.

6. Add any other image attributes as desired and then type the final **>**.

7. Type the clickable text that should appear next to the image, if any.

8. Type **</A>** to complete the link.

✔ Tip

■ For information on creating sets of coordinates for server-side image maps, consult your Internet service provider. They'll be able to tell you what kind of server they have and in what format the coordinates should be.

```
code.html

<A HREF="http://www.castro.com/cgi-
bin/imagemap/lcastro/banner.map">

<IMG SRC="clickimage.gif" ALT="SE banner"
ISMAP></A>

<H1>Starsearch Enterprises</H1>

<UL><LI><A HREF="http://www.castro.com/
lcastro/ newinfo.html">New programs</A>

<LI><A HREF="http://www.castro.com/
lcastro/pressrelease.html">Press releases</A>

<LI><A HREF="http://www.castro.com/lcastro
/events.html">Upcoming events</A>

<LI><A HREF="http://www.castro.com/lcastro
/infoSE.html">About Starsearch
```

Figure 7.32 *Notice how the text-based alternate links below the image point to the same URLs as the buttons in the clickable image. This gives equal access to your users who can't see the images.*

Figure 7.33 *In Netscape, when your user points at a part of a clickable image, the cursor changes into a hand and the corresponding URL shows in the status area at the bottom of the window.*

Figure 7.34 *In Internet Explorer, the cursor changes to a hand when placed over a clickable image, but the status line does not show the particular coordinates.*

```
code.html

<HTML><HEAD><TITLE>Creating Colored
Links</TITLE></HEAD>

<BODY BGCOLOR="#000000"
TEXT="#FFFFFF" ALINK="#242424"
VLINK="#616161" LINK="#bababa">

My eyes are green, my hair is bright purple. The
text is white, the background is black, the links
should be light gray to start with, dark gray when
clicked on and medium gray when visited. If
these colors don't look right to you, blame the
Linotronic.

<P><A HREF="newlink.html">New Link</A>
<BR>

<A HREF="newlink2.html">New Link that I'm
clicking on right now</A><BR>

<A HREF="visitedlink.html">Visited Link</A>
<BR>

</BODY></HTML>
```

Figure 7.35 *You may select a color for new links, visited links, and active links (one that is being clicked).*

Figure 7.36 *It is important to choose colors (or shades of gray, as in this example) that have enough contrast so that you can see all the items on the page, but not so much (especially with colors) as to be garish and distracting.*

Changing the Color of Links

The LINK tags let you change the color of links. Although certain standard link colors have already been established—like blue for links that have not yet been visited—you can use whatever color you want. But don't forget: people will only click on a link if they know it's a link.

To change the color of links:

1. Place the cursor inside the BODY tag.

2. To change the color of links that have not yet been visited, type **LINK**.

   To change the color of links that have already been visited, type **VLINK**.

   To change the color of a link when the user clicks on it, type **ALINK.**

3. Type **="#rrggbb"**, where *rrggbb* is the hexadecimal representation of the desired color.

   Or type **=color**, where *color* is one of the 16 predefined colors.

4. Repeat steps 2–3 for each kind of link.

✔ Tips

- See Appendix C and the inside back cover for a complete listing of hexadecimal values and the equivalents for many common colors.

- Make sure you test the colors of your text, links, and background together. Also test your color page on a black and white and a grayscale monitor.

- Be careful when choosing different colors for links from page to page. If your visitors can't tell what to click on or which pages they've already visited, they may decide not to click on anything.

Lists

The HTML specifications contain special codes for creating lists of items. You can create plain, numbered, or bulleted lists, as well as lists of definitions. You can also nest one kind of list inside another. In the sometimes sketchy shorthand of the Internet, lists come in very handy.

All lists are formed by a principal code to specify what sort of list you want to create (OL for ordered list, DL for definition list, etc.) and a secondary code to specify what sort of items you want to create (LI for list item, DT for definition term, etc.).

Although the W3C does not recommend the use of List codes for simply indenting paragraphs, they *are* rather handy in this regard. You can find more information about that in Chapter 6, *Page Layout*, under *Creating Indents (with Lists)* on page 107.

Creating Ordered Lists

The ordered list is perfect for explaining step-by-step instructions for how to complete a particular task or for creating an outline (complete with links to corresponding sections, if desired) of a larger document. You may create an ordered list anywhere in the BODY section of your HTML document.

To create ordered lists:

1. Type the title of the ordered list.

2. Type **<OL**.

3. If desired, type **TYPE=X**, where *X* represents the kind of symbols that should be used in the ordered list: *A* for capital letters, *a* for small letters, *I* for capital roman numerals, *i* for small roman numerals, and *1* for numbers, which is the default.

4. If desired, type **START=n**, where *n* represents the initial value for this list item. The START value is always numeric and is converted automatically, according to the TYPE value.

5. Type **>** to finish the ordered list definition. Any text entered after the OL tag and before the first LI tag will appear with the same indentation as the first item in the list, but without a number.

6. Type **<LI**.

7. If desired, type **TYPE=X**, where *X* represents the kind of symbols that should be used for this and subsequent list items. Changing the TYPE here overrides the value chosen in step 3.

```
code.html
<HTML><HEAD><TITLE>Creating Ordered
Lists</TITLE></HEAD><BODY>

Ordered lists are the most common kinds of lists,
perfect for explaining step by step instructions or
for giving an outline (complete with links to the
corresponding sections, if desired) for a larger
document.

<H1>Changing a light bulb</H1>

<OL>

<LI>Make sure you have unplugged the lamp.
<LI>Unscrew the old bulb.
<LI>Get the new bulb out of the package.
<LI>Check the wattage to make sure it's correct.
<LI>Screw in the new bulb.
<LI>Plug in the lamp and turn it on!

</OL>

</BODY></HTML>
```

Figure 8.1 *There is no special way to format a list's title. Just use a regular header (see page 38).*

Figure 8.2 *This list uses the default TYPE=1 attribute to create a numbered list.*

Creating Ordered Lists

```
code.html
<HTML><HEAD><TITLE>Creating Ordered
Lists</TITLE></HEAD><BODY>

<H1>The Great American Novel</H1>

<OL TYPE=I>

<LI>Introduction
<LI>Denouement
<LI>Climax
<LI>End
<LI>Epilogue

</OL>

</BODY></HTML>
```

Figure 8.3 *To use roman numerals for each of the list's items, insert TYPE=I in the OL tag.*

The Great American Novel

   I.   Introduction
  II.   Development
 III.   Climax
 IV.   Denouement
  V.   Epilogue

Figure 8.4 *Roman numerals are great for outlines. Note how they are automatically right-aligned.*

8. If desired, type **VALUE=n**, where *n* represents the initial value for this list item. The VALUE is always specified numerically and is converted automatically by the browser to the type of symbol specified by the TYPE value. The VALUE attribute overrides the START value chosen in step 4.

9. Type the final **>** to complete the list item definition.

10. Type the text to be included in the list item.

11. Repeat steps 6–10 for each new list item.

12. Type **</OL>** to complete the ordered list.

✔ Tips

- Unless you specify otherwise (with the TYPE attribute), items will be numbered with Arabic numerals (1, 2, 3, etc.).

- Keep the text in your list items short. If you have more than a few lines of text in each item, you may have better luck using headers (H1, H2, etc.) and paragraphs (P).

- Inserting a line break (BR) in a list item breaks the text to the next line, but maintains the same indenting.

- Text placed after the OL tag appears indented by the same amount as the following list item, but without a number or letter.

- You may create one type of list inside another. For more information, consult *Creating Nested Lists* on page 141.

- You should know that the W3C discourages the use of the START, TYPE, and VALUE attributes in favor of style sheets *(see page 289)*.

Creating Ordered Lists

Creating Unordered Lists

Unordered lists are probably the most widely used lists on the Web. Use them to list any series of items that have no particular order, such as hot Web sites or names.

To create unordered lists:

1. Type the introductory text for the unordered list, if desired.

2. Type **<UL**.

3. If desired, type **TYPE=shape**, where *shape* represents the kind of bullet that should be used with each list item. You may choose *disc* for a solid round bullet (the default for first level lists), *circle* for an empty round bullet (the default for second level lists), or *square* for square bullets (the default for third and subsequent level lists).

4. Type **>** to finish the unordered list definition. Any text entered after the UL tag and before the first LI tag will appear with the same indentation as the first item in the list, but without a bullet.

5. Type **<LI**.

6. Type **TYPE=shape**, where *shape* represents the kind of bullet (*disc, circle,* or *square*) that should be used in this list item. You only need to specify the shape here if it differs from the one you've chosen in step 3.

7. Type **>** to finish the list item definition.

8. Type the text to be included in the list item.

9. Repeat steps 5–7 for each list item.

10. Type **</UL>** to complete the unordered list.

```
code.html

<HTML><HEAD><TITLE>Creating Unordered
Lists</TITLE></HEAD><BODY>

Unordered lists are probably the most widely
used lists on the Web. Use them to list any series
of items that have no particular order, such as hot
web sites or names.

<H1>PageWhacker, version 12.0--
Features</H1>

<UL><EM><FONT SIZE=-1>New or improved
features marked with a solid bullet. <BR>(All
features may show the same bullets in some
browsers.)</FONT></EM>

<LI TYPE=round>One click page layout
<LI TYPE=disc>Spell checker for 327 major
languages
<LI>Image retouching plug-in
<LI TYPE=round>Special HTML filters
<LI>Unlimited Undo's and Redo's
<LI TYPE=disc>Automatic book writing

</UL>

</BODY></HTML>
```

Figure 8.5 *Notice that there is no TYPE specified for the third and fifth items. They will have the default bullet.*

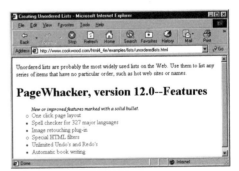

Figure 8.6 *Notice that the third and fifth items are displayed with the default bullet (a disc).*

Creating Unordered Lists

```
┌─────────── code.html ───────────┐
<HTML><HEAD><TITLE>Creating Unordered
Lists</TITLE></HEAD><BODY>

<H1>The hotel offers the following entertainment
choices:</H1>

<UL>

<LI>Live music and dancing in the Starlight
Lounge
<LI TYPE=square>Midnight snacks in Balladier
Hall
<LI TYPE=disc>Free HBO and Cinemax
<LI TYPE=square>Moonlight swim in the rooftop
pool
<LI TYPE=disc>Specialty room service
<LI TYPE=square>Friday night Bingo in the
Green room

</UL>

</BODY></HTML>
```

Figure 8.7 *There is no TYPE specified for the first item. It will be displayed with the default bullet: a disc (solid round).*

Figure 8.8 *It's hard to tell the difference between discs and squares in Explorer.*

Figure 8.9 *Netscape displays discs slightly smaller than squares, which gives a little variety to this list.*

✔ **Tips**

■ You can use any image you want for bullets—if you use style sheets. For more details, consult *Setting List Properties* on page 289.

■ Keep the text in your list items short. If you have more than a couple of lines of text in each item, you may have better luck using headers (H1, H2, etc.) and paragraphs (P).

■ Inserting a line break (BR) in a list item breaks the text to the next line, but maintains the same indenting.

■ Text placed after the UL tag appears indented by the same amount as the following list item, but without a bullet. In fact, many people use the UL tag for indenting text *(see page 107).*

■ The TYPE attribute in an LI tag overrides the TYPE attribute used in a UL tag.

■ You may create one type of list inside another. For more information, consult *Creating Nested Lists* on page 141.

■ You should know that the W3C discourages the use of the TYPE attribute in favor of style sheets *(see page 289).* However, I doubt that the major browsers will stop supporting it any time soon.

■ There is one more value possible for the TYPE attribute: *round*. However, Netscape displays it the same as circle while Explorer displays it as a disc.

■ Netscape displays discs and circles at a smaller size than Explorer **(Figures 8.8 and 8.9)**.

Creating Unordered Lists

Creating Definition Lists

HTML provides a special tag for creating definition lists. This type of list is particularly suited to glossaries, but works well with any list that pairs a word or phrase with a longer description. Imagine, for example, a list of Classical Greek verb tenses, each followed by an explanation of proper usage.

To create definition lists:

1. Type the introductory text for the definition list.

2. Type **<DL>**. You may enter text after the DL tag. It will appear on its own line, aligned to the left margin.

3. Type **<DT>**.

4. Type the word or short phrase that will be defined or explained, including any logical or physical formatting desired.

5. Type **<DD>**.

6. Type the definition of the term entered in step 4. Browsers generally indent definitions on a new line below your definition term.

7. Repeat steps 3–6 for each pair of terms and definitions.

8. Type **</DL>** to complete the list of definitions.

✔ Tip

- You can create more than one DL line or more than one DT line to accommodate multiple words or multiple definitions.

```
<HTML><HEAD><TITLE>Creating Definition
Lists</TITLE></HEAD><BODY>

<H1>Classical Greek Verb Tenses</H1>

<DL>

<DT><STRONG>Present</STRONG><BR>

<DD><EM>e.g. .luo, luomai</EM>. The present
usually shows the pure verb stem in verbs with
strong stems. In many verbs it undergoes drastic
phonetical changes due to the union of the
thematic vowels to the tense suffixes.

<DT><STRONG>Future</STRONG><BR>

<DD><EM>e.g. luso, lusomai, luthesomai
</EM>. The future has the characteristic s in
between the verb stem and the thematic vowels,
which gives: verb stem + s (-the- in passive voice)
+ thematic vowel + personal ending.

<DT><STRONG>Aorist</STRONG><BR>

<DD><EM>e.g. .elusa, eluthen, elusamen</EM>.
The aorist (from a-orizo, aoristos: indefinite,
limitless) is the equivalent to the indefinite past in
several languages. Its main characteristic is the
temporal suffix -sa- (in the active and middle
voice) and -the- in the passive voice. The -s- from
sa may change to accomodate different stem
endings. For example: kopto = ekops (ps = psi)a.

</DL>

</BODY></HTML>
```

Figure 8.10 *You may want to add formatting to your definition term to help it stand out.*

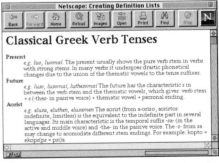

Figure 8.11 *The defined word (marked with DT) is aligned to the left. The definition (marked with DD) is indented.*

Creating Definition Lists

```
┌─────────── code.html ──────────────┐
<HTML><HEAD><TITLE>Creating Nested
Lists</TITLE></HEAD><BODY>

<H1>The Great American Novel</H1>

<OL TYPE=I>
<LI>Introduction
    <OL TYPE=A>
        <LI>Boy's childhood
        <LI>Girl's childhood
    </OL>
<LI>Development
    <OL TYPE=A>
        <LI>Boy meets Girl
        <LI>Boy and Girl fall in love
        <LI>Boy and Girl have fight
    </OL>
<LI>Climax
    <OL TYPE=A>
        <LI>Boy gives Girl ultimatum
            <OL TYPE=1>
                <LI>Girl can't believe her ears
                <LI>Boy is indignant at Girl's
                indignance
            </OL>
        <LI>Girl tells Boy to get lost
    </OL>
<LI>Denouement
<LI>Epilogue
</OL>

</BODY></HTML>
```

Figure 8.12 *Browsers automatically indent nested lists, but if you use tabs to indent them in your HTML document, they'll be easier to organize and set up.*

Figure 8.13 *You, the designer, can choose the type of numbering for each level of your outline.*

Creating Nested Lists

You may insert one type of list into another. This is particularly useful with an outline rendered with ordered lists, where you may want several levels of items.

To create nested lists:

1. Create your first list.

2. Place the cursor inside your first list where you want your nested list to appear.

3. Create your nested list in the same way you created the regular list.

4. Continue with the principal list.

✔ Tips

■ Use tabs to indent the nested list in your HTML document so that it is easier to see what you're doing **(Figure 8.12)**. Nested lists are automatically indented by browsers.

■ The numbering for nested ordered lists automatically starts at 1 unless you specify a new value with the START attribute.

■ By default, each and every level of an ordered list will be numbered with Arabic numerals. You'll have to use the TYPE attribute to override them. According to *The Chicago Manual of Style* the correct nesting order is I, A, 1, a, 1.

■ By default, the first level of an unordered list will have solid round bullets, the next will have empty round bullets and the third and subsequent levels will have square bullets. Use the TYPE tag to specify the type of bullet you want *(see page 138)*.

Tables

Figure 9.1 *Tables let you create fancy professional-looking layouts that will wow your visitors.*

In earlier editions of this book, I tried to stick to the straight and narrow of table design by explaining how to use them only in the context of tabular data. However, what most people use tables for has nothing to do with columns of numbers. So I've completely revamped this chapter in order to show you how to use tables in a non-standard way—to create multicolumn text, captions for images, sidebars, and more.

Tables might seem a bit daunting at first, especially when used for layout. However, if you carefully map out your page *(see page 144)* before you start in on the HTML code, your life will be a lot easier. The second most important step is to specify the width of the whole table as well as of the individual cells *(see page 148)*. Setting the width keeps the table's size constant (instead of letting the browser figure it out in its own indomitable way) and keeps your elements the way you intended.

If tables really make you miserable, you can cheat. You can use PageMill or FrontPage or some other Web page program, create the table in that program, and then tweak the HTML code by hand afterwards as necessary.

If you do want to use tables for displaying rows and columns of tabular data, consult the end of this chapter *(see pages 160–165)* for some special tools for structuring that data and consolidating the formatting.

Mapping Out Your Page

Before you create a complicated table, it's really important to have a vision of what you're about to construct. You need to know how many rows and columns you need, how big these should be, and where each of the items on your page should go.

To map out your page:

1. Design your page on a piece of paper—with a pen!

2. Figure out how many rows and columns you will need. Identify any rows or columns that will span more than one space.

3. If necessary, you can nest one table inside another. However, you should keep this nesting to a minimum as it tends to slow browsers down—and sometimes cause them to break down altogether.

4. Measure how wide your table should be (the standard is around 600 pixels) and then decide how many pixels wide each column should be.

5. Create the skeleton of your page with just the table tags but little or no content.

6. Finally, create or insert the content.

✔ Tip

■ One good way to get ideas for table structure is to look at how others do it *(see page 310)*. However, there are some very complicated setups out there. One way to get a handle on what's going on in someone else's page is to download the source code and then change the BGCOLOR of each nested table *(see page 158)* so you can better see which parts of the layout belong to which table.

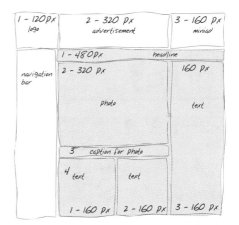

Figure 9.2 *Here's a map of the main example used in this chapter. The main outer table has three columns and two rows. (The second row is the navigation bar and the cell that contains the inner table.) The inner (shaded) table has three columns and four rows.*

```
                code.html
<HTML><HEAD><TITLE>Table</TITLE>
</HEAD><BODY>

<TABLE>

<TR>

<TD><IMG SRC="elephant.jpg" WIDTH=312
HEIGHT=234 ALT="Elephant Baby"></TD>

</TR>

<TR>

<TD><FONT SIZE=-1><I>A baby elephant
hanging out with its mom, aunts and greataunts,
and maybe even its grandmother</I></FONT>
</TD></TR>

</TABLE>

</BODY></HTML>
```

Figure 9.3 *This very simple table has two rows, each of which has only one cell. Notice that I've added extra size formatting to the caption to keep it unobtrusive.*

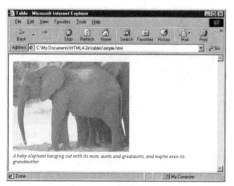

Figure 9.4 *A simple table like this is a great way to keep a photo and its caption forever joined.*

Creating a Simple Table

Tables are made up of rows of cells. The number of cells in each row determine the table's shape.

To create a simple table:

1. Type **<TABLE>**.

2. Type **<TR>** to define the beginning of the first row. If desired, press Return and Tab to visually distinguish the row elements.

3. Type **<TD>** to define the beginning of the cell.

4. Type the contents of the cell.

5. Type **</TD>** to complete the cell.

6. Repeat steps 3–5 for each cell in the row.

7. Type **</TR>** to complete the row.

8. Repeat steps 2-7 for each row.

9. To finish the table, type **</TABLE>**.

✔ Tips

■ The </TABLE> tag is *not* optional. Netscape won't display tables without it.

■ Officially, you can omit the closing tag for cells (</TD>) and rows (</TR>). However, leaving them out makes some browsers display extra spaces between cells.

■ There is also a TH tag for creating *header* cells. But, all it does is center the contents of a cell and format it in boldface. If you're mostly using tables to help layout your page, TH is not very useful.

■ You can create a caption for the table in opening and closing CAPTION tags. Use ALIGN=direction, where *direction* is top, bottom, left, or right to align the caption. Personally, I think it's ugly and not very useful for layout purposes.

Creating a Simple Table

Adding a Border

A border helps separate your table from the rest of the text. However, if you're laying out your page with tables, you may not want to call so much attention to the border. It's up to you.

To create a border:

1. Inside the initial TABLE tag, type **BORDER**.

2. If desired, type **=n**, where *n* is the thickness in pixels of the border. The default thickness for the border is 2 pixels.

✔ Tips

■ You get a border (that is, it takes up space) whether you use the BORDER tag or not. The BORDER tag simply determines whether your visitors can *see* the border or not.

■ To get rid of the border completely, use **BORDER=0**.

■ Tables naturally expand to the edge of the elements they contain or to the edge of the browser window, whichever comes first. That's sometimes hard to see unless you view the border.

■ It's not a bad idea to use the BORDER tag while you're constructing your table and then banish it once you have everything in its place. Just remember that the BORDER takes up 2 pixels of space on each side and 2 pixels between each cell.

```
code.html
<HTML><HEAD><TITLE>Table</TITLE>
</HEAD><BODY>
<TABLE BORDER=10>
<TR>
<TD><IMG SRC="elephant.jpg" WIDTH=312
HEIGHT=234 ALT="Elephant Baby"></TD>
</TR>
<TR>
<TD><FONT SIZE=-1><I>A baby elephant
hanging out with its mom, aunts and greataunts,
and maybe even its grandmother</I></FONT>
</TD></TR>
</TABLE>
</BODY></HTML>
```

Figure 9.5 *Remember that the BORDER attribute affects not only the external border but also the divisions between cells.*

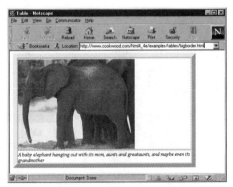

Figure 9.6 *Although borders are not usually shown in tables used for layout, they are often temporarily useful for showing exactly what's happening with a table. Here for example, you can see that the word "grandmother" in the caption wouldn't fit on one line even if the table extended itself all the way to the edge of the window. Therefore, the table shrunk to the limit of the first line of text with "grandmother" on the next line by itself.*

```
code.html
<HTML><HEAD><TITLE>Table</TITLE>
</HEAD><BODY>

<TABLE BORDER=10
BORDERCOLORLIGHT="#00FF00"
BORDERCOLORDARK="#189234">

<TR>

<TD><IMG SRC="elephant.jpg" WIDTH=312
HEIGHT=234 ALT="Elephant Baby"></TD>

</TR>

<TR>

<TD><FONT SIZE=-1><I>A baby elephant
hanging out with its mom, aunts and greataunts,
and maybe even its grandmother</I></FONT>
</TD></TR>

</TABLE>

</BODY></HTML>
```

Figure 9.7 *You have to use the BORDER tag (see page 146) for the BORDERCOLOR tags to have effect.*

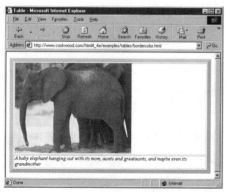

Figure 9.8 *Explorer lets you choose the colors for the border. This one's green. You'd see it that way too if you were looking at it on my Web site (see page 20).*

Changing the Border Color

Generally, a table's border is generated from the color of the background. Microsoft added a few silly extensions to Explorer for changing the color of the border (including the shading). If you really get into fiddling around with your borders, you'll be thrilled.

To make a solid colored border:

Type **BORDERCOLOR= "#rrggbb"**, where *rrggbb* is the hexadecimal representation of the desired color for the border.

To make a shaded colored border:

1. Type **BORDERCOLORDARK ="#rrggbb"**, where *rrggbb* is the hexadecimal representation of the color that you want to use for the darker parts of the border (top and left borders of cells, bottom and right borders of the table itself).

2. Type **BORDERCOLORLIGHT ="#rrggbb"**, where *rrggbb* is the hexadecimal representation of the color that you want to use for the lighter parts of the border (bottom and right borders of cells, top and left borders of the table itself).

✔ Tips

■ You won't get any border at all unless you use the BORDER tag *(see page 146).*

■ With no BORDERCOLOR tags, most browsers shade the border based on the background color. With just the BORDER-COLOR tag, the table will have no shading and will be a solid color.

■ You can also use color names to specify the color. For more information, see Appendix C.

Setting the Width

A browser will automatically determine the width of your table by calculating the width of the elements and text it contains. Somehow, it always seems to add a little extra. It's particularly important to manually set the width of each cell *and* of the table as a whole in order to eliminate this extra space.

To set the width of a cell or table:

In the TD or TABLE tag, type **WIDTH=n**, where *n* is the desired width of the cell or of the entire table, in pixels.

✔ Tips

■ You can also set the size of a cell or table as a percentage of the table or browser, respectively. The table will expand as the browser window is resized.

■ You can't make the table too small for its contents; the browser will just ignore you.

■ The width of the table should be the sum of the width of the columns and their elements, the width of the border *(see page 146)*, and the width of the cell spacing and cell padding *(see page 155)*

■ There is also a HEIGHT tag but it is non-standard, and not very well supported.

■ Generally, you only need to use the WIDTH tag with the first cell in each column. However, if you have cells that span columns or rows *(see pages 152–153)*, it may be necessary to add the WIDTH attribute explicitly to every cell.

■ If you make the table wider than the browser's window, the visitor may not be able to see the parts of the table that extend off to the right. I don't recommend making tables any wider than 600 pixels.

```
<TABLE WIDTH=320 BORDER=0>

<TR>

<TD WIDTH=320><IMG SRC="elephant.jpg"
WIDTH=312 HEIGHT=234 ALT="Elephant
Baby"></TD></TR>

<TR>

<TD><FONT SIZE=-1><I>A baby elephant
hanging out with its mom, aunts and greataunts,
and maybe even its grandmother</I></FONT>
</TD></TR>

</TABLE>
```

Figure 9.9 *Specify the width of each cell as well as of the entire table as a whole.*

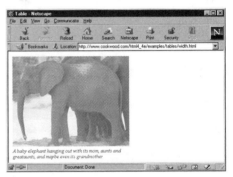

Figure 9.10 *By setting the width of the entire table, the caption is divided into two lines—and looks much better.*

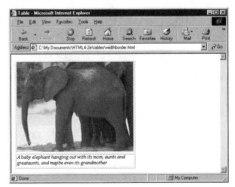

Figure 9.11 *Here I've revealed the border so you can see what's going on.*

```
code.html
<HTML><HEAD><TITLE>Table</TITLE>
</HEAD><BODY>

<TABLE  ALIGN=center WIDTH=320>

<TR>

<TD WIDTH=320><IMG SRC="elephant.jpg"
WIDTH=312 HEIGHT=234 ALT="Elephant
Baby"></TD>

</TR>

<TR>

<TD><FONT SIZE=-1><I>A baby elephant
hanging out with its mom, aunts and greataunts,
and maybe even its grandmother</I></FONT>
</TD></TR>

</TABLE>

</BODY></HTML>
```

Figure 9.12 *Add the ALIGN=center attribute to the TABLE tag in order to center the table on the page.*

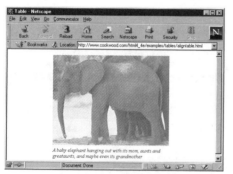

Figure 9.13 *You can center a table to show it off.*

Centering a Table on the Page

You can draw attention to a table by centering it in the browser window.

To center a table on the page:

In the TABLE tag, type **ALIGN=center**.

✔ Tips

- You could also center the table by enclosing the entire table in opening and closing CENTER tags *(see page 100)*.

- You could conceivably center one table within another. For more information, consult *Nesting One Table in Another* on page 156.

- You can also wrap text to the right or left of a table. For more details, consult *Wrapping Text around a Table* on page 150.

- You can't align a table to the top or middle line of text as you can with images.

Centering a Table on the Page

Wrapping Text around a Table

You can wrap text around a table in much the same way you can with images. While there are more sophisticated layout techniques, wrapping text around a table is helpful for keeping images together with captions in a long flow of text.

To wrap text around a table:

1. Type **<TABLE**.

2. Either type **ALIGN=left** to align the table to the left of the screen while the text flows to the right or type **ALIGN=right** to align the table to the right of the browser window while the text flows on the left side of the table.

3. Type **>**.

4. Create the rest of the table.

5. Type **</TABLE>**.

6. Type the text that should flow around the table.

To stop text wrap:

1. Place the cursor where you want to stop wrapping text to the side of the table.

2. *Either* type **<BR CLEAR=left>** to stop flowing text until there are no more tables aligned to the left margin.

   Or type **<BR CLEAR=right>** to stop flowing text until there are no more tables aligned to the right margin.

   Or type **<BR CLEAR=all>** to stop flowing text until there are no more tables on either margin.

✔ Tip

- For more details about wrapping text, see pages 88–90.

```
                      code.html
<HTML><HEAD><TITLE>Table</TITLE>
</HEAD><BODY>

It's hard to tell what goes through a baby
elephant's mind [snip]

<TABLE ALIGN=left WIDTH=320>

<TR><TD WIDTH=320><IMG SRC=
"elephant.jpg" WIDTH=312 HEIGHT=234
ALT="Elephant Baby"></TD></TR>

<TR><TD><FONT SIZE=-1><I>A baby elephant
hanging out with its mom, aunts and greataunts,
and maybe even its grandmother</I></FONT>
</TD></TR>

</TABLE>

And what about gorillas? Today in the paper
there's a story about a new gorilla [snip]

<P>Why is it so easy for them? Are they better
parents? Do they just not worry [snip]

</BODY></HTML>
```

Figure 9.14 *Just as with images, the text that will wrap around the table comes* after *the table itself. Note that I have snipped out some of the text in order to show you the important parts of the page.*

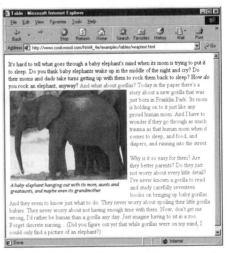

Figure 9.15 *The text flows around the image and the caption as if they were one unit. In a sense, they are: they're a table.*

Wrapping Text around a Table

```
code.html
<HTML><HEAD><TITLE>Table</TITLE>
</HEAD><BODY>

It's hard to tell what goes through a baby
elephant's mind when its mom is trying to put it
to sleep. Do you think baby elephants wake up in
the middle of the night and cry? Do their moms
and dads take turns getting up with them to rock
them back to sleep? How <EM>do</EM> you
rock an elephant, anyway?

<TABLE  ALIGN=left WIDTH=320 HSPACE=20
VSPACE=20>

<TR><TD WIDTH=320>
```

Figure 9.16 *You can use either the HSPACE attribute, the VSPACE attribute, or both at once.*

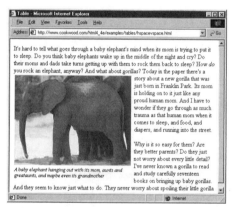

Figure 9.17 *Explorer doesn't recognize the HSPACE and VSPACE attributes when applied to tables. Notice that this illustration is identical to Figure 9.15.*

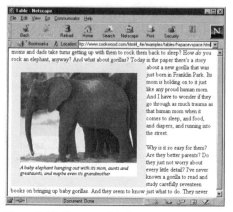

Figure 9.18 *Netscape adds the extra space around the table just as if it were an image.*

Adding Space around a Table

 If your table is surrounded by other elements on your page, you may wish to pad it with a little extra space to help it stand out from the rest of the page.

To add space around a table:

1. Type **<TABLE**.

2. If desired, type **HSPACE=h** where *h* is the number of pixels of space to add on *both* the right and left sides of the table.

3. If desired, type **VSPACE=v** where *v* is the number of pixels of space to add on *both* the top and bottom of the table.

4. Type **>**

5. Create the table's contents.

6. Type **</TABLE>**.

✔ Tips

- You don't have to add both HSPACE and VSPACE at the same time.

- Neither HSPACE nor VSPACE is a standard attribute for the TABLE tag. Explorer doesn't support them here **(Figure 9.17)** but Netscape does **(Figure 9.18)**.

- One alternative to HSPACE and VSPACE that both browsers do support is pixel shims. For more details, consult *Using Pixel Shims* on page 109.

Adding Space around a Table

Spanning a Cell across Columns

With a table, it's often necessary to straddle or span one cell across a few columns. For example, with multicolumn text, you could span a headline across the columns of text.

To span a cell across two columns:

1. When you get to the point in which you need to define the cell that spans more than one column, type **<TD**.

2. Type **COLSPAN=n>**, where *n* equals the number of columns the cell should span.

3. Type the cell's contents.

4. Type **</TD>**.

5. Complete the rest of the table. If you create a cell that spans 2 columns, you will need to define one less cell in that row. If you create a cell that spans 3 columns, you will define two less cells for the row. And so on.

✔ Tip

■ Writing the HTML code for a table from scratch is, uh, challenging—especially when you start spanning columns and rows. It helps to sketch it out on paper first, as described on page 144, to get a handle on which information goes in which row and column. Or you can cheat and use a Web page editing program like FrontPage or PageMill to get started. You can always open the file and edit the HTML by hand later.

```
code.html

<TABLE WIDTH=320>

<TR><TD COLSPAN=2 WIDTH=320><FONT
SIZE=+2 FACE="Verdana,Arial,Helvetica,sans-
serif">The Truth about Elephants</FONT></TD>
</TR>

<TR><TD COLSPAN=2 WIDTH=320><IMG
SRC= "elephant.jpg" WIDTH=312 HEIGHT=234
ALT="Elephant Baby"></TD></TR>

<TR><TD COLSPAN=2><FONT SIZE=-1><I>A
baby elephant hanging out with its mom, aunts
and greataunts, and maybe even its
grandmother</I></FONT></TD></TR>

<TR><TD>It's hard to tell what goes through a
baby elephant's mind [snip] </TD>

<TD>And what about gorillas? Today in the
paper [snip] </TD></TR>

</TABLE>

<P>Why is it so easy for them? Are they better
parents? [snip]
```

Figure 9.19 *Notice that it was necessary to add the COLSPAN tag to the new header, the photo, and the caption since they all span across the two columns of text. The third bit of text ("Why is it so easy...") is still separate and will appear below the table.*

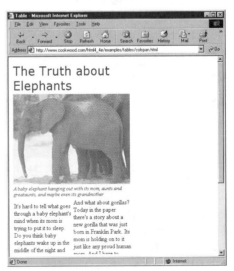

Figure 9.20 *The three highlighted cells span two columns. The two columns of text are simply individual TD cells.*

```
                    code.html
<TABLE WIDTH=480 >

<TR><TD COLSPAN=3 VALIGN=BOTTOM
WIDTH=480><FONT SIZE=+3 FACE=
"Verdana,Arial,Helvetica,sans-serif">The Truth
about Elephants</FONT></TD></TR>

<TR><TD COLSPAN=2 WIDTH=320><IMG
SRC="elephant.jpg" WIDTH=312 HEIGHT=234
ALT="Elephant Baby"></TD>

<TD ROWSPAN=3 WIDTH=160>Why is it so
easy for them? Are they better parents? [snip]
</TD></TR>

<TR><TD COLSPAN=2  WIDTH=320><FONT
SIZE=-1><I>A baby elephant hanging out with
its mom, aunts and greataunts, and maybe even
its grandmother</I></FONT></TD></TR>

<TR><TD WIDTH=160>It's hard to tell what goes
through a baby elephant's mind [snip]</TD>

<TD WIDTH=160>And what about gorillas?
Today in the paper [snip]</TD></TR>

</TABLE>
```

Figure 9.21 *Now we're getting somewhere. I've added the third column of text and spanned it across the three rows of the photo, caption, and two other columns of text. I've also adjusted the widths of the cells and of the table as necessary.*

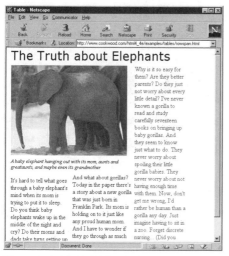

Figure 9.22 *The highlighted column spans three rows: the row with the photo, the row with the caption, and the row of two cells of text.*

Spanning a Cell across Rows

Creating a cell that spans more than one row is essentially identical to spanning cells over more than one column—just from another direction.

To span a cell across two or more rows:

1. When you get to the point in which you need to define the cell that spans more than one row, type **<TD**.

2. Type **ROWSPAN=n>**, where *n* equals the number of rows the cell should span.

3. Type the cell's contents.

4. Type **</TD>**.

5. Complete the rest of the table. If you define a cell with a rowspan of 2, you will not need to define the corresponding cell in the next row. If you define a cell with a rowspan of 3, you will not need to define the corresponding cells in the next two rows.

Aligning a Cell's Contents

By default, a cell's contents are aligned two ways: horizontally to the left and vertically in the middle. To gain a little more control over the alignment of a cell's contents, use the ALIGN and VALIGN tags.

To align the contents of cells horizontally:

1. Place the cursor in the initial tag for the cell, row, or section, after the name of the tag but before the final >.

2. If desired, type **ALIGN=direction**, where *direction* is left, center, or right.

3. Type **VALIGN=direction**, where *direction* is either top, middle, bottom, or baseline.

✔ Tips

■ You can align all of the cells in one or more rows or columns by inserting the ALIGN or VALIGN attribute in the appropriate tag (TR, THEAD, TFOOT, TBODY, COLGROUP, or COL).

■ The default value for ALIGN is *left*. The default for VALIGN is *middle*.

■ Officially, you can also justify a cell's contents with both margins (**ALIGN=justify**) or align the contents with respect to any character you choose (**ALIGN=char CHAR=x**). Unfortunately, no browser I've seen supports either feature.

■ The baseline value aligns the contents of each cell with the baseline of the first line of text that it contains. *Baseline* is the same as *top* when there are several lines of text and no images. *Baseline* is the same as *bottom* when the cells contain both images and text. Only Netscape supports the baseline value.

```
code.html
<TABLE WIDTH=480>

<TR><TD COLSPAN=3 VALIGN=BOTTOM
WIDTH=480><FONT SIZE=+3 FACE=
"Verdana,Arial,Helvetica,sans-serif">The Truth
about Elephants</FONT></TD></TR>

<TR><TD COLSPAN=2 WIDTH=320><IMG
SRC="elephant.jpg" WIDTH=312 HEIGHT=234
ALT="Elephant Baby"></TD>

<TD ROWSPAN=3 WIDTH=160 VALIGN=TOP>
Why is it so easy for them? Are they better
parents? [snip] </TD></TR>

<TR><TD COLSPAN=2  ALIGN=RIGHT
WIDTH=320><FONT SIZE=-1><I>A baby
elephant hanging out with its mom, aunts and
greataunts, and maybe even its grandmother
</I></FONT></TD></TR>

<TR><TD WIDTH=160 VALIGN=TOP>It's hard
to tell what goes through a baby elephant's mind
[snip] </TD>

<TD WIDTH=160 VALIGN=TOP>And what
about gorillas? Today in the [snip] </TD></TR>

</TABLE>
```

Figure 9.23 *You can add different alignment attributes to any cell in your table.*

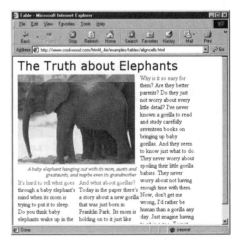

Figure 9.24 *Compare the tops of the columns of text in this illustration with the ones in Figure 9.22. Now that I've aligned them all to the top, they look much better. Also note that I've aligned the caption to the right.*

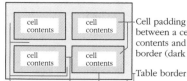

Cell spacing is between the borders of each cell (light pink)

Figure 9.25 *Cell spacing adds space between cells. Cell padding adds space between a cell's contents and its border. When using tables for layout, you often want to eliminate both types so that your elements are right up next to one another.*

```
code.html
<TABLE WIDTH=480 CELLSPACING=0
CELLPADDING=4 BORDER=0>

<TR><TD COLSPAN=3 VALIGN=BOTTOM
WIDTH=480><FONT SIZE=+3
FACE="Verdana,Arial,Helvetica,sans-serif">The
Truth about Elephants</FONT></TD></TR>

<TR><TD COLSPAN=2 WIDTH=312 ><IMG
SRC="elephant.jpg" WIDTH=312 HEIGHT=234
ALT="Elephant Baby"></TD>
```

Figure 9.26 *Since this table contains columns of text, we need a little bit of spacing between the text and the cell's borders. There's no need for space between the cells themselves.*

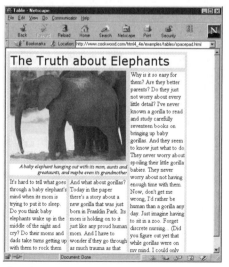

Figure 9.27 *Cell spacing and padding help make columns of text more readable. (It's invisible; I've just highlighted it here for your reference.)*

Controlling Space in and Around Cells

Cell spacing adds space *between* cells, making the table bigger without changing the size of individual cells. Cell padding adds space *around* the contents of a cell, in effect, pushing the walls of the cell outward. When using tables for layout, you often want to eliminate both kinds of spacing.

To control space in and around cells:

1. Place the cursor in the TABLE tag before the final >.

2. Type **CELLSPACING=n**, where *n* is the number of pixels desired between each cell. (The attribute *cellspacing* is one word.)

3. Type **CELLPADDING=n**, where *n* is the number of pixels desired between the contents and the walls of the cell. (The attribute *cellpadding* is one word.)

✔ Tips

- To eliminate space between the contents of one cell and the next, use **CELLSPACING=0 CELLPADDING=0**. This is the most common value in a table used for layout.

- The default for cell spacing is 2 pixels. The default for cell padding is 1 pixel.

- The alignment options *(see page 154)* consider the cell padding as the actual cell limits, and thus, may give unexpected results.

- If, after eliminating cell spacing and padding, there's still a little bit of space between your elements, make sure you've set your BORDER to 0 pixels *(see page 146)* and that you've set the width of your table and of each of the cells it contains *(see page 148)*.

Controlling Space in and Around Cells

Nesting One Table in Another

In some circumstances, you'll need to put one table inside another. For instance, in our example, we want to insert the multicolumn text table with cell spacing into a table that has no spacing between the columns.

To nest one table in another:

1. Create the inner table.

2. Create the outer table. Determine which cell of the outer table will hold the inner table and type **placeholder** (or some other easily identifiable text) there as a placeholder.

3. Test both tables separately to make sure they look the way you want them to.

4. Replace the word *placeholder* with the inner table by copying and pasting.

✔ Tips

- The width of the cell that contains the inner table should match the width of the inner table. Be sure to also set the widths of all of the surrounding cells as well as the outer table.

- Creating the tables separately before nesting them helps pinpoint where problems may lie, should they occur.

- Only nest tables where it's absolutely necessary. They can slow down a browser considerably or even make it crash.

- You can also use ** ** in any cell that should remain empty. Otherwise, it may not display at all.

```
code.html

<TABLE border=0 cellspacing=0 cellpadding=0
WIDTH=600>

<TR>

<TD WIDTH=120><IMG SRC=logo.jpg
width=120 height=100></TD>

<TD WIDTH=320><IMG SRC=ad2.gif
width=320 height=100></TD>

<TD WIDTH=160><IMG SRC=miniad.jpg
WIDTH=160></TD></TR>

<TR><TD  valign=top><FONT FACE=
"Verdana,Arial,Helvetica,sans-serif">

<A HREF="lions.html">Lions</A>
<BR><A HREF="armadillos.html">
Armadillos</A>
<BR><A HREF="hyenas.html">Hyenas</A>
<BR><A HREF="elephants.html">
Elephants</A>
<BR><A HREF="giraffes.html">Giraffes</A>
<BR><A HREF="gorillas.html">Gorillas</A>
</FONT></TD>

<TD COLSPAN=2 WIDTH=480>this is where the
inner table will go</TD></TR>

</TABLE>
```

Figure 9.28 *Construct the outer table separately, leaving an empty cell where the inner table should go. Notice how the width of the table and of each individual cell is set properly.*

Figure 9.29 *The outer table is 600 pixels wide. The space for our inner table is 480 pixels wide. It'll fit perfectly.*

```
┌────────────────────────────────┐
│ ▦          code.html         ▣ │
├────────────────────────────────┤
<BR><A HREF="gorillas.html">
Gorillas</A></FONT></TD>

<TD COLSPAN=2 WIDTH=480>

<TABLE WIDTH=480 CELLSPACING=0
CELLPADDING=4 border=0>

<TR><TD colspan=3 VALIGN=bottom
WIDTH=480><FONT SIZE=+3
FACE="Verdana,Arial,Helvetica,sans-serif">The
Truth about Elephants</FONT></TD></TR>

<TR><TD COLSPAN=2 width=312><IMG
SRC="elephant.jpg" WIDTH=312 HEIGHT=234
ALT="Elephant Baby"></TD>

<TD ROWSPAN=3 WIDTH=152
VALIGN=top>Why is it so easy for them? Are
```

Figure 9.30 *Copy the inner table to the space reserved for it in the cell of the outer table.*

Figure 9.31 *This page is really made up of two tables, the outer table and the inner, highlighted table. The inner table is exactly the same as the one shown in Figure 9.27 on page 155.*

- Don't nest a table in a table in a table. Simplify your design instead.

- When studying other people's nested tables, download the source code *(see page 310)* and then change the background color *(see page 158)* of the individual tables to make it easier to tell which table belongs to which part of the layout.

- Don't forget to close each table with its own closing </TABLE> tag. Otherwise, your table will display correctly in Explorer but Netscape won't show a thing.

- You may need to slightly adjust the positioning of particular elements. For more information, consult *Using Pixel Shims* on page 109.

Changing a Cell's Color

Changing the color of one or more cells is a great way to add visual clarity and structure to your table.

To change a cell's color:

1. Within the TD tag, type **BGCOLOR=**.

2. Type **"#rrggbb"**, where *rrggbb* is the hexadecimal representation of the desired color.

   Or type **color**, where *color* is one of the sixteen predefined color names *(see inside back cover)*.

✔ Tips

- You can change the color of the cells in one or more rows or columns by adding the BGCOLOR attribute to the appropriate tag (TR, THEAD, TFOOT, TBODY, COLGROUP, or COL).

- Explorer supports using BGCOLOR in the TABLE tag for changing the background of the whole table.

- The BGCOLOR in an individual cell (TH or TD) overrides the color specified in a row (in a TR tag), which in turn overrides the color specified for a group of rows or columns (in THEAD, COLGROUP, etc.), which, as you might expect, overrides the color specified for the entire table (in the TABLE tag).

- Consult *Colors in Hex* on page 357 and the inside back cover for help choosing colors.

- BGCOLOR has been deprecated in HTML 4. The W3C recommends the use of styles to change the background color *(see page 286)*

```
code.html
<HTML><HEAD><TITLE>Using tables for
layout</TITLE></HEAD>

<BODY LINK="#FFFFFF">

<TABLE BORDER=0 CELLSPACING=0
CELLPADDING=0  WIDTH=600>

<TR><TD WIDTH=120><IMG SRC=logo.jpg
WIDTH=120 HEIGHT=100></TD>

<TD WIDTH=320><IMG SRC=ad2.gif
WIDTH=320 HEIGHT=100></TD>

<TD WIDTH=160><IMG SRC=miniad.jpg
WIDTH=160></TD>

</TR>

<TR><TD BGCOLOR="#339966"
VALIGN=TOP><FONT FACE=
"Verdana,Arial,Helvetica,sans-serif">
```

Figure 9.32 *I've changed the background color of the navigation bar to help tie it to the logo in the upper left-hand corner. I've also changed the link's color on the page to make the links stand out better on the dark green background chosen.*

Figure 9.33 *Changing the color of a column really makes it stand out. Since it matches the color in the logo, it helps to pull the whole design together as well.*

```
                code.html
<BODY >

<TABLE BORDER=0 CELLSPACING=0
CELLPADDING=0  WIDTH=600>

<TR><TD WIDTH=120><IMG SRC=logo.jpg
WIDTH=120 HEIGHT=100></TD>

<TD WIDTH=320><IMG SRC=ad2.gif
WIDTH=320 HEIGHT=100></TD>

<TD WIDTH=160><IMG SRC=miniad.jpg
WIDTH=160></TD></TR>

<TR><TD BACKGROUND="fishlight.jpg"
VALIGN=TOP><FONT FACE=
"Verdana,Arial,Helvetica,sans-serif">
```

Figure 9.34 *Add the BACKGROUND tag to the cell that you want to fill with an image.*

Figure 9.35 *This fish image* almost *works design-wise because it is so dark that the white links show up quite nicely. Still, I think it's a little busy—like most background images.*

Using a Background Image

I am not very fond of background images, either in cells, tables, or an entire page *(see page 99)*. If you do decide to use one, make sure it contrasts enough with the cell's contents so that the contents are legible.

To use a background image for a cell:

Within the TD tag, type **BACKGROUND= "image.gif"** where *image.gif* is the URL of the image that you wish to use as the backdrop for your cell.

To use a background image for the entire table:

Within the TABLE tag, type **BACKGROUND= "image.gif"** where *image.gif* is the URL of the image that you wish to use as the backdrop for your table.

✔ Tips

- You can add both a background image and a background color to a cell. The background color will both display before the image and then continue to shine through the transparent parts of the image, if there are any.

- If you set a background image for the whole table, beware! Explorer uses one image for the background while Netscape copies the whole image into each cell individually.

- In Explorer, the BGCOLOR attribute overrides the background image—except in the cell spacing area *(see page 155)*. If you view the same page with Netscape, you'll find that background colors disappear completely if you specify a background image. Can we say "consensus" please?

Dividing Your Table into Column Groups

When using tables for displaying tabular data (their classic purpose), you can divide your table into two kinds of column groups: structural and non-structural. The former control where dividing lines, or rules, are drawn *(see page 164)*. The latter do not. Both let you apply formatting to an entire column (or groups of columns) of cells all at once.

To divide a table into structural column groups:

1. After the <TABLE> and <CAPTION> tags, type **<COLGROUP**.

2. If the column group has more than one column, type **SPAN=n**, where *n* is the number of columns in the group.

3. If desired, define the attributes for the column group.

4. Type the final **>**.

5. Repeat steps 1–4 for each column group that you wish to define.

To divide a table into non-structural column groups:

1. After the <TABLE> and <CAPTION> tags, type **<COL**.

2. If the column group has more than one column, type **SPAN=n**, where *n* is the number of columns in the group.

3. If desired, define the attributes for the column group.

4. Type the final **>**.

5. Repeat steps 1–4 for each column group that you wish to define.

```
code.html

<TABLE>

<CAPTION ALIGN=top>Bear sightings in
Western Massachusetts</CAPTION>

<COLGROUP ALIGN=LEFT STYLE="font: 10pt
Lithos Regular">

<COLGROUP SPAN=3 ALIGN=CENTER>

<TR><TD><BR>

<TH>Babies
```

Figure 9.36 *This table is divided into two column groups. The first column group contains just one column (the one with the city names). It will be aligned to the left and set in 10pt Lithos Regular. The second column group spans 3 columns and its contents will be centered.*

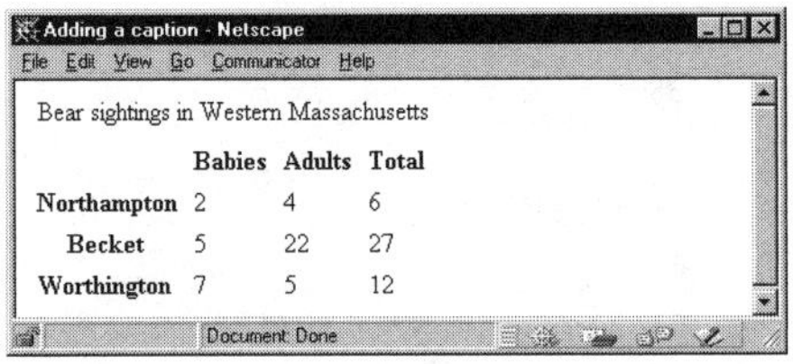

Figure 9.37 *Netscape does not support the COLGROUP tag yet.*

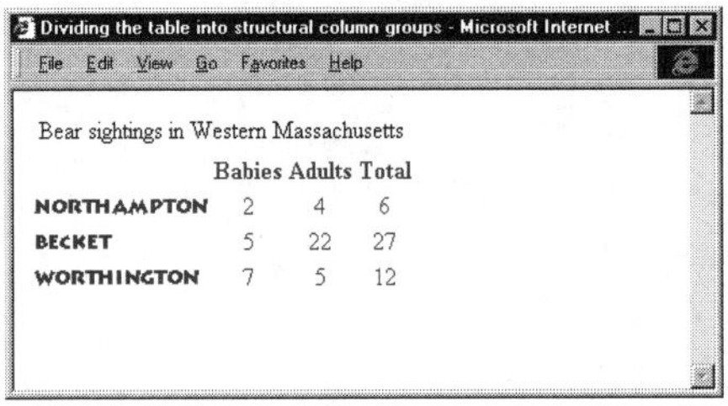

Figure 9.38 *The first column group is now properly aligned to the left and in Lithos. The contents of the second column group (the remaining three columns) are centered.*

```
code.html
<TABLE>

<CAPTION ALIGN=top>Bear sightings in
Western Massachusetts</CAPTION>

<COLGROUP ALIGN=LEFT STYLE="font: 10pt
Lithos Regular">

<COLGROUP SPAN=3 ALIGN=CENTER>

<COL SPAN=2>

<COL STYLE="font-weight:900">

<TR>

<TD><BR>

<TH>Babies
```

Figure 9.39 *Now I divide the second column group into two separate non-structural column groups (with COL) so that I can format an entire column at a time without affecting how rules (see page 164) will be drawn.*

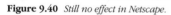

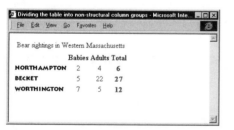

Figure 9.40 *Still no effect in Netscape.*

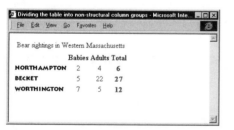

Figure 9.41 *I've used the second non-structural column group to format the last column in bold type so that the totals stand out a bit more.*

✔ Tips

- Both types of column group definitions are completely ignored by Netscape.

- Use COLGROUP when you want to determine where dividing lines (rules) should go. Use COL for *everything but* deciding where dividing lines go. For more information on drawing dividing lines, consult page 164.

- You can use many attributes to format column groups, including BGCOLOR, STYLE, and others.

- You can divide COLGROUPs into COLs in order to add non-structural information (like size, alignment, or whatever) to individual columns within structural column groups. Simply type the COL tag *after* the parent COLGROUP tag **(Figure 9.39)**. Note that COL tags' attributes override the attributes in the COLGROUP tag.

- If the column group only contains one column, you don't need to use the SPAN attribute. Its default is 1.

- Header cells—those marked with the TH tag—are not affected by the alignment specified in a column group. For more information on aligning cells, consult *Aligning a Cell's Contents* on page 154.

- COLGROUP has an optional closing tag. COL has none.

Dividing Your Table into Column Groups

Dividing the Table into Horizontal Sections

You can also mark a horizontal section of your table—one or more rows—and then format it all at once. Then draw dividing lines (rules) between sections, instead of between individual rows.

To divide the table into horizontal sections:

1. Before the first <TR> tag of the section you want to create, type **<THEAD**, **<TBODY**, or **<TFOOT**.

2. If desired, define the desired attributes for the section.

3. Type **>**.

4. If necessary, create the section's contents.

5. Close the section with **</THEAD>**, **</TBODY>**, or **</TFOOT>**.

✔ Tips

■ Netscape does not yet recognize horizontal section tags.

■ You can use many cell attributes (BGCOLOR, STYLE, etc.) to format horizontal sections of cells, but IE doesn't support HEIGHT or WIDTH.

■ Horizontal section tags go *after* column group tags *(see page 160)*.

■ Theoretically, at least one TBODY tag is required in every table. Create more than one if you like. You can only have one THEAD and one TFOOT.

■ The closing tags are optional. A section is automatically closed when you begin the next **(Figure 9.44)**.

■ For more on rules, see page 164.

```
                  code.html
<TABLE>
<CAPTION ALIGN=top>Bear sightings in
Western Massachusetts</CAPTION>

<COLGROUP ALIGN=LEFT STYLE="font: 10pt
Lithos Regular">
<COLGROUP SPAN=3 ALIGN=CENTER>
<COL SPAN=2>
<COL STYLE="font-weight:900">

<THEAD STYLE="font: 10pt Lithos Regular">

<TR>
<TD><BR>
<TH>Babies
<TH>Adults
<TH>Total

<TBODY>
<TR>
<TH>Northampton
```

Figure 9.42 *I want the column titles in the THEAD section and the rest of the table in the TBODY.*

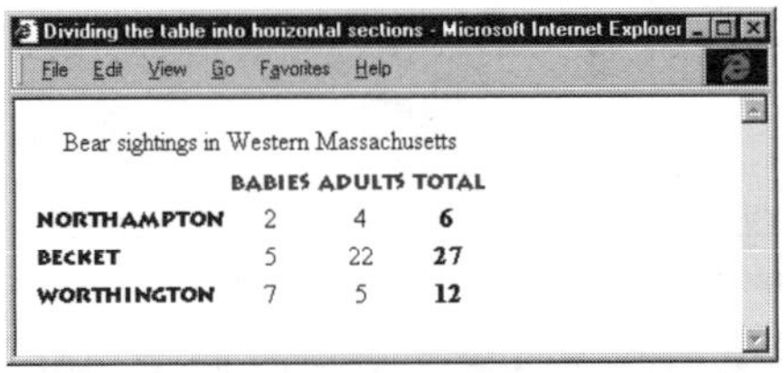

Figure 9.43 *The entire THEAD section is now formatted in Lithos Regular.*

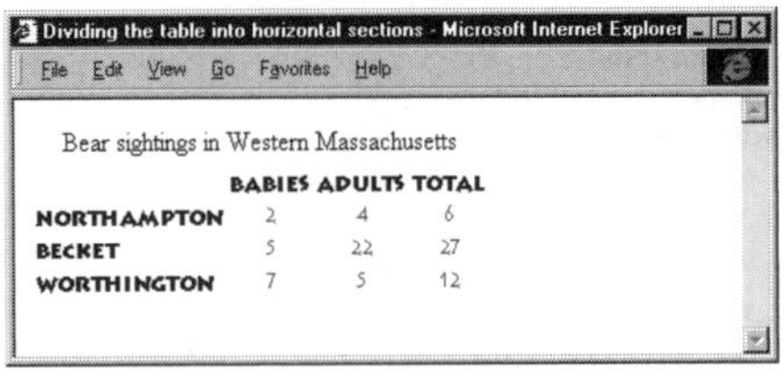

Figure 9.44 *Note that in Figure 9.42, the TBODY tag closes the THEAD tag. If it weren't there, the whole table would be considered part of the THEAD. The result is shown here— not a tragedy certainly, but notice how the entire table is now formatted in Lithos Regular (and the bold formatting specified in the COL tag has been overridden).*

```
                code.html
<HTML><HEAD><TITLE>Choosing which
exterior borders to display</TITLE></HEAD>

<BODY>

<TABLE BORDER FRAME=vsides>

<CAPTION ALIGN=top>Bear sightings in
Western Massachusetts</CAPTION>

<COLGROUP ALIGN=LEFT STYLE="font: 10pt
Lithos Regular">

<COLGROUP SPAN=3 ALIGN=CENTER>

<COL SPAN=2>

<COL STYLE="font-weight:900">

<THEAD STYLE="font: 10pt Lithos Regular">

<TR>
```

Figure 9.45 *Add the FRAME attribute just after the BORDER attribute within the TABLE tag.*

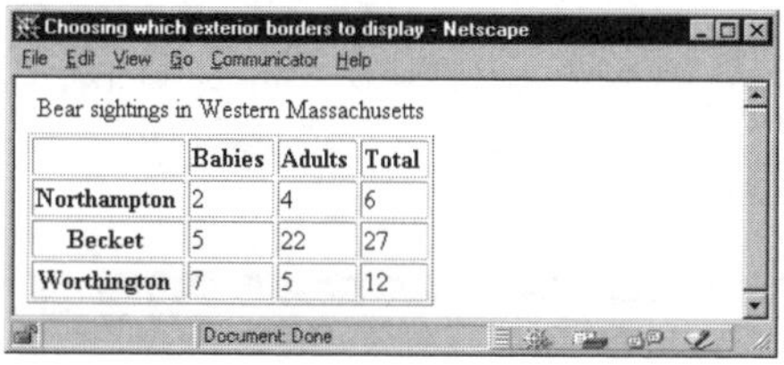

Figure 9.46 *The FRAME attribute has no effect in Netscape; the table appears with the complete border as usual.*

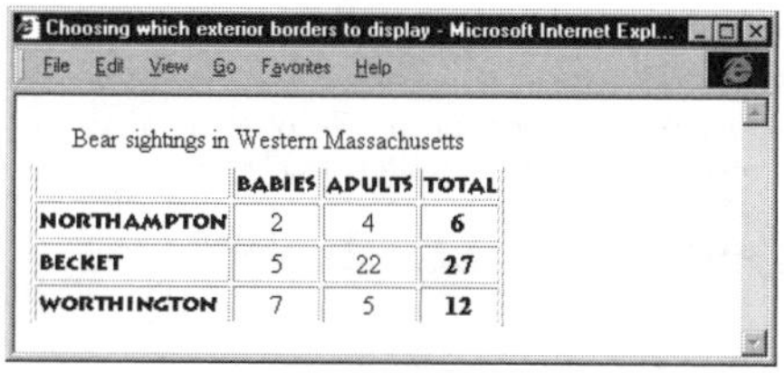

Figure 9.47 *In Internet Explorer, with a FRAME value of* vsides, *the external border appears only on the right and left sides of the table. The internal border appears as usual (and if you ask me, it looks kind of funny). To control the internal borders, use the RULES attribute described on page 164.*

Choosing Which Borders to Display

When you use the BORDER tag *(see page 146)*, a border appears between each cell and also around the table itself. HTML 4 lets you choose which external sides of the table should have a border as well as which internal borders should be displayed.

To choose which external sides should have a border:

In the TABLE tag, after the required BORDER attribute, type **FRAME=location**, where *location* is one of the values listed below:

- *void*, for no external borders
- *above*, for a single border on top
- *below*, for a single border on bottom
- *hsides*, for a border on both the top and bottom sides
- *vsides*, for a border on both the right and left sides
- *rhs*, for a single border on the right side
- *lhs*, for a single border on the left side
- *box* or *border*, for a border on all sides (default)

Chapter 9

To choose which internal borders should be displayed:

In the TABLE tag, after the required BORDER attribute, type **RULES=area**, where *area* is one of the following values:

- *none*, for no internal rules

- *rows*, for horizontal rules between each row in the table

- *cols*, for vertical rules between each column in the table **(Figures 9.49 and 9.50)**

- *groups*, for rules between column groups and horizontal sections as defined by the tags described on pages 160–162 **(Figure 9.51)**

- *all*, for rules between each row and column in the table (default)

✔ Tips

■ You must use the BORDER tag in order for any of the FRAME or RULES attributes to have effect.

■ The *Void* value for FRAME seems rather pointless (you could just skip the BORDER attribute if you didn't want a border) until you pair it up with a value for RULES. The same goes for the *None* value for RULES, which makes most sense when you pair it with a positive value for FRAME.

■ The default values, *box* and *border* for FRAME and *all* for RULES, *are* pretty superfluous. If you want all the external borders, skip the FRAME attribute altogether. If you want all the internal borders, skip the RULES attribute. Don't forget to use the BORDER tag, of course. Without it, no borders will be drawn, no matter what you use for FRAME and RULES.

Figure 9.48 *The RULES attribute goes in the TABLE tag, after the BORDER attribute, which is required for the RULES attribute to have an effect.*

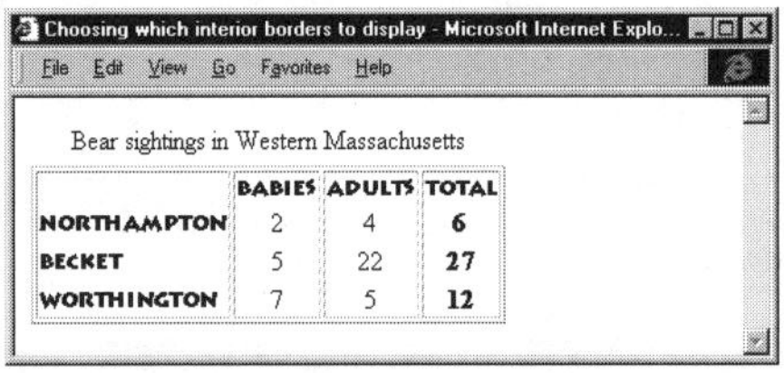

Figure 9.49 *With* RULES=cols, *only the vertical rules are displayed. Notice that the line around the perimeter of the table is part of the external border and is not affected by RULES.*

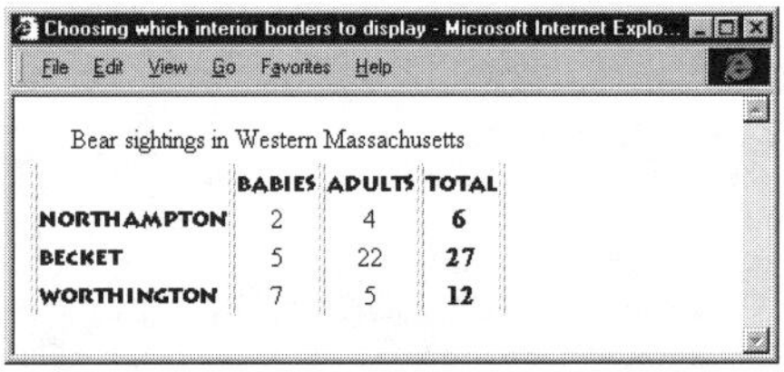

Figure 9.50 *To display only the vertical borders, combine* FRAME=vsides *with* RULES=cols.

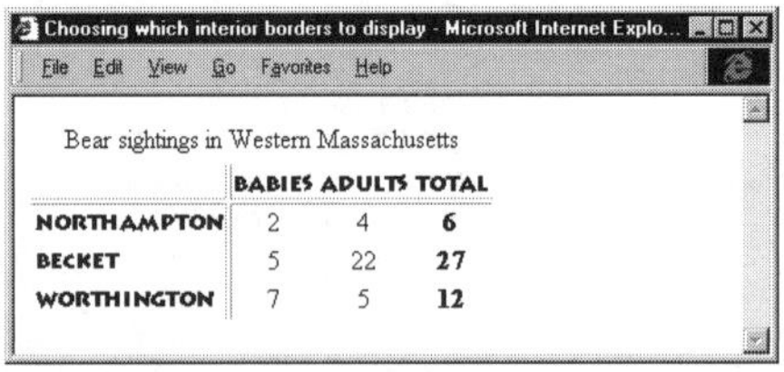

Figure 9.51 *The* attribute RULES=groups *is particularly useful when you've divided the table into column and row groups (see pages 160–162). Instead of rules between each column, rules are only displayed between groups. (I've also set* FRAME=void *in this example, to get rid of the external borders.)*

Choosing Which Borders to Display

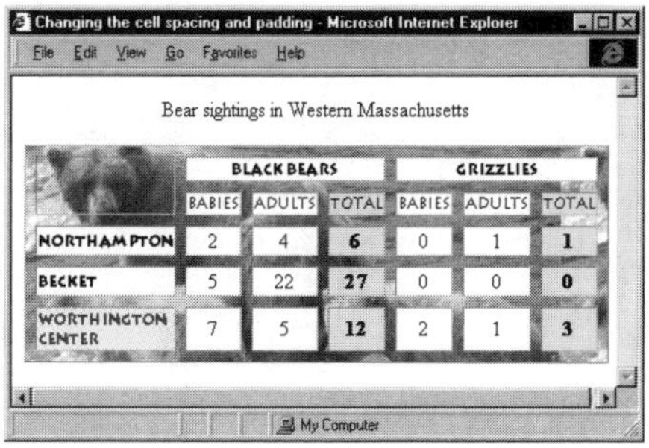

Figure 9.52 *Imagine if the name of the third city were longer than would fit on one line.*

```
code.html
<TD BGCOLOR=yellow>27

<TD>0

<TD>0

<TD BGCOLOR=yellow>0

<TR ALIGN=CENTER>

<TH ALIGN=LEFT NOWRAP>Worthington
Center

<TD>7
```

Figure 9.53 *Simply add NOWRAP to the TD or TH tag of the offending cell.*

Figure 9.54 *Now the entire city name fits on one line. Note that the whole table is a bit bigger—I've reduced it here to fit in the margin.*

Controlling Line Breaks in a Cell

Unless you specify otherwise, a browser will divide the lines of text in a cell as it decides on the height and width of each column and row. The NOWRAP attribute forces the browser to keep all the text in a cell on one line.

To keep text in a cell on one single line:

1. Place the cursor in the initial tag for the cell, after <TD or <TH, but before the final >.

2. Type **NOWRAP**.

✔ Tips

■ Browsers will make the cell (and the table that contains it) as wide as it needs to accommodate the single line of text—even if it looks really ugly. I don't recommend using the NOWRAP tag with tables used for layout. It overrides the WIDTH attribute.

■ You can use regular line breaks (BR) between words to mark where you *do* want the text to break.

■ You can also type ** ** instead of a regular space to connect pairs of words or other elements with non-breaking spaces.

■ For more information on line breaks, consult *Creating a Line Break* on page 102, *Keeping Lines Together* on page 103, and *Creating Discretionary Line Breaks* on page 104.

Controlling Line Breaks in a Cell

Speeding up Table Display

Although tables are extremely powerful, they can be very slow to appear in your visitor's browser. The major factor is that the browser must calculate the width and height of the table before it can begin to display the cells. So, if you can keep the browser's calculations to a minimum, the table will appear more quickly and your visitors may actually wait to see it.

To speed up table display:

- Keep tables as small as possible. Where you can, divide large tables into smaller ones.

- Specify the width of the table in pixels *(see page 148)*.

- Use absolute values (in pixels) or percentages for determining cell width.

- Only specify proportional widths for cells, columns, and horizontal sections when you've already set a fixed width in pixels for the entire table.

- Divide your table into column groups.

Frames

One of the trickier parts of creating a Web site is giving your visitors an idea of the scope of information contained in your site and then making that information easily accessible without confusing or overwhelming them. Frames can be the key to organizing your site and making it easy to navigate.

By dividing a page, called a *frameset*, into frames, you allow the visitor to see more than one page at a time, without completely cluttering up their screen. Each frame contains its own Web page, and theoretically could be viewed independently in a separate window.

The beauty of having several Web pages open on a screen at a time, however, lies in the ability to interrelate the information in each of the pages. For example, you can have a stationary banner frame across the top of the window that includes your company name and logo. Meanwhile, a dynamic frame on the left side of the window can include a table of contents. Finally, the main area of the window will be devoted to the *contents frame*, whose data changes each time your visitor clicks on a new topic in the table of contents.

As of version 4, frames are finally part of standard HTML. Most browsers support them.

Creating a Simple Frameset

Think of a frameset as a window with individual panes. Each pane shows different information. You decide how many panes your window will have, what size each pane will be, how its borders should look and if it should have scroll bars or not. Once you've built the window, you create the initial landscape behind the window by assigning individual URLs to each pane, that is, frame.

First, you'll learn to create a simple frameset with three horizontal rows all in the same column.

To create a simple frameset:

1. Type **<FRAMESET** after the </HEAD> tag on the frameset page.

2. Type **ROWS="a** where *a* is the height of the first row. The value may either be a percentage (40%), an exact number of pixels (35), or completely variable (with an asterisk *), depending on the size of the other rows.

3. Type **, b** where *b* is the height of the second row, again expressed as a percentage, an absolute value in pixels, or a variable (with an asterisk: *).

4. Repeat step 3 for each additional row.

5. Type **">** to complete the row definition.

6. Type **<FRAME** to assign a URL and other attributes to the top row/pane.

7. Type **NAME="name"** where *name* is a word that identifies this particular frame's use, like *banner*, *index*, or *contents*.

8. Type **SRC="content.html">** where *content.html* is the URL for the page that will be initially displayed in this frame when the visitor first navigates to this frameset.

9. Repeat steps 6–8 for each row you defined in steps 2–4.

```
                  code.html
<HTML><HEAD><TITLE>Frames in
Rows</TITLE></HEAD>

<FRAMESET ROWS="65,*,60">

<FRAME NAME="banner" SRC="banner.html">

<FRAME NAME="photos"
SRC="openingpage.html">

<FRAME NAME="buttons" SRC="buttons.html">

</FRAMESET>
```

Figure 10.1 *The frameset page has no actual content. Instead, it defines the frames and links them with the pages that hold the content.*

```
                  buttons.html
<HTML><HEAD><TITLE>Buttons</TITLE></HEAD>
<BODY BGCOLOR=#000000>
<TABLE CELLPADDING=5 CELLSPACING=0 WIDTH=100%>
<TR>
                  banner.html
<HTML><HEAD><TITLE>Barcelona Tours</TITLE></HEAD>
<BODY>
<IMG SRC="flag.gif" WIDTH=30 HEIGHT=25 ALIGN=LEFT>
<B>Welcome to <EM>Barcelona Tours </EM>
                  openingpage.html
<HTML><HEAD><TITLE>Barcelona Tours--Viatges per
Barcelona</TITLE></HEAD>
<BODY>
<H1>Welcome--Benvinguts</H1>
<IMG SRC="batllo.jpeg" ALIGN=LEFT WIDTH=221 HEIGHT=165 HSPACE=5>
One of the most striking things you notice when you walk around
Barcelona is its fabulous architecture. Most of the Barcelonians just
walk on by, completely oblivious--or accustomed?--to the beauty around
them.
<P>In this photo, you can see the Casa Amatller and the Casa Batll&#243;
sitting side by side along the busy main thoroughfare, the Passeig de
Gr&#224;cia. The Casa Amatller was designed by Puig i Cadalfalch, the
same architect responsible for the Pointed House (Casa de les Punxes)
among many other Barcelona landmarks. Casa Batll&#243;, of course, is
Antoni Gaud&#237;'s creation, and has many of the undulating surfaces
and animal imagery present in much of Gaud&#237;'s work.
<A HREF="rambles.html">Next stop</A>
</BODY>
</HTML>
```

Figure 10.2 *Once you've created a frameset, the next step is to create the pages that will appear within the frames.*

Figure 10.3 *Viewed individually, the pages shown in Figure 10.2 appear just as any other Web page.*

Figure 10.4 *By default, Netscape displays the frames with rather thick borders.*

Figure 10.5 *Internet Explorer's frames have thinner default borders.*

10. Type **</FRAMESET>** to complete the frameset and the construction of your "window".

11. Create the pages that will be displayed initially in the frames, that is, those referenced by the SRC tag in step 8 **(Figures 10.2 and 10.3)**. This is the "landscape" behind the window.

✔ Tips

- Don't forget the closing </FRAMESET> tag! If you do, Netscape will show a blank page. (Explorer is less strict.)

- The name you define in step 7 is used when you're targeting links to this frame. For more details, see page 181.

- Use the asterisk (*) to allocate to a frame whatever leftover space there is available in the window. That is, if the first two frames occupy 40 and 60 pixels respectively, and the window size is 250 pixels, the frame with the asterisk will occupy 150 pixels.

- You can use more than one asterisk at a time. The remaining space will be divided equally among the frames marked with an asterisk. To divide the remaining space unequally, add a number to the asterisk, e.g., **2***. In this case, two thirds of the remaining space will go to the frame marked 2* and the last third will go to the frame marked with just a plain asterisk.

- The BODY tag is not used at all in frameset pages.

- To provide information for visitors whose browsers don't support frames, see page 185.

Creating Frames in Columns

Another simple way to divide a frameset is into columns instead of rows.

To create frames in columns:

1. Type **<FRAMESET** after the </HEAD> tag in the frameset page.

2. Type **COLS="a,b">** where *a* and *b* (and any others) represent the width of the corresponding column, as a percentage, number of pixels, or variable (*).

3. Type **<FRAME** to define the leftmost frame/column.

4. Type **NAME="name"** where *name* is a word that identifies this particular frame's use, like *banner*, *index*, or *contents*.

5. Type **SRC="content.html">** where *content.html* is the URL of the page that you want to be displayed in this frame when the visitor initially navigates to this frameset.

6. Repeat steps 3–5 for each frame/column.

7. Type **</FRAMESET>**.

8. Create the Web pages that will be shown initially in the frameset page.

✔ Tips

- Consult the tips on page 169 for details on allocating the space among frames with variables (*).

- A frame's name is used when you're targeting links to appear in the frame. For details, consult *Targeting Links to Particular Frames* on page 181.

```
code.html
<FRAMESET COLS="110,*,100">

<FRAME NAME="banner"
SRC="bannercols.html">

<FRAME NAME="photos"
SRC="openingpagecols.html">

<FRAME NAME="buttons"
SRC="buttonscols.html">

</FRAMESET>
```

Figure 10.6 *To create a page with frames in columns, use the COLS attribute instead of ROWS.*

```
buttonsCOLS.html
<TABLE CELLPADDING=5 CELLSPACING=0 WIDTH=90%>
<TR>
<TH BGCOLOR="#F3D7E3" NOWRAP><A HREF="openingpage.html"><FONT
SIZE=-2>City Tour</A>
```
```
bannerCOLS.html
<HTML><HEAD><TITLE>Barcelona Tours</TITLE></HEAD>
<BODY>
<IMG SRC="flag.gif" WIDTH=30 HEIGHT=25>
<BR><B>Welcome to <EM>Barcelona Tours </EM>
```
```
openingpageCOLS.html
<HTML><HEAD><TITLE>Barcelona Tours--Viatges per
Barcelona</TITLE></HEAD>
<BODY>
<H1>Benvinguts!</H1>
<IMG SRC="batllo.jpeg" WIDTH=221 HEIGHT=165 HSPACE=5>
One of the most striking things you notice when you walk around
Barcelona is its fabulous architecture. Most of the Barcelonians just
walk on by, completely oblivious--or accustomed?--to the beauty around
them.
<P>In this photo, you can see the Casa Amatller and the Casa Batll&#243;
sitting side by side along the busy main thoroughfare, the Passeig de
Gr&#224;cia. The Casa Amatller was designed by Puig i Cadalfalch, the
same architect responsible for the Pointed House (Casa de les Punxes)
among many other Barcelona landmarks. Casa Batll&#243;, of course, is
Antoni Gaud&#237;'s creation, and has many of the undulating surfaces
and animal imagery present in much of Gaud&#237;'s work.
<A HREF="rambles.html">Next stop</A>
</BODY>
</HTML>
```

Figure 10.7 *Don't forget to create the content for the frames. Although these pages are very similar to the ones shown in Figure 10.2, they have been adjusted slightly to fit better vertically.*

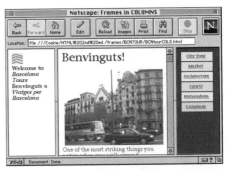

Figure 10.8 *Both Netscape (shown here) and Internet Explorer show the columns of frames in very much the same way as they show frames in rows.*

```
                code.html
<FRAMESET FRAMEBORDER=0
ROWS="*, 193, 104, 165, *"
COLS="*, 110, 110, 110, *" >

<FRAME NAME=border1 SRC="border.html"
SCROLLING="NO" MARGINWIDTH=1
MARGINHEIGHT=1>

<FRAME NAME=border2 SRC="border.html"
SCROLLING="NO" MARGINWIDTH=1
MARGINHEIGHT=1>

<FRAME NAME=border3 SRC="border.html"
SCROLLING="NO" MARGINWIDTH=1
MARGINHEIGHT=1>

<FRAME NAME=border4 SRC="border.html"
SCROLLING="NO" MARGINWIDTH=1
MARGINHEIGHT=1>
```

Figure 10.9 *You set the size of rows and columns in the FRAMESET tag. Then define each row from left to right, and from top to bottom.*

Figure 10.10 *Notice that the first and last rows and first and last columns of frames are set to take up all the leftover space not used up by the photos. Then I set each of those frames to display an empty page with a white background. No matter what size window my visitors look at this page with, the outside frames will expand or contract, but the photo filled frames will stay the same size.*

Creating Frames in Rows and Columns

Some information is best displayed horizontally while some looks better vertically. You can create both rows and columns in the same frameset to accommodate different kinds of information.

To create a frameset with both rows and columns:

1. Type **<FRAMESET** to begin.

2. Type **ROWS "a, b"** where *a* and *b* (and any others) represent the height of the corresponding rows.

3. Type **COLS="x, y"** where *x* and *y* (and any others) represent the width of the corresponding columns.

4. Type **>**.

5. Define the first frame in the first row by typing **<FRAME NAME="name" SRC="initialurl.html">**.

6. Define the rest of the frames in the first row from left to right.

7. Repeat steps 5–6 for each row, from top to bottom.

8. Type **</FRAMESET>** to complete the frameset.

✔ Tips

- Defining rows and columns in this way limits you to the same number of frames in each row or column. To create one row with two frames and another row with three, you'll have to combine multiple framesets *(see page 172)*.

- There is more about this technique (and this particular example) on the Web site *(see page 20)*.

Creating Frames in Rows and Columns

Combining Framesets

One of the most common layouts for frames you'll see on the Web is to have one row at the top that spans the width of the browser, and then a second row divided into two frames. This effect is achieved by inserting a frameset in the second row.

To combine framesets:

1. Make a sketch of your frameset and determine how many rows and columns you will need.

2. Type **<FRAMESET** to begin.

3. Type **ROWS="a, b">** where *a* and *b* (and any others) represent the height of the corresponding rows.

4. In the example in Figure 10.11, the first and third rows are a single frame while the second row is divided into columns. For a row with just a single frame, type **<FRAME NAME="name" SRC="contents.html">** in the usual way.

5. For the second row, which is divided into columns in this example, type **<FRAMESET COLS="a, b">** where *a* and *b* (and any others) represent the width of each column in the row.

6. Type **<FRAME NAME="name" SRC="contents.html">** where *name* is the reference for the frame and *contents.html* is the page that will be initially shown in that frame.

7. Repeat step 6 for each frame in the column. (In this example, there are two columns, so you'll have to define two frames in the inner frameset.)

8. When you've finished defining the frames/columns in the divided row, type **</FRAMESET>**.

```
                    code.html
<HTML><HEAD><TITLE>Targeting particular
frames</TITLE></HEAD>

<FRAMESET ROWS="45,*,45">

<FRAME NAME="banner" SRC="banner.html">

<FRAMESET COLS="120,*">

<FRAME NAME="index" SRC="indexcity.html">

<FRAME NAME="photos"
SRC="openingpage.html">

</FRAMESET>

<FRAME NAME="buttons" SRC="buttons.html">

</FRAMESET>

</HTML>
```

Figure 10.11 *First create the outer frameset. Then define each row from top to bottom. For rows that will be divided, use an inner frameset. The highlighted area here corresponds to just the second row of the Web page.*

Combining Framesets

Figure 10.12 *In this example, the first and third rows are simple frames while the second row is a frameset divided into two columns.*

9. Continue defining each row individually. For a row with just one frame (i.e., just one column), just use a FRAME tag. For rows divided into multiple columns, repeat steps 5–8.

10. Type **</FRAMESET>** to complete the outer frameset.

✔ Tips

- It's absolutely crucial that you add a closing </FRAMESET> tag for each opening <FRAMESET> that you create. Otherwise, Netscape won't show anything at all.

- Although I've defined the rows first and then the columns in this example, you can define the columns first if it works better for your particular layout. In fact, when adjusting the borders, both methods have distinct advantages (see the tips on page 179).

- It is important to stress that not every row need be divided into columns. For rows with a single frame (i.e., that span the entire window from left to right), just use a FRAME tag. For rows divided into columns, use an inner frameset.

- If you want to create the *same number* of frames in each row and each column, you don't need to combine multiple framesets. For details, consult *Creating Frames in Rows and Columns* on page 171.

- You can use combined framesets to change more than one frame at a time. For more information, consult *Changing Multiple Frames with One Link* on page 304.

Combining Framesets

Creating an Inline Frame

If you want to mix text, graphics, and a frame all on one page, you'll need to create a floating or *inline* frame—and hope that your visitors view the page with Explorer (although it *is* standard HTML 4).

To create an inline frame:

1. In the container page, type **<IFRAME SRC="frame.url"**, where *frame.url* is the page that should be initially displayed in the inline frame.

2. Type **NAME="name"**, where *name* is a word that identifies this inline frame's use.

3. Type **WIDTH=x HEIGHT=y** where *x* and *y* represent the width and height, respectively, of the inline frame as a percentage or as an absolute value in pixels.

4. If desired, type **ALIGN=LEFT** or **ALIGN=RIGHT** to wrap the text that comes after the frame around the frame.

5. Type **>**.

6. Type the text that should appear if the browser doesn't support inline frames.

7. Type **</IFRAME>** to complete the inline frame.

✔ Tips

- You can also use the FRAMEBORDER *(see page 179)*, HSPACE/VSPACE *(see page 91)*, SCROLLING *(see page 176)*, and MARGINWIDTH/MARGINHEIGHT *(see page 175)* tags with inline frames.

- Netscape (as of version 4) does not support inline frames.

```
code.html

<BODY BGCOLOR="#FFFFFF">

<H1>Barcelona Tours</H1>

Here's an idea of what the Barcelona Tours home
page looks like:

<HR><P><CENTER>

<IFRAME SRC="bcntourrc.html" NAME="float"
WIDTH=90% HEIGHT=70% >

The <A HREF="bcntourrc.html">Barcelona
Tours</A> page contains great photos and
essential tips for making your vacation a success.

</IFRAME>
```

Figure 10.13 *Because many Web surfers use Netscape, and Netscape doesn't support inline frames, it's important to add alternate text between the opening and closing IFRAME tags.*

Figure 10.14 *Floating frames won't appear in Netscape but the alternate text (here with a link to the frameset) will.*

Figure 10.15 *Floating frames function similarly to images, flowing with the rest of the content on the page.*

Figure 10.16 *In this illustration you can see the default margins. Note how the contents of each frame begins slightly down and to the right.*

```
code.html
<FRAMESET ROWS="65,*,60">

<FRAME NAME="banner" SRC="banner.html"
MARGINWIDTH=0 MARGINHEIGHT=0>

<FRAMESET COLS="120,*">
<FRAME NAME="index" SRC="indexcity.html"
MARGINWIDTH=0 MARGINHEIGHT=0>
<FRAME NAME="photos" SRC="openingpage.html"
MARGINWIDTH=0 MARGINHEIGHT=0>
</FRAMESET>

<FRAME NAME="buttons" SRC="buttons.html"
MARGINWIDTH=0 MARGINHEIGHT=0>
</FRAMESET>
```

Figure 10.17 *Adjust the margins of each frame by adding a MARGINWIDTH and/or MARGINHEIGHT tag to the desired FRAME tags. In this case, all the margins have been set to 0.*

Figure 10.18 *With the margins at 0, each frame's contents start in the top-left corner of each frame.*

Adjusting a Frame's Margins

By default, both Netscape and Explorer display a frame's contents with a margin of 8 pixels on each side **(Figure 10.16)**. You can adjust the margin so that there is more space, or, if you prefer, so that the frame's contents begin in the top-left corner.

To adjust a frame's margins:

1. In the desired FRAME tag, before the final >, type **MARGINWIDTH=w** where *w* is the desired amount of space, in pixels, between the left and right edges of the frame and the frame's contents **(Figure 10.17)**.

2. Type **MARGINHEIGHT=h** where *h* is the desired amount of space, in pixels, between the top and bottom edges of the frame and the frame's contents.

✔ Tip

- The margin is transparent and thus always appears to be the same color as the background of the page displayed in the frame.

Adjusting a Frame's Margins

Showing or Hiding Scroll Bars

You can decide whether each individual frame should have a scroll bar all the time, never, or only when needed. *Only when needed* means that the scroll bars will appear only when there is more information than can be shown at one time in the frame. If the visitor makes the window big enough, these scroll bars will eventually disappear.

To show scroll bars all the time:

In the FRAME tag of the particular frame for which you wish to show the scroll bar, type **SCROLLING=YES**.

To hide scroll bars all the time:

In the FRAME tag of the particular frame for which you wish to hide the scroll bar, type **SCROLLING=NO**.

✔ Tips

- The default is for scroll bars to appear only when necessary, that is, when there is more information than can fit in the frame. To use the default, you can type **SCROLLING=AUTO** or, more simply, don't type any SCROLLING tag at all.

- There are few things more frustrating than jumping to a frameset page with tiny little frames that make it impossible to view the entire contents. Even worse is when you cannot scroll around (or make the frame bigger—see page 180) to make the hidden information visible. To avoid frustrating *your* visitors, make sure you test your frameset page in a small window and ensure that all the frames without scroll bars are big enough to display their entire contents.

```
<FRAMESET ROWS="65,*,60">

<FRAME NAME="banner" SRC="banner.html"
SCROLLING=NO>

<FRAMESET COLS="120,*">
<FRAME NAME="index" SRC="indexcity.html">
<FRAME NAME="photos"
SRC="openingpage.html">
</FRAMESET>

<FRAME NAME="buttons" SRC="buttons.html"
SCROLLING=NO>

</FRAMESET>
```

Figure 10.19 *So that the top and bottom frames never display scroll bars, add SCROLLING=NO to their FRAME tags.*

Figure 10.20 *Eliminating scroll bars from certain areas makes the information much clearer and more attractive. But be careful not to take away scroll bars from areas that need them. Remember, you can't control the size of your visitor's window.*

Showing or Hiding Scroll Bars

```
═════════ code.html ═════════
<FRAMESET BORDERCOLOR="#FF0000"
ROWS="65,*,60">

<FRAME NAME="banner" SRC="banner.html"
SCROLLING=NO>

<FRAMESET COLS="120,*">

<FRAME NAME="index" SRC="indexcity.html">
```

Figure 10.21 *You can add the BORDERCOLOR tag to any frameset or frame tag. Here it's been added to the topmost frameset tag so that it will affect all the frames contained within.*

Figure 10.22 *Both Netscape and Explorer can display colored frame borders (This is Netscape.)*

Adjusting the Color of the Borders

In theory, you can change the color of each frame individually. In practice, however, since the borders are shared between frames, the possibilities are more limited.

To adjust the color of all the borders in the frameset:

Inside the topmost FRAMESET tag before the final >, type **BORDERCOLOR=color**, where *color* is one of the sixteen predefined colors *(see page 357)*.

To change the color of rows, columns, or individual frames:

In the appropriate FRAMESET or FRAME tag, type **BORDERCOLOR=color**.

✔ Tips

- You can also type **BORDERCOLOR= "#rrggbb"**. Consult *Colors in Hex* starting on page 357 for more details.

- A BORDERCOLOR tag in an individual frame overrides a BORDERCOLOR tag in a row or column, which in turn overrides the tag defined in the topmost FRAMESET. If two BORDERCOLOR tags at the same level conflict, the one that comes first in your HTML file takes precedence.

- When you change the border of an individual frame, other frames that share its borders are also affected.

- The BORDERCOLOR tag is not standard HTML but it is supported by both Netscape and Explorer.

Adjusting the Color of the Borders

Adjusting the Frame Borders

By default, your visitor's browser will draw sculpted borders around each frame in your frameset. The BORDER tag lets you control the width of the space between frames. The FRAMEBORDER tag lets you choose to fill that space with sculpted borders or leave it blank.

To adjust the amount of space between frames:

Inside the topmost FRAMESET tag, before the final >, type **BORDER=n** where *n* is the desired width of the space between frames, in pixels.

✔ Tips

- You can use **BORDER=0** to make the borders completely disappear.

- The default border width is 5 pixels.

- You cannot set the thickness for individual frames.

- Explorer won't show borders between 1 and 5 pixels wide. Instead, it shows nothing.

- The best way to make frames jut right up next to each other is to use both BORDER=0 and FRAMEBORDER=0 *(see page 179)*. While BORDER=0 is enough for today's browsers, older programs will appreciate the redundancy.

- You can change the color of the borders (or the space between the frames) as well. For details, consult *Adjusting the Color of the Borders* on page 177.

- Explorer also supports a FRAMESPACING attribute which works essentially like the BORDER attribute (which earlier versions of Explorer did not support).

- BORDER is not standard HTML, but is still well supported.

Figure 10.23 *Add the BORDER tag to any frameset or frame tag to adjust its borders' thickness. Here, I've added the tag to the topmost frameset tag so that all the frames are affected.*

Figure 10.24 *Thick, colored borders can help divide information into understandable chunks.*

Figure 10.25 *With a value between 1 and 5, Explorer shows no borders at all.*

Adjusting the Frame Borders

```
code.html
<FRAMESET BORDERCOLOR="#FF0000"
BORDER=0 FRAMEBORDER=0
ROWS="65,*,60">

<FRAME NAME="banner" SRC="banner.html"
SCROLLING=NO>

<FRAMESET COLS="120,*">
```

Figure 10.26 *If you want to be sure that your page has no borders, whether it is viewed in Netscape or Internet Explorer, set both the BORDER and FRAME-BORDER tags to 0.*

Figure 10.27 *To have each frame right up next to the adjacent one, use FRAMEBORDER=0 BORDER=0.*

Figure 10.28 *With just FRAMEBORDER=0, you can still see a separation below the City Tour frame.*

To hide the sculpted borders:

Type **FRAMEBORDER=0** inside the topmost FRAMESET tag, before the final >.

✔ Tips

■ **FRAMEBORDER=0** makes the sculpted borders disappear but it does not get rid of all of the space between frames. To get rid of both borders and space, use **FRAMEBORDER=0** and **BORDER=0**.

■ To view *some* borders when the topmost frameset is set for none, type **FRAMEBORDER=1** in the desired FRAME or FRAMESET tag.

■ To make the horizontal borders disappear, define the columns in the outer frameset and the rows in the inner frameset and then type **FRAMEBOR-DER=0** within each of the FRAME tags in the desired column.

■ You can use the FRAMEBORDER tag with individual frames. Explorer will display the border around an individual frame, but Netscape will show the border for the entire row.

Adjusting the Frame Borders

Keeping Visitors from Resizing Frames

Frames with relative or variable sizes are always resized when the visitor changes the size of the browser window. However, you can also choose whether to let the visitor resize individual frames.

To keep visitors from resizing your frames:

Type **NORESIZE** in the FRAME tag for the desired frame.

✔ Tips

■ Netscape displays resizable frames with a small hash mark in the middle of the border. The mark disappears if you've used the NORESIZE attribute. Explorer displays both resizable and non-resizable borders exactly the same way.

■ If you use very small pixel values for your frames and the visitor views the frameset page in a very large window, the width of the frames will probably not be quite as you wished. The entire frameset is always stretched to fill the window.

■ If you set the border width to 0 with the BORDER attribute *(see page 178)*, visitors won't be able to resize the frames at all. (The same goes for the FRAMEBORDER and FRAMESPACING attributes.)

■ In Explorer, if you set the BORDER width to less than 5, the borders disappear, and again visitors won't be able to resize frames at all, regardless of whether you use the NORESIZE attribute or not.

Figure 10.29 *Normally when the visitor places the pointer over a border, it changes into a double-headed arrow with which she can change the size of the frame. Also notice the hash mark which indicates the frame can be resized.*

```
<FRAMESET BORDERCOLOR="#FF0000"
BORDER=6 ROWS="65,*,60">

<FRAME NAME="banner" SRC="banner.html"
SCROLLING=NO NORESIZE>

<FRAMESET COLS="120,*">
<FRAME NAME="index" SRC="indexcity.html">
<FRAME NAME="photos"
SRC="openingpage.html">
</FRAMESET>

<FRAME NAME="buttons" SRC="buttons.html"
SCROLLING=NO NORESIZE>
```

Figure 10.30 *Add the NORESIZE tag to any frames that you don't want the visitor to be able to resize. Here, I've modified the top and bottom frames and left the middle frames flexible.*

Figure 10.31 *Once you've restricted the resizability, the pointer will not turn into a double-pointed arrow and the visitor can't change the size of the frame. (In Netscape, the hash mark disappears also.)*

Keeping Visitors from Resizing Frames

```
code.html
<FRAMESET ROWS="65,*,60">

<FRAME NAME="banner" SRC="banner.html">

<FRAME NAME="photos"
SRC="openingpage.html">
```

Figure 10.32 *Targets will only work if the frame in which you want the page to appear has a name.*

```
code.html
<TR><TD BGCOLOR="#F3D7E3"><A
HREF="openingpage.html" TARGET=photos>
Beginning</A>

<TR><TD BGCOLOR="#F6D5C3">
<A HREF="rambles.html" TARGET=photos>Les
Rambles Boulevard</A>
```

Figure 10.33 *In the link, specify the name of the frame in which the destination page should open.*

Figure 10.34 *The original contents of the photos frame is the* Welcome *page. But when the visitor clicks the* Les Rambles *link (which is targeted to appear in the* photos *frame)...*

Figure 10.35 *...the* Les Rambles *page replaces the* Welcome *page in the* photos *frame.*

Targeting Links to Particular Frames

The initial content of a given frame is specified in the frameset page with the SRC tag. However, you can have other pages appear in that same frame. The trick is to add a pointer, called a *target*, to the links to those pages. The target says "open this link in the *photos* frame" (or whatever it's called).

To target a link to a particular frame:

1. Make sure the target frame has a name **(Figure 10.32)**. For more information, consult *Creating a Simple Frameset* on page 168.

2. On the page where the link should appear, type **<A HREF="page.html"** where *page.html* is the file that should be displayed in the target frame.

3. Type **TARGET="name"** where *name* is the reference given to the target frame within the FRAME tag **(Figure 10.33)**.

4. Add any other attributes as desired to the link and then type the final **>**. For more information on creating links, see Chapter 7, *Links*.

✔ Tips

- The frame must have a name to be targeted. For more information on naming frames, consult *Creating a Simple Frameset* on page 168.

- Frame names must begin with an alphanumeric character (except the special names described on page 182).

- If you don't specify a target, the link will open in the frame that contains the link.

Targeting Links to Particular Frames

Targeting Links to Special Spots

Although many times you'll be happy targeting a link to a particular frame, as described on page 181, other times you will want to make more general instructions, like having the link open in a new window, or opening the link in the same window that contained the link.

To target a link to a special spot:

1. Type **<A HREF="contents.html"** where *contents.html* is the page that you wish to be displayed in the special spot.

2. Type **TARGET=_blank** to have the link open in a new, blank window. This is the ideal targeting for links to other sites which may not fit very well inside your frames.

   Or type **TARGET=_self** to open the link in the same frame that contains the link **(Figure 10.36)**. The information in the frame (including the link itself) will be replaced by the *contents.html* file specified in step 1.

   Or type **TARGET=_top** to open the link in the current browser window but independently of the rest of the frameset to which it currently belongs.

   Or type **TARGET=_parent** to open the link in the frame that contains the current frameset. This will only be different from _top when you are using nested framesets. For more information on nested framesets, consult *Nesting Framesets* on page 184.

```
                    code.html

you'll see older couples checking out the bird and
flower stalls, younger people arguing at the
political booths, mimes and bands, beggars and
pickpockets (well, maybe you won't
<em>see</em> them). If I were there, I'd be
drinking an orxata at the Caf&#233; de
l'&#211;pera watching all the people go by.

<BR>

<A HREF="rambles2.html" TARGET=_self>More
about Les Rambles</A>

<A HREF="plcat.html">Next stop</A>
```

Figure 10.36 *In this example, the link accesses a second page of information. It makes sense to display this second page in the same frame.*

Figure 10.37 *When the visitor clicks a link that is targeted to the same frame that contains the link...*

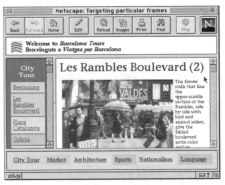

Figure 10.38 *...the frame's contents are replaced with the new contents from the link.*

Targeting Links to Special Spots

```
code.html
<HTML><HEAD><TITLE>Buttons</TITLE>
</HEAD><BODY BGCOLOR="#FF0000">

<TABLE CELLPADDING=5 CELLSPACING=0
WIDTH=100%>

<TR><TH><FONT COLOR="#FFFFFF"
SIZE=+1>City Tour</FONT></A>

<TR><TD BGCOLOR="#F3D7E3"><A
HREF="openingpage.html"
TARGET=photos>Beginning</A>

<TR><TD BGCOLOR="#F6D5C3"><A
HREF="rambles.html" TARGET=photos>Les
Rambles Boulevard</A>

<TR><TD BGCOLOR="#D8E9D6"><A
HREF="plcat.html" TARGET=photos>
Pla&#231;a Catalunya</A>
```

Figure 10.39 *In the original document, I've set the target for each link individually.*

```
code.html
<HTML><HEAD><TITLE>Buttons</TITLE>

<BASE TARGET=photos></HEAD>

<BODY BGCOLOR="#FF0000">

<TABLE CELLPADDING=5 CELLSPACING=0
WIDTH=100%>

<TR><TH><FONT COLOR="#FFFFFF"
SIZE=+1>City Tour</FONT></A>

<TR><TD BGCOLOR="#F3D7E3"><A
HREF="openingpage.html">Beginning</A>

<TR><TD BGCOLOR="#F6D5C3"><A
HREF="rambles.html">Les Rambles
Boulevard</A>

<TR><TD BGCOLOR="#D8E9D6"><A
HREF="plcat.html">Pla&#231;a
Catalunya</A>
```

Figure 10.40 *You can save a lot of typing by using the BASE tag to set the default target for every link on the page. This document is equivalent to the one shown in Figure 10.39.*

Changing the Default Target

If a frame contains a link, the link will open up in that same frame, by default, unless you change the target as described on pages 181–182. You can change the default target for all of the links on a page by using the BASE tag.

To change the default target:

1. In the HEAD section of the page that contains the links, type **<BASE**.

2. Type **TARGET="name"**, where *name* is the word that identifies the frame or window in which you want the links to appear, by default.

3. Type **>** to complete the BASE tag.

✔ Tip

■ You can override the target specified in the BASE tag by choosing a target in the link itself *(see page 181)*.

Nesting Framesets

As if frames and framesets weren't complicated enough, you can nest framesets inside of frames to achieve special effects.

To nest framesets:

1. Build the child, or inner, frameset *(see page 168)*.

2. Build the parent, or outer, frameset **(Figure 10.41)**. When you reach the frame in which you wish to nest the child frameset, type **SRC="child.html"** in the FRAME tag, where *child.html* is the file that you built in step 1.

✔ Tips

■ You can target a link to open in the parent frame of a frameset (in this example, the right column is the parent frame of the Barcelona tour frameset). For more information, consult *Targeting Links to Special Spots* on page 182.

■ You can't nest a frameset inside a frame that is in that same frameset. Hey, and why would you want to?

■ You can use nested framesets to change two frames with one link (a common desire). Simply create a special frameset that references the two pages that you want to appear. Then point the link at the new frameset. It's a bit slower than the JavaScript way, but it's pure HTML. (For the JavaScript way, consult *Changing Multiple Frames with One Link* on page 304.)

```
code.html
<HTML><HEAD><TITLE>Nesting
Frames</TITLE></HEAD>

<FRAMESET COLS="*,4*">

<FRAME SRC="bigindex.html">

<FRAME NAME="main"
SRC="bcntourrc.html">

</FRAMESET>

</HTML>
```

Figure 10.41 *The frameset shown has two columns. The first column will contain a simple index page, while the second column will contain a distinct frameset (in fact, the one used in most of the previous examples in this chapter).*

Figure 10.42 *In this example, the Barcelona tour is easily integrated into a larger group of topics just by nesting its frameset into the larger one.*

```
code.html
<FRAMESET ROWS="65,*,60">
<FRAME NAME="banner" SRC="banner.html"
NORESIZE SCROLLING=NO >
<FRAMESET COLS="120,*">
<FRAME NAME="index" SRC="indexcity.html">
<FRAME NAME="photos"
SRC="openingpage.html">
</FRAMESET>

<FRAME NAME="buttons" SRC="buttons.html"
NORESIZE SCROLLING=NO>

<NOFRAMES>
The information on this page is displayed in
frames. Your browser can't view frames (or if
you're using Internet Explorer, you've turned
frame viewing off--go to Preferences under Edit
and then Web Content and check Show Frames).
Sorry!
</NOFRAMES>

</FRAMESET></HTML>
```

Figure 10.43 *The NOFRAMES tags come after all of the framesets and frames have been defined.*

Figure 10.44 *Netscape always displays frames, and thus* never *shows the NOFRAMES information.*

Figure 10.45 *When you turn frames off in Internet Explorer, the alternate information is displayed. This is a good way to test how this information will appear.*

Creating Alternatives to Frames

Although Netscape and Internet Explorer have been able to display frames since version 2, and frames have been added to the official HTML specifications with version 4, some browsers (OK, not many) still do not support them. You can create alternate content that will appear if your visitor's browser doesn't support frames.

To create alternatives to frames:

1. Type **<NOFRAMES>** just before the last </FRAMESET> tag **(Figure 10.43)**.

2. Create the content that you want to appear if the frames do not.

3. When you've finished creating the alternate content, type **</NOFRAMES>**.

✔ Tips

- The NOFRAMES section will not be shown in browsers that can interpret frames, like Netscape **(Figure 10.44)** and Internet Explorer. Instead, the frames will be shown.

- Although this example is rather simple, don't be misled: you can put practically anything in the NOFRAMES section.

- Some visitors set up Explorer so that it doesn't view frames (by unchecking Frames in the Web Content preferences). They will see the NOFRAMES content.

- If you don't create a NOFRAMES section, beware! When visitors jump to your page with a browser that can't read frames, instead of an error message, they simply won't see anything! If nothing else, the NOFRAMES section can be used to explain what the problem is **(Figure 10.45)**.

Creating Alternatives to Frames

Forms

✔ **What you can do with forms:**

- get feedback

- have a guestbook

- take a survey

- see who's visiting you

- sell stuff

- and much more!

Up to now, all the HTML you have learned has helped you communicate *your* ideas with your visitors. In this chapter, you'll learn how to create forms which enable your visitors to communicate with you.

There are two basic parts of a form: the structure or shell, that consists of fields, labels, and buttons that the visitor sees on a page and hopefully fills out, and the processing script that takes that information and converts it into a format that you can read or tally.

Constructing a form's shell is straightforward and similar to creating any other part of the Web page. You can create text boxes, special password boxes, radio buttons, checkboxes, drop-down menus, larger text areas, and even clickable images. You will give each element a name that will serve as a label to identify the data once it is processed. Constructing forms is discussed on pages 193–210.

Processing the data from a form is a bit more complicated. The principal tool, the *CGI script*, is typically written in Perl or some other programming language. Although Perl programming is beyond the scope of this book, and even explaining how to use existing Perl scripts stretches its limits a bit, I've added a few simple ready-made Perl CGI scripts for your use to get you started *(see page 191)*.

If this all seems a bit daunting, or if your ISP doesn't allow you to run CGI scripts, you might decide to have visitors submit form data via e-mail *(see page 194)* or use a public form host *(see page 195)*.

About CGI Scripts

If you're a non-programmer, the phrase *CGI script* may make you want to quickly close this book and forget about forms altogether. Hold on. What's CGI? What's a script? It's not as impossible as it sounds. First, a script is another word for a program, just like Microsoft Word or Adobe Photoshop. Of course, the scripts you'll use to process forms are a good deal simpler than commercial applications that cost hundreds of dollars. But they work in a similar way.

CGI, which stands for *Common Gateway Interface*, is simply a standardized way for sending information between the server and the script. So, to resume, a CGI script is a program (usually written in a programming language called Perl) that communicates with the server in a standard (CGI-like) way.

Perl is the most common language used for CGI scripts, partly because it's easily ported from one platform to another, partly because it's great for massaging data into understandable information, and partly because it has this reputation as a cool language—really! Perl programmers love to brag about how they can do anything with Perl, on one line, in a million different ways.

You can use other programming languages, like C++, tcl, Visual Basic, or even AppleScript to create CGI scripts. My advice is that if you know one of these languages, you should use it; otherwise, use Perl.

One extra nice thing about Perl programmers is that they often like to share. You can find tons of ready-to-use CGI scripts written in Perl all over the Web *(see page 190)*. Many are free, many are not.

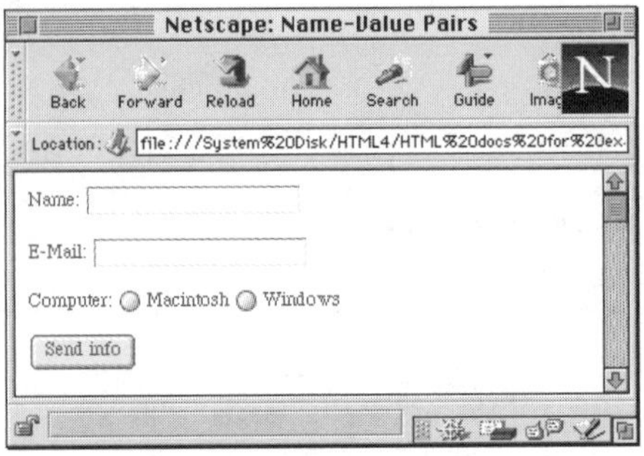

Figure 11.1 *Here's your basic form. There are two text fields, one set of radio buttons and a submit button. The words Name, E-Mail, Computer, Macintosh, and Windows are all labels. They do not affect the data that is collected in any way.*

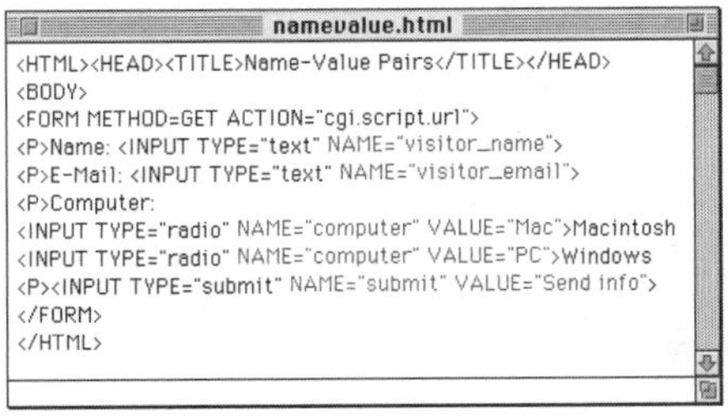

namevalue.html

```
<HTML><HEAD><TITLE>Name-Value Pairs</TITLE></HEAD>
<BODY>
<FORM METHOD=GET ACTION="cgi.script.url">
<P>Name: <INPUT TYPE="text" NAME="visitor_name">
<P>E-Mail: <INPUT TYPE="text" NAME="visitor_email">
<P>Computer:
<INPUT TYPE="radio" NAME="computer" VALUE="Mac">Macintosh
<INPUT TYPE="radio" NAME="computer" VALUE="PC">Windows
<P><INPUT TYPE="submit" NAME="submit" VALUE="Send info">
</FORM>
</HTML>
```

Figure 11.2 *Here's the HTML code that is behind the form in Figure 11.1. Just focus on the NAME and VALUE attributes for now. (You'll learn how to create form elements later on in the chapter.) First, notice how each form element has a NAME attribute, but only some have a VALUE. The VALUE attribute determines the data that is sent to the server for that element. Some form elements allow the visitor to type in any value (like text boxes) while others do not (like radio buttons). Form elements that work by checking or selecting must have the value specified in the VALUE attribute.*

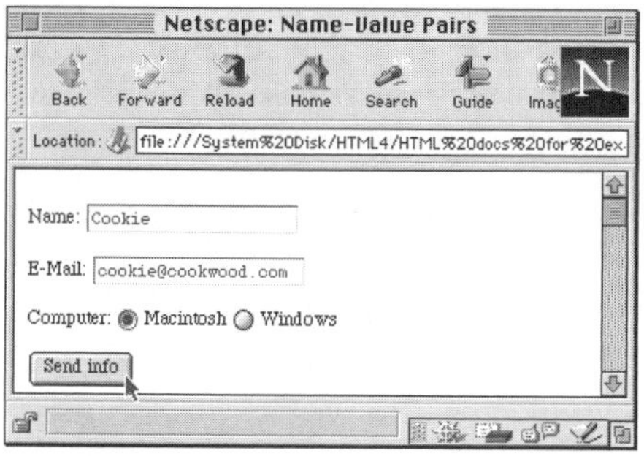

Figure 11.3 *When the visitor enters information in the text fields and chooses a radio button, the name-value pairs are set. Clicking the submit button (labeled here "Send info") will send the name-value pairs to the CGI-script on the server.*

Label	Name	Value
Name	visitor_name	Cookie
E-Mail	visitor_email	cookie@cookwood.com
Computer	computer	Mac
Send info	submit	Send info

Figure 11.4 *These are the actual name-value pairs that will be sent when the visitor clicks the submit button in Figure 11.3. Be sure not to confuse* label *with* name. *Also, notice that the values for the first two fields correspond to what the visitor has typed. The value for the radio button—Mac, not Macintosh (which is the label)—was set by me, the author of this Web page (see Figure 11.2) since the visitor can only click the button (and not type).*

visitor_name=Cookie&
visitor_email=cookie@cookwood.com
&computer=Mac&submit=Send+info

Figure 11.5 *This is what the data that is sent to the CGI script looks like. Notice that each name is linked with its value with an equals sign (=). An ampersand (&) separates each name-value pair and spaces are marked with plus signs.*

What does the CGI script do?

Each element on your form will have a *name* and a *value* associated with it. The name identifies the data that is being sent. It might be something like *visitor_name*. The value is the data (say, *Castro*), and can either come from you, the Web page designer, or from the visitor who types it in a field **(Figures 11.1 and 11.2)**. When a visitor clicks the submit button (or an active image—see page 210), the name-value pair of each form element is sent to the server (it might look like *visitor_name=Castro*).

CGI scripts generally have two functions. The first is to take all those name-value pairs and separate them out into individual intelligible pieces. The second is to actually do something with that data—like print it out, multiply fields together, send an e-mail confirmation, store it on a server, or whatever. There are CGI scripts that create guestbooks, bulletin boards, chat areas, counters, games, postcard senders, image randomizers, scripts that work with databases, let you edit Web pages, and many, many more.

Security

Before you get too excited, you should know that CGI scripts can leave your server wide open to invaders. That's one reason some ISPs do not allow their users to use CGI scripts. If this is your case, one alternative is to use a form hosting service, as described on page 195.

If your ISP does allow you to run CGI-scripts, you should still read up on security issues. You might start with *http://www.go2net.com/people/paulp/cgi-security/* for more information on what CGI scripts can make you vulnerable to.

About CGI Scripts

Getting a Script

If your ISP okays your use of CGI scripts, your next step is to get your hands on one. You might start with the scripts included with this book *(see page 191)*. Or you can either write your own or adapt one of the hundreds of scripts available on the Web. Some of these scripts are free, others require some sort of compensation to the programmer. While you can find scripts all over the Web, I've found four particularly good places to look.

The CGI Resource Index

The CGI Resource Index, published by Matt's Script Archive, Inc. (see below), lists hundreds of links to Perl CGI scripts, documentation, books, magazine articles, programmers, and jobs. It's at *www.cgi-resources.com* **(Figure 11.6)**.

Matt's Script Archive

Also known as MSA, Matt's Script Archive— *www.worldwidemart.com/scripts*—is one of the most popular script repositories on the Web. Created by teenager Matt Wright, the site offers several useful, free Perl CGI scripts.

Extropia.com

Another famous source for free Perl CGI scripts is Extropia.com, created by Selena Sol and Gunther Birznieks. Though recently sporting a more commercial look, Extropia offers many useful scripts that its authors have generously released to the public domain. They now offer support for those scripts—for a fee. You can find them at *www.extropia.com*.

The WebScripts Archive

While not the biggest or perhaps the most popular, Darryl Burgdorf's site houses what I think is the best documented and easiest to implement collection of Perl CGI scripts. You'll find them at: *www.awsd.com/scripts*.

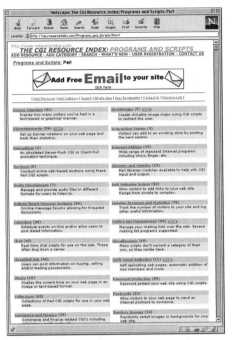

Figure 11.6 *You'll find more than 1600 Perl CGI scripts available for download from The CGI Resource Index (http://www.cgi-resources.com). Some are free. Some are not.*

```
1    #!/usr/local/bin/perl
2
3    if ($ENV{'REQUEST_METHOD'} eq 'GET')
     {
4       @pairs = split(/&/,
         $ENV{'QUERY_STRING'});
5    } elsif ($ENV{'REQUEST_METHOD'} eq
     'POST') {
6       read (STDIN, $buffer,
         $ENV{'CONTENT_LENGTH'});
7       @pairs = split(/&/, $buffer);
8    } else {
9       print "Content-type:
         text/html\n\n";
10      print "<P>Use Post or Get";
11   }
12
13   foreach $pair (@pairs) {
14      ($key, $value) = split (/=/, $pair);
15      $key =~ tr/+/ /;
16      $key =~ s/%([a-fA-F0-9] [a-fA-F0-
         9])/ pack("C", hex($1))/eg;
17      $value =~ tr/+/ /;
18      $value =~ s/%([a-fA-F0-9] [a-fA-F
         0-9])/pack("C", hex($1))/eg;
19
20      $value =~s/<!--(.|\n)*-->//g;
21
22      if ($formdata{$key}) {
23         $formdata{$key} .= ", $value";
24      } else {
25         $formdata{$key} = $value;
26      }
27   }
28
29   print "Content-type: text/html\n\n";
30   foreach $key (sort keys(%formdata)) {
31      print "<P>The field named <B>$key</B>
         contained <B>$formdata{$key}</B>";
32   }
```

Figure 11.7 *Here is one rendition of the all-important script that parses form data. The highlighted portion is the essential part. The rest of it is for displaying the results in a simple way. You can find this script and others at http://www.cookwood.com/ html4_4e/cgiscripts/.*

Using the Scripts Included with This Book

With this book, I have included a set of very simple scripts that you can use to process the data that visitors submit to your Web site. These scripts are designed to help you understand how forms work and get you started. To really get some use out of them, you will have to know a little Perl (or be willing to learn). If you're just interested in getting the data from a form, you're probably better off using e-mail *(see page 194).*

To use the scripts included with this book:

1. Download the desired scripts from my Web site: *www.cookwood.com/html4_4e/ cgiscripts/.*

2. Read and follow the instructions in *Preparing a Script* on page 192.

3. Reference the script (from your server) in step 2 on page 193.

4. Get a visitor to go to your site and press the Submit button!

✔ Tips

- To get more high-powered scripts, consult *Getting a Script* on page 190.

- If you are intrigued by writing your own scripts, you might be interested in my other book: *Perl and CGI for the World Wide Web: Visual QuickStart Guide,* also published by Peachpit Press. With the same clear, concise, and visually-oriented format as the book you have in your hands, it is a perfect starting place for the non-programmer who wants to make their Web pages interactive. For more details, check out *www.cookwood.com/ perl/.* End of commercial.

Preparing a Script

Whether you've written your own script or are using someone else's, you'll have to do a couple of things to get it ready for use with your form.

Adapting scripts for your use

If you're using a Perl script that you've downloaded from someone else, you'll have to open it up and see what variables and path names it uses. You will have to change these to reflect your particular situation.

Transferring the script to the server

The next step is to copy the script to the server, generally with an FTP program like WS_FTP *(see page 334)* or Fetch *(see page 336)*. Some servers require that all CGI scripts be located in a central cgi-bin directory. Others provide a personal cgi-bin directory for each user. Still others let you store CGI scripts wherever you want, as long as you add a particular extension to them for identification. You'll have to ask your ISP.

Permissions

If your page is on a Unix server, you will have to use a program called chmod to make the CGI script accessible and executable. For more details type **man chmod** at the Unix prompt.

Add it to your form!

So you've got your CGI script on your server, ready to go. The only thing left is to add it to your form *(see page 193)*.

```
code.html
<FORM METHOD=POST
ACTION="http://www.cookwood.com/
cgi-bin/lcastro/namevalue.cgi" >
```

```
<HR>Please share any suggestions or comments
with us:
<TEXTAREA NAME="comments" ROWS=3
COLS=65 WRAP>Comments?</TEXTAREA>
<HR>
<INPUT TYPE="submit" VALUE="Order Bed">
<INPUT TYPE="reset" VALUE="Start Over">
</FORM>
```

Figure 11.8 *Every form has three parts: the FORM tag, the actual form elements where the visitor enters information, and the SUBMIT tag which creates the button that sends the collected information to the server (or an active image).*

Figure 11.9 *A form gives you a great way to get information and feedback from your visitors.*

Creating a Form

A form has three important parts: the FORM tag, which includes the URL of the CGI script that will process the form; the form elements, like fields and menus; and the submit button which sends the data to the CGI script on the server.

To create a form:

1. Type **<FORM METHOD=POST**.

2. Type **ACTION="script.url">** where *script.url* is the location on the server of the CGI script that will run when the form is submitted *(see pages 188–192)*.

3. Create the form's contents, as described on pages 196–216, including a submit button *(see page 206)* or active image *(see page 210)*.

4. Type **</FORM>** to complete the form.

✔ Tips

- In order for your visitor to send you the data on the form, you'll need either a submit button (if your form contains fields, buttons, and other elements that your visitors will fill in) or an active image. For more on submit buttons, consult *Creating the Submit Button* on page 206. For details on active images, consult *Using an Image to Submit Data* on page 210.

- You can use tables to lay out your form elements more precisely. For more information, consult Chapter 9, *Tables*.

- You can also use the GET method to process information gathered with a form. However, since the GET method limits the amount of data that you can collect at one time, I recommend using POST.

Creating a Form

Sending Form Data via E-mail

If you don't feel like messing with CGI scripts and can deal with not having your data perfectly formatted (or pre-processed by a script), you can have a visitor's data be sent to you via e-mail.

To send form data via e-mail:

1. Type **<FORM METHOD=POST**.
2. Type **ENCTYPE="text/plain"** in order to format the incoming text.
3. Type **ACTION="mailto:you@site.com**, where *you@site.com* is the e-mail address where you want data from the form to be sent.
4. Type **>**.
5. Create the form's contents, as described on pages 196–216.
6. Type **</FORM>**.

✔ Tips

- This technique doesn't work with pre-version 4 browsers.
- When the visitor clicks the submit button, an alert appears warning them that their e-mail address will be submitted along with the data and that the data will not be encrypted. They have to click OK to continue submitting the data.
- Consult *Souping Up Mailto Links* on page 313 for tips on changing the subject line (and other fields) in the incoming e-mail messages.
- The From field's value depends on what the visitor has entered in their browser's preferences. It may or may not be truthful.

code.html

```
<H2>Ordering your new bed</H2>
<FORM METHOD=POST ENCTYPE="text/plain"
ACTION="mailto:lcastro@cookwood.com">
Name: <INPUT TYPE="text" NAME="name">
Address: <INPUT TYPE="text" NAME="address"
SIZE=30>
<P>City: <INPUT TYPE="text" NAME="city">
State: <INPUT TYPE="text" NAME="state"
SIZE=2 MAXLENGTH=2>
```

Figure 11.10 *One way to get around the complications of CGI scripts is to have the data that is submitted with the form sent to your e-mail address.*

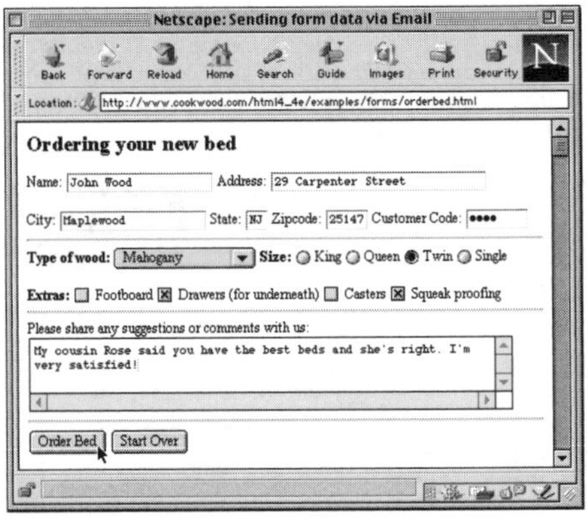

Figure 11.11 *Forms that will be submitted via e-mail look precisely the same as those that are processed with a CGI script.*

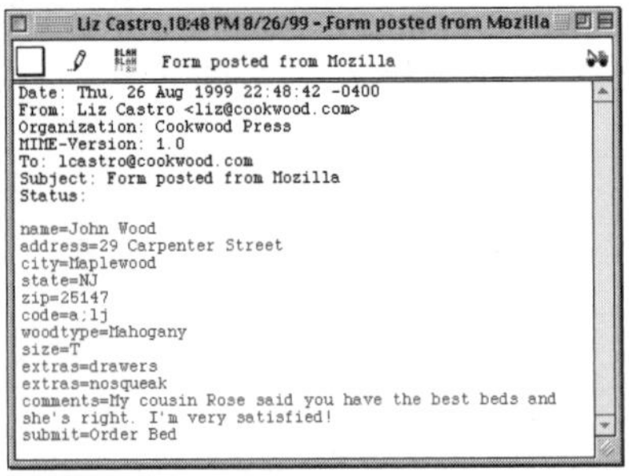

Liz Castro,10:48 PM 8/26/99 -,Form posted from Mozilla

Form posted from Mozilla

```
Date: Thu, 26 Aug 1999 22:48:42 -0400
From: Liz Castro <liz@cookwood.com>
Organization: Cookwood Press
MIME-Version: 1.0
To: lcastro@cookwood.com
Subject: Form posted from Mozilla
Status:

name=John Wood
address=29 Carpenter Street
city=Maplewood
state=NJ
zip=25147
code=a;lj
woodtype=Mahogany
size=T
extras=drawers
extras=nosqueak
comments=My cousin Rose said you have the best beds and
she's right. I'm very satisfied!
submit=Order Bed
```

Figure 11.12 *The data is contained in the body of the e-mail message. Note that the default Subject line depends on the browser your visitor uses (in this example, it was Netscape, code name Mozilla). The From field should reveal the visitor's e-mail address. The To field will correspond to the address you entered for the ACTION attribute.*

Figure 11.13 *This is Response-O-Matic's home page (www.response-o-matic.com). They're one of the better form hosting services I've seen.*

Figure 11.14 *Response-O-Matic gets you started by asking you a few questions and then creating a template, as shown in Figure 11.15.*

Figure 11.15 *Save the template to your hard disk and edit it as necessary. (Just don't change the hidden fields.)*

Using a Form Hosting Service

Another option for those who cannot or don't want to use a CGI script is a form hosting service. There are several such companies that create forms for you, give you access to CGI scripts that process the forms, or process the forms directly and send you the results via e-mail. You generally "pay" for the service by including some sort of advertisement on your page.

To use a form hosting service:

1. Search for a form hosting service on AltaVista or Yahoo.

2. Connect to the form hosting service.

3. Read their site to answer the following questions:

   - Who creates the form: you or them?

   - What do you have to do in exchange for them processing your forms?

   - Is it OK to use their processing for commercial sites, or just personal ones?

4. Follow their instructions for setting up your form. Consult the rest of this chapter for more information about creating form elements.

✔ Tips

- Most form hosting services send you the gathered data in an e-mail message.

- Not all form hosting services are the same. Although they generally all process forms in exchange for advertising, some ads are not as intrusive as others. For example, Response-o-Matic **(Figure 11.13)** only shows their ad in the Thank You page and e-mail, not on the form itself. That means you can design the form to fit in perfectly with the rest of your site.

Find extra tips, the source code for examples, and more at www.cookwood.com

Creating Text Boxes

Text boxes can contain one line of free-form text—that is, anything that the visitor wants to type—and are typically used for names, addresses, and the like.

To create a text box:

1. If desired, type the label that will identify the text box to your visitor (for example, **Name:**).

2. Type **<INPUT TYPE="text"**.

3. Type **NAME="name"**, where *name* is the text that will identify the input data to the server (and your script).

4. If desired, type **VALUE="value"**, where *value* is the data that will initially be shown in the field and that will be sent to the server if the visitor doesn't type something else.

5. If desired, define the size of the box on your form by typing **SIZE=n**, replacing *n* with the desired width of the box, measured in characters.

6. If desired, type **MAXLENGTH=n**, where n is the maximum number of characters that can be entered in the box.

7. Finish the text box by typing a final **>**.

✔ Tips

- Even if your visitor skips the field (and you haven't set the default text with the VALUE attribute), the NAME attribute is still sent to the server (with an undefined, empty VALUE).

- The default SIZE is 20. However, visitors can type up to the limit imposed by the MAXLENGTH attribute. Still, for larger, multi-line entries, it's better to use text areas *(see page 198)*.

---

code.html

Name: <INPUT TYPE="text" NAME="name">

Address: <INPUT TYPE="text" NAME="address" SIZE=30>

<P>City: <INPUT TYPE="text" NAME="city">

State: <INPUT TYPE="text" NAME="state" SIZE=2 MAXLENGTH=2>

Zipcode: <INPUT TYPE="text" NAME="zip" SIZE=5 MAXLENGTH=5>

Figure 11.16 *While it's essential to set the NAME attribute for each text box, you only have to set the VALUE attribute when you want to add default values for a text box.*

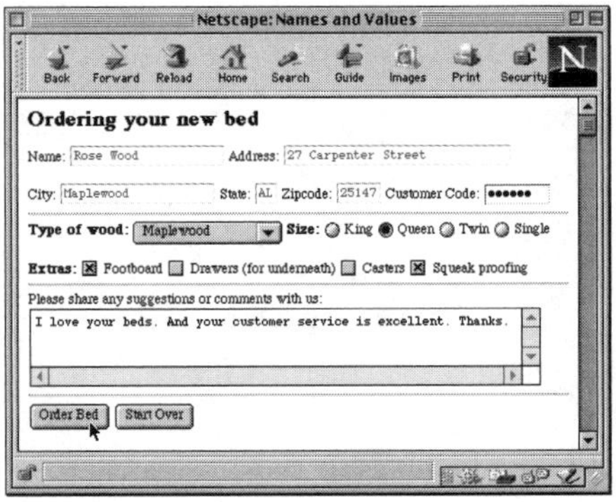

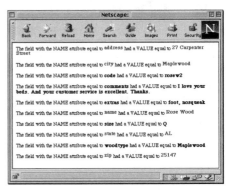

Figure 11.17 *Text boxes can be different sizes to accommodate different types of fields.*

Figure 11.18 *It's important to give descriptive names to your text boxes (with the NAME attribute) so that you know what information you're receiving.*

code.html

Customer Code: <INPUT TYPE="password" NAME="code" SIZE=8>

Figure 11.19 *The NAME attribute identifies the password when you compile the data with your form-parsing script.*

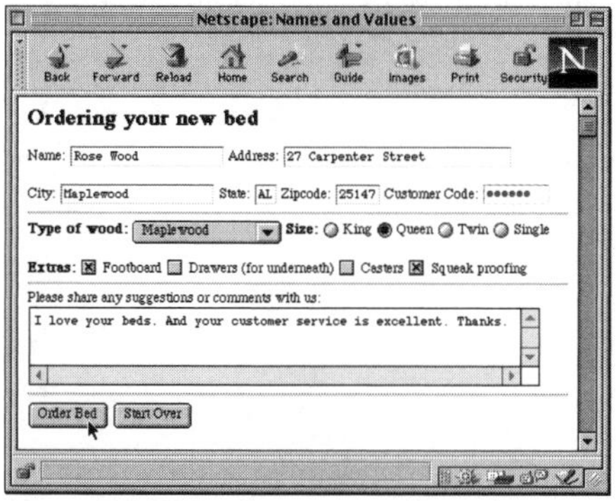

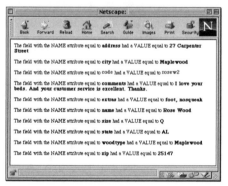

Figure 11.20 *When the visitor enters a password in a form, the password is hidden with bullets.*

Figure 11.21 *The password data appears as regular text after processing by a form-parsing script. Password boxes are not high-security! (See second to last tip.)*

Creating Password Boxes

The only difference between a password box and a text box is that whatever is typed in the former is hidden by bullets or asterisks. The information is *not* encrypted when sent to the server.

To create password boxes:

1. If desired, type the label that will identify the password box to your visitor (for example, **Enter password:**).

2. Type **<INPUT TYPE="password"**.

3. Type **NAME="name"**, where *name* is the text that will identify the input data to the server (and your script).

4. If desired, define the size of the box on your form by typing **SIZE=n**, replacing *n* with the desired width of the box, measured in characters.

5. If desired, type **MAXLENGTH=n**, where n is the maximum number of characters that can be entered in the box.

6. Finish the text box by typing a final **>**.

✔ Tips

- Even if nothing is entered in the password box, the NAME is still sent to the server (with an undefined VALUE).

- You could set default text for VALUE (as in step 4 on page 196), but that kind of defeats the purpose of a password.

- The only protection the password box offers is from folks peering over your visitor's shoulder as she types in her password. Since the data is not encrypted when it is sent to the server, moderately experienced crackers can discover the password without much trouble.

- To password protect a page, see page 311.

Creating Password Boxes

Creating Larger Text Areas

In some cases, you want to give the visitor more room to write. Unlike text boxes *(see page 196)*, text areas may be as large as your page, and will expand as needed if the person enters more text than can fit in the display area. They're perfect for eliciting questions and comments.

To create larger text areas:

1. If desired, type the explanatory text that will identify the text area.

2. Type **<TEXTAREA**.

3. Type **NAME="name"**, where *name* is the text that will identify the input data to the server (and your script).

4. If desired, type **ROWS=n**, where *n* is the height of the text area in rows. The default value is 4.

5. If desired, type **COLS=n**, where *n* is the width of the text area in characters. The default value is 40.

6. If desired, type **WRAP** so that when the visitor types, the lines are automatically wrapped within the margins.

7. Type **>**.

8. Type the default text, if any, for the text area. You may not add any HTML coding here.

9. Type **</TEXTAREA>** to complete the text area.

✔ Tips

- There is no use for the VALUE attribute with text areas.

- Visitors can enter up to 32,700 characters in a text area. Scroll bars will appear when necessary.

Figure 11.22 *The VALUE attribute is not used with the TEXTAREA tag. Default values are set by adding text between the opening and closing tags (as in "Comments?" here).*

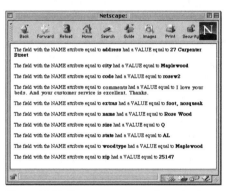

Figure 11.23 *The visitor can override the default text simply by typing over it.*

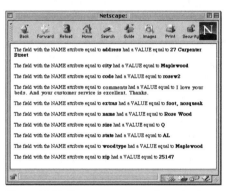

Figure 11.24 *Text areas are great for getting longer comments and suggestions from visitors. They are typically used in guestbooks and bulletin boards.*

Creating Larger Text Areas

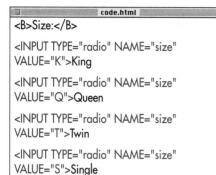

```
code.html
<B>Size:</B>

<INPUT TYPE="radio" NAME="size"
VALUE="K">King

<INPUT TYPE="radio" NAME="size"
VALUE="Q">Queen

<INPUT TYPE="radio" NAME="size"
VALUE="T">Twin

<INPUT TYPE="radio" NAME="size"
VALUE="S">Single
```

Figure 11.25 *The NAME attribute serves a dual purpose for radio buttons: it links the radio buttons in a given set and it identifies the values when they are sent to the script. The VALUE attribute is crucial since the visitor has no way of typing a value.*

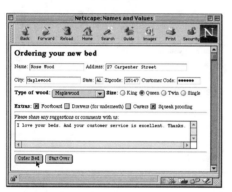

Figure 11.26 *The radio buttons themselves are created with the HTML tags. The labels (King, Queen, etc.) are created with plain text alongside the HTML tags.*

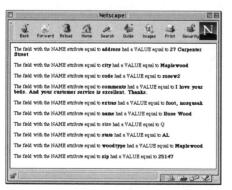

Figure 11.27 *Note that it is the VALUE (Q) and not the label (Queen) that gets sent to the script.*

Creating Radio Buttons

Remember those old-time car radios with big black plastic buttons? Push one to listen to WFCR; push another for WRNX. You can never push two buttons at once. Radio buttons on forms work the same way (except you can't listen to the radio).

To create a radio button:

1. If desired, type the introductory text for your radio buttons. You might use something like **Select one of the following**.

2. Type **<INPUT TYPE="radio"**.

3. Type **NAME="radioset"**, where *radioset* both identifies the data sent to the script and also links the radio buttons together, ensuring that only one per set can be checked.

4. Type **VALUE="data"**, where *data* is the text that will be sent to the server if the radio button is checked, either by you (in step 5) or by the visitor.

5. If desired, type **CHECKED** to make the radio button active by default when the page is opened. (You can only do this to one radio button in the set.)

6. Type the final **>**.

7. Type the text that identifies the radio button to the visitor. This is often the same as VALUE, but doesn't have to be.

8. Repeat steps 2-7 for each radio button in the set.

✔ Tip

■ If you don't set the VALUE attribute, the word "on" is sent to the script. It's not particularly useful since you can't tell which button in the set was pressed.

Creating Radio Buttons

Creating Checkboxes

While radio buttons can accept only one answer per set, a visitor can check as many checkboxes in a set as they like. Like radio buttons, checkboxes are linked by the value of the NAME attribute.

To create checkboxes:

1. If desired, type the introductory text (something like **Select one or more of the following**) for your checkboxes.

2. Type **<INPUT TYPE="checkbox"**. (Notice there is no space in the word *checkbox*.)

3. Type **NAME="boxset"**, where *boxset* both identifies the data sent to the script and also links the checkboxes together.

4. Type **VALUE="value"** to define a value for each checkbox. The value will be sent to the server if the checkbox is checked (either by the visitor, or by you as described in step 5).

5. Type **CHECKED** to make the checkbox checked by default when the page is opened. You (or the visitor) may check as many checkboxes as desired.

6. Type **>** to complete the checkbox.

7. Type the text that identifies the checkbox to the user. This is often the same as the VALUE, but doesn't have to be.

8. Repeat steps 2-7 for each checkbox in the set.

✔ Tip

■ If you don't set the VALUE attribute, the word "on" is sent to the script. It's not particularly useful since you can't tell which box in the set was checked.

```
code.html
<P><B>Extras:</B>

<INPUT TYPE="checkbox" NAME="extras"
VALUE="foot">Footboard

<INPUT TYPE="checkbox" NAME="extras"
VALUE="drawers">Drawers (for underneath)

<INPUT TYPE="checkbox" NAME="extras"
VALUE="casters">Casters

<INPUT TYPE="checkbox" NAME="extras"
VALUE="nosqueak">Squeak proofing
```

Figure 11.28 *Notice how the label text (not highlighted) does not need to match the VALUE attribute. That's because the label text identifies the checkboxes to the visitor in the browser while the VALUE identifies the data to the script.*

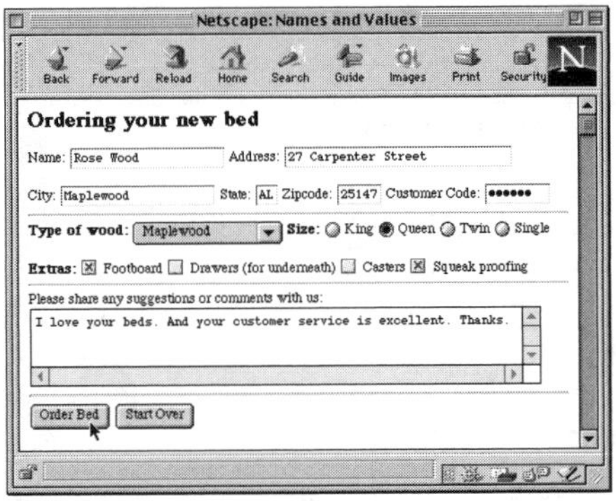

Figure 11.29 *The visitor can check as many boxes as necessary. Each corresponding value will be sent to the script, together with the checkbox set's name.*

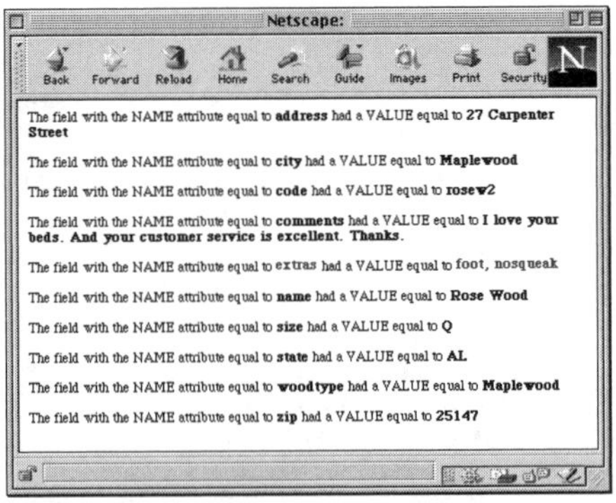

Figure 11.30 *Since the visitor has chosen two checkboxes, both values (but not their labels, of course) are sent to the script. This particular script separates multiple values with a comma.*

```
┌──────────────────────────────────┐
│▒▒▒         code.html         ▒▒▒│
├──────────────────────────────────┤
<B>Type of wood:</B>

<SELECT NAME="woodtype">

<OPTION VALUE="Mahogany">Mahogany

<OPTION VALUE="Maplewood">Maplewood

<OPTION VALUE="Pine">Pine

<OPTION VALUE="Cherry">Cherry

</SELECT>
└──────────────────────────────────┘
```

Figure 11.31 *Menus are made up of two HTML tags: SELECT and OPTION. You set the common NAME attribute in the SELECT tag and the individual VALUE attribute in each of the OPTION tags.*

Figure 11.32 *There's no way for a visitor to select nothing in a menu unless you set the SIZE attribute. The default selection is either the first option in the menu or the one you've set as SELECTED in step 8.*

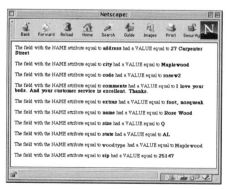

Figure 11.33 *Notice that the NAME attribute (wood-type) and not the label (Type of wood:) is what gets sent to the script.*

Creating Menus

Menus are perfect for offering your visitors a choice from a given set of options.

To create menus:

1. Type the introductory text, if desired.

2. Type **<SELECT**.

3. Type **NAME="name"**, where *name* will identify the data collected from the menu when it is sent to the server.

4. If desired, type **SIZE=n**, where *n* represents the height (in lines) of the menu.

5. If desired, type **MULTIPLE** to allow your visitor to select more than one menu option (with Ctrl or Command).

6. Type **>**.

7. Type **<OPTION**.

8. Type **SELECTED** if you want the option to be selected by default.

9. Type **VALUE="value"**, where *value* specifies the data that will be sent to the server if the option is selected.

10. Type **>**.

11. Type the option name as you wish it to appear in the menu.

12. Repeat steps 7-11 for each option.

13. Type **</SELECT>**.

✔ Tips

■ If you add the SIZE attribute in step 4, the menu appears more like a list, and there is no automatically selected option (unless you use SELECTED—see step 8).

■ If SIZE *(see step 4)* is bigger than the number of options, visitors can deselect all values by clicking in the empty space.

Creating Menus

If you have a particularly large menu with many options, you may want to group the options into categories and place them in submenus.

To create a menu with submenus:

1. Create a menu as described on page 201.

2. Before the first <OPTION> tag in the first group that you wish to place together in a submenu, type **<OPTGROUP**.

3. Type **LABEL="submenutitle">**, where *submenutitle* is the header for the submenu.

4. After the last <OPTION> tag in the group, type **</OPTGROUP>**.

5. Repeat steps 2–4 for each submenu.

✔ Tips

- You can add **LABEL="option_name"** to the OPTION tag to specify what the menu option should say. However, while this is standard HTML 4, neither Explorer nor Navigator uses this information properly. If there is no LABEL attribute, the browser automatically uses the text that follows the OPTION tag (as described in step 11 on page 201).

- Submenus, despite being part of the official HTML 4 specifications, are not yet supported by Explorer or Netscape.

```
code.html

How old are you?

<SELECT NAME=menu SIZE=5 MULTPLE>

<OPTGROUP LABEL="10-19">
<OPTION VALUE="10">10
<OPTION VALUE="11">11
<OPTION VALUE="12">12
<OPTION VALUE="13">13
<OPTION VALUE="14">14
<OPTION VALUE="15">15
<OPTION VALUE="16">16
<OPTION VALUE="17">17
<OPTION VALUE="18">18
<OPTION VALUE="19">19
</OPTGROUP>

<OPTGROUP LABEL="20-29">
<OPTION VALUE="20">20
```

Figure 11.34 *Each submenu has a title, specified in the LABEL attribute of the OPTGROUP tag, and a series of options (defined with OPTION tags and regular text).*

Creating Menus

```
code.html
<FORM METHOD=POST
ACTION="http://www.yoursite.com/cgi-bin/
uploadfile.cgi" ENCTYPE="multipart/form-data" >

Name: <INPUT TYPE="text" NAME="firstname"
SIZE=20>

<P><B>What files are you sending?</B>

<BR><INPUT TYPE="file" NAME="files"
SIZE=40>

<INPUT TYPE="submit" Name="Submit"
```

Figure 11.35 *There are two crucial steps in allowing visitors to upload files. First, make sure you use the POST method in the FORM tag. Second, don't forget to add the ENCTYPE attribute.*

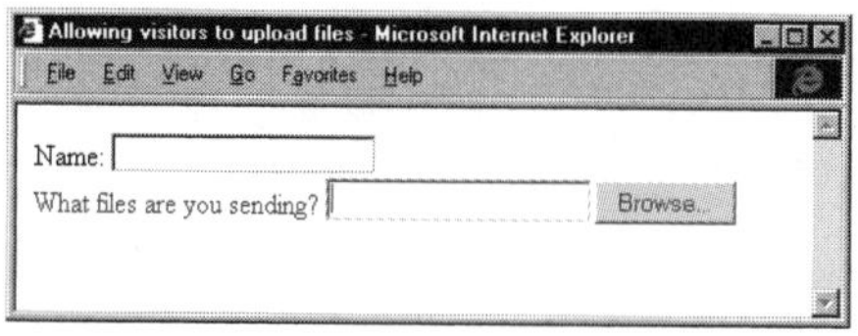

Figure 11.36 *When you create a file upload area, both a field where the visitor can type the path to the file and a Browse button (so the visitor can use an Open dialog box to choose the file) appear on your page.*

Allowing Visitors to Upload Files

If the information you need from the folks filling out your form is complicated, you might want to have them upload an entire file to your server.

To allow visitors to upload files:

1. Type **<FORM METHOD=POST ACTION= "upload.cgi">** where *upload.cgi* is the URL of a special CGI script that processes incoming files. Most regular form parsing scripts won't be enough.

2. Type **ENCTYPE="multipart/form-data"**. The ENCTYPE attribute ensures that the file is uploaded in the proper format.

3. Type the caption for the file upload area so your visitors know what to do. Something like **What file would you like to upload?** would work well.

4. Type **<INPUT TYPE="file"** to create a file upload box and a Browse button.

5. Type **NAME="title"**, where *title* identifies to the server the files being uploaded.

6. If desired, type **SIZE=n**, where *n* is the width, in characters, of the field in which the visitor will enter the path and file name.

7. Type the final **>**.

8. Complete the form as usual.

✔ Tips

- The SIZE attribute is optional, but since most paths and file names are pretty long, it's a good idea to set it at 40 or 50. The default is 20.

- You can't use the GET method for forms that allow file uploading.

- You can find CGI scripts for uploading files at *www.cgi-resources.com*.

Allowing Visitors to Upload Files

About Hidden Fields

HTML forms allow for a special kind of field that doesn't appear in the browser, and yet is part of the form. These hidden fields seem counterproductive at first glance: if your visitors can't see them, how will they fill them in? The answer is they won't. Instead, you will use hidden fields to store information gathered from an earlier form so that it can be combined with the present form's data.

Imagine, for example, that on the first page, you ask for a visitor's name, address, and telephone number. You then want to send them to your catalog page where they can choose which piece of furniture they wish to order. Instead of asking them for their personal data a second time, you can use a CGI script to collect the data from the first form and then generate the hidden fields that will contain this data in the second form. Then, when you go to process the data from the second form, all of the fields, including both the items ordered and the personal data, will be analyzed.

Don't get carried away by the word *hidden*. While hidden fields are not shown by the browser, they still form part of the HTML code that makes up the page (so the CGI script can get at them), and thus are not at all invisible if someone should look at the source code for your page *(see page 310)*.

```
code.html
<FORM METHOD=POST
ACTION="whatever.cgi">

<INPUT TYPE="hidden" NAME="name"
VALUE="value">

<INPUT TYPE=submit VALUE="Submit Data">
```

Figure 11.37 *An excerpt from the HTML file used to create the form shows the syntax for hidden elements. It doesn't make much sense to write such code yourself and thus I'm reluctant to create such an example. Instead, your CGI script should generate this code.*

Adding Hidden Fields to a Form

Although you hardly ever add hidden fields to an HTML document yourself, you'll have to know how to do it in order to write a CGI script that generates the code for the fields.

To add hidden fields to a form:

1. Within the form on your HTML page, type **<INPUT TYPE="hidden"**.

2. Type **NAME="name"**, where *name* is a short description of the information to be stored.

3. Type **VALUE="value"**, where *value* is the information itself that is to be stored.

4. Type **>**.

✔ Tips

■ It doesn't matter where the hidden fields appear in your form since they won't appear in the browser anyway. As long as they are within the opening and closing FORM tags, you're OK.

■ You don't have to use the quotation marks around the name and value if the name and value are comprised of only alphanumeric characters—that is, no spaces and no funny symbols. Since quotation marks have a special meaning in a Perl script and will thus need to be backslashed to get rid of that special meaning, it's often simpler to leave them out altogether where possible.

■ To create an element that will be submitted with the rest of the data when the visitor clicks the submit button but that is also visible to the visitor, create a regular form element and use the READONLY attribute *(see page 216)*.

Creating the Submit Button

All the information that your visitors enter won't be any good to you unless they send it to the server. You should always create a submit button for your forms so that the visitor can deliver the information to you. (If you use images as active elements in a FORM area, see page 210.)

To create a submit button:

1. Type **<INPUT TYPE="submit"**.

2. If desired, type **VALUE="submit message"** where *submit message* is the text that will appear in the button.

3. Type the final **>**.

✔ Tips

- If you leave out the VALUE attribute, the submit button will be labeled *Submit Query*, by default.

- The name-value pair for the submit button is only sent to the script if you set the NAME attribute. Therefore, if you omit the NAME attribute, you won't have to deal with the extra, usually superfluous submit data.

- On the other hand, you can create multiple submit buttons (with both the NAME and VALUE attributes) and then write your CGI script to react according to which submit button the visitor presses. Of course, it would be much easier just to use a set of radio buttons for the same purpose.

```
code.html
<INPUT TYPE="submit" VALUE="Order Bed">
```

Figure 11.38 *If you leave out the NAME attribute, the name-value pair for the submit button will not be passed to the script. Since you usually don't need this information, that's a good thing.*

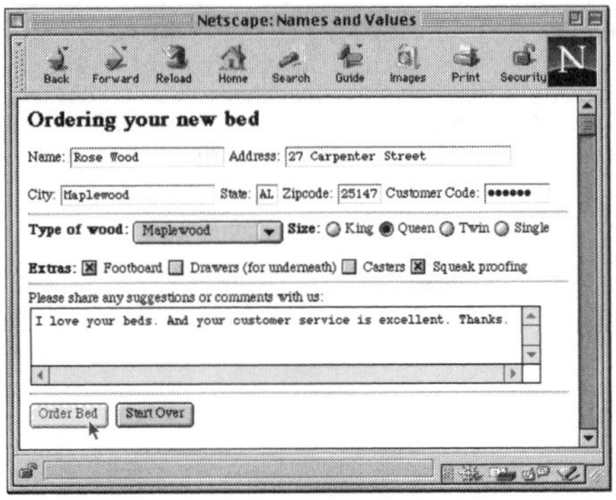

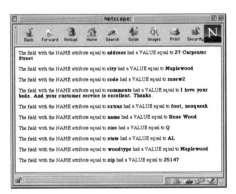

Figure 11.39 *The most important function of the submit button is to activate the script that will collect the data from the other fields. You can personalize the button's contents with the VALUE attribute. (The phrase* Order Bed *is clearer for your visitors than the default* Submit Query*).*

Figure 11.40 *If there is no NAME attribute specified for the submit button, not even the submit button's VALUE attribute will be gathered by the script. But, hey, what do you need it for anyway?*

```
                    code.html
<FORM ACTION="processform.cgi"
METHOD=POST>

<INPUT TYPE="radio" NAME="cats"
ACCESSKEY=w>Woody

<BR><INPUT TYPE="radio" NAME="cats"
ACCESSKEY=c>Cookie

<BR><INPUT TYPE="radio" NAME="cats"
ACCESSKEY=x>Xixona

<BR><INPUT TYPE="radio" NAME="cats"
ACCESSKEY=l>Llumeta

<BR><INPUT TYPE="radio" NAME="cats"
ACCESSKEY=a>All of them (Don't make me
choose!)

<P><BUTTON TYPE="submit" NAME="submit"
VALUE="submit" STYLE="font: 24pt Arial Black;
background:yellow"><IMG SRC="check.gif"
WIDTH=40 HEIGHT=40>Vote</BUTTON>

</FORM>

</BODY></HTML>
```

Figure 11.41 *If you want a submit button with an image, you'll have to create it with the BUTTON tag. It's probably a good idea to make the background transparent and save the image in GIF format so that it blends in with the button.*

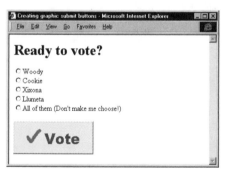

Figure 11.42 *The HTML code for a submit button with an image is a little more complicated, but looks so snazzy. (Although it would help if I could actually draw.)*

HTML 4 includes several tags that let you create prettier submit buttons. You can add an image, change the font, or even change the background color. That'll get them to submit that form!

To create a submit button with an image:

1. Type **<BUTTON TYPE="submit" NAME="submit" VALUE="submit"**

2. If desired, type **STYLE="font: 24pt Arial Black; background:yellow"** (or whatever) to change the appearance of the button text *(see page 257)*.

3. Type **>**.

4. Type the text, if any, that should appear on the left side of the image in the button.

5. Type **<IMG SRC="image.gif"** where *image.gif* is the name of the image that will appear on the button.

6. If desired, add any other image attributes.

7. Type **>** to complete the image.

8. Type the text, if any, that should appear on the right side of the image in the button.

9. Type **</BUTTON>**.

✔ Tips

- You can also use the BUTTON tag to create a submit button without an image. Just skip steps 5–7.

- For information on creating buttons with scripts, consult *Creating a Button that Executes a Script* on page 296.

- Only Explorer for Windows currently supports the BUTTON tag, despite the fact that it is a standard part of HTML 4.

Creating the Submit Button

Resetting the Form

If humans could fill out forms perfectly on the first try, there would be no erasers on pencils and no backspace key on your computer keyboard. You can give your visitors a reset button so that they can start over with a fresh form (including all the default values you've set).

To create a reset button:

1. Type **<INPUT TYPE="reset"**.
2. If desired, type **VALUE="reset message"** where *reset message* is the text that appears in the button. The default reset message is *Reset*.
3. Type **>**.

✔ Tip

- The name-value pair for the reset button is only sent to the script if you set the NAME attribute. Therefore, if you omit the NAME attribute, you won't have to deal with the completely superfluous reset data—which is usually something like "reset, Reset".

code.html
```
<INPUT TYPE="reset" VALUE="Start Over">
```

Figure 11.43 *You can use the VALUE attribute to set any text you wish for the reset button.*

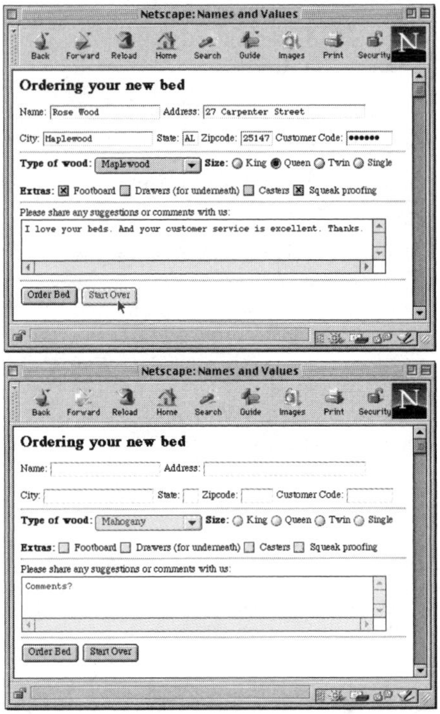

Figure 11.44 *If your visitor clicks the reset button, all the fields are set to their default values.*

```
code.html
<BR><INPUT TYPE="radio" NAME="cats"
ACCESSKEY=x>Xixona

<BR><INPUT TYPE="radio" NAME="cats"
ACCESSKEY=l>Llumeta

<BR><INPUT TYPE="radio" NAME="cats"
ACCESSKEY=a>All of them (Don't make me
choose!)

<P>

<BUTTON TYPE="submit" NAME="submit"
VALUE="Submit" STYLE="font: 24pt Arial Black;
background:yellow"><IMG SRC="check.gif"
WIDTH=40 HEIGHT=40
ALT="">Vote</BUTTON>

<BUTTON TYPE="reset" NAME="reset"
VALUE="reset" STYLE="font: 24pt Arial Black;
background:yellow"><IMG SRC="reset.gif"
WIDTH=40 HEIGHT=40
ALT="">Reset</BUTTON>
```

Figure 11.45 *Make sure you set the TYPE to* reset. *Otherwise, the button won't actually do anything at all.*

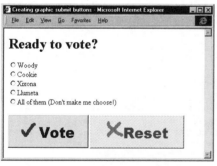

Figure 11.46 *You can also use the BUTTON tag to create a reset button with an image (and you can probably create a much prettier image than mine).*

With HTML 4 (and Explorer for the time being), you can add images, font choices, and even a background color to your reset button.

To create a reset button with an image:

1. Type **<BUTTON TYPE="reset" NAME="reset" VALUE="reset"**

2. If desired, type **STYLE="font: 24pt Arial Black; background:yellow"** (or whatever) to change the appearance of the button text *(see page 257)*.

3. Type **>**.

4. Type the text, if any, that should appear on the left side of the image in the button.

5. Type **<IMG SRC="image.gif"**, where *image.gif* is the name of the image that will appear on the button.

6. If desired, add any other image attributes.

7. Type **>** to complete the image.

8. Type the text, if any, that should appear on the right side of the image in the button.

9. Type **</BUTTON>**.

✔ Tips

■ You can also use the BUTTON tag to create a reset button without an image. Just skip steps 5–7.

■ For information on creating buttons with scripts, consult *Creating a Button that Executes a Script* on page 296.

■ Only Explorer 4 for Windows currently supports the BUTTON tag, despite the fact that it is a standard part of HTML 4.

Resetting the Form

Using an Image to Submit Data

You may use an image—called an active image—as a combination input element and submit button. In addition to submitting the data from the other fields in the form, a click on the image sends the current mouse coordinates to the server in two name-value pairs. The names are generated by adding .x and .y to the value of the NAME attribute. The values correspond to the actual horizontal and vertical locations (where 0,0 is the top-left corner) of the cursor.

To use an image to submit data:

1. Create a GIF or JPEG image *(see page 57)*.

2. Type **<INPUT TYPE="image"**.

3. Type **SRC="image.url"**, where *image.url* is the location of the image on the server.

4. Type **NAME="name"**. When the visitor clicks on the image, the x and y coordinates of the mouse will be appended to the name defined here and sent to the server.

5. Type the final **>** to finish the active image definition for the form.

✔ Tips

■ Setting the VALUE attribute has no effect. The values are set to the mouse coordinates automatically.

■ *All* the form data is sent when the visitor clicks the active image **(Figure 11.49)**. Therefore, it's a good idea to explain how to use the active image and to place the image at the end of the form so that the visitor completes the other form elements before clicking the image and sending the data.

```
                    code.html
<BR><INPUT TYPE="radio" NAME="infotype"
VALUE="time">Local time

<INPUT TYPE="radio" NAME="infotype"
VALUE="weather">Local weather

<INPUT TYPE="radio" NAME="infotype"
VALUE="directions">Directions

<INPUT TYPE="radio" NAME="infotype"
VALUE="statistics">City statistics

<P><INPUT TYPE="image" SRC="zonemap.gif"
NAME="coord">

</FORM>
```

Figure 11.47 *If you use an active image, you don't need a submit button.*

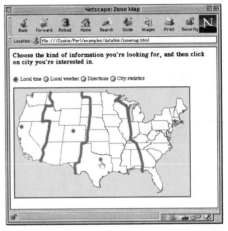

Figure 11.48 *You can have both regular form elements (like the radio buttons) and an image map in the same form. When the visitor clicks the map, all of the data is sent to the script.*

Figure 11.49 *The browser appends a period and an x to the NAME attribute (coord) and uses this name (coord.x) to identify the x coordinate of the location where the visitor clicked. The same happens with the y coordinate. Notice that the information from the radio button is also collected.*

```
code.html
<FIELDSET>

<LEGEND>Personal Information</LEGEND>

<P>Name: <INPUT TYPE="text"
NAME="firstname" SIZE=15><BR>

E-mail: <INPUT TYPE="text" NAME="email"
SIZE=25>

</FIELDSET>

<FIELDSET>

<LEGEND ALIGN=right>Comments</LEGEND>

Please let us know what you think:<BR>

<TEXTAREA COLS="40" ROWS="7"
NAME="comments" WRAP><B>I</B> think
your cats are...

</TEXTAREA>

</FIELDSET>

<INPUT TYPE="submit" NAME="Submit"
VALUE="Send info">

</FORM>
```

Figure 11.50 *The FIELDSET tag is ideal for separating your form into smaller, more easily understood chunks.*

Figure 11.51 *The fieldsets are outlined with a thin line. The legend appears at the top right or top left.*

Organizing the Form Elements

If you have a lot of information to fill out on a form, you can group related elements together to make the form easier to follow. The easier it is for your visitors to understand the form, the more likely they are to fill it out correctly.

To organize the form elements:

1. Below the FORM tag but above any form elements that you wish to have contained in the first group, type **<FIELDSET>**.

2. Type **<LEGEND**.

3. If desired, type **ALIGN=direction** where *direction* is top, bottom, left, or right.

4. Type **>**.

5. Type the text for the legend.

6. Type **</LEGEND>** to complete the legend.

7. Create the form elements that should belong in the first group. For more information, see pages 196–210.

8. Type **</FIELDSET>** to complete the first group of form elements.

9. Repeat steps 1-8 for each group of form elements.

✔ Tips

- You don't have to create a legend. To omit it, skip steps 2-6. In fact, you don't have to organize your form into groups at all. While it is a useful tool, it's completely optional.

- At press time, only Internet Explorer for Windows recognized field set definitions. And it only aligns legends to the left or right.

Formally Labeling Form Parts

As you've seen, the explanatory information next to a form element is generally just plain text. For example, you might type "First name" before the Text field where the visitor should type her name. HTML 4 provides a method for marking up labels so that you can formally link them to the associated element and use them for scripting or other purposes.

To formally label form parts:

1. Type **<LABEL**.

2. Type **FOR="idname">**, where *idname* is the value of the ID attribute in the corresponding form element.

3. Type the contents of the label.

4. Type **</LABEL>**.

✔ Tips

■ You have to use the ID attribute in the form element's tag in order to mark it with a LABEL. For example, you might have <INPUT TYPE=text SIZE=15 ID=firstname>. For more details about the ID attribute, consult *Identifying Particular Tags* on page 250.

■ Labels are part of HTML 4, but at press time, neither Explorer nor Communicator supports them. And frankly, they're rather a pain for what they're worth. Personally, I'd leave them out.

■ A more effective labeling technique uses the TITLE attribute. For more information, consult *Labeling Elements in a Web Page* on page 320.

```
code.html
<HTML><HEAD><TITLE>Formally labeling form
parts</TITLE></HEAD>

<BODY>

<FORM METHOD=POST
ACTION="processform.cgi">

<LABEL FOR="firstname">Name: </LABEL>

<INPUT TYPE="text" NAME="firstname"
ID="firstname" SIZE=20><BR>

<LABEL FOR="email">E-mail address:</LABEL>

<INPUT TYPE="text" NAME="email"
ID="email">

</FORM>

</BODY></HTML>
```

Figure 11.52 *You link a label to its form element with the FOR and ID attributes.*

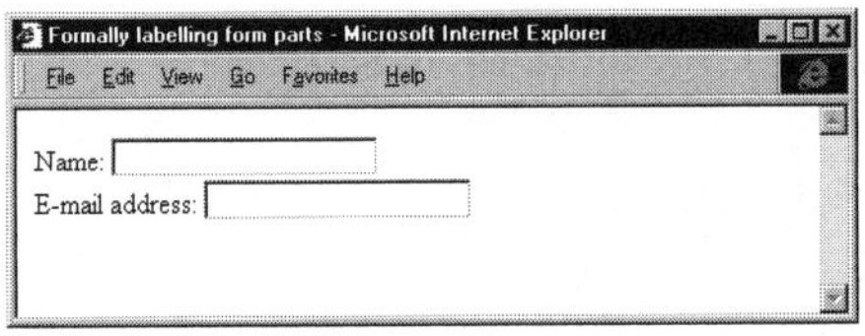

Figure 11.53 *There's no outward difference in appearance when you use labels—at least not yet.*

```
┌────────────────────────────────────┐
│░░░░░░░░░░░ code.html ░░░░░░░░░░░░░ ▓│
├────────────────────────────────────┤
│ <HTML><HEAD><TITLE>Setting the tab │
│ order</TITLE></HEAD>               │
│                                    │
│ <BODY>                             │
│                                    │
│ <A HREF="moreinfo.html" TABINDEX=4>About │
│ our company</A>                    │
│                                    │
│ <H1>Please tell us more about yourself:</H1> │
│                                    │
│ <FORM METHOD=POST                  │
│ ACTION="processform.cgi" >         │
│                                    │
│ <BR>Name: <INPUT TYPE="text"       │
│ NAME="firstname" SIZE=20 TABINDEX=1> │
│                                    │
│ <BR>E-mail address: <INPUT TYPE="text" │
│ NAME="email" TABINDEX=2>           │
│                                    │
│ <BR>Hobbies: <INPUT TYPE="text"    │
│ NAME="hobbies" TABINDEX=3>         │
│                                    │
│ </FORM>                            │
│                                    │
│ </BODY></HTML>                     │
└────────────────────────────────────┘
```

Figure 11.54 *You can add the TABINDEX attribute to links, form elements, and client-side image maps.*

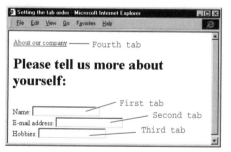

Figure 11.55 *With forms on a page that begins with a link, you may want to change the tab order so that the first tab takes you to the first field, not the first link.*

Setting the Tab Order

By pressing the Tab key, visitors can move through the fields in your form from top to bottom. Depending on your form's layout, you may prefer to set the tab order yourself so that the visitor fills out all the fields in a particular group before going on to the next group.

To set the tab order:

In the form element's tag, type **TABINDEX=n**, where *n* is the number that indicates the tab order.

✔ Tips

- The value for TABINDEX can be any number between 0 and 32767.

- By default, the tab order depends on the order of the elements in the HTML code. When you change the tab order, the lower numbered elements are activated first, followed by higher numbered elements.

- In a form, you can assign tab order to text fields, password fields, checkboxes, radio buttons, text blocks, menus, and buttons.

- You can also assign tab order to links and client-side image maps. For more information, consult *Setting the Tab Order for Links* on page 127 or *Creating a Client-Side Image Map* on page 130, respectively.

- OK, I cannot tell a lie. The first time your visitor hits the Tab key, the Address field (where the current URL is displayed) is activated (even if its toolbar is hidden). Then, the next tab brings the visitor where *you* say.

Setting the Tab Order

Adding Keyboard Shortcuts

One great new feature of HTML 4 is the ability to add keyboard shortcuts to different parts of your page, including form elements. When the visitor types the keyboard shortcut, the form element is made active for further input (in the case of a text field) or selected (like a radio button).

To add a keyboard shortcut to a form element:

1. Inside the form element's tag, type **ACCESSKEY="**.

2. Type the keyboard shortcut (any letter or number).

3. Type the final **"**.

4. If desired, add information about the keyboard shortcut to the text so that the visitor knows that it exists.

✔ Tips

- I've only been able to get this to work on Internet Explorer for Windows (4 and 5).

- On Windows systems, to invoke the keyboard shortcut, visitors use the Alt key plus the letter you've assigned. On Macs, visitors will probably use the Command key (although it doesn't work yet).

- Keyboard shortcuts that you choose may override the browser's shortcuts. If you assign a popular shortcut used in a browser to some part of your form (like S for Save), you may annoy your visitors. Keep in mind though, that at least on Windows machines, the important browser keyboard shortcuts go with the Ctrl key, not Alt.

```
code.html
<H1>Vote for the cutest cat:</H1>

<FORM ACTION="processform.cgi"
METHOD="POST">

<BR><INPUT TYPE="radio" NAME="cats"
ACCESSKEY=w>Woody (Alt-W)

<BR><INPUT TYPE="radio" NAME="cats"
ACCESSKEY=c>Cookie (Alt-C)

<BR><INPUT TYPE="radio" NAME="cats"
ACCESSKEY=x>Xixona (Alt-X)

<BR><INPUT TYPE="radio" NAME="cats"
ACCESSKEY=l>Llumeta (Alt-L)

<BR><INPUT TYPE="radio" NAME="cats"
ACCESSKEY=a>All of them (Don't make me
choose!) (Alt-A)<BR><INPUT TYPE="submit"
NAME="submit" VALUE="Vote">

</FORM>
```

Figure 11.56 *Add keyboard shortcuts to your form elements with the ACCESSKEY attribute.*

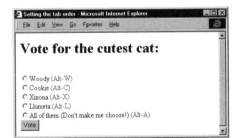

Figure 11.57 *When the visitor views the page, no item is selected. It's a good idea to show the keyboard shortcuts so that the visitor knows they're available.*

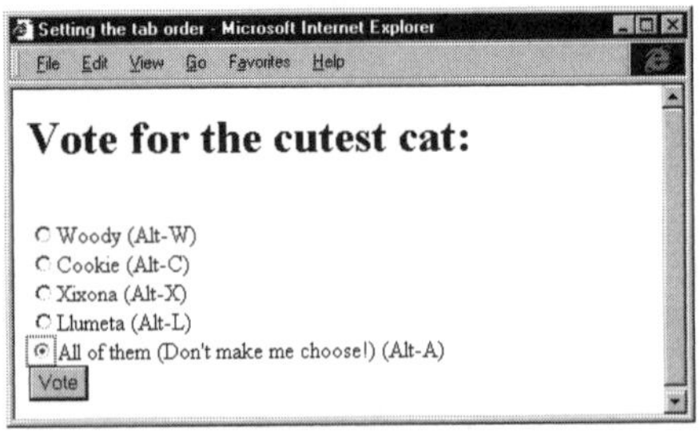

Figure 11.58 *Once the visitor uses the keyboard shortcut (Alt-A in this case), the radio button is activated and actually selected. In the case of a text box or text area, the cursor would be placed in the field, and the visitor could proceed to type in the information.*

Adding Keyboard Shortcuts

```
                code.html
<H1>Vote for the cutest cat:</H1>

<FORM ACTION="processform.cgi"
METHOD="POST">

<BR><INPUT TYPE="radio" NAME="cats"
ACCESSKEY=w>Woody

<BR><INPUT TYPE="radio" NAME="cats"
ACCESSKEY=c>Cookie

<BR><INPUT TYPE="radio" NAME="cats"
ACCESSKEY=x>Xixona

<BR><INPUT TYPE="radio" NAME="cats"
ACCESSKEY=l>Llumeta

<BR><INPUT TYPE="radio" NAME="cats"
ACCESSKEY=a>All of them (Don't make me
choose!)

<BR><INPUT TYPE="submit" NAME="submit"
VALUE="Vote" DISABLED>

</FORM>
```

Figure 11.59 *You can add the DISABLED attribute to any form element, but it probably makes most sense in the INPUT tag for a submit button.*

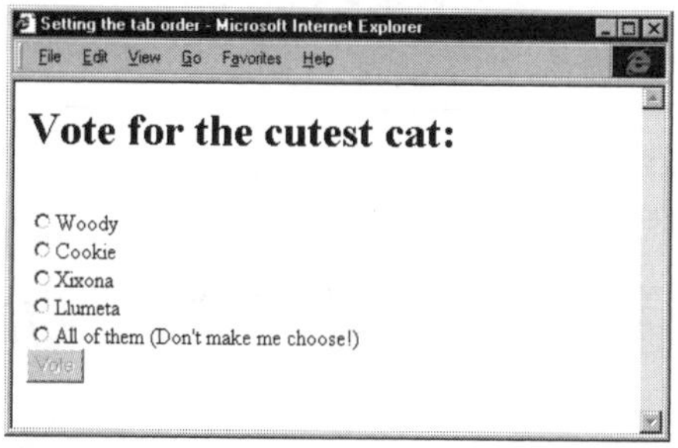

Figure 11.60 *In this example, the Vote button is grayed out because the visitor has not yet chosen any of the radio buttons. A script will be necessary to enable the submit button once a choice is made.*

Disabling Form Elements

In some cases, you may not want visitors to use certain parts of your form. For example, you might want to disable a submit button until all the required fields have been filled out.

To disable a form element:

In the form element's tag, type **DISABLED**.

✔ Tips

- The only way you can change the contents of a disabled form element is with a script. For more information on scripting, consult Chapter 17, *Scripts*. You'll also need some JavaScript expertise.

- If you disable a form element, its keyboard shortcut is also disabled. For more information on keyboard shortcuts, consult *Adding Keyboard Shortcuts* on page 214.

Keeping Elements from Being Changed

Sometimes it may be necessary to automatically set the contents of a form element and keep the visitor from changing it. For example, you could have the visitor confirm information, or you could show a past history of transactions and then submit that information again with the new data collected. You can do this by making the element "read-only".

To keep elements from being changed:

Type **READONLY** in the form element's tag.

✔ Tips

- You can use the READONLY attribute in text boxes, password boxes, checkboxes, radio buttons, and text areas.

- Setting the READONLY attribute is something like using a hidden field without making it hidden. For more information on hidden fields, consult *About Hidden Fields* on page 204.

```
code.html
<H1>Vote again:</H1>

<FORM METHOD=POST
ACTION="processform.cgi">

<BR>So far you've voted for

<TEXTAREA NAME="votehistory" COLS=25
ROWS=3 READONLY>Woody on Monday,
Cookie on Tuesday, Xixona on Thursday, and
Llumeta on Wednesday</TEXTAREA>

<BR><INPUT TYPE="radio" NAME="cats"
ACCESSKEY=w>Woody

<BR><INPUT TYPE="radio" NAME="cats"
ACCESSKEY=c>Cookie

<BR><INPUT TYPE="radio" NAME="cats"
ACCESSKEY=x>Xixona

<BR><INPUT TYPE="radio" NAME="cats"
ACCESSKEY=l>Llumeta

<BR><INPUT TYPE="radio" NAME="cats"
ACCESSKEY=a>All of them (Don't make me
choose!)

<BR><INPUT TYPE="submit" NAME="submit"
VALUE="Vote" DISABLED>

</FORM>
```

Figure 11.61 *Add the READONLY attribute to any form element that you want to show to visitors but that you don't want them to change.*

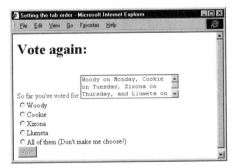

Figure 11.62 *In this example, the visitor's prior votes are displayed in the read-only text area. They can be viewed by the visitor and then submitted with the new vote.*

Multimedia

One of the things that has made the Web so popular is the fact that you can add graphics, sound, animations, and movies to your Web pages. While in the past, the prohibitive size of such files limited their effectiveness, newer technologies—including streaming audio and video, Flash, and Shockwave—make pages with dynamic multimedia effects much more accessible to those of us who don't have the latest, fastest Pentiums and G4s.

Multimedia files, however, continue to be very large, and as technology improves, they seem to get bigger still. Ten seconds of medium quality sound take up more than 200K, which will take your average visitor about a minute to download. A ten second file of a movie displayed in a tiny 2" x 3" window would be considerably larger.

In addition, since the Web population is diverse, and uses many different kinds of computers, you have to make sure that the files you provide can be viewed and heard by your visitors (or the largest number possible of them). The fact that the developers of multimedia technologies can't seem to agree on standards doesn't help in the least.

Please note that this chapter is meant to be an introduction to multimedia Web files, with a strong emphasis on the HTML code you need. I highly recommend a look at *Audio on the Web* by Jeff Patterson and Ryan Melcher and *Animation on the Web* by Sean Wagstaff. Both books are published by Peachpit Press.

Helper Applications and Plug-ins

Browsers are generally limited to displaying HTML, text, GIF, and JPEG files in the browser window. When a browser comes across any other kind of file—a strange image format, a sound or video, even an Excel file—it relies on two kinds of support: plug-ins and external helper applications.

You must use the proper extension for each file so that the browser knows what to do with it. The system of standardized extensions is known as MIME—Multipurpose Internet Mail Extensions *(see Table 12.1)*.

Plug-ins are mini-programs that add consoles or controls within a page itself in order to play a sound or display a movie. Your visitors might not even realize that the plug-in is even present since it seems like the multimedia effect is just another part of the page—all wholly enclosed in the browser window.

If there is no plug-in available, the browser will attempt to launch an external application, sometimes called a *helper app*, that can display the file. Visitors can use virtually any program as a helper app, though fast, small programs—specializing in viewing rather than creating—are probably the best choice **(Figure 12.2)**.

Finally, if the browser cannot find a suitable helper application, it will give the visitor the opportunity to save the file to their hard disk.

While some plug-ins are included with the browser software upon download, many others are not. If your visitors don't have the appropriate plug-in or helper application, they won't be able to view your files until they download such a program. While this may be easy and free, it still takes time. It's important to remember that including unusual files that require such a download may cost you some of your visitors.

MIME type	Extension(s)
image/gif	.gif
image/jpeg	.jpeg .jpg .jpe
image/pict	.pic .pict
image/tiff	.tif .tiff
image/x-xbitmap	.xbm
audio/basic	.au .snd
audio/aiff	.aiff .aif
audio/x-wav	.wav
video/quicktime	.qt .mov
video/mpeg	.mpg .mpeg .mpe
video/x-msvideo	.avi
application/mac-binhex40	.hqx
application/x-stuffit	.sit
application/x-macbinary	.bin
application/octet-stream	.exe
application/postscript	.ai .eps .ps
application/rtf	.rtf
application/x-compressed	.zip .z .gz .tgz
application/x-tar	.tar

Table 12.1: *It is extremely important to use the proper extension to identify your external files. If there is more than one possible extension, you can generally use whichever you prefer, as long as you follow the naming limitations of the server (e.g., DOS servers insist on three letter extensions).*

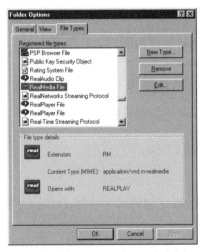

Figure 12.2 *Visitors can choose which helper application should be linked to which kinds of files by choosing View > Folder Options in the Windows Explorer window and then clicking the File Types tab.*

```
code.html
<HTML><HEAD><TITLE>Opening TIFFs</TITLE>
</HEAD><BODY>

Woody went through his own particular
psychedelic stage:<BR>

<A HREF="woodycolor.tiff">
<IMG SRC="woodycoloricon.gif"> 225K Tiff
image</A>

</BODY></HTML>
```

Figure 12.3 *Since a visitor has to take the time to download large images like the one referenced here, you should at least give them an idea of how big the image is.*

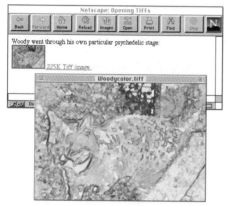

Figure 12.4 *Once the visitor clicks on the icon, the browser launches the helper application (in this case JPEGView) and the helper application shows the TIFF file.*

Non-Supported Images

While the major browsers can all display GIF, JPEG, and PNG images without much difficulty, you'll have to create a link to view any other kind of images with an external helper application.

To create a link to a non-supported image:

1. Create an image and save it in the desired format with the proper extension. *(See Table 12.1 on page 218.)*

2. In your HTML document where you want the image to appear, type **<A HREF="image.ext">** where *image.ext* is the name of the image file on the server with the appropriate extension.

3. If desired, use an icon to indicate the external image by typing **<IMG SRC="icon.gif">** where *icon.gif* is the location on the server of the icon.

4. Give a description of the image, including its size and format.

5. Complete the link by typing **</A>**.

✔ Tips

- Why bother with other formats besides GIF, JPEG, or PNG? Perhaps you want to provide non-expert visitors with a certain type of graphic image (TIFF, say) and you don't want them to have to bother with converting it.

- Since non-GIF/JPEG images generally will not appear inline, there is little advantage to using additional image formatting, like ALIGN or LOWSRC.

Non-Supported Images

Sound

You can add sound to your Web page in two ways: either as a file that is downloaded all at once to your visitor's computer and then replayed, or as a streaming file that is downloaded little bits at a time, and that starts to play even as it continues downloading. Both systems have advantages and disadvantages.

Non-streaming sound files are good for short, discrete sounds—including noises, spoken phrases, and short music clips. They are simpler to use, easier to set up, and require less effort for your visitor, that is, no plug-in is usually required. When creating or choosing non-streaming audio files, you should consider the quality, size, compression, and format of the files. The higher the quality, the larger the size, which affects the time the files take to download. Compression can help get files back down to a reasonable size but may create compatibility problems on various platforms. Perhaps the most important issue is format. I recommend using WAV format for all your non-streaming sound files. They are readable by both Macs and Windows.

Streaming audio is great for longer sounds that, because of their download time, would try your visitor's patience. Instead, folks can listen to the first part while the rest is downloading. Streaming audio is the only option for live broadcast. On the downside, it is slightly more complicated to create and sometimes requires a special server for delivery to your page. And your visitors may need to download a special plug-in the first time they try to listen to streaming audio. The most common streaming audio format is RealMedia.

You'll learn how to include both types of sound on your Web site in this section.

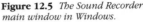

Click here to start recording.

Figure 12.5 *The Sound Recorder main window in Windows.*

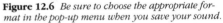

Figure 12.6 *Be sure to choose the appropriate format in the pop-up menu when you save your sound.*

Figure 12.7 *To create a sound with the Macintosh's Sound control panel, click Add.*

Figure 12.8 *Click Record to start recording your sound and Stop when you are finished. Then click Save to save your sound.*

Figure 12.9 *Finally, give your sound a name.*

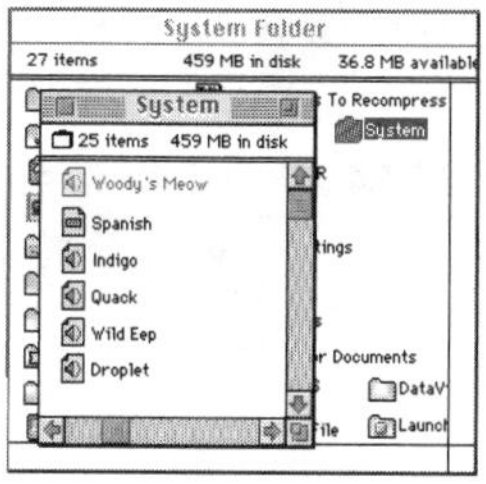

Figure 12.10 *Once you have created the sound, you can find it in the System file icon inside the System Folder. Drag it out and place it in the folder with the rest of your HTML files.*

Getting Sound

There are several ways you can get your hands on sound files.

- If your computer has a sound board and a microphone, you can record your own sounds. The most basic programs are Sound Recorder for Windows **(Figures 12.5–12.6)** or the Sound control panel for Macintosh **(Figures 12.7–12.10)**. For more advanced software with many more features, try taking a look at Syntrillium Software's Cool Edit *(www.syntrillium.com)* or Macromedia's SoundEdit *(www.macromedia.com)*

- For streaming audio, you'll need to download RealNetwork's RealProducer *(www.real.com)*.

- Or search for sounds at AltaVista by clicking the Audio button. At Yahoo, try *http://dir.yahoo.com/Computers_and_ Internet/Multimedia/Audio/Archives*.

✔ Tips

- The most popular sound formats on the Internet today are WAV (Microsoft's default sound format) and RA or RM (RealAudio or RealMedia). I recommend using the former for basic sound files and the latter for streaming audio.

- You can use CoolEdit or SoundEdit to convert an existing sound file into one of these more common formats.

- Just because you have the technology to copy your favorite band's CD and place it on your Web site, doesn't mean they won't sue your pants off. For an extremely helpful discussion of copyrights and electronic rights, I recommend you check out Ivan Hoffman's site: *www.ivanhoffman.com*.

Getting Sound

Embedding Sound in a Page

Both major browsers come with plug-ins that let them play sound right in the Web page itself without it being necessary for the visitor to download anything extra.

To embed sound in a page:

1. In your HTML document, type **<EMBED SRC="sound.url"**, where *sound.url* is the complete file name and extension for the sound file.

2. If desired, type **CONTROLS="form"**, where *form* determines how the sound controls should appear. The available options are *console*, *smallconsole*, *playbutton*, *pausebutton*, *stopbutton*, and *volumelever*.

   If you choose a kind of control, type **WIDTH=w HEIGHT=h** where *w* and *h* represent the width and height, respectively, of the type of control.

3. If desired, type **AUTOSTART=false** so that the sound doesn't play automatically when the visitor jumps to the page.

4. If desired, type **LOOP=n** to repeat the sound automatically *n* number of times. Or type **LOOP=true** to repeat the sound until the visitor clicks the Stop button (if you've provided one) or jumps to another page.

5. If desired, type **ALIGN=direction** to align the controls on the page. The ALIGN tag works the same for embedded sound as it does for images. For more information, see page 93.

6. Type the final **>**.

```
code.html
<HTML><HEAD><TITLE>Using LiveAudio to
embed sound on a page</TITLE></HEAD>
<BODY>
<H1>Pronunciation</H1>
Lots of people have asked me to add sound to my
"Learn Catalan" page so that they can hear how
you pronounce <EMBED SRC="bondia.wav"
CONTROLS="playbutton" WIDTH=25
HEIGHT=25 AUTOSTART=false>"Bon Dia" ,
<EMBED SRC="patom.wav"
CONTROLS="playbutton" WIDTH=25
HEIGHT=25 AUTOSTART=false>"Pa amb
tom&agrave;quet" and <EMBED
SRC="visca.wav" CONTROLS="playbutton"
WIDTH=25 HEIGHT=25 AUTOSTART=false >
"Visca Catalunya". Have a party. (Una festa...)
</BODY></HTML>
```

Figure 12.11 *If you're going to put a lot of sounds on one page, you can use just the play button to save space.*

Figure 12.12 *In this example, I've created three buttons so that visitors can easily play a short, individual sound.*

```
code.html
<HTML><HEAD><TITLE>Using LiveAudio to
embed sound on a page</TITLE></HEAD>

<BODY>

<H1>Dakota</H1>

<EMBED SRC="dakota.wav" AUTOSTART=true
LOOP=3 CONTROLS="smallconsole"
WIDTH=144 HEIGHT=15 ALIGN=right>

Dakota is Kevin's lovable golden lab. I haven't
actually met him, though I'm looking forward to
it. But I know he sounds something like this.

<P><EMBED SRC="dakota.wav"
CONTROLS="playbutton" WIDTH=37
HEIGHT=22 ALIGN=left HSPACE=10>

Click on the playbutton at left to hear Dakota
when he sees a squirrel outside.

</BODY></HTML>
```

Figure 12.13 *If you're going to put a lot of sounds on one page, you can use just the play button to save space.*

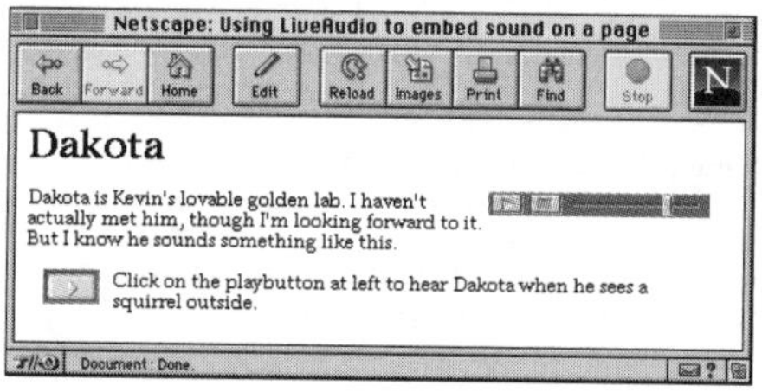

Figure 12.14 *The small console (right) contains, from right to left, a play button, stop button, and progress indicator. The independent play button is shown at bottom left.*

✔ Tips

- Netscape seems to be in a state of flux about the EMBED tag. I had a horrible time getting it to work consistently. Explorer, on the other hand, though it doesn't claim to support the EMBED tag at all, does so quite nicely.

- You can create a background sound that works with Netscape browsers by using the EMBED tag together with AUTOSTART=true but omitting the CONTROLS, HEIGHT, and WIDTH tags.

- The EMBED tag is an inline tag. It will not start a new line automatically. Instead, you'll have to precede it with a BR or P tag.

- You can also use the HSPACE and VSPACE tags to leave more space between the console and the surrounding text.

- There is also a more standard but less used OBJECT tag for embedding sound (and other files), but Netscape doesn't support it.

Embedding Sound in a Page

Adding a Link to a Sound

An easy way to add sound to your page is by adding a link to that sound. The user will then have to click the link to listen to the sound.

To add a link to a sound:

1. If desired, create a small icon that you can use to indicate the link to the sound and call it *soundicon.gif.*

2. Create the sound file. I recommend saving the file in WAV format *(see page 220).*

3. In your HTML document where you wish to place the link to the sound file, type **<A HREF="sound.wav">** where *sound.wav* is the location of the sound file on the server.

4. Type **<IMG SRC="soundicon.gif">** where *soundicon.gif* is the icon that will indicate the link to the sound that you created in step 1.

5. If desired, type the description, size, and format of the audio file.

6. Type **</A>** to complete the link.

✔ Tips

■ When your visitors click a link to an external sound, their browser will attempt to launch an appropriate helper application to play the sound. If there is no such application available, the browser will give the visitor the chance to simply save the sound file to their hard disk.

■ Give extra information to your visitors, including the format and size of the audio file, so that they can decide whether or not to download the sound.

■ Find out how big a sound file is by selecting it on the Desktop and choosing Properties (W) or Get Info (M).

```
code.html

<HTML><HEAD><TITLE>Listening to
sounds</TITLE></HEAD><BODY>

At night, Woody serenades the neighborhood
with his latest hit caterwaul:<P>

<A HREF="soundwoody.wav"><IMG
SRC="victrola.gif" WIDTH=52 HEIGHT=73>
40K Sound @ 22.3kHz</A>

<P>OK, I admit it. That's not Woody. It's me.
Makes the cats come investigate, just the same,
though.

</BODY></HTML>
```

Figure 12.15 *Always include information on your page about the size and recording quality of your sound.*

Figure 12.16 *When the visitor clicks the sound icon (the victrola) or the clickable text description of the sound, the browser downloads the sound and launches the helper application (in this case SoundMachine) which plays the sound.*

Adding a Link to a Sound

```
                code.html
<HTML><HEAD><TITLE>Inserting a background
sound for IE</TITLE></HEAD>

<BODY>

<H1>Dakota</H1>

<BGSOUND SRC="dakota.wav" LOOP=2>

Dakota is Kevin's lovable golden lab. I haven't
actually met him, though I'm looking forward to
it. But I know he sounds something like this.

</BODY></HTML>
```

Figure 12.17 *The BGSOUND tag can be placed any-where on the page. However, since Internet Explorer will play the sound as soon as it encounters the tag you may want to place the tag at the end of the page so that the visitor sees the page before hearing the sound.*

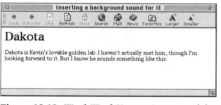

Figure 12.18 *Woof, Woof. You can't see sound, but trust me, if you play it loud enough, your cats will disappear.*

Adding Background Sound for Explorer

IE ONLY Internet Explorer has a special, non-standard tag that lets you link a sound to a page and have the sound play automatically whenever a visitor jumps to the page.

To add background sound:

1. In the HTML document, type **<BGSOUND SRC="sound.url"** where *sound.url* is the complete file name, including the extension of the sound.

2. If desired, type **LOOP=n** where *n* is the number of times you wish the sound to be played. Use **LOOP=-1** or **LOOP=infinite** to play the sound over and over.

3. Type the final **>**.

✔ Tips

- To create background sounds for both Explorer and Netscape users, use both the technique on this page as well as that described in the tip on page 223.

- Don't use a really obnoxious, annoying, or long sound (or even a particularly loud one) if you want people to come back to your page with any regularity.

- The BGSOUND tag recognizes WAV, AU, or MIDI formatted sounds.

Adding Background Sound for Explorer

Find extra tips, the source code for examples, and more at www.cookwood.com   **225**

Creating RealMedia Files

RealMedia files are not downloaded all at once but instead are streamed bit by bit to your visitors so that they don't have to wait for a complete download before listening. Although you can download the official RealServer—or your ISP may already have it installed on your server—you can also stream RealMedia files to your visitors for free with a regular Web server.

There are three components to adding Real-Media sound to your pages: the sound itself, a text file called a metafile that references the sound on your server, and the HTML code that points to the metafile.

To create a RealMedia sound:

1. Download RealProducer from RealMe-dia's site: *proforma.real.com/mario/ tools/producer.html?wp=699tools& src=prod.* (Or try *www.real.com.*)

2. Open RealProducer.

3. If you see the New Session - Choose Recording Wizard dialog box, check Don't Use Recording Wizards in the bottom-left corner **(Figure 12.19)**.

4. On the left side of the New Session dialog box that appears, choose Media Device to record a new sound or click File to convert an existing one **(Figure 12.20)**.

5. On the right side of the dialog box, choose a name for the RealMedia file.

6. Click OK.

7. In the main RealProducer window, fill out all the boxes in the dialog box as nec-essary **(Figure 12.21)**. If you're using a regular Web server (and not RealServer) choose Single-rate for Web Servers under File Type.

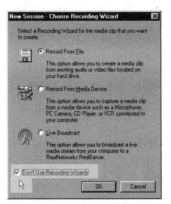

Figure 12.19 *Click the Don't Use Recording Wiz-ards option to have more control over your RealMedia sound.*

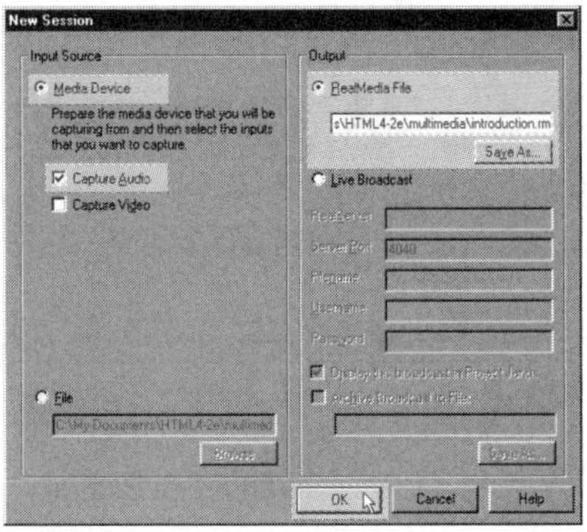

Figure 12.20 *In the left side of the box, choose whether to record a new sound or convert an exist-ing one. On the right side choose a file name for the new RealMedia file. Then click OK.*

Creating RealMedia Files

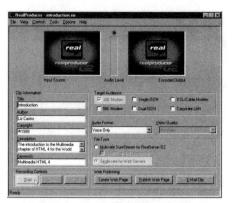

Figure 12.21 *In the main RealProducer window, fill in the boxes as desired. Be sure to select the proper speed for your target audience, and mark Single-rate for Web Servers in the lower center area of the window. Then click Start when you're ready to begin recording or encoding.*

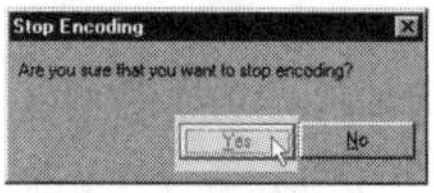

Figure 12.22 *After you click Stop in the main recording window, you'll have to click Yes here.*

8. Then click Start. If you're recording a new sound, you're on. If you're converting an existing sound it will be processed now.

9. If you're recording, click Stop to complete the recording and click Yes in the dialog box that appears **(Figure 12.22)**.

10. The RealMedia file with the name you chose in step 5 is created.

✔ Tips

- If you like, take advantage of the Recording Wizards that RealProducer provides you with to create your sound, metafile, and even your HTML page. Then, if you need to make any changes, consult the rest of this section.

- You can find more information about using RealMedia files with your Web pages at *www.real.com/devzone/library/ stream/index.html*.

- There are several versions available of RealProducer. The most basic is free and is the one I used in these examples.

- RealMedia sounds used to be called RealAudio. Now, since you can create streaming video, the files are more generically called RealMedia. You still may see many files out on the Web with the .ra extension (instead of .rm).

Creating RealMedia Files

Creating a RealMedia Metafile

A link or embedded RealMedia file does not point to the file itself, but rather to a file that points to the RealMedia file. The intermediary file is called a *metafile* and is simply a text file that lists the path of one or more RealMedia files.

Figure 12.23 *Open a text document and type the path to the RealMedia file, including the server, on its own line. You may list as many RealMedia files as you like.*

To create a metafile:

1. With your text editor, create a new blank file.

2. At the very top, type **http://www.your-server.com/path/realmediafile.rm**, where *http://www.yourserver.com/path* is the path to the directory on your server that contains the RealMedia files you created in step 5 on page 226 and *realmediafile.rm* is the actual name of the RealMedia file.

3. Repeat step 2 for each RealMedia sound that you want to play.

4. If you want to have the sound played in an independent RealMedia helper application (called RealPlayer), save the file as Text Only with the .ram extension.

   Or, if you want the console embedded in the page, save the metafile as Text Only with the .rpm extension.

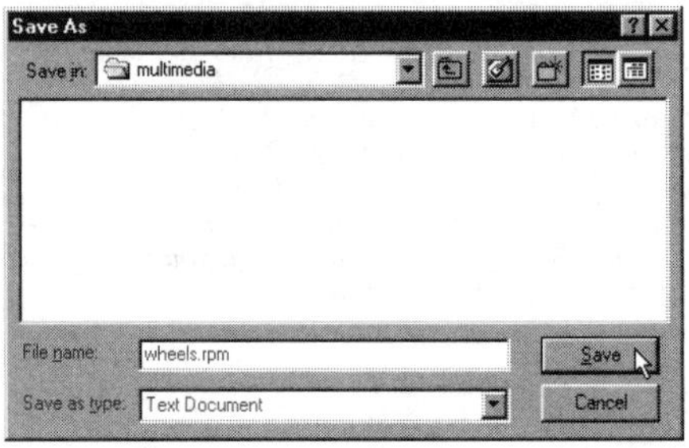

Figure 12.24 *Be sure to save the file in Text Only (also called Text Document or ASCII) format. Use the .ram if you're going to link to the sound; use .rpm for embedded sound.*

✔ Tips

- Be sure to save the file with the .ram extension when *linking* to a RealMedia sound *(see page 229)* and the .rpm extension when *embedding* RealMedia sound on a page *(see page 230)*.

- You may list as many RealMedia files as you like. They will play successively.

- Be sure to upload metafiles in ASCII mode. They're just text after all *(see page 334)*.

Creating a RealMedia Metafile

```
code.html
<HTML><HEAD><TITLE>Learning
Catalan</TITLE></HEAD><BODY>

<H1>Pronunciation</H1>

People are constantly asking me to add sound to
my Learn Catalan page so that they can hear
how words really sound. Well, now you can hear
me recite a <A HREF="pla.ram">whole
paragraph</A> in Catalan.

</BODY></HTML>
```

Figure 12.25 *Use the .ram extension when linking to RealMedia sounds that should be played with the external RealPlayer helper application.*

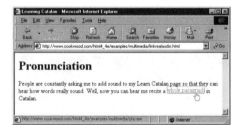

Figure 12.26 *A link to a RealMedia sound looks just like any other link.*

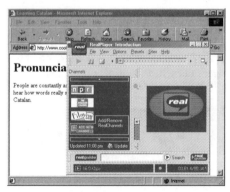

Figure 12.27 *When the visitor clicks a link to a RealMedia file, the external RealPlayer application is automatically launched and the sound is played.*

Linking to a RealMedia Sound

There are two ways to give your visitors access to RealMedia sounds. You can either create a link to them, in which case the browser will launch a helper application to deal with the file. Or you can embed the sound in the page *(see page 230)*.

To link to a RealMedia sound:

In your HTML page, type **<A HREF="meta-file.ram">click here</A>**, where *metafile.ram* is the name of the file you created in step 4 on page 228.

✔ Tip

■ Linking to a RealMedia sound is better supported than embedding the sound in the page.

Linking to a RealMedia Sound

Embedding RealMedia Files in Your Page

You can add a console to your page so that the effect is better integrated with the rest of your content.

To embed RealMedia sound in your page:

1. In your HTML page, type **<EMBED SRC="metafile.rpm"**, where *metafile.rpm* is the name of the file you saved in step 4 on page 228.

2. Type **TYPE="audio/x-pn-realaudio-plugin"**. (All three hyphens are required.)

3. Type **CONSOLE="label"**, where label identifies this and other related RealMedia sound controls.

4. Type **CONTROLS="form" HEIGHT=h WIDTH=w**, where *form*, *h*, and *w* correspond to the values shown here, respectively:

   All, 125, 275

   StopButton, 25, 35

   PlayButton, 25, 35

   ControlPanel, 40, 275

   ControlPanel,StatusBar, 60, 275

   ControlPanel,InfoVolumePanel, 105, 275

5. Type **LOOP=true** to have the sound or sounds play over and over again.

6. Type **NUMLOOP=n**, where *n* is the number of times the sound or sounds should be played.

```
<HTML><HEAD><TITLE>The start of a
career</TITLE></HEAD><BODY>

<H1>The Wheels on the Bus</H1>

Dear Auntie Becky:

<P>I've been learning lots of new songs lately,
but my favorite is still the one that you taught me:
<I>The Wheels on the Bus</I>.

<P><EMBED SRC="wheels.rpm"
TYPE="audio/x-pn-realaudio-plugin"
HEIGHT=60 WIDTH=275 CONSOLE="wheels"
CONTROLS="ControlPanel,StatusBar">

</BODY></HTML>
```

Figure 12.28 *Be sure to include the TYPE attribute so that the proper RealPlayer plug-in is used.*

Figure 12.29 *In this example, I've created a console with just the control panel and status bar.*

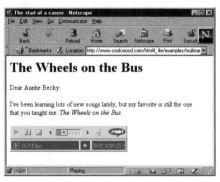

Figure 12.30 *Once the visitor presses the play button (left-pointing arrow), the status bar keeps them abreast of any problems transmitting the sound.*

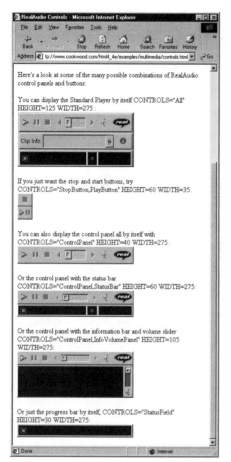

Figure 12.31 *You can customize the RealPlayer console to your page's needs.*

7. Type **SHUFFLE** to have multiple sounds played back in random order.

8. Type **NOLABELS=true** to hide the words "Title", "Author", and "Copyright" in the plug-in.

9. Type **>** to complete the EMBED tag.

✔ Tips

■ You can wrap text around an EMBED tag, just like an image. Use ALIGN=right or ALIGN=left. The HSPACE and VSPACE attributes also work the same way as they do for images.

■ If you have a lot of sounds on your page, you should probably ask your ISP if they have or can get the RealServer software. Using a regular Web server to stream RealMedia files only works for small quantities of data.

■ Remember that EMBED is an inline tag. To have a console or button begin on its own line, you'll have to precede the EMBED tag with a P or BR.

Video

If you listen to the Web hype long enough, you'll believe you can tune into Paramount's home page and watch previews to their new movies. Unfortunately, thanks to the huge size of video files and the relative minuscule speed of most home modems, although you might be *able* to do this, you might be gray before the opening credits finish rolling.

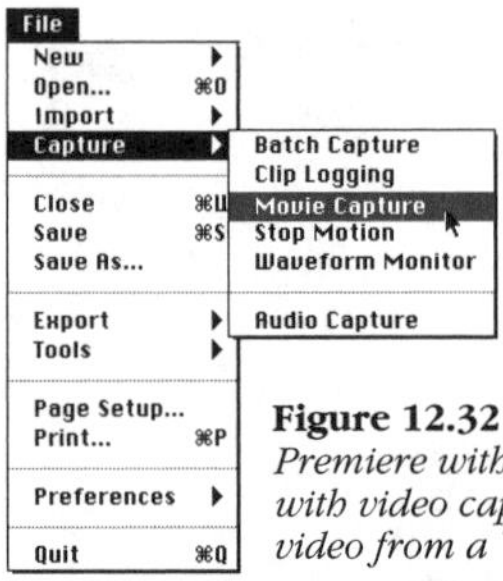

Nevertheless, it is possible to add links to video on your Web pages. As with sound files, you have to be especially careful to provide video in a format that your visitors will be able to use: QuickTime and MPEG for Mac and Windows, AVI just for Windows.

Capturing video

If you have an AV Mac or PowerMac or a video capture card for your PC, you can create video files by copying clips from your VCR to your computer. Along with the video-specific hardware, you will need a fast computer and a big, fast, hard disk.

The actual process, although not difficult, is a bit beyond the scope of this book. Your AV Mac or Video card should have instructions on how to digitize video. In my experience, the hardest part is figuring out where to connect all the cables.

Once again, you have to be careful about just what you copy. Most broadcast television is copyrighted and may not be published without permission. Of course, you are welcome to insert videos on your page that you've filmed yourself.

You may also find video files online or in a commercial library on CD-ROM.

Figure 12.32 *You can use Adobe Premiere with an AV Mac or a PC with video capture card to capture video from a VCR.*

Figure 12.33 *If you don't have your own home movies, you can use copyright free clips included in CD-ROM collections, like this short movie, which is included in the Adobe Premiere Deluxe CD-ROM.*

```
code.html
<HTML><HEAD><TITLE>Linking to
video</TITLE></HEAD><BODY>

Woody is a carnivore and although he's a bit
nearsighted, does his best to terrorize the
feathered contingent in the neighborhood. <P>

<A HREF="video.woody.mov"><IMG
SRC="movieicon.gif" WIDTH=67 HEIGHT=55>
5.2 Mb QuickTime Movie</A>

<P><EM>OK, I admit it. This is hardly a movie,
with only one frame. I just don't happen to have
a video camera. Sorry. You get the HTML idea,
though.</EM>

</BODY></HTML>
```

Figure 12.34 *It's a good idea to tell your visitors how big the video file is so that they know how long it will take to download.*

Figure 12.35 *A click by the visitor on the icon or text downloads the video file, launches the video player, and then plays the video.*

Adding External Video to Your Page

To make video accessible to your visitors regardless of their browser, you might consider using, or at least adding, a link to an external video file. When the visitor clicks the link, the browser downloads the video file and opens the appropriate helper program which then views the video.

To add a link to external video:

1. Create a small icon that you can use as an inline image on your page to indicate the link to the video and call it *video.gif*.

2. Make sure the video file has the correct extension (even for Macintosh files). Otherwise, the visitor's browser will not know what kind of file it is and may be unable to open it. (Use .qt or .mov for QuickTime files, .avi for AVI files, and .mpeg or .mpg for MPEG files.)

3. In your HTML document, where you wish to place the link to the video file, type **<A HREF="video.ext">** where *video.ext* is the location of the video file, including the correct extension, on the server.

4. Type **<IMG SRC="video.gif">** where *video.gif* is the location of the icon that will indicate the link to the video. (Add any other IMG attributes as desired.)

5. Type the size and format of the video file, for example, **5.2 Mb QuickTime movie**.

6. Type **</A>** to complete the link to the video file.

Adding External Video to Your Page

Adding Internal Video

Miracle of miracles, there is a way to insert video and animations on a page in a way that both Netscape and Explorer recognize.

To add internal video:

1. Create a movie or animation. You can also convert an existing movie.

2. In your HTML document, type **<EMBED SRC="movie.ext"**, where *movie.ext* is the URL for the desired movie file, including the extension.

3. Type **WIDTH=w HEIGHT=h** where *w* and *h* are the width and height, respectively, in pixels, of the movie.

4. If desired, type **AUTOSTART=true** to have the movie play automatically when the visitor jumps to the page.

5. If desired, type **LOOP=true** to have the movie play continuously until the visitor clicks on the movie or jumps to a different page.

6. If desired, type **ALIGN=direction**. The ALIGN tag works the same for video as it does for images. For more information, see page 93.

7. Type **>**.

✔ Tips

■ You can use the EMBED tag to include Shockwave movies on your page. For more on creating animations, you might want to consult the excellent *Animation on the Web* by Sean Wagstaff, also published by Peachpit Press.

■ You have to make sure the HEIGHT and WIDTH attributes are specified correctly in order for the controls in a QuickTime movie to appear.

```
code.html
<HTML><HEAD><TITLE>Adding internal video</TITLE></HEAD>
<BODY>
<EMBED SRC="nature.avi" WIDTH=85 HEIGHT=120 AUTOSTART=true ALIGN=right>
<H1>Ashfield and Conway</H1>
The Hilltowns of Ashfield and Conway have some of the prettiest fall colors I've ever seen. For all of you who love dull, sunny California weather, you don't know what you're missing!
```

Figure 12.36 *Since videos inserted on a page with the EMBED tag do not always have controls, you might want to add the AUTOSTART attribute so that they project automatically. Otherwise, instruct your visitors to click the video to play it.*

Figure 12.37 *To play a movie that is inserted with the EMBED tag, just click it.*

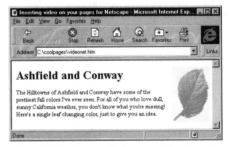

Figure 12.38 *Internet Explorer can also view videos inserted with the EMBED tag, although it offers more flexibility with the DYNSRC tag described on page 235.*

```
code.html
<HTML><HEAD><TITLE>Inserting video on your
pages for IE</TITLE></HEAD>

<BODY>

<IMG SRC="leaf.gif" DYNSRC="nature.avi"
CONTROLS ALIGN=right>

<H1>Ashfield and Conway</H1>

The Hilltowns of Ashfield and Conway have
some of the prettiest fall colors I've ever seen. For
all of you who love dull, sunny California
weather, you don't know what you're missing!
```

Figure 12.39 *You can specify a regular image with the SRC attribute as usual. It will be displayed as the movie is loading, as well as in browsers (like Netscape) that don't recognize the DYNSRC attribute.*

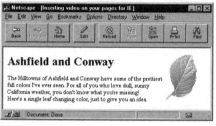

Figure 12.40 *Since Netscape can't view the video, it just shows the static image.*

Figure 12.41 *If you use the CONTROLS attribute (see step 5), a play button and progress bar appear below the video.*

Adding Internal Video for Explorer

 Internet Explorer supports a special, non-standard attribute of the IMG tag that allows you to insert video on a page.

To add video for Internet Explorer:

1. Create an AVI movie. Create a static image, perhaps of the first frame of the movie.

2. In your HTML document, type **<IMG SRC="image.gif"** where *image.gif* is the static image that will be displayed before and after the movie is played.

3. Type **DYNSRC="movie.avi"** where *movie.avi* is the URL of the desired movie.

4. If desired, type **LOOP=n** where *n* is the number of times the movie should be projected. Use **LOOP=-1** or **LOOP=infinite** to project the movie continuously.

5. If desired, type **CONTROLS** to show the play button and progress bar under the movie.

6. If desired, type **START=event**, where *event* is either **FILEOPEN** to project the movie when the visitor jumps to the page, or **MOUSEOVER**, to project the movie when the visitor points at the link with the mouse.

7. Type the final **>**.

✔ Tip

- To add video that can be accessed by most browsers (although not internally), consult *Adding External Video to Your Page* on page 233.

Adding Internal Video for Explorer

Creating a Marquee

A marquee is text that starts at one part of the screen and floats across to the left, rather like the messages that advertise sales in the window of a 24-hour gas station. Internet Explorer lets you put marquees on your Web page.

To create a marquee:

1. Type **<MARQUEE**.

2. If desired, type **BEHAVIOR=type** where *type* is **scroll**, for text that starts at one side of the screen and disappears off the other, **slide** for text that starts at one side of the screen and stops when it reaches the other, or **alternate** for text that starts at one side of the screen and bounces back when it reaches the other side.

3. To determine which direction the text starts from, type **DIRECTION=left** or **DIRECTION=right**.

4. If desired, type **LOOP=n**, where *n* is the number of times the text will pass across the screen. Use **LOOP=infinite** to have the text appear continuously.

5. Type **SCROLLAMOUNT=n** to determine how much space, in pixels, is left between each pass of the text.

6. Type **SCROLLDELAY=n** to determine how much time, in milliseconds, passes before the text scrolls again.

7. Use the **HEIGHT**, **WIDTH**, **HSPACE**, **VSPACE**, **ALIGN**, and **BGCOLOR** attributes as usual, if desired.

8. Type the final **>**.

9. Type the scrolling text.

10. Type **</MARQUEE>**.

```
code.html
<H1>The Quabbin Reservoir</H1>

They had to flood four towns and three [snip]

<MARQUEE WIDTH=75% HEIGHT=15
BEHAVIOR=scroll DIRECTION=left
LOOP=infinite BGCOLOR=yellow>

Attention: Quabbin Enthusiasts General Meeting
Dec 9 at 7pm

</MARQUEE>
```

Figure 12.42 *A marquee begins with an opening tag that contains the attributes. It is followed by the text that will scroll and then the closing tag.*

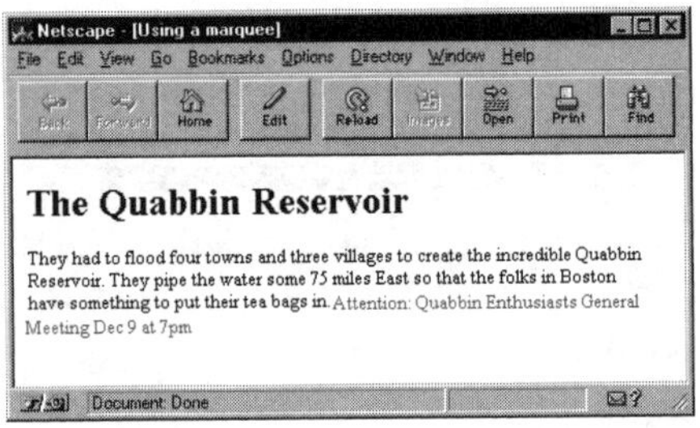

Figure 12.43 *Netscape does not recognize the MARQUEE tag and instead displays plain text.*

Figure 12.44 *With the attributes BEHAVIOR=scroll and DIRECTION=left, the text begins at the left and then disappears off the right. You can also use the CENTER and FONT tags to change the appearance of the marquee.*

Creating a Marquee

```
┌─────────────────────────────────┐
│ code.html                       │
├─────────────────────────────────┤
│ <HTML><HEAD><TITLE>Using        │
│ applets</TITLE></HEAD>          │
│                                 │
│ <BODY>                          │
│                                 │
│ Does anybody really know what time it is? │
│                                 │
│ <APPLET CODE="Clock2.class" WIDTH=170 │
│ HEIGHT=150>                     │
│                                 │
│ </APPLET>                       │
│                                 │
│ </BODY></HTML>                  │
└─────────────────────────────────┘
```

Figure 12.45 *The most important attribute in the APPLET tag is CODE. Make sure that it points to the proper Java compiled applet (not the source).*

Figure 12.46 *Applets let you create interactive, multimedia effects on your page without having to know how to program or script. (For information about JavaScript, see Chapter 17, Scripts and Chapter 18, JavaScript Essentials.)*

Inserting Applets

Java applets are little applications (hence the term *applets*) that can run in your browser to create special effects on your page, like clocks, calculators, and interactive events. There are whole books devoted to Java; here we'll restrict the topic to how to insert applets on your page once you've written or copied them from another source.

To insert an applet:

1. Type **<APPLET CODE="applet.class"** where *applet.class* is the name of the compiled applet.

2. If desired, type **WIDTH=w HEIGHT=h** to specify the applet size in pixels.

3. Type **></APPLET>**.

✔ Tips

- If you don't know how to write your own applets, you can download freeware applets from many sources on the Web. For starters, try *http://www.gamelan.com*.

- You can also download the Java Development Kit (for Macintosh and Windows, among others) from Sun, its developer *(http://java.sun.com)*.

- Even if you don't know how to write Java applets from scratch, you can use the JDK for making minor changes to existing applets. Simply download the source (if it is available), make the desired changes, and then compile the new class file with the Java Compiler that comes with the JDK.

- The APPLET tag has been deprecated in HTML 4 in favor of the more generic OBJECT, but is still supported.

Inserting Applets

An Introduction to Cascading Style Sheets

HTML was originally developed primarily as a universal coding system that would enable anyone to view the same pages, regardless of the computer platform they were using. HTML offered structural formatting (this line is a heading, that word should be emphasized) but did not allow designers much control over the appearance of the page. While the original inhabitants of the Web—mostly scientists and other academics—were more concerned with content, the second generation—Web designers and the rest of us—insisted on being able to change the color of a word or choose a particular font.

While the browser manufacturers were trying to satisfy this thirst for aesthetic control by slapping on new proprietary, non-standard HTML tags left and right, and the Web design elite were appropriating tables as a layout tool, the World Wide Web Consortium went to work on a system that would keep HTML universal while allowing designers more control over the look of their pages. The result of that effort is called Cascading Style Sheets.

Cascading Style Sheets, also known as *CSS*, or simply *styles*, let you assign several properties at once to all the elements on your page marked with a particular tag. For example, you can display all your H1 headers in a particular size, font, and color. Although you could conceivably use HTML tags to achieve at least some of this formatting (say with FONT or BIG), styles offer several advantages.

The Advantages of Using Style Sheets

First, styles save time. Imagine setting the font for each header and each paragraph in a long Web page **(Figure 13.1)**. Don't forget the closing </FONT> tags! With styles, you type a single line for each element at the top of the page **(Figure 13.2)**.

Second, styles are easy to change. Go back to your page and change the font, size, and color of each paragraph by hand. With styles, you make edits quickly—in just one place.

Third, computers are better at applying styles consistently than you are. Really. Did you remember to format each and every paragraph? You can be sure that the computer did.

Next, styles let you control text in ways that are out of reach of HTML tags. You can set line spacing (leading), background color, and remove bold and italic formatting, among other things.

You can also use styles together with JavaScript to create dynamic effects known as DHTML.

Finally, styles make it easy to create a common format for all your Web pages. And you still only have to define the styles once. Make changes in one centralized place and—voilà!—all the pages are updated right away.

```
code.html
<HTML><HEAD><TITLE>Why bother with
styles?</TITLE></HEAD>

<BODY>

<P><FONT FACE="Myriad Roman, Verdana"
SIZE=-1><EM><B>On this page, you'll learn a
little about each of our cats, and how they have
created </EM>their own<EM>
style</EM></B></FONT>.

<H1><FONT FACE="Nueva Roman, Lithos
Regular" SIZE=+2>Llumi, the
Huntress</FONT></H1>

<P><FONT FACE="Myriad Roman, Verdana"
SIZE=-1>Llumi is our sweet, but
<EM>ferocious</EM> hunter-kitty. Maybe it's
because she was born out in the wild (OK, the
parking lot of the <A
HREF="commonwealth.htm">place my brother-
in-law works</A>) or maybe because she was
an orphan (he found her when she and her six
brothers and sisters were just two days old.) Then
again, maybe it's because we brought her home
to a rather hostile environment: a fiercely
territorial <A HREF="cookie.html">Catalan
cat</A> who had just had a baby of her own,
who didn't see any reason why she should share
her bed (that is, <EM>our</EM> bed), with this
outsider, an American, no less.</FONT>

<H1><FONT FACE="Nueva Roman, Lithos
Regular" SIZE=+2>Xixona, the Hungry
</FONT></H1>

<P><FONT FACE="Myriad Roman, Verdana"
SIZE=-1>Xixona, we call her Xixo (pronounced
Shi-shoe) for short, looks like a carbon-copy of
her mother, <A
HREF="cookie.html">Cookie</A>, if a bit
darker. It's very easy to tell them apart, though,
all you have to do is start feeding her. Xixo is
```

Figure 13.1 *When you format text with HTML tags, apart from invoking the wrath of the W3C—which has deprecated those tags—you spend an inordinate amount of time typing while being limited to very basic styles.*

```
code.html
<HTML><HEAD><TITLE>Setting all font values at
once</TITLE>

<STYLE>

H1 {font: normal 20pt "Nueva Roman", "Lithos
Regular"}

P {font: 10pt/15pt "Myriad Roman", "Verdana"}

P.intro {font: italic bold}

P.intro EM {font-style:normal}

</STYLE>

</HEAD>

<BODY>

<P class=intro>On this page, you'll learn a little
about each of our cats, and how they have
created <EM>their own</EM> style.

<H1> Llumi, the Huntress</H1>

<P>Llumi is our sweet, but <EM>ferocious</EM>
hunter-kitty. Maybe it's because she was born out
in the wild (OK, the parking lot of the <A
HREF="commonwealth.htm">place my brother-
in-law works</A>) or maybe because she was
an orphan (he found her when she and her six
brothers and sisters were just two days old.) Then
again, maybe it's because we brought her home
to a rather hostile environment: a fiercely
territorial <A HREF="cookie.html">Catalan
cat</A> who had just had a baby of her own,
who didn't see any reason why she should share
her bed (that is, <EM>our</EM> bed), with this
outsider, an American, no less.

<H1>Xixona, the Hungry </H1>

<P>Xixona, we call her Xixo (pronounced Shi-
shoe) for short, looks like a carbon-copy of her
mother, <A HREF="cookie.html">Cookie</A>, if
a bit darker. It's very easy to tell them apart,
```

Figure 13.2 *With styles, all the formatting information is centralized either at the top of the page or in a
separate document. Changes are easy, fast, and
global.*

The Downside of Style Sheets

The biggest disadvantage of using style sheets
is that no browser supports them completely.
Even Internet Explorer 5, while supporting
most of the specification, does not support it
all. Netscape 4, in particular, does not support
style sheets very well, although they've promised complete support in the upcoming
version 5.

According to The Web Standards Project *(see
page 15)*, the browser that correctly interprets
the most CSS is Opera, a new, lean, fast
browser from Norway, whose chief technical
officer just happens to be Håkon Lie, one of
the major forces behind CSS at the W3C. You
can get more information about Opera at
www.opera.com.

Since browsers are in a constant state of flux,
I haven't wanted to add compatibility information in this printed book. Instead, you can
go to my Web site *(www.cookwood.com/
html4_4e/browser_tests/)* to see which browsers support which parts of CSS. I've also
created a series of tester pages that you can
point a browser at in order to see how those
features are supported. While it's a great way
to tell if a problematic page is your fault—or
theirs—you still have to remember that the key
is which browser your *visitors* use. You want
them to be able to see your page properly.

Note that CSS is also in a state of change.
While CSS Level 1 (CSS1) and CSS Level 2
(CSS2) have already been officially recommended by the W3C, there is currently work
underway on CSS Level 3.

Another impediment to using style sheets is
that you have to take the time to learn how
to use them. They're not that complicated,
but they have their own distinct syntax. It's
not HTML. Luckily, you have this book in
front of you. Let's get to it.

The Anatomy of a Style

A style is made up of a tag name (H1, P, etc.) and one or more definitions* that determine how the elements marked with that tag should be displayed—perhaps in red, at 12 points, with Lithos Regular.

Each definition contains a property, a colon, and one or more values. For example, to change the color of text, you use the *color* property with a value of say, *red*. The definition would read **color: red**. The space after the colon is not required. Multiple definitions must be separated by semicolons **(Figure 13.3)**.

Some properties can be grouped together with a special umbrella property (like, *font*, *background*, and *border*, among others). For example, **font: bold 12pt Tekton** is the same as writing **font-size: 12pt; font-weight: bold; font-family: Tekton**.

Definitions (and thus, the properties and values) always look the same, whether the style is applied locally *(see page 248)*, internally *(see page 244)*, or externally *(see page 246)*. The only difference is in the punctuation surrounding them—curly brackets vs. quote marks **(Figure 13.4)**.

The available properties and corresponding values that you use in defining styles are described in detail on pages 257–289.

Some properties are automatically inherited from tag to tag. For example, if you define H1 tagged text as blue, any text marked with an EM tag that is inside the H1 tag will also be blue. Of course, EM tagged text inside a paragraph defined with P (or any other tag) will not be blue.

*(The W3C uses fancier words than I do: the tag name is called a *selector* and the definitions are called *declarations*.)

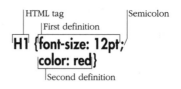

Figure 13.3 *A style is made up of a tag name (H1) and one or more definitions (font-size: 12pt and color: red) that specify how you want to display elements marked with that tag.*

Figure 13.4 *The outer parts of this style look a bit different from the one in Figure 13.3 because this style is being applied locally (see page 248). Note, more importantly, how the definition has exactly the same appearance: a property, a colon, and a value.*

Setting up Style Sheets

There are three ways to apply style sheets: locally, internally, and externally. You can use any one or all three of these methods. The local method will override any internal styles while the internal styles will override styles applied from an external sheet. Indeed, this is where Cascading Style Sheets get their name.

This chapter explains how to set up and apply style sheets. To get more information about writing the style definitions themselves, consult Chapter 15, *Formatting Text with Styles* and Chapter 16, *Layout with Styles*.

Creating an Internal Style Sheet

Internal style sheets are ideal for individual pages with lots of text. They let you set the styles at the top of your page that should be used throughout an HTML document. If you plan to apply the style sheet to more than one page, you're better off using external style sheets *(see page 246)*.

To create an internal style sheet:

1. At the top of your HTML document, between the <HEAD> and </HEAD> tags, type **<STYLE>**.

2. Type the name of the tag whose properties you wish to define (**H1**, **P**, or whatever).

3. Type **{** to mark the beginning of this tag's properties.

4. Define as many properties as desired for this tag, using the steps described on pages 257–290. Separate each property with a semicolon.

5. Type **}** to mark the end of this tag's properties.

6. Repeat steps 2–5 for each tag for which you wish to define properties.

7. Type **</STYLE>** to complete the style sheet.

```
<HTML><HEAD><TITLE>Creating an internal
style sheet</TITLE>

<STYLE>

H1 {text-align:center; letter-spacing:.5em;
background:green; color:yellow; font: normal
20pt "Nueva Roman", "Lithos Regular"}

P {text-align:justify; text-indent:8pt; font:
10pt/15pt "Myriad Roman", "Verdana"}

P.intro {text-indent:0;font: italic bold}

P.intro EM {font-style:normal}

A:link {background:yellow;color:green;
text-decoration:none}

A:visited {background:orange; color:yellow;text-
decoration:none}

A:hover {background:red;color:white;text-
decoration:none}

A:active {background:white;color:black;text-
decoration:none}

</STYLE>

</HEAD><BODY>

<P class=intro>On this page, you'll learn a little
about each of our cats, and how they have
created <EM>their own</EM> style.
```

Figure 14.1 *An internal style sheet goes in the HEAD section of your HTML document.*

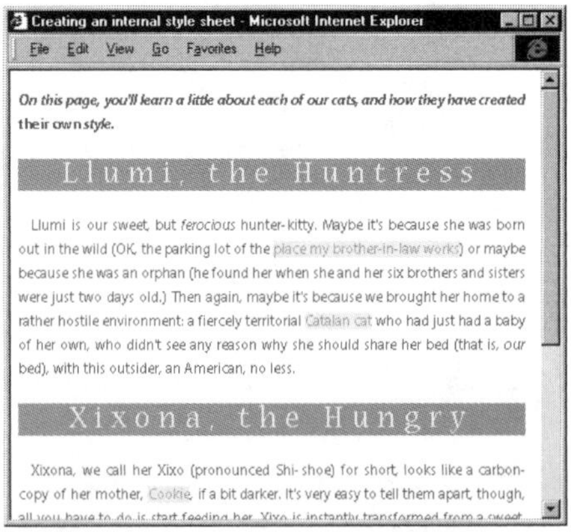

Figure 14.2 *Each element is displayed according to the styles defined at the top of the HTML page.*

```
                code.html
<HTML><HEAD><TITLE>Creating an internal
style sheet</TITLE>

<STYLE>

<!--

H1 {text-align:center; letter-spacing:.5em;
background:green; color:yellow; font: normal
20pt "Nueva Roman", "Lithos Regular"}

P {text-align:justify; text-indent:8pt; font:
10pt/15pt "Myriad Roman", "Verdana"}

P.intro {text-indent:0;font: italic bold}

P.intro EM {font-style:normal}

A:link {background:yellow;color:green; text-
decoration:none}

A:visited {background:orange; color:yellow;text-
decoration:none}

A:hover {background:red;color:white;text-
decoration:none}

A:active {background:white;color:black;text-
decoration:none}

-->

</STYLE>

</HEAD><BODY>

<P class=intro>On this page, you'll learn a little
about each of our cats, and how they have
created <EM>their own</EM> style.

<H1>Llumi, the Huntress</H1>

<P>Llumi is our sweet, but <EM>ferocious</EM>
```

Figure 14.3 *To hide styles from browsers that don't support them, add comment tags just after the initial STYLE tag and before the final one.*

✔ Tips

- For more details on property syntax, consult *The Anatomy of a Style* on page 242.

- Each set of properties must begin with an opening curly bracket "**{**" and end with a closing curly bracket "**}**". Each property and its values must be separated with a semicolon "**;**".

- You can define properties for several tags at once by separating each tag with a comma: **H1, H2, H3 {color:red}** will display the three levels of headers in red.

- Define the properties for a tag that depends on another by typing the dependent tag after the parent one, separated by just a space: **H1 EM {color:red}** means that all text marked with the EM tag *that is found within the H1 tags* should be shown in red. EM tags found anywhere else (say, in a P tag) will not be red.

- Add comment tags after (**<!--**) the initial <STYLE> tag and before (**-->**) the final </STYLE> tag to hide styles from browsers that don't yet understand them **(Figure 14.3)**. Otherwise, the errant browser may show the style definitions to your visitors. For more information on comments, consult *Hiding Text (Adding Comments)* on page 56.

- You can also apply styles to individual HTML tags. For more details, consult *Applying Styles Locally* on page 248.

- If you want to apply your styles to more than one Web page, you should use an external style sheet. For more information, consult *Creating an External Style Sheet* on page 246 and *Using an External Style Sheet* on page 247.

Creating an External Style Sheet

External style sheets are ideal for giving all the pages on your Web site a common look. Instead of getting their styles from individual internal style sheets, you can set each page to consult the external sheet, thus ensuring that each will have the same settings.

To create an external style sheet:

1. Create a new text document.

2. Type the name of the tag whose properties you wish to define (**H1**, **P**, or whatever).

3. Type **{** to mark the beginning of this tag's properties.

4. Define as many properties as desired for this tag, using the steps described on pages 257–289. Separate each property with a semicolon.

5. Type **}** to mark the end of this tag's properties.

6. Repeat steps 2–5 for each tag for which you wish to define properties.

7. Save the document in Text Only format in the desired directory. Give the document the extension .css to designate the document as a Cascading Style Sheet.

✔ Tips

- Make sure you save the style sheet as Text Only (sometimes called Text Document or ASCII) and give it the .css extension. It should be uploaded in ASCII—not Binary—mode *(see pages 335 and 336)*. This goes for Mac folks too!

- All the tips listed on page 245 also apply to external style sheets.

```
styles.css
H1 {text-align:center;letter-spacing:.5em;
background:green; color:yellow; font: normal 20pt
"Nueva Roman", "Lithos Regular"}

P {text-align:justify; text-indent:8pt;
font: 10pt/15pt "Myriad Roman", "Verdana"}

P.intro {text-indent:0;font: italic bold}

P.intro EM {font-style:normal}

A:link {background:yellow; color:green;
text-decoration:none}

A:visited {background:orange; color:yellow;
text-decoration:none}

A:hover {background:red;color:white;
text-decoration:none}

A:active {background:white;color:black;text-
decoration:none}
```

Figure 14.4 *The external style sheet contains precisely the same information as the internal one—but no HTML tags.*

```
code.html
<HTML><HEAD><TITLE>Creating an external style
sheet</TITLE>

<LINK REL=stylesheet TYPE="text/css"
HREF="styles.css">

</HEAD><BODY>

<P class=intro>On this page, you'll learn a little
about each of our cats, and how they have created
```

Figure 14.5 *An external style sheet is linked to a given Web page with the LINK tag (see page 247).*

Figure 14.6 *A page linked to an external style sheet looks just as it would if the style sheet were right in the page itself (see Figure 14.2).*

Creating an External Style Sheet

```
┌─────────── code.html ───────────┐
<HTML><HEAD><TITLE>Creating an external style
sheet</TITLE>

<LINK REL=stylesheet TYPE="text/css"
HREF="styles.css">

</HEAD>

<BODY>

<P class=intro>On this page, you'll learn a little
about Cookie, our Catalan cat.

<H1>Cookie, the Invisible</H1>

<P>When we lived in Barcelona, people would
come to our house and rave about our big,
American cat, <A HREF="woody.htm">Woody
</A>. Poor Cookie never got even a mention. Of
course, that was because as soon as she heard the
doorbell, she ran under the bed and stayed there
until the guests had long gone home. I'm not sure
why she was so shy with people. It might have to do
with the fact that she was born in a planter on the
busiest street in Barcelona, and I abducted her from
```

Figure 14.7 *Here is a second page that I will link to the same external style sheet.*

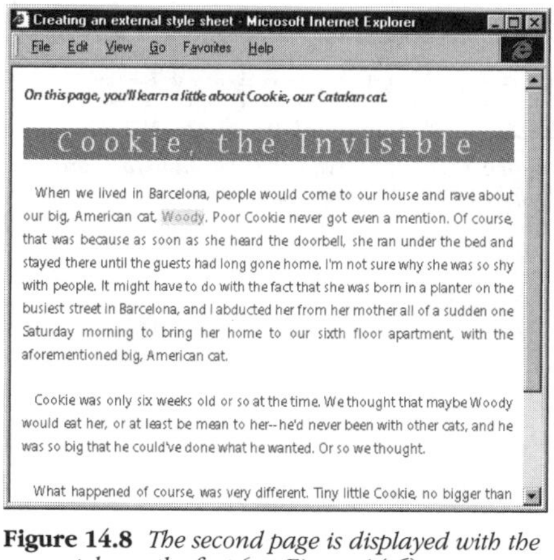

Figure 14.8 *The second page is displayed with the same styles as the first (see Figure 14.6).*

Using an External Style Sheet

Once you've created an external style sheet *(see page 246)*, you link it to each page it should format.

To use an external style sheet:

1. In the HEAD section of each and every HTML page in which you wish to use the style sheet, type **<LINK REL=stylesheet TYPE="text/css"**.

2. Type **HREF="url.css"**, where *url.css* is the name you used in step 7 on page 246.

3. Type the final **>**.

✔ Tips

- When you make a change to the style sheet, all the pages that reference it are automatically updated as well.

- Theoretically, you can also import an external style sheet. However, I don't recommend it. It requires more typing than the method described above, and neither Netscape nor Explorer supports it.

- URLs in an external style sheet are relative to the location of the style sheet file on the server, not to the HTML page's location. For more information about relative URLs, consult *URLs* on page 27.

- You can link an external style sheet, include an internal style sheet, and apply local styles all in the same HTML document. Local styles override internal style sheets which, in turn, override external style sheets.

Applying Styles Locally

If you are new to style sheets and would like to experiment a bit before taking the plunge, applying styles locally is an easy, small-scale, and rather safe way to begin. Although it doesn't centralize all your formatting information for easy editing and global updating, it does open the door to the additional formatting that is impossible to create with conventional HTML tags.

To apply styles locally:

1. Within the HTML tag that you want to format, type **STYLE="**.

2. Type **property:value**, using the steps described on pages 257–290.

3. To create additional style definitions, type a semicolon **;** and repeat step 2.

4. Type the final quote mark **"**.

✔ Tips

- Be careful not to confuse the equals signs with the colon. Since they both assign values it's easy to interchange them without thinking.

- Don't forget to separate multiple property definitions with a semicolon.

- Don't forget to enclose your style definitions in straight quote marks.

```
code.html

<HTML><HEAD><TITLE>Applying styles
locally</TITLE></HEAD>

<BODY>

<P STYLE="background:yellow;color:red;text-
transform:capitalize;border:double medium
green;font-weight:900;padding:0.5em">On this
page, you'll learn a little about each of our cats,
and how they have created their own style.

<H1> Llumi, the Huntress</H1>

<P>Llumi is our sweet, but <EM>ferocious</EM>
hunter-kitty. Maybe it's because she was born out
```

Figure 14.9 *Except for coloring the text red, all the other styles applied here are not available through HTML tags. You need CSS!*

Figure 14.10 *The styles are applied to the paragraph. Hopefully, you'll have better taste.*

```
                code.html
<HTML><HEAD><TITLE>Applying styles to a
class</TITLE>

<STYLE>

H1 {text-align:center; letter-spacing:.5em;
background:green; color:yellow; font: normal
20pt "Nueva Roman", "Lithos Regular"}

P {text-align:justify; text-indent:8pt;
font: 10pt/15pt "Myriad Roman", "Verdana"}

P.intro {text-indent:0;font: italic bold}

P.intro EM {font-style:normal}

</STYLE>

</HEAD><BODY>

<P CLASS=intro>On this page, you'll learn a
little about each of our cats, and how they have
created <EM>their own</EM> style.

<H1>Llumi, the Huntress</H1>

<P>Llumi is our sweet, but <EM>ferocious</EM>
hunter-kitty. Maybe it's because she was born out
```

Figure 14.11 *In this example, regular P tags are indented. Those of class intro will not be indented, and will be displayed in italic bold.*

Figure 14.12 *Only the paragraph marked with the P tag as intro class will be formatted as intro. Paragraphs with the P tag without any class will be formatted as usual, as is the case with the last paragraph shown on this page.*

Defining Styles for Classes

You can divide your HTML elements into categories or *classes* in order to apply styles to them selectively. For example, you can create a class of introductory paragraphs that will have slightly different formatting than regular paragraphs.

To define styles for classes:

1. Mark the elements in your HTML page that belong to the class by adding **CLASS=classname** (where *classname* is the identifying word for the class) to the appropriate HTML tags.

2. In the STYLE section of your HTML page, type **parenttag.classname**, where *parenttag* is the tag that the class is a subset of, and *classname* is the same as in step 1. (Yes, that's a period between the parent tag and the class name.)

3. Type a curly bracket **{** to begin the definitions.

4. Type **property:value** to specify the additional properties that should be applied to elements of this class.

5. If desired, type a semicolon **;** and then specify additional properties and values *(see pages 257–290)*.

6. Type a right curly bracket **}** to complete the class definition.

✔ Tips

- You can only define styles for classes in internal or external style sheets. It doesn't make sense to define them locally since the whole point is to format a whole group of elements at once.

- The class name should not be a JavaScript keyword. Check my Web site for the list: *www.cookwood.com/html4_4e/.*

Identifying Particular Tags

Instead of creating a whole class of HTML tags, you can also identify individual tags, and then either apply style sheet information or JavaScript functions to them.

To identify particular tags:

1. Identify the element in your HTML page by adding **ID=idname** (where *idname* is the identifying word for the tag) to the appropriate HTML tag.

2. In the STYLE section of your HTML page, type **parenttag#idname**, where *parenttag* is the kind of HTML tag that is identified with the ID attribute, and *idname* is the same as in step 1. (Yes, that's a number sign between the parent tag and the ID name.)

3. Type a curly bracket **{** to begin the definitions.

4. Type **property:value** to specify the additional properties that should be applied to elements of this class.

5. If desired, type a semicolon **;** and then specify additional properties and values *(see pages 257–290).*

6. Type a right curly bracket **}** to complete the ID definition.

✔ Tips

- ■ Each ID in an HTML document must be unique.

- ■ IDs are especially useful for applying JavaScript to particular parts of your Web page.

```
code.html
<HTML><HEAD><TITLE>Applying styles to a
class</TITLE>
<STYLE>
H1 {text-align:center; letter-spacing:.5em;
background:green; color:yellow; font: normal
20pt "Nueva Roman", "Lithos Regular"}
P {text-align:justify; text-indent:8pt;
font: 10pt/15pt "Myriad Roman", "Verdana"}
P#intro {text-indent:0;font: italic bold}
P.intro EM {font-style:normal}
</STYLE>
</HEAD><BODY>
<P ID=intro>On this page, you'll learn a little
about each of our cats, and how they have
created <EM>their own</EM> style.
<H1>Llumi, the Huntress</H1>
<P>Llumi is our sweet, but <EM>ferocious</EM>
hunter-kitty. Maybe it's because she was born out
in the wild (OK, the parking lot of the <A
```

Figure 14.13 *In this example, regular P tags are indented. The one marked with ID intro will not be indented, and will be displayed in italic bold.*

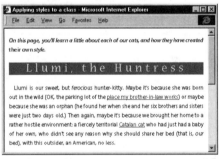

Figure 14.14 *Only the one paragraph with the unique ID of intro will be formatted.*

Identifying Particular Tags

Creating Custom HTML Tags

HTML 4 includes two generic tags that can be combined with classes *(see page 249)* and ID *(see page 250)* in order to create custom HTML tags.

Block-level vs. Inline

It's important to note the distinction between block-level and inline HTML elements. Block-level elements, like paragraphs, generally begin on a new line, and can contain other block-level elements, inline elements, and text. The P tag is the quintessential block-level tag, as are BODY, H1, TABLE, and others.

Inline elements, in contrast, usually do not begin a new line, and can only contain other inline elements or text. Inline elements like B or FONT add formatting to bits and pieces of the text. IMG is also an inline tag.

DIV and SPAN

The HTML tags DIV and SPAN don't do much at all by themselves. However, you can combine them with classes and IDs to create your own custom HTML tags. DIV is for block-level elements and SPAN is for inline elements.

Creating Custom Block-Level HTML Tags

You can create a custom block-level HTML tag by adding a class or ID to the DIV tag and then defining the styles that it should apply.

To create a custom block-level HTML tag:

1. In the STYLE section at the top of your HTML document or in an external style sheet, type **DIV.classname**, where *classname* is the identifying word for the class you're going to use.

   Or type **DIV#IDname**, where *IDname* is the identifying word for this particular instance of the DIV tag.

2. Type **{property:value**, using the information on pages 257–290.

3. Create additional definitions, if desired, separating each with a **;**.

4. Add the final **}**.

✔ Tips

■ You can create word processor type style sheets with custom block-level tags. Instead of being limited to just the P and Hn tags, you could create an INTRO tag or a CHAPTERTITLE tag. The possibilities are endless.

■ When you apply a custom tag to your HTML content, the tag will look like <DIV CLASS=INTRO> or <DIV CLASS=CHAPTERTITLE> and not like <INTRO> or <CHAPTERTITLE> *(see page 253)*.

```
code.html
<HTML><HEAD><TITLE>Dividing your
document into sections</TITLE>

<STYLE>

DIV.llumi {background: aqua}

DIV.xixo {background: lime}

H1  {text-align:center;letter-spacing:.5em;
background:green; color:yellow; font: normal
20pt "Nueva Roman", "Lithos Regular"}

P  {text-align:justify; text-indent:8pt;
font: 10pt/15pt "Myriad Roman", "Verdana"}

P.intro {text-indent:0;font: italic bold}

P.intro EM {font-style:normal}

</STYLE>
```

Figure 14.15 *Define the DIV styles in the STYLE section at the top of your HTML document.*

```
code.html
<P class=intro>On this page, you'll learn a little
about each of our cats, and how they have
created <EM>their own</EM> style.

<DIV CLASS="llumi">

<H1>Llumi, the Huntress</H1>

<P>Llumi is our sweet, but <EM>ferocious</EM>
hunter-kitty. Maybe it's because she was born out
in the wild (OK, the parking lot of the <A
HREF="commonwealth.htm">place my brother-
in-law works</A>) or maybe because she was
an orphan (he found her when she and her six
brothers and sisters were just two days old.) Then
again, maybe it's because we brought her home
to a rather hostile environment: a fiercely
territorial <A HREF="cookie.html">Catalan
cat</A> who had just had a baby of her own,
who didn't see any reason why she should share
her bed (that is, <EM>our</EM> bed), with this
outsider, an American, no less.

</DIV>

<DIV CLASS="xixo">

<H1>Xixona, the Hungry </H1>

<P>Xixona, we call her Xixo (pronounced Shi-
```

Figure 14.16 *Then mark the appropriate sections in your HTML page with DIV tags.*

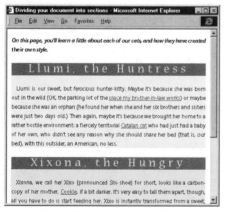

Figure 14.17 *DIV tags are great for dividing your document into thematic sections.*

Using Custom Block-Level HTML Tags

Using a custom block-level tag is not much different from using any other HTML tag. You just have to specify the class or ID.

To use the custom block-level tag:

1. At the beginning of the desired section of your document, type **<DIV**.

2. Type **CLASS="classname"**, where *class-name* identifies the type of section.

   Or type **ID="idname"**, where *idname* identifies this particular section.

3. Type the final **>**.

4. Create the contents of this section.

5. At the end of the desired section, type **</DIV>**.

✔ Tips

- For some reason, you can't apply certain CSS features to any other tag besides the DIV tag. For example, if you want to specify the width of a text block, that text must be enclosed in a DIV tag *(see page 278)*. Applying it to the P tag won't have any effect.

- The DIV and SPAN *(see page 254)* tags let you create custom styles without co-opting any existing tags and their corresponding styles.

- Notice that the closing tag is always </DIV>. It does not change according to the class or ID.

- Internet Explorer 5 also recognizes the non-standard NOWRAP attribute in the DIV tag. It has the same effect as enclosing the contents in NOBR tags *(see page 103)* but doesn't work in Netscape.

Using Custom Block-Level HTML Tags

Creating Custom Inline HTML Tags

A custom inline HTML tag is like a character style in a word processor or layout program. It's particularly useful for combining a set of text formatting characteristics in one tag.

To create a custom inline tag:

1. In the STYLE section at the top of your HTML document or in an external style sheet, type **SPAN.classname**, where *classname* is the identifying word for the class you're going to use.

   Or type **SPAN#idname**, where *idname* is the word that identifies this particular text.

2. Type **{property:value**, using the information on pages 257–289.

3. Create additional definitions, if desired, separating each with a **;**.

4. Add the final **}**.

✔ Tip

■ For details on applying your new tags, consult *Using Custom Inline HTML Tags* on page 255.

```
code.html
<STYLE>
DIV.llumi {background: aqua}
DIV.xixo {background: lime}
SPAN.initialcap {font-size:200%}
SPAN.allcaps {font-variant:small-caps}
H1  {text-align:center; letter-spacing:.5em;
    background:green; color:yellow; font: normal
    20pt "Nueva Roman", "Lithos Regular"}
P  {text-align:justify; text-indent:8pt; font:
    10pt/15pt "Myriad Roman", "Verdana"}
P.intro {text-indent:0;font: italic bold}
P.intro EM {font-style:normal}
</STYLE>
```

Figure 14.18 *Notice that the text affected by the SPAN tags here could not really be styled with any other tag without adding unwanted extra formatting.*

```
code.html
<BODY>

<P class="intro">
<SPAN CLASS="initialcap">O</SPAN>
<SPAN CLASS="allcaps">n this page, you'll
</SPAN> learn a little about each of our cats,
and how they have created <EM>their
own</EM> style.

<DIV CLASS="llumi">

<H1>Llumi, the Huntress</H1>

<P>Llumi is our sweet, but <EM>ferocious</EM>
hunter-kitty. Maybe it's because she was born out
in the wild (OK, the parking lot of the <A
HREF="commonwealth.htm">place my brother-
```

Figure 14.19 *You can use the SPAN tag for format-ting any piece of text. You can also nest other inline HTML tags (like B or FONT) within the SPAN tag.*

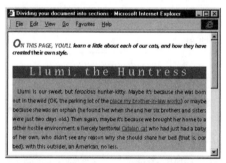

Figure 14.20 *SPAN tags are great for applying focused effects on individual letters or words.*

Using Custom Inline HTML Tags

Once you've defined your custom inline tags, you apply them to your HTML document.

To use a custom inline HTML tag:

1. At the beginning of the desired words, type **<SPAN**.

2. Type **CLASS="classname"**, where *class-name* identifies the type of text.

Or type **ID="idname"**, where *idname* identifies this particular text.

3. Type the final **>**.

4. Create the text you wish to affect.

5. Type **</SPAN>**.

✔ Tips

■ The SPAN tag has no properties of its own. That is, unless you define styles for it, it will have no effect on the text that it encloses.

■ The DIV *(see page 252)* and SPAN tags let you create custom styles without co-opting any existing tags and their cor-responding styles.

■ Notice that the closing tag is always </SPAN>. It does not change according to the class or ID.

Defining Styles for Links

If you don't like underlined links, you can change the background and foreground color of your links to make them stand out without looking so ugly. Link styles have a special syntax.

To define styles for links:

1. Type **A:**.

2. Type **link** to change the appearance of links that haven't yet been or currently aren't being clicked or pointed at.

   Or type **visited** to change the appearance of links that the visitor has already clicked.

   Or type **active** to change the appearance of links when clicked.

   Or type **hover** to change the appearance of links when pointed to.

3. Type a curly bracket **{** to begin the definitions.

4. Type **property:value** to specify how the links should look. You might try changing the color *(see page 265)*, the background color *(see page 266)*, and the underlining *(see page 270)*.

5. If desired, type a semicolon **;** and then specify additional properties and values.

6. Type a right curly bracket **}** to complete the link definition.

✔ Tips

- To change the appearance of all the links (in all states) at once, just type **A {property:value}**.

- Netscape Communicator 4 does not support the hover feature.

```
                    code.html

P {text-align:justify;
    text-indent:8pt;
    font: 10pt/15pt "Myriad Roman", "Verdana"}
P.intro {text-indent:0;font: italic bold}
P.intro EM {font-style:normal}
A:link {background:yellow;
        color:green;
        text-decoration:none}
A:visited {background:orange; color:yellow;text-
decoration:none}
A:hover {background:red;color:white;text-
decoration:none}
A:active {background:white;color:black;text-
decoration:none}
</STYLE>
</HEAD>
```

Figure 14.21 *You can create a different style for each state of a link.*

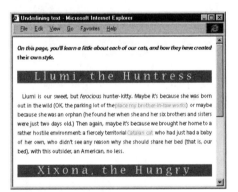

Figure 14.22 *In this example, I've created a background for links so they're visible, but gotten rid of the underlining so they're not so ugly.*

Formatting Text with Styles

Many Tags Deprecated

The W3 Consortium wants you to stop using the FONT tag and about 20 other tags and attributes that add formatting to text, lists, tables, and the rest of your Web page. Instead, they think you should consolidate all that formatting information in one step: the style. And while leaving your familiar tags behind may take some practice, you'll soon find that styles save you time and typing. For more about deprecated tags, see page 44.

Styles offer many more possibilities than HTML tags and extensions ever did. Now you can change the size, weight, slant, line height, foreground and background color, spacing, and alignment of text, decide whether it should be underlined, overlined, struck through, or blinking, and convert it to all uppercase, all lowercase, or small-caps.

Note: This chapter explains how to create individual styles. You can use these styles locally *(see page 248)*, in an internal style sheet *(see page 244)*, or in an external style sheet *(see page 246)*.

Choosing a Font Family

Because not everyone has the same set of fonts, the font-family property has a special characteristic: you can specify more than one font, in case the first is not available in your visitor's system. You can also have a last ditch attempt at controlling the display in the visitor's system by specifying a generic font style like *serif* or *monospace*.

To set the font family:

1. Type **font-family: familyname**, where *familyname* is your first choice of font.

2. If desired, type **, familyname2**, where *familyname2* is your second font choice. Separate each choice with a comma and a space.

3. Repeat step 2 as desired.

✔ Tips

■ It's a good idea to specify at least two font choices, one of them a common font, so that you maintain some control over how the document is displayed. Common fonts in Macintosh systems are Times and Palatino for serif fonts and Helvetica for sans-serif. Most Windows systems contain Times as well, but Arial is more prevalent as a sans-serif choice.

■ You can use the following generic font names—**serif**, **sans-serif**, **cursive**, **fantasy**, and **monospace**—as a last ditch attempt to influence which font is used for display.

■ You can set the font family, font size, and line height all at once, using the general font style *(see page 264).*

■ You can use very specific font names, like *Futura Condensed Bold Italic.*

■ Double quotes are not required around even multi-word font names.

```
code.html
<HTML><HEAD><TITLE>Choosing a font
family</TITLE>
<STYLE>
H1 {font-family: "Nueva Roman", "Lithos
Regular"}
P {font-family: "Myriad Roman", "Verdana"}
</STYLE></HEAD><BODY>
<P>On this page, you'll learn a little about each
of our cats, and how they have created their own
style.
<H1> Llumi, the Huntress</H1>
<P>Llumi is our sweet, but <EM>ferocious</EM>
hunter-kitty. Maybe it's because she was born out
in the wild (OK, the parking lot of the <A
```

Figure 15.1 *For the header, Nueva Roman is the first choice. If the user doesn't have Nueva Roman, Lithos Regular will be used. Similarly for P paragraphs, Myriad Roman is the first choice and Verdana is the second choice.*

Figure 15.2 *On this system, both first choices were available: Nueva Roman for headers and Myriad Roman for the P paragraphs.*

```
code.html
<HTML><HEAD><TITLE>Embedding a font
family</TITLE>

<STYLE>

@font-face {font-family: "Nueva Roman";
src: url(NUEVAR1.eot)}

H1 {font-family: "Nueva Roman", "Lithos
Regular"}

P {font-family: "Myriad Roman", "Verdana"}

</STYLE></HEAD><BODY>

<P>On this page, you'll learn a little about each
of our cats, and how they have created their own
style.

<H1> Llumi, the Huntress</H1>

<P>Llumi is our sweet, but <EM>ferocious</EM>
hunter-kitty. Maybe it's because she was born out
```

Figure 15.3 *To embed a font for Explorer users,
insert the @font-face line within the STYLE tags in the
HEAD of your Web page. The src URL points to a special version of the font that can be downloaded to
your visitor's system.*

Figure 15.4 *The result looks exactly the same as
Figure 15.2—even if your visitor doesn't have the
fonts installed on their system.*

Embedding Fonts on a Page

You can choose whatever font you want, but
if your visitors don't have it installed on their
computers, they won't be able to view it. One
solution is to embed a font in a page.

To embed fonts on a page:

1. Type **@font-face {font-family: "**.

2. Type the full name of the font that you
   wish to embed.

3. Type **"; src: url(**.

4. Type the URL of the font.

5. Type **)}**.

6. Use the font name from step 2 in other
   style definitions, as desired.

✔ Tips

- You can't just choose any font file as the
  source for an embedded font (in step 4).
  You have to use a special format of the
  font. Internet Explorer requires fonts to
  be in the .eot format. You can convert
  your installed fonts into .eot with a program called WEFT. For more information,
  see *www.microsoft.com/typography/
  web/embedding/weft2/*.

- Bitstream has developed a technology
  called TrueDoc that allows you to embed
  fonts in Web pages for viewing in both
  Netscape and Explorer. However, in my
  tests, it didn't look so great in Explorer.
  Check out *www.truedoc.com* for more
  details.

Embedding Fonts on a Page

Creating Italics

There are two ways to apply italic formatting. Either choose Garamond Italic or Palatino Italic (or whatever) for the font *(see page 258)*, or first choose the font (Garamond or Palatino) and then choose Italics. If all of your text in a given font should be in italics, the first method is simpler. But if you want to use the font in both its roman and italic forms, the second method, described here, will prove more flexible.

To create italics:

1. Type **font-style:**.

2. Type **oblique** for oblique text, or **italic** for italic text.

To remove italics:

1. Type **font-style:**.

2. Type **normal**.

✔ Tips

■ It used to be that the italic version of a font was created by a font designer from scratch, while the oblique version was created by the computer, on the fly. This distinction has blurred somewhat, but generally holds.

■ If you set the font style as italic and there is no italic style available, the browser should try to display the text in oblique style.

■ One reason you might want to remove italics is to emphasize some text in a paragraph that has inherited italic formatting from a parent tag. For information on inherited styles, see page 242.

```
code.html
<HTML><HEAD><TITLE>Creating
italics</TITLE>

<STYLE>

H1 {font-family: "Nueva Roman", "Lithos
Regular"}

P {font-family: "Myriad Roman", "Verdana"}

P.intro {font-style:italic}

P.intro EM {font-style:normal}

</STYLE>

</HEAD><BODY>

<P class=intro>On this page, you'll learn a little
about each of our cats, and how they have
created <EM>their own</EM> style.
```

Figure 15.5 *In this example, I've set all the P elements of class "intro" in italics. Then I eliminated the italics from EM elements within P.intro elements, so that they will continue to stand out.*

Figure 15.6 *Notice that the P paragraph marked with the intro class (the first paragraph) is in italics. The text in that paragraph marked with the EM tag ("their own") is in roman face.*

```
code.html
<HTML><HEAD><TITLE>Applying bold
formatting</TITLE>

<STYLE>

H1 {font-weight:normal; font-family: "Nueva
Roman", "Lithos Regular"}

P {font-family: "Myriad Roman", "Verdana"}

P.intro {font-style:italic;
font-weight:bold}

P.intro EM {font-style:normal}

</STYLE>

</HEAD><BODY>

<P class=intro>On this page, you'll learn a little
about each of our cats, and how they have
created <EM>their own</EM> style.

<H1> Llumi, the Huntress</H1>
```

Figure 15.7 *The H1 elements are automatically bold faced, but if I'm not crazy about how they look, I can override the bold formatting by using a value of "normal". I've also added bold formatting to the P.intro elements.*

Figure 15.8 *The headers are now shown in normal weight. The P intro paragraph is now both bold and italic (see page 260).*

Applying Bold Formatting

Bold formatting is probably the most common and effective way to make text stand out. Using style sheets gives you much more flexibility with bold text, providing relative values or allowing you to get rid of it altogether.

To apply bold formatting:

1. Type **font-weight:**.

2. Type **bold** to give an average bold weight to the text.

3. Or type **bolder** or **lighter** to use a value relative to the current weight.

4. Or type a multiple of **100** between 100 and 900, where 400 represents book weight and 700 represents bold.

To remove bold formatting:

1. Type **font-weight**.

2. Type **normal**.

✔ Tips

- Since the way weights are defined varies from font to font, the values may not be relative from font to font. They are designed to be relative *within* a given font family.

- If the font family has fewer than nine weights, or if they are concentrated on one end of the scale, it is possible that some numeric values correspond to the same font weight.

- What can you remove bold formatting from? Any tag where it's been applied automatically (B and H1 come to mind) and where it's been inherited from a parent tag *(see page 242).*

Applying Bold Formatting

Setting the Font Size

You can set the font size of text marked with a particular HTML tag (or class) by specifying an exact size in points or pixels, or with descriptive words, or by specifying a relative size, with respect to a parent element.

To set the font size:

1. Type **font-size:**.

2. Type an absolute font size: **xx-small**, **x-small**, **small**, **medium**, **large**, **x-large**, or **xx-large**.

   Or type a relative font size: **larger** or **smaller**.

   Or type an exact size: say, **12pt** or **15px**.

   Or type a percentage relative to any parent style: e.g., **150%**.

✔ Tips

- There should not be any spaces between the number and the unit.

- The relative values (larger, smaller, and the percentage) depend on the size of the parent style. For example, if we defined a value of 150% for the P tag's intro class, it would mean 150% of 14pt, the defined size for the P tag in general, or 21pt.

- You can set font size together with other font values (see page 264).

```
code.html

<HTML><HEAD><TITLE>Setting the font
size</TITLE>

<STYLE>

H1 {font-size:20pt;font-weight:normal;
font-family: "Nueva Roman", "Lithos Regular"}

P {font-size:10pt; font-family: "Myriad Roman",
"Verdana"}

P.intro {font-style:italic; font-weight:bold}

P.intro EM {font-style:normal}

</STYLE>

</HEAD><BODY>

<P class=intro>On this page, you'll learn a little
about each of our cats, and how they have
created <EM>their own</EM> style.

<H1> Llumi, the Huntress</H1>
```

Figure 15.9 *I'm going to make all the text a bit smaller in order to fit more on a page and reduce the amount of scrolling my visitors have to do. Don't forget the semicolon at the end of each style.*

Figure 15.10 *You can start to get an idea of the power that styles give you. Just two lines change every marked paragraph on your page (compare with Figure 15.8).*

```
┌─────────────────────────────────┐
│▓▓▓▓▓▓▓▓ code.html ▓▓▓▓▓▓▓▓      █│
├─────────────────────────────────┤
<HTML><HEAD><TITLE>Setting the line
height</TITLE>

<STYLE>

H1 {font-size:20pt; font-weight:normal;
font-family: "Nueva Roman", "Lithos Regular"}

P {line-height:15pt; font-size:10pt;
font-family: "Myriad Roman", "Verdana"}

P.intro {font-style:italic;font-weight:bold}

P.intro EM {font-style:normal}

</STYLE>

</HEAD><BODY>

<P class=intro>On this page, you'll learn a little
about each of our cats, and how they have
created <EM>their own</EM> style.

<H1> Llumi, the Huntress</H1>

<P>Llumi is our sweet, but <EM>ferocious</EM>
hunter-kitty. Maybe it's because she was born out
```

Figure 15.11 *The line-height determines the amount of leading, or space between lines.*

Figure 15.12 *Spacing out the lines makes them easier to read.*

Setting the Line Height

Line height refers to a paragraph's leading, that is, the amount of space between each line in a paragraph. Using a large line height can sometimes make your body text easier to read. A small line height for headers (with more than one line) often makes them look classier.

To set the line height:

1. Type **line-height:**.

2. Type **n**, where *n* is a number that will be multiplied by the font-size to obtain the desired line height.

   Or type **p%** where *p%* is a percentage of the font size.

   Or type **a**, where *a* is an absolute value in points, pixels, or whatever.

✔ Tips

- You can specify the line height together with the font family, size, weight, style, and variant, as described on page 264.

- If you use a number to determine the line height, this factor is inherited by all child items. If you use a percentage, only the resulting size is inherited, not the percentage factor.

Setting All Font Values at Once

You can set the font style, weight, variant, size, line height, and family all at once.

To set all font values at once:

1. Type **font:**.

2. If desired, type **normal**, **oblique**, or **italic** to set the font-style *(see page 260)*.

3. If desired, type **normal**, **bold**, **bolder**, **lighter**, or a multiple of **100** (up to 900) to set the font-weight *(see page 260)*.

4. If desired, type **small-caps** to use a small cap font variant *(see page 272)*.

5. Type the desired font size, using the values given in step 2 on page 262.

6. If desired, type **/lineheight**, where *lineheight* is expressed in the same form as the font size *(see page 262)*.

7. Type a space followed by the desired font family or families, in order of preference, separated by commas, as described on page 258.

✔ Tips

- You can also set each option separately. See the page referenced with that step.

- The order I've outlined above is required by the official specifications and by Netscape. Explorer doesn't care.

- Only the size and family are required. All the other definitions may be omitted—in which case they'll be set to their default values.

- You can only set the line height if you have also set the font size. The line height must come directly after the font size and the slash.

```
                    code.html
<HTML><HEAD><TITLE>Setting all font values at
once</TITLE>

<STYLE>

H1 {font: normal 20pt "Nueva Roman", "Lithos
Regular"}

P {font: 10pt/15pt "Myriad Roman", "Verdana"}

P.intro {font: italic bold}

P.intro EM {font-style:normal}

</STYLE></HEAD><BODY>

<P class=intro>On this page, you'll learn a little
about each of our cats, and how they have
created <EM>their own</EM> style.
```

Figure 15.13 *The styles defined for H1, P, and P.intro are exactly the same as on the preceding page (Figure 15.11). This method simply combines them all in one place.*

Figure 15.14 *The result is exactly the same as if you had defined each characteristic separately (cf. Figure 15.12).*

```
                    code.html
<HTML><HEAD><TITLE>Setting the
color</TITLE>

<STYLE>

H1 {color:yellow; font: normal 20pt "Nueva
Roman", "Lithos Regular"}

P {font: 10pt/15pt "Myriad Roman", "Verdana"}

P.intro {font: italic bold}

P.intro EM {font-style:normal}

</STYLE>

</HEAD><BODY>

<P class=intro>On this page, you'll learn a little
about each of our cats, and how they have
created <EM>their own</EM> style.

<H1> Llumi, the Huntress</H1>
```

Figure 15.15 *You can use either color names, like* yellow, *in this example, or hexadecimal representations of colors.*

Figure 15.16 *These headers really are yellow! You can see it better on the Web (see page 20).*

Setting the Text Color

You can change the color of any tagged text, whether it be an entire paragraph, or just a few words.

To set the text color:

1. Type **color:**.

2. Type **colorname**, where *colorname* is one of the 16 predefined colors.

   Or type **#rrggbb**, where *rrggbb* is the hexadecimal representation of the desired color.

   Or type **rgb(r, g, b)** where *r*, *g*, and *b* are integers from 0-255 that specify the amount of red, green, or blue, respectively, in the desired color.

   Or type **rgb(r%, g%, b%)** where *r*, *g*, and *b* specify the percentage of red, green, and blue, respectively, in the desired color.

✔ Tips

- If you type a value for r, g, or b higher than 255 it will be replaced with 255. Similarly a percentage higher than 100% will be replaced with 100%.

- You can use the color property to change the color of any HTML element. For more information, consult *Changing the Foreground Color* on page 285.

- You can also use #rgb to set the color where the hexadecimal values are repeated digits. So you could write #FF0099 as #F09.

- The hexadecimal number should *not* be enclosed in double quotes (as it is when used in an HTML tag).

Changing the Text's Background

The background refers not to the background of the entire page, but to the background of the specified tag. In other words, you can change the background of just a few paragraphs or words, by setting the background of those words to a different color.

To change the text's background:

1. Type **background:**.

2. Type **transparent** or **color**, where *color* is a color name or hex color.

3. If desired, type **url(image.gif)**, to use an image for the background.

   If desired, type **repeat** to tile the image both horizontally and vertically, **repeat-x** to tile the image only horizontally, **repeat-y** to tile the image only vertically, and **no-repeat** to not tile the image.

   If desired, type **fixed** or **scroll** to determine whether the background should scroll along with the canvas.

   If desired, type **x y** to set the position of the background image, where *x* and *y* can be expressed as a percentage or an absolute distance from the top-left corner. Or use values of *top*, *center*, or *bottom* for *x* and *left*, *center*, and *right* for *y*.

✔ Tip

■ You can specify both a color and a GIF image's URL for the background. The color will be used until the image is loaded—or if it can't be loaded for any reason—and will be seen through any transparent portions of the image.

```
code.html
<HTML><HEAD><TITLE>Changing the text's
background color or image</TITLE>

<STYLE>

H1 {background:green; color:yellow; font:
normal 20pt "Nueva Roman", "Lithos Regular"}

P {font: 10pt/15pt "Myriad Roman", "Verdana"}

P.intro {font: italic bold}

P.intro EM {font-style:normal}

</STYLE>

</HEAD><BODY>

<P class=intro>On this page, you'll learn a little
about each of our cats, and how they have
created <EM>their own</EM> style.
```

Figure 15.17 *In this example, the background of just the headers is set to green to offset the yellow text.*

Figure 15.18 *Be sure to use a background color that contrasts enough with the color of the text and the background of the page itself.*

```
code.html
<HTML><HEAD><TITLE>Controlling
spacing</TITLE>

<STYLE>

H1 {letter-spacing:.5em; background:green;
color:yellow; font: normal 20pt "Nueva Roman",
"Lithos Regular"}

P {text-indent:8pt; font: 10pt/15pt "Myriad
Roman", "Verdana"}

P.intro {text-indent:0;font: italic bold}

P.intro EM {font-style:normal}

</STYLE>

</HEAD><BODY>

<P class=intro>On this page, you'll learn a little
about each of our cats, and how they have
created <EM>their own</EM> style.
```

Figure 15.19 *You can specify tracking and kerning by using the letter-spacing and word-spacing tags, respectively. Indenting is defined with the text-indent property.*

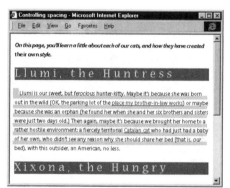

Figure 15.20 *Explorer currently supports text indents (notice the body text) and letter spacing (in the headers), but not word spacing. Netscape only supports text-indent. (Note that the space is highlighted here in red, but normally it's transparent.)*

Controlling Spacing

You can add or reduce space between words (tracking) or between letters (kerning). You can also add a chunk of space, or an indent, before particular paragraphs.

To specify tracking:

1. Type **word-spacing:**.

2. Type **length**, where *length* is a numerical value in pixels, points, ems, etc.

To specify kerning:

1. Type **letter-spacing:**.

2. Type **length**, where *length* is a numerical value in pixels, points, ems, etc.

To add indents:

1. Type **text-indent:**.

2. Type a value for the text indent, either as an absolute value (either positive or negative) or as a percentage.

✔ Tips

- You may use negative values for word and letter spacing, although the actual display always depends on the browser's capabilities.

- Word and letter spacing values may also be affected by your choice of alignment.

- Use a value of normal to set the letter and word spacing to their defaults.

- To avoid gaping holes in justified text, use a value of 0 for letter spacing.

- Currently, Netscape only supports text-indent. You can check my Web site to see if there have been any changes (*see page 241*).

Controlling Spacing

Setting White Space Properties

Normally browsers will simply ignore any extra spaces or returns that you type in an HTML document. You can set certain tags to behave like the PRE tag, taking into account all this extra white space.

To set white space properties:

1. Type **white-space:**.

2. Type **pre** to have browsers take all extra spaces and returns into account.

   Or type **nowrap** to keep all elements on the same line, except where you've inserted BR tags.

   Or type **normal** to treat white space as usual.

✔ Tip

- The PRE tag is explained in more detail on page 113.

Setting White Space Properties

```
code.html
<HTML><HEAD><TITLE>Setting white space
properties</TITLE>

<STYLE>

H1 {white-space:pre; letter-spacing:.5em;
background:green; color:yellow; font: normal
20pt "Nueva Roman", "Lithos Regular"}

P {text-indent:8pt; font: 10pt/15pt "Myriad
Roman", "Verdana"}

P.intro {text-indent:0;font: italic bold}

P.intro EM {font-style:normal}

</STYLE>

</HEAD><BODY>

<P class=intro>On this page, you'll learn a little
about each of our cats, and how they have
created <EM>their own</EM> style.

<H1>      Llumi,

       the

   Huntress</H1>

<P>Llumi is our sweet, but <EM>ferocious</EM>
hunter-kitty. Maybe it's because she was born
```

Figure 15.21 *A value of pre for white space means that the browser will conserve all extra spaces and returns that you type in the HTML document—as if you had formatted the text with the PRE tag, but without the monospace font.*

Figure 15.22 *Netscape supports the white-space property while Explorer does not.*

```
code.html
<HTML><HEAD><TITLE>Aligning text</TITLE>
<STYLE>
H1 {text-align:center; letter-spacing:.5em;
background:green; color:yellow; font: normal
20pt "Nueva Roman", "Lithos Regular"}
P {text-align:justify; text-indent:8pt; font:
10pt/15pt "Myriad Roman", "Verdana"}
P.intro {text-indent:0;font: italic bold}
P.intro EM {font-style:normal}
</STYLE>
</HEAD><BODY>
<P class=intro>On this page, you'll learn a little
about each of our cats, and how they have
created <EM>their own</EM> style.
<H1>Llumi, the Huntress</H1>
<P>Llumi is our sweet, but <EM>ferocious</EM>
```

Figure 15.23 *Set the default alignment for each tag by using the text-align property.*

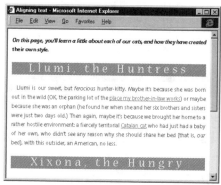

Figure 15.24 *Here I've centered the headlines and justified the P paragraphs.*

Aligning Text

You can set up certain HTML tags to always be aligned to the right, left, center, or justified, as desired.

To align text:

1. Type **text-align:**.

2. Type **left** to align the text to the left.

   Or type **right** to align the text to the right.

   Or type **center** to center the text in the middle of the screen.

   Or type **justify** to align the text on both the right and left.

✔ Tip

■ If you choose to justify the text, be aware that the word spacing and letter spacing may be adversely affected. For more information, consult *Controlling Spacing* on page 267.

Underlining Text

Style sheets let you underline text and get rid of underlining (say, with links). You can also add a line over the text or through it.

To underline text:

1. Type **text-decoration:**.

2. To underline text, type **underline**.

   Or, for a line above the text, type **overline**.

   Or, to strike out the text, type **line-through**.

To get rid of underlining, overlining, or strike through text:

1. Type **text-decoration:**.

2. Type **none**.

✔ Tips

■ You can eliminate the lines from tags that normally have lines (like U, STRIKE, DEL, INS, or A) or from tags that you've formatted earlier with lines with another style.

■ Most graphic designers hate underlining and consider it a relic from the typewriter age. Such designers might want to use the *none* option for text-decoration. However, the links will have to be marked in some other way (background color, perhaps, as in the example) or nobody will know to click on them **(Figure 15.26)**.

■ If you do get rid of the underlining below your links, make sure you also eliminate underlining under visited links, active links, and hovering *(see page 256)*.

```
code.html
<STYLE>

H1 {text-align:center; letter-spacing:.5em;
background:green; color:yellow; font: normal
20pt "Nueva Roman", "Lithos Regular"}

P {text-align:justify; text-indent:8pt; font:
10pt/15pt "Myriad Roman", "Verdana"}

P.intro {text-indent:0;font: italic bold}

P.intro EM {font-style:normal}

A:link {background:yellow; color:green;
text-decoration:none}

A:visited {background:orange; color:yellow;
text-decoration:none}

A:hover {background:red;color:white;
text-decoration:none}

A:active {background:white;color:black;
text-decoration:none}

</STYLE>

</HEAD><BODY>

<P class=intro>On this page, you'll learn a little
```

Figure 15.25 *In this example, I've decided to high-light links with color and thus have chosen to eliminate the underlining.*

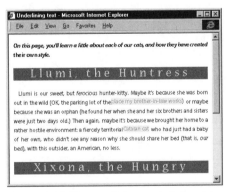

Figure 15.26 *If you really hate underlining, style sheets make it easy to get rid of it—and replace it with something that makes your links stand out without making them ugly.*

```
                code.html
<HTML><HEAD><TITLE>Making text
blink</TITLE>

<STYLE>

H1 {text-align:center; letter-spacing:.5em;
background:green; color:yellow; font: normal
20pt "Nueva Roman", "Lithos Regular"}

P {text-align:justify; text-indent:8pt; font:
10pt/15pt "Myriad Roman", "Verdana"}

P.latest {text-decoration:blink}

[snip]

</STYLE></HEAD><BODY>

<P CLASS=latest>And now, this late breaking
news!<P>
```

Figure 15.27 *I've created a new class of P tag and made it blink.*

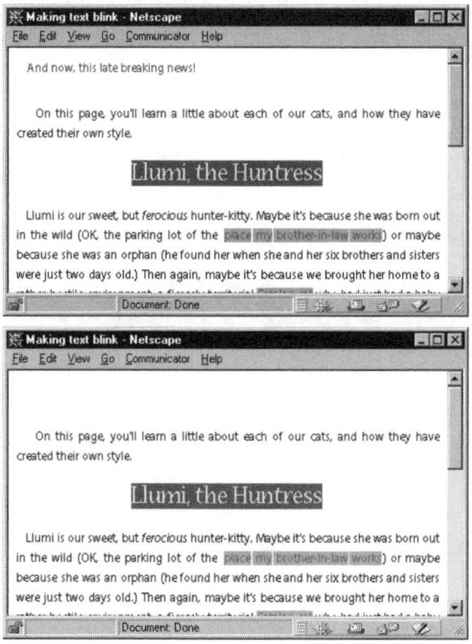

Figure 15.28 *Now you see it, now you don't. Remember though, that you'll never see text blink in Internet Explorer.*

Making Text Blink

Personally, I think the blink tag was one of the keys to Netscape's success. It added an element of animation to otherwise completely static pages. Nowadays, of course, you can add all sorts of moving objects to your pages, and blinking text is a bit out of fashion. But, just in case you still go for blinking text, you might as well use style sheets to create it.

To make text blink:

1. Type **text-decoration:**.

2. Type **blink**.

✔ Tips

■ Although the blink option has been somewhat legitimized by its inclusion in the official specification for Cascading Style Sheets (level 2), Internet Explorer does not recognize the *blink* option. Perhaps the fact that it is a descendant of arch rival Netscape's wildly popular BLINK tag *(see page 55)* has something to do with it.

■ You should also know that blinking text—and other high contrast images on your page—can provoke seizures in people with epilepsy. It's also considered a bit gauche in the sophisticated world of Web design. You might want to be careful where and how much you use it.

Making Text Blink

Changing the Text Case

You can define the text case for your style by using the text-transform property. In this way, you can display the text either with initial capital letters, in all capital letters, in all small letters, or as it was typed.

To change the text case:

1. Type **text-transform:**.

2. Type **capitalize** to put the first character of each word in uppercase.

    Or type **uppercase** to change all the letters to uppercase.

    Or type **lowercase** to change all the letters to lowercase.

    Or type **none** to leave the text as is (possibly canceling out an inherited value).

Many fonts have a corresponding small caps variant that includes uppercase versions of the letters proportionately reduced to small caps size. You can call up the small caps variant with the font-variant property.

To use a small caps font:

1. Type **font-variant:**.

2. Type **small-caps**.

✔ Tips

- To stop using the small caps variant for a dependent style, use **font-variant: none**.

- I've had trouble using text-transform in combination with a variety of font values *(see page 264)*. If you plan to use text-transform, I advise specifying the font values separately.

```
code.html
<HTML><HEAD><TITLE>Changing the text
case</TITLE>

<STYLE>

H1 {text-transform:uppercase ; text-align:center;
letter-spacing:.5em; background:green;
color:yellow; font-size: 20pt; font-weight:
normal; font-family: "Nueva Roman", "Lithos
Regular"}

P {text-align:justify; text-indent:8pt; font:
10pt/15pt "Myriad Roman", "Verdana"}

P.intro {text-indent:0;font: italic bold}

P.intro EM {font-style:normal}

EM {text-transform:uppercase}
```

Figure 15.29 *I've decided to display the headers and emphasized text in all uppercase letters.*

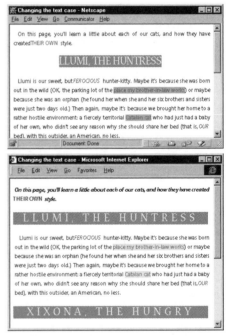

Figure 15.30 *You can see how important it is to test your pages with both browsers. Although both support the text-transform property, the fact that Netscape (top) doesn't support letter-spacing might make you decide not to display the headers in uppercase letters.*

Layout with Styles

```
code.html
<HTML><HEAD><TITLE>Displaying
elements</TITLE>
<LINK REL=stylesheet HREF="llumxixo.css">
</HEAD><BODY>
<P class=intro>On this page, you'll learn a little
about each of our cats, and how they have created
<EM>their own</EM> style.
<H1>Llumi, the Huntress</H1>
<IMG SRC="llumineu.gif" ALT="Llumi in the
snow"><IMG SRC="llumgesp.gif" ALT="Llumi in the
jungle">
```

Figure 16.1 *This is the document I use for most of this chapter. Notice that I have linked the page to an external style sheet that contains the formatting from Chapter 15, Formatting Text with Styles, in order to keep the focus on what we're doing here.*

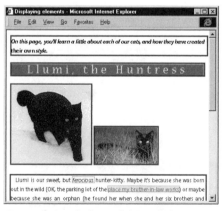

Figure 16.2 *Each element has its own box. Some boxes are block-level and automatically start a new paragraph (like the text paragraphs and header). Others are inline and do not start a new paragraph (like the EM element containing the word "ferocious").*

Every item that you create with styles sheets is enclosed in an invisible box. You can control the size, color, and spacing of the box, as well as the way it flows with respect to other objects on the page.

An element's box may be *block-level* (thereby generating a new paragraph) or *inline* (not generating a new paragraph).

There are three special areas of the box that you can control. First, surrounding the contents is a space called the *padding*. You can control the padding's width. Around the padding is the *border*. The border can be colored and thickened, and can also have texture. Around the border is a transparent space called the *margin*. Although you can't color the margin, you can change its width and height, thereby controlling the position of the elements on the page.

Some layout styles, especially percentage values, depend on an element's parent. A *parent* is the element that contains the current element. For example, the BODY might contain H1 and P tags, and thus is a parent to them. However, if the BODY is sectioned into DIV tags and the P tags are enclosed in one of the DIVs, then the DIV is the P's parent (and the BODY is the DIV's parent). Finally, the P tag might contain an EM, and, in turn, be its parent.

Offsetting Elements In the Natural Flow

Each element has a natural location in a page's flow. Moving the element with respect to this original location is called *relative positioning*. The surrounding elements are not affected—at all.

To offset elements within the natural flow:

1. Type **position:relative;** (don't forget the semicolon).

2. Type **top**, **right**, **bottom**, or **left**.

3. Type **:v**, where *v* is the desired distance that you want to offset the element from its natural location, either as an absolute or relative value (10pt, or 2em, for example).

4. If desired, type **;** (semicolon) and repeat steps 2 and 3 for additional directions.

✔ Tips

■ The "relative" in *relative positioning* refers to the element's original position, not the surrounding elements **(Figure 16.5)**. You can't move an element with respect to other elements. Instead, you move it with respect to where it used to be. Yes, this is important!

■ The other elements are not affected by the offsets—they flow with respect to the *original* containing box of the element, and may even be overlapped.

■ To flow text around an image, the image must be positioned relatively.

■ Including **position:relative** enables offsets. Without it, the offsets may not work. (In Explorer, they definitely won't.)

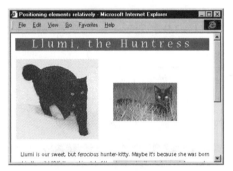

```
code.html
<STYLE>
IMG {position:relative;top:0;left:0}
IMG.off {position:relative;top:-40;left:30}
</STYLE></HEAD><BODY>

<P class=intro>On this page, you'll learn a little
about each of our cats, and how they have
created <EM>their own</EM> style.

<H1>Llumi, the Huntress</H1>

<IMG SRC="llumineu.gif" ALT="Llumi in the
snow"><IMG SRC="llumgesp.gif" ALT="Llumi in
the jungle" CLASS=off>
```

Figure 16.3 *The offsets for a relatively positioned element are with respect to where the element would have gone had you omitted the offsets. They don't have any relationship to other elements on the page.*

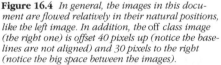

Figure 16.4 *In general, the images in this document are flowed relatively in their natural positions, like the left image. In addition, the* off *class image (the right one) is offset 40 pixels up (notice the baselines are not aligned) and 30 pixels to the right (notice the big space between the images).*

Figure 16.5 *An element is moved with respect to its natural position in the flow, not with respect to other elements.*

Offsetting Elements In the Natural Flow

```
code.html

<HTML><HEAD><TITLE>Positioning
elements</TITLE>

<LINK REL=stylesheet HREF="llumxixo.css">

<STYLE>

IMG {position:absolute; left:0; top:0}

</STYLE></HEAD><BODY>

<P class=intro>On this page, you'll learn a little
about each of our cats, and how they have
created <EM>their own</EM> style.

<H1>Llumi, the Huntress</H1>

<IMG SRC="llumineu.gif" ALT="Llumi in the
snow">

<IMG SRC="llumgesp.gif" ALT="Llumi in the
jungle">

<P>Llumi is our sweet, but <EM>ferocious</EM>
```

Figure 16.6 *You can apply the* position *property to any element. In this example, with offsets of 0 for both top and left, the images will appear at the upper-left corner of the parent element, in this case the BODY.*

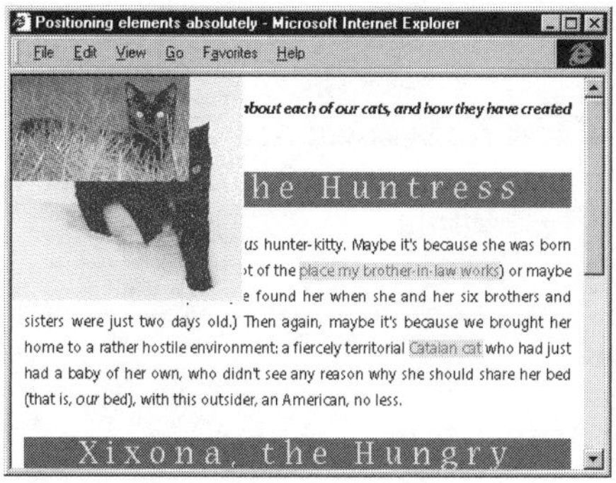

Figure 16.7 *Absolutely positioned elements are taken out of the flow—and as you can see here, the rest of the elements flow as if the images were not there, creating overlapped and covered elements. You can use offsets to determine the exact position of the elements—and avoid or control overlapping, as desired.*

Positioning Elements Absolutely

The elements in your Web page generally flow in the order in which they appear. That is, if the IMG tag comes before the P, the image appears before the paragraph. This is called the normal flow. You can take elements out of the normal flow—and position them *absolutely*—by specifying their precise position with respect to their parent element.

To absolutely position elements:

1. Type **position:absolute;** (don't forget the semicolon).

2. Type **top**, **right**, **bottom**, or **left**.

3. Type **:v**, where *v* is the desired distance that you want to offset the element from its parent element, either expressed as an absolute or relative value (10pt, or 2em, for example), or as a percentage of the parent element.

4. If desired, type **;** (semicolon) and repeat steps 2 and 3 for additional directions.

✔ Tips

■ For more information on parent elements, see page 273.

■ Because absolutely positioned elements are taken out of the flow of the document, they can overlap each other. (This is not always bad.)

■ If you don't specify an offset for an absolutely positioned item, the item appears in its natural position (after the header in this example), but does not affect the flow of subsequent items.

Positioning Elements in 3D

Once you start fiddling with relative and absolute positioning, it's quite possible to find that your elements have overlapped. You can choose which element should be on top.

To position elements in 3D:

1. Type **z-index:**.

2. Type **n**, where *n* is a number that indicates the element's level in the stack of objects.

✔ Tips

■ The higher the z-index, the higher up the element will be in the stack.

■ You can use both positive and negative values for z-index.

```
code.html

<HTML><HEAD><TITLE>Positioning elements in
3D</TITLE>

<LINK REL=stylesheet HREF="llumxixo.css">

<STYLE>

IMG {position:absolute}

</STYLE></HEAD><BODY>

<P class=intro>On this page, you'll learn a little
about each of our cats, and how they have
created <EM>their own</EM> style.

<H1>Llumi, the Huntress</H1>

<IMG SRC="llumineu.gif" ALT="Llumi in the
snow">

<IMG SRC="llumgesp.gif" ALT="Llumi in the
jungle" STYLE="z-index:-1">

<DIV STYLE="position:relative;left:200;
width:240">
```

Figure 16.8 *By using a negative value for the second image's z-index, I ensure that it will be placed below other images. (I also adjusted the width of the DIV so that it wouldn't overlap the images in this example.)*

Figure 16.9 *The second image is underneath the first one and thus cannot be seen.*

Positioning Elements in 3D

```
code.html

<HTML><HEAD><TITLE>Positioning
elements</TITLE>

<LINK REL=stylesheet HREF="llumxixo.css">

<STYLE>

IMG {display:none}

</STYLE></HEAD><BODY>

<P class=intro>On this page, you'll learn a little
about each of our cats, and how they have
created <EM>their own</EM> style.

<H1>Llumi, the Huntress</H1>

<IMG SRC="llumineu.gif" ALT="Llumi in the
snow">

<IMG SRC="llumgesp.gif" ALT="Llumi in the
jungle">

<P>Llumi is our sweet, but <EM>ferocious</EM>
hunter-kitty. Maybe it's because she was born out
in the wild (OK, the parking lot
```

Figure 16.10 *Setting the IMG tag to display none means that any images inserted in the HTML document (like the two shown here) will be hidden from the visitor.*

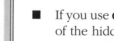

Figure 16.11 *The images are nowhere to be seen. Notice that the remaining elements flow right over the space where the images would have been displayed. It's as if the images were not part of the HTML document at all.*

Displaying and Hiding Elements

The display property is useful for hiding or revealing particular elements depending on the visitor's browser, language preference, or other criteria. You can also set elements to display as block-level or inline. Or you can display an element as a list item—even without the LI tag.

To specify how elements should be displayed:

1. Type **display:**.

2. Type **none** to hide the given elements.

   Or type **block** to display the element as a block-level (thus starting a new paragraph).

   Or type **inline** to display the element as inline (not starting a new paragraph).

   Or type **list-item** to display the element as if you had used the LI tag (*see pages 135–141*).

✔ Tips

- If you use **display:none**, no trace remains of the hidden element in the browser window. There is no empty space.

- The **display:none** definition, combined with scripts, is ideal for hiding elements that belong to one of several versions contained in the same HTML document.

Setting the Height or Width for an Element

You can set the height and width for most elements, including images, form elements, and even blocks of text. If you have several elements on a page that are the same size, you can set their height and width simultaneously. This information helps browsers set aside the proper amount of space necessary and thus view the rest of the page—generally, the text—more quickly.

To set the height or width for an element:

1. Type **width:w**, where *w* is the width of the element, and can be expressed either as an absolute value or as a percentage of the parent element.

2. Type **height:h**, where *h* is the height of the element, and can be expressed only as an absolute value.

✔ Tips

■ Using a percentage value for the width property is a little tricky. If you are used to the WIDTH attribute for the IMG tag, you might think 50% means half of the original image size. Not so. It means half of the width *of the parent element—*no matter what the original width of the image was. *(For more on parent elements, see page 273.)*

■ You cannot set the WIDTH property for most text tags (like P and H1). To set the width of a block of text, enclose your P or H1 tags (or whatever) in DIV tags.

```
                    code.html
<HTML><HEAD><TITLE>Positioning elements
relatively</TITLE>

<LINK REL=stylesheet HREF="llumxixo.css">

<STYLE>

IMG {position:relative;top:0;left:0}

IMG.off {position:relative;top:-40;left:30}

</STYLE></HEAD><BODY>

<DIV STYLE="position:relative; left:100;
width:200">

<P class=intro>On this page, you'll learn a little
about each of our cats, and how they have
created <EM>their own</EM> style.</DIV>

<H1>Llumi, the Huntress</H1>

<IMG SRC="llumineu.gif" ALT="Llumi in the
snow">
```

Figure 16.12 *For this example, I've created a DIV section (since the width property doesn't work with P and H1 tags, among others).*

Figure 16.13 *The DIV section is restricted to a width of 200 pixels.*

```
code.html
<HTML><HEAD><TITLE>Setting the
border</TITLE>

<LINK REL=stylesheet HREF="llumxixo.css">

<STYLE>

IMG {position:relative;top:0;left:0;border:thick
double green}

IMG.off {position:relative;top:-40;left:30}

</STYLE></HEAD><BODY>

<DIV STYLE="position:relative;left:100;
width:200">

<P class=intro>On this page, you'll learn a little
about each of our cats, and how they have
created <EM>their own</EM> style.</DIV>

<H1>Llumi, the Huntress</H1>

<IMG SRC="llumineu.gif" ALT="Llumi in the
```

Figure 16.14 *Here I've applied the border property to the IMG tag so that all images will have a thick double green border.*

Figure 16.15 *Double borders are something you can not achieve with HTML tags alone.*

Setting the Border

You can create a border around an element and then set its thickness, style, and color. If you've specified any padding *(see page 281)* the border encloses both the padding and the contents of the element.

To set the border:

1. Type **border**.

2. If desired, type **-top**, **-bottom**, **-left**, or **-right**, (with no space after **border**) to limit where the border should go.

3. If desired, type **thin**, **medium**, **thick**, or an absolute value (like **4px**) to determine the thickness of the border. Medium is the default.

4. If desired, type **none**, **dotted**, **dashed**, **solid**, **double**, **groove**, **ridge**, **inset**, or **outset** to determine the border style.

5. If desired, type **color**, where *color* is either one of the 16 color names or is expressed as described on page 265.

✔ Tips

■ You can define any part of the border individually. For example, you can use **border-left-width:5** to set just the width of just the left border. Or use **border-color:red** to set just the color of all four sides. The twenty different properties are border-style (border-top-style, border-right-style, etc.), border-color (border-top-color, etc.), border-width (border-top-width, etc.), and border (border-top, etc.)

■ If you don't set the color of the border, the browser should use the color you have specified for the element's contents *(see page 265).*

Adding Padding Around an Element

Padding is just what it sounds like: extra space around the contents of an element but inside the border. Think of Santa Claus' belly—nicely padded, while being held in by his belt (the border). You can change the padding's thickness, but not its color or texture.

To add padding around an element:

1. Type **padding**.

2. If desired, type **-top**, **-bottom**, **-left**, or **-right**, (with no space after **padding**) to limit the padding to one side of the object.

3. Type **:x**, where *x* is the amount of desired space to be added, expressed in units or as a percentage of the parent element.

✔ Tips

- There are several shortcuts available for setting the padding values. You can use **padding: t r b l** to set the top, right, bottom, and left values at once, in that order (with just a space separating each value). Or **padding: v h** to set the top and bottom values (v) equally and the right and left values (h) equally. Or type **padding: t h b** to set the top value (t), the left and right values to a single value (h), and then the bottom value (b). Or type **padding: a**, where *a* is the value for all sides.

- The values may be expressed in absolute terms or as a percentage of the corresponding width in the parent element.

```
code.html
<HTML><HEAD><TITLE>Setting the
padding</TITLE>
<LINK REL=stylesheet HREF="llumxixo.css">
<STYLE>
IMG {position:relative;top:0;left:0;border: thick
double green}
IMG.off {position:relative;top:-40;left:30}
H1 {padding:10}
</STYLE></HEAD><BODY>
<DIV STYLE="position:relative; left:100;
width:200">
<P class=intro>On this page, you'll learn a little
about each of our cats, and how they have
created <EM>their own</EM> style.</DIV>
```

Figure 16.16 *I've added some padding to the header to create a larger background around the text.*

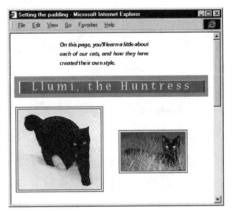

Figure 16.17 *Ten pixels of padding have been added all around the text in the header.*

```
                code.html
<HTML><HEAD><TITLE>Setting the
margin</TITLE>

<LINK REL=stylesheet HREF="llumxixo.css">

<STYLE>

IMG {position:relative;top:0;left:0;border: thick
double green}

IMG.off {position:relative;top:-30;left:30}

H1 {padding:10;margin:30}

</STYLE></HEAD><BODY>

<DIV STYLE="position:relative; left:100;
width:200">

<P class=intro>On this page, you'll learn a little
about each of our cats, and how they have
created <EM>their own</EM> style.</DIV>

<H1>Llumi, the Huntress</H1>
```

Figure 16.18 *To indent an element on all sides, increase the size of its margins.*

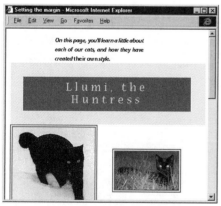

Figure 16.19 *Increasing the size of the margin (the transparent space around the header) means there isn't enough room to fit the header on one line. (Although I highlight the margin here in color, it is actually transparent.)*

Setting the Margins around an Element

The margin is the amount of transparent space between one element and the next, in addition to and outside of any padding *(see page 280)* or border *(see page 279)* around the element.

To set an element's margins:

1. Type **margin**.

2. If desired, type **-top**, **-bottom**, **-left**, or **-right**, (with no space after **margin**) to limit where space should be added.

3. Type **:x**, where *x* is the amount of desired space to be added, expressed in units or as a percentage of the width of the corresponding value of the parent element.

✔ Tips

- You can also use **margin: t r b l** to set the top, right, bottom, and left values at once, in that order (with just a space separating each value). Or **margin: v h** to set the top and bottom values (v) equally and the right and left values (h) equally. Or type **margin: t h b** to set the top value (t), the left and right values to a single value (h), and then the bottom value (b). Last but not least, you can type **margin: a**, where *a* is the value to be used for all sides.

- The values may be expressed in absolute terms or as a percentage of the corresponding width in the parent element.

- Margin values for absolutely positioned boxes are specified with the offset properties—top, bottom, right, and left *(see page 275)*.

Aligning Elements Vertically

If you have elements (like images) on your page that you would like aligned in the same way, you can use the vertical-align property to set the tag, or a class of the tag, accordingly.

To position text:

1. Type **vertical-align:**

2. Type **baseline** to align the element's baseline with the parent's baseline.

   Or type **middle** to align the middle of the element with the middle of the parent.

   Or type **sub** to position the element as a subscript of the parent.

   Or type **super** to position the element as a superscript of the parent.

   Or type **text-top** to align the top of the element with the top of the parent.

   Or type **text-bottom** to align the bottom of the element with the bottom of the parent.

   Or type **top** to align the top of the element with the top of the tallest element on the line.

   Or type **bottom** to align the bottom of the element to the bottom of the lowest element on the line.

   Or type a percentage of the line height of the element, which may be positive or negative.

```
code.html

<HTML><HEAD><TITLE>Aligning elements
vertically</TITLE>

<LINK REL=stylesheet HREF="llumxixo.css">

<STYLE>

IMG {position:relative;top:0;left:0;border: thick
double green;vertical-align:top}

IMG.off {position:relative;left:30}

H1 {padding:10;margin:30}

</STYLE></HEAD><BODY>

<DIV STYLE="position:relative;left:100;
width:200">

<P class=intro>On this page, you'll learn a little
about each of our cats, and how they have
created <EM>their own</EM> style.</DIV>

<H1>Llumi, the Huntress</H1>

<IMG SRC="llumineu.gif" ALT="Llumi in the
snow">

<IMG SRC="llumgesp.gif" ALT="Llumi in the
jungle" CLASS=off>

<P>Llumi is our sweet, but <EM>ferocious</EM>
```

Figure 16.20 *I've eliminated the top offset from the* off *class images in order to show the full effect of vertically aligning all the images on this page. Notice that all the images in the document are affected by the vertical-align property. The* off *class images simply have additional properties of their own.*

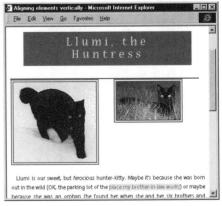

Figure 16.21 *The images are aligned with respect to their top edges.*

```
                    code.html
<STYLE>

IMG {position:relative;top:0;left:0; border: thick
double green; vertical-align:middle; float:left}

IMG.right {float:right}

H1 {padding:10;margin:30}

</STYLE></HEAD><BODY>

<DIV STYLE="position:relative;left:100;
width:200">

<P class=intro>On this page, you'll learn a little
about each of our cats, and how they have
created <EM>their own</EM> style.</DIV>

<H1>Llumi, the Huntress</H1>

<IMG SRC="llumineu.gif" ALT="Llumi in the
snow">

<P>Llumi is our sweet, but <EM>ferocious</EM>
hunter-kitty. Maybe it's because she was born out
in the wild (OK, the parking lot of the [snip]
rather hostile environment:

<IMG SRC="llumgesp.gif" ALT="Llumi in the
jungle" CLASS=right>
```

Figure 16.22 *Please note that I moved the second image (llumgesp.gif) lower down on the page for aesthetic reasons.*

Figure 16.23 *By default, images will allow text to flow to the right. Images that belong to the "right" class, like the image of Llumi in the grass, will let text flow to the left.*

Wrapping Text around Elements

You can define your images (or other elements) so that text always wraps around them to the left or right, down both sides, or never at all.

To wrap text around elements:

1. Type **float:**.

2. Type **left** if you want the element on the left and the text to flow to its right.

   Or type **right** if you want the element on the right and the text to flow to its left.

✔ Tips

- Remember, the direction you choose applies to the element you're floating, not to the text that flows around it. When you **float: left**, the text flows to the right, and vice-versa.

- The trick to making text flow between elements is to always put the image directly before the text that should flow next to it.

- For more information about flowing text between images, consult *Wrapping Text around Images* on page 88. The CSS properties work the same way as the regular HTML tags.

Stopping Text Wrap

When you flow text around images with HTML tags, you can create a line break that effectively stops text from flowing. With style sheets you can mark a particular tag so that other elements (like text) cannot flow around it.

To stop text wrap:

1. Type **clear:**.

2. Type **left** to stop the flow until the left side is clear of all elements.

   Or type **right** to stop the flow until the right side is clear of elements.

   Or type **both** to stop the flow until both sides are clear.

   Or type **none** to continue the flow.

✔ Tips

■ If you're like me and can never correctly answer 50-50 Trivial Pursuit questions like "Which hand is God holding out to Adam in the Sistine Chapel, his right or his left?", then perhaps this clarification will be useful: When you use **clear: right**, you mean you want to stop text flow *until the right is clear*. Confusingly, the result is that the left *looks clear*. Look at Figure 16.25 again. That big space on the left next to the second image only appears because the text must stop flowing until the right is clear. At that point, the text continues to flow again.

■ The use of the clear style is analogous to the BR tag with the CLEAR attribute *(see page 90)*.

```
code.html
<STYLE>
IMG {position:relative;top:0;left:0; border: thick
double green;vertical-align:middle; float:left}
IMG.right {float:right;clear:right}
H1 {padding:10;margin:30}
</STYLE></HEAD><BODY>
<DIV STYLE="position:relative;left:100;
width:200">
<P class=intro>On this page, you'll learn a little
about each of our cats, and how they have
created <EM>their own</EM> style.</DIV>
<H1>Llumi, the Huntress</H1>
<IMG SRC="llumineu.gif" ALT="Llumi in the
snow">
<P>Llumi is our sweet, but <EM>ferocious</EM>
hunter-kitty. Maybe it's because she was born out
in the wild (OK, the parking lot of the [snip]
rather hostile environment:
<IMG SRC="llumgesp.gif" ALT="Llumi in the
jungle" CLASS=right>a fiercely territorial
```

Figure 16.24 *To keep text from flowing to the left of the second image, I've added the clear:right definition to the images that belong to the* right *class.*

Figure 16.25 *When you clear right, you actually generate an empty (clear) space to the left, since the flow must stop until the right side is clear.*

```
╔══════════ code.html ═══════════╗
<HTML><HEAD><TITLE>Stopping text
wrap</TITLE>

<LINK REL=stylesheet HREF="llumxixo.css">

<STYLE>

IMG {position:relative;top:0;left:0;border: thick
double green;vertical-align:middle;float:left}

IMG.right {float:right}

H1 {padding:10;margin:30}

HR {color:red;height:10}

</STYLE></HEAD><BODY>

<DIV STYLE="position:relative;left:100;
width:200">

<P class=intro>On this page, you'll learn a little
about each of our cats, and how they have
created <EM>their own</EM> style.

<HR>

</DIV>
```

Figure 16.26 *You can add color to horizontal lines (as shown here), or to any other element—except images.*

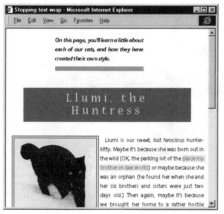

Figure 16.27 *The horizontal line shown below the first paragraph is red. Don't believe me? Check out the Web site (see page 20). Notice that the line has the same width as the paragraph of text that it follows. That's because it belongs to the DIV which we limited to 200 pixels wide (see page 278).*

Changing the Foreground Color

You can change the color of any element, including horizontal lines, form elements, and tables.

To change the foreground color:

1. Type **color:**.

2. Type **colorname**, where *colorname* is one of the 16 predefined colors.

   Or type **#rrggbb**, where *rrggbb* is the hexadecimal representation of the desired color.

   Or type **rgb(r, g, b)**, where *r, g,* and *b* are integers from 0-255 that specify the amount of red, green, or blue, respectively, in the desired color.

   Or type **rgb(r%, g%, b%)**, where *r, g,* and *b* specify the percentage of red, green, and blue, respectively, in the desired color.

✔ Tips

- If you type a value for r, g, or b higher than 255 it will be replaced with 255. Similarly a percentage higher than 100% will be replaced with 100%.

- You can also use the color property to change the color of text. For more information, consult *Setting the Text Color* on page 265.

- Changing the foreground color of an image doesn't have any effect. (You'll have to do that in an image editing program.) You can, however, change the background color (that is, what will appear through transparent areas). For more information, consult *Changing the Background* on page 286.

Changing the Background

The background refers not to the background of the entire page, but to the background of a particular tag. In other words, you can change the background of any element—including images, form elements, and tables.

To change the background color or image:

1. Type **background:**.

2. Type **transparent** or **color**, where *color* is a color name or hex color.

3. If desired, type **url(image.gif)**, to use an image for the background.

   If desired, type **repeat** to tile the image both horizontally and vertically, **repeat-x** to tile the image only horizontally, **repeat-y** to tile the image only vertically, or **no-repeat** to not tile the image.

   If desired, type **fixed** or **scroll** to determine whether the background should scroll along with the canvas.

   If desired, type **x y** to set the position of the background image, where *x* and *y* can be expressed as a percentage or as an absolute distance. Or use values of *top*, *center*, or *bottom* for *x* and *left*, *center*, and *right* for *y*.

✔ Tips

■ Set the background for the BODY tag to create a background for the entire page. (It's the only way Netscape will apply the background definition.)

■ If you specify both a color and a URL for the background, the color will be used until the URL is loaded, and will be seen through any transparent portions of the background image. (If you don't specify a color, Netscape will use black.)

```
code.html
<HTML><HEAD><TITLE>Changing the
background</TITLE>

<LINK REL=stylesheet HREF="llumxixo.css">

<STYLE>

IMG {position:relative;top:0;left:0; border: thick
double green; vertical-align:middle;float:left}

IMG.right {float:right}

H1 {padding:10;margin:30}

HR {color:red;height:10}

BODY {background:url(llumgesp.gif)}

P {background:white;padding:5}

</STYLE></HEAD><BODY>

<DIV STYLE="position:relative;left:100;
width:200">
```

Figure 16.28 *I've added the background property to the BODY tag to create a background for the entire page. To keep the text legible, I added a white background to all the P tags (which will be added to and may override any P definitions from the external style sheet).*

Figure 16.29 *I'm continually amazed at how ugly I can make a page look by simply adding a background. Note that since the background image is smaller than the browser window, the image is automatically tiled to fill the window. Oh joy.*

```
┌─────────────────────────────────────┐
│ ▨          code.html         ▨      │
├─────────────────────────────────────┤
│ <STYLE>                             │
│                                     │
│ IMG {position:relative;top:0;left:0;border: thick
│ double green;vertical-align:middle;float:left}
│                                     │
│ IMG.right {float:right}             │
│                                     │
│ H1 {padding:10;margin:30}           │
│                                     │
│ HR {color:red;height:10}            │
│                                     │
│ BODY {background:url(llumgesp.gif)} │
│                                     │
│ P {background:white;padding:5}      │
│                                     │
│ </STYLE></HEAD><BODY>               │
│                                     │
│ <DIV STYLE="position:relative;left:100;
│ width:100; height:100;overflow:scroll ">
│                                     │
│ <P class=intro>On this page, you'll learn a little
```

Figure 16.30 *After limiting the height to 100 pixels, I used the overflow property to keep the text block the desired size while enabling visitors to access the hidden contents with scroll bars.*

Figure 16.31 *Scroll bars appear both below and to the right of the DIV section.*

Figure 16.32 *If you set overflow to hidden, no scroll bars appear, and the extra contents cannot be viewed by your visitors.*

Determining Where Overflow Should Go

If you make an element's box smaller than its contents with the height and width properties *(see page 278)*, the excess content has to go somewhere. You can decide where it should go with the overflow property.

To determine where overflow should go:

1. Type **overflow:**.

2. Type **visible** to expand the element box so that its contents fit. This is the default option.

   Or type **hidden** to hide any contents that don't fit in the element box.

   Or type **scroll** to add scroll bars to the element so that the visitor can access the overflow if they so desire.

✔ **Tip**

■ If you don't specify the overflow property, excess content will flow below (but not to the right of) the element's box. This is one of the reasons that assigning a height to text sometimes seems like it has no effect. (The other reason is that the height and width properties have no effect on many text tags, like P and H1. Instead use a DIV tag. See page 253 for details.)

Clipping an Element

You can create a window that only reveals a particular section of the element. Currently, the window must be a rectangle, but the idea is that other shapes will be available in future revisions of CSS.

To clip an element:

1. Type **clip: rect(**.

2. Type **t r b l**, where *t*, *r*, *b*, and *l* are the top, right, bottom, and left coordinates of the rectangular portion of the element that you want to display **(Figure 16.35)**.

3. Type the final **)**.

✔ Tips

■ Presently, an element has to be positioned absolutely *(see page 275)* before you can clip it.

■ Remember not to add commas between the offset values.

■ The offset values can be absolute (3px) or relative (3em).

■ Clipping does not just affect the element's content. It also hides padding and borders.

■ Clipping is currently under review by the World Wide Web Consortium and may have changed by the time you read this.

```
code.html

<STYLE>

IMG {position:relative;top:0;left:0;border: thick
double green;vertical-align:middle;float:left}
IMG.right {float:right}

IMG.clip {position:absolute;top:150;
clip:rect(0 180 130 40)}

H1 {padding:10;margin:30}
HR {color:red;height:10}
BODY {background:url(llumgesp.gif)}
P {background:white;padding:5}

</STYLE></HEAD><BODY>

<DIV STYLE="position:absolute;left:100;
width:200;clip:rect(0 50 100 0)">
```

Figure 16.33 *The clipping information from the image means we will start at the very top (0) and go down 130 pixels. Then we'll start at pixel 40 and go across to the right until pixel 180.*

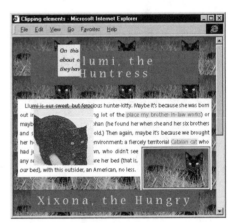

Figure 16.34 *There must be a useful way to implement clipping, but I haven't found it yet. Certainly hiding bits of text and images isn't it.*

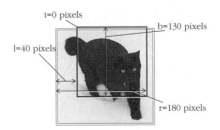

Figure 16.35 *The values for left and top are the parts you clip out. The right and bottom values minus the left and top determine what remains.*

```
┌─────────────────────────────────────┐
│▓▓▓▓▓▓▓▓▓     code.html     ▓▓▓▓▓▓▓▓▓█│
├─────────────────────────────────────┤
│<HTML><HEAD><TITLE>Controlling        │
│overflow</TITLE>                      │
│                                      │
│<LINK REL=stylesheet HREF="llumxixo.css">│
│                                      │
│<STYLE>                               │
│                                      │
│UL {list-style:url(xixo.gif) inside}  │
│                                      │
│OL {list-style:lower-alpha}           │
│                                      │
│</STYLE></HEAD><BODY>                 │
│                                      │
│<H1>Great Things about Cats</H1>      │
│                                      │
│<UL>                                  │
│<LI>They're beautiful and elegant [snip]│
│<LI>You don't ever need an alarm clock [snip]│
│<LI>If you're ever hungry, they're sure to [snip]│
│</UL>                                 │
│                                      │
│<H1>A Day in the Life</H1>            │
│                                      │
│<OL>                                  │
│<LI>Wake Liz up for food              │
└─────────────────────────────────────┘
```

Figure 16.36 *Here I've set the bullet for unordered lists to an image (yes, it's a cat). I've also decided to number ordered lists with lowercase letters. (The example text is snipped to fit on this page.)*

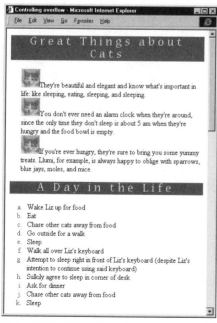

Figure 16.37 *Being able to choose your own bullets for unordered lists is so cool!*

Setting List Properties

There are several bullet styles for unordered lists, and several number styles for numbered lists. You can set these styles globally with the list-style property.

To set list properties:

1. Type **list-style:**.

2. If desired, to set the list item property to a solid, round circle, type **disc**.

    Or type **circle** to use an empty, round circle.

    Or type **square** to use a solid square.

    Or type **decimal** to use arabic numerals (1, 2, 3, etc.).

    Or type **lower-alpha** to use lowercase letters (a, b,c, etc.).

    Or type **upper-alpha** to use uppercase letters (A, B, C, etc.).

    Or type **lower-roman** to use lowercase Roman numerals (i, ii, iii, etc.).

    Or type **upper-roman** to use uppercase Roman numerals (I, II, III, etc.).

    Or type **url(image.gif)**, where *image.gif* is the URL of the image that you want to use as a marker for your lists.

3. If desired, type **outside** to hang the marker to the left of the list items. Type **inside** to align the marker flush left together with all the other lines in the list item paragraph.

✔ Tip

■ The **outside** value won't create hanging indents properly if you use big images for bullets like I did in Figure 16.37. Until it does, **inside** looks better.

Specifying Page Breaks

At some point, your visitors may decide to print your Web page. Most browsers will automatically adjust the contents on a page in order to best fit the paper size the visitor has chosen in the Page Setup dialog box. With CSS2 you can specify exactly where you want the page to break when your visitor goes to print it out.

To specify a page break after a given tag:

Type **page-break-after:always**.

To specify a page break before a given tag:

Type **page-break-before:always**.

To remove page breaks:

Type **page-break-after:auto** or **page-break-before:auto**.

```
code.html

<HTML><HEAD><TITLE>Setting page
breaks</TITLE>

<LINK REL=stylesheet HREF="llumxixo.css">

<STYLE>

UL {list-style:url(xixo.gif) inside}

OL {list-style:lower-alpha}

H1 {page-break-before:always}

</STYLE></HEAD><BODY>

<H1 STYLE="page-break-before:auto">Great
Things about Cats</H1>

<UL>

<LI>They're beautiful and elegant and know
what's important in life: like sleeping, eating,
```

Figure 16.38 *To make each list print on a separate page, I've added a page break to the header tag. To avoid creating an empty page before the first header, I've used a local style to override the page break in the first header.*

Scripts

Scripts are little programs that add interactivity to your page. You can write simple scripts to add an alert box or a bit of text to your page, or more complicated scripts that load particular pages according to your visitor's browser or change a frame's background color depending on where they point the mouse. Because scripts are perfect for moving elements around on a page, they are the backbone of dynamic HTML, also known as DHTML.

Most scripts are written in JavaScript, which was developed by Netscape Communications (the same folks who created Netscape Navigator and Netscape Communicator). That's because JavaScript is the scripting language that is supported by most browsers, including Communicator and Explorer. VBScript, developed by Microsoft, currently works only with Explorer for Windows.

Of course, there are entire books written about JavaScript and VBScript—and some very fine ones indeed, including *JavaScript for the World Wide Web: Visual QuickStart Guide, 3rd Edition* by Dori Smith and Tom Negrino, and *VBScript for the World Wide Web* by Paul Thurrott. In this chapter, rather than talking about how to write scripts, I'll stick to explaining how to insert those scripts, once created, into your HTML documents.

For a look at a few important scripts that you can use in your pages, consult Chapter 18, *JavaScript Essentials*.

Adding an "Automatic" Script

There are two kinds of scripts—those that are executed without the visitor having to do anything and those that react to something the visitor has done. The first group might be called "automatic scripts" and are executed by the browser when the page is loaded. You can have as many automatic scripts as you like on a page. They will run in the order they appear. (The second group, "triggered scripts", is discussed on page 294.)

To add an automatic script:

1. In your HTML document, type **<SCRIPT**.

2. Type **LANGUAGE="script"**, where *script* is the name of the scripting language you'll be using: *JavaScript, VBScript,* etc.

3. Type **TYPE="text/language-name"**, where *language-name* identifies the scripting language you're using: *javascript, vbscript,* etc.

4. Type **>**.

5. Type the content of the script.

6. Type **</SCRIPT>**.

✔ Tips

■ Although the LANGUAGE attribute has been deprecated in HTML 4 in favor of **TYPE="text/language-name"**, it remains the de facto standard. Using both covers all your bases.

■ The location of the script on the HTML page determines when it will load. Scripts are loaded in the order in which they appear in the HTML document. If you want your script to load before anything else, be sure to place it in the HEAD section.

```
<HTML><HEAD><TITLE>Simple Scripts</TITLE>
</HEAD><BODY>
<SCRIPT LANGUAGE="JavaScript"
TYPE="text/javascript">
document.write("Visca Catalunya!")
</SCRIPT>
<P>Here's the rest of the page.
</BODY></HTML>
```

Figure 17.1 *A script may appear anywhere in your HTML document, however, where it appears determines when it will be executed.*

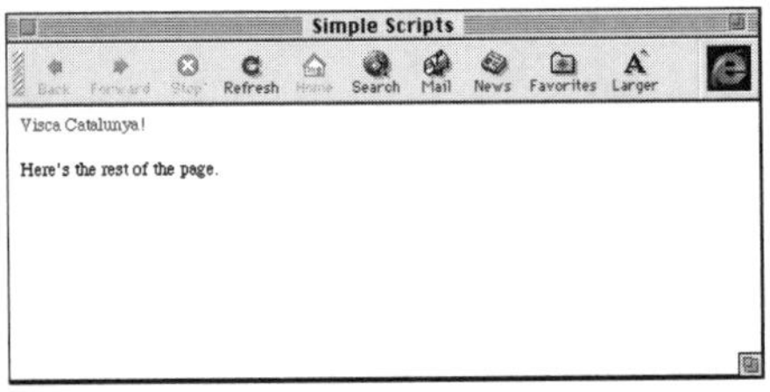

Figure 17.2 *This simple JavaScript script is output to the browser window itself. Other scripts send their results elsewhere.*

```
extscript.txt
document.write("Visca Catalunya!")
```

Figure 17.3 *Here I've created an independent text file with the same script as in Figure 17.1. I can reference this external script from inside any HTML document.*

```
code.html
<HTML><HEAD><TITLE>Simple Scripts</TITLE>
</HEAD><BODY>
<SCRIPT LANGUAGE="JavaScript"
TYPE="text/javascript" SRC="extscript.txt">
</SCRIPT>
<P>Here's the rest of the page.
</BODY></HTML>
```

Figure 17.4 *The SRC attribute not only references the script, it also automatically hides it from browsers that don't recognize the SCRIPT tag.*

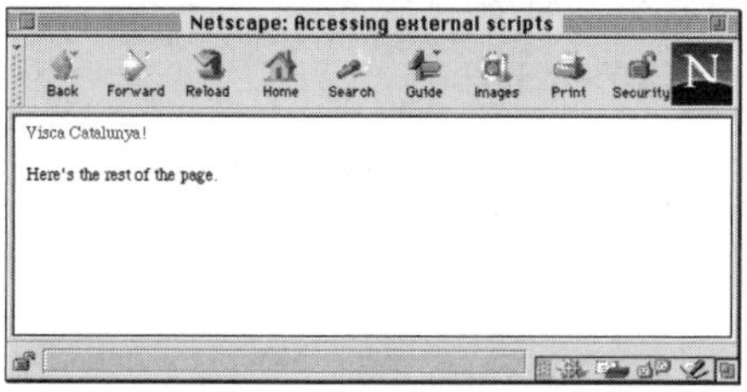

Figure 17.5 *External scripts are no different from internal ones. But they are often much more convenient.*

Calling an External Automatic Script

If you use a script in several different Web pages, you'll save time (and avoid typos) by linking the script to each page instead of typing it in each.

To call an external automatic script:

1. Type **<SCRIPT**.

2. Type **LANGUAGE="script"**, where *script* is the name of the scripting language you'll be using: *JavaScript, VBScript,* or whatever.

3. Type **TYPE="text/language-name"**, where *language-name* identifies the scripting language you're using: *javascript, vbscript,* etc.

4. Type **SRC="script.url"**, where *script.url* is the location on the server of the external script.

5. If desired, type **CHARSET=code**, where *code* is the official name for the set of characters used in the external script.

6. Type **>**.

7. Type **</SCRIPT>**.

✔ Tips

■ Using external scripts is a great way to keep older browsers from displaying your scripts as text. Since they don't understand the SCRIPT tag, they ignore it (and the SRC attribute) completely. Use NOSCRIPT to give those visitors using the older browsers an idea of what they're missing *(see page 298).*

■ Explorer for Macintosh does not yet support external scripts. Explorer for Windows has no problem with them.

Calling an External Automatic Script

Triggering a Script

Sometimes you won't want a script to run until the visitor does something to trigger it. For example, perhaps you want to run a script when the visitor mouses over a particular picture or link, or when a page is loaded. These actions—mousing over or loading a page—are called *intrinsic events*. There are currently 18 predefined intrinsic events. You use them as triggers to determine when a script will run.

To trigger a script:

1. Create the HTML tag that the intrinsic event depends on **(Figure 17.16)**.

2. Within the tag created in step 1, type **EVENT**, where *event* is an intrinsic event as defined below **(Figure 17.17)**. Unless otherwise noted, most events can be used with most HTML tags.

   ONLOAD occurs when a browser loads a page or frameset. **ONUNLOAD** occurs when it unloads. They can be used in the BODY or FRAMESET tags.

   ONCLICK occurs when the visitor clicks an element. **ONDBLCLICK** occurs when they double click it.

   ONMOUSEDOWN occurs when the visitor points at an HTML element and presses the mouse button down. **ONMOUSEUP** occurs when they let go.

   ONMOUSEOVER occurs when the visitor points at an element. **ONMOUSEMOVE** occurs when the visitor moves the pointer that is already over an element. **ONMOUSEOUT** occurs when the visitor moves the pointer away from the element.

   ONSELECT occurs when the visitor selects some text in a form element.

```
code.html
<HTML><HEAD><TITLE>Triggering
scripts</TITLE>
</HEAD><BODY>
What <A HREF="time.html">time</A> is it?
<P>Here's the rest of the page.
</BODY></HTML>
```

Figure 17.6 *First, create the HTML tag that the intrinsic event depends on. In this case, I want the script to occur when a visitor clicks the link. Therefore, I have to start with the link tag.*

```
code.html
<HTML><HEAD>
<TITLE>Triggering scripts</TITLE>
</HEAD><BODY>
What <A HREF="time.html" ONCLICK=
"alert('Today is '+ Date())">time</A> is it?
<P>Here's the rest of the page.
</BODY></HTML>
```

Figure 17.7 *The event name and the script itself go right inside the HTML tag. Make sure to enclose the script in double quotation marks.*

Figure 17.8 *A triggered script doesn't run until the visitor completes the required action. In this case, they have to click the link.*

Figure 17.9 *Once the visitor clicks the link, the script runs. In this case, an alert appears, giving the current date and time.*

ONFOCUS occurs when the visitor selects or tabs to an element. **ONBLUR** occurs when the visitor leaves an element that was "in focus".

ONKEYPRESS occurs when the visitor types any character in a form element. **ONKEYDOWN** occurs even before the visitor lets go of the key and **ONKEYUP** waits until the visitor lets go of the key. As you might imagine, these only work with form elements that you can type in.

ONSUBMIT occurs when the visitor clicks the submit button in a form *(see page 206)*. **ONRESET** occurs when the visitor resets the form *(see page 208)*.

ONCHANGE occurs when the visitor has changed the form element's value and has left that element (by tabbing out or selecting another).

3. Next, type **="script"**, where *script* is the actual script that should run when the event occurs.

✔ Tips

- ■ If your script requires quotation marks, use single quotation marks so that they're not confused with the quotation marks that enclose the entire script (in step 3).

- ■ If you need to use quotes within text that is already enclosed in single quotation marks, you can backslash them. So, you could use **ONCLICK="alert('Here is today\'s date:' + Date())"**. Without the backslash, the apostrophe in *today's* would mess up the script.

- ■ For a complete listing of which intrinsic events work with which HTML tags, consult the table on page 368.

Triggering a Script

Creating a Button that Executes a Script

HTML 4 offers a new kind of button, not restricted to a FORM element *(see page 193)* that you can add to your Web page. You can associate the button with a script to give your visitor full control over when the script should be executed.

To create a button that executes a script:

1. Type **<BUTTON TYPE="button"**.

2. Type **NAME="name"**, where *name* is the identifier for the button.

3. Type **ONCLICK="script"**, where *script* is the code (usually JavaScript) that will run when the visitor clicks the button.

4. If desired, type **STYLE="font: 14pt Lithos Regular; background:red"** (or whatever) to change the appearance of the text on the button.

5. Type **>**.

6. If desired, type the text that should appear on the button.

7. Type **</BUTTON>**.

✔ Tips

■ You can use other intrinsic events with buttons, but ONCLICK makes the most sense.

■ You can also add images to buttons. Simply insert the image between the opening and closing BUTTON tags (that is, after step 5 or 6).

■ You can also use buttons with forms *(see pages 207 and 209)*.

■ Although BUTTON is standard HTML, only Internet Explorer currently supports it.

```
code.html
<HTML><HEAD><TITLE>Associating scripts with
a button</TITLE></HEAD>

<BODY>

<BUTTON TYPE="button" NAME="Check Time"
ONCLICK="alert('Today is '+ Date())"
STYLE="font: 14pt Lithos Regular;
background:white;color:red">What time is
it?</BUTTON>

</BODY></HTML>
```

Figure 17.10 *Notice that the script is the same as the one used in the example in Figure 17.7. The style information here is optional, but it does make the button stand out. I also could have added an image.*

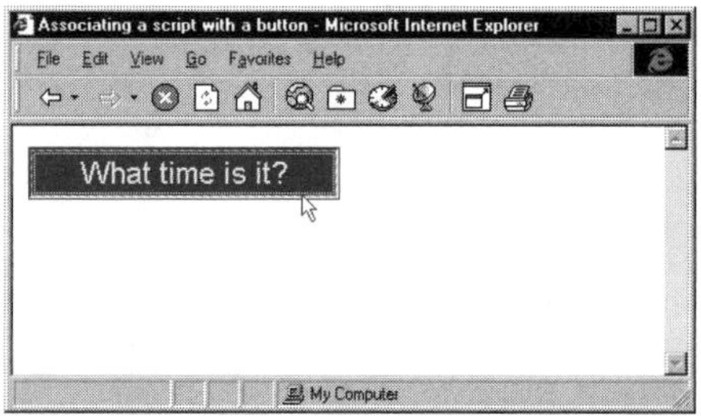

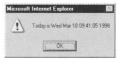

Figure 17.11 *Although the BUTTON tag is a standard part of HTML 4, only Explorer for Windows currently supports it (with or without scripts).*

Figure 17.12 *A click on the button executes the script, as shown here.*

Figure 17.13 *This is Mosaic 1. Because it doesn't understand the SCRIPT tag, it ignores it and prints out the script as if it were regular text. Ugly!*

```
code.html
<HTML><HEAD><TITLE>Llumi's big cat
dreams</TITLE>

<SCRIPT LANGUAGE="JavaScript"
TYPE="text/javascript">

<!--

    littlecat = new Image(143,83)
    littlecat.src = "real.jpg"
    bigcat = new Image(143,83)
    bigcat.src = "dream.jpg"

// end comments to hide scripts -->

</SCRIPT>

</HEAD><BODY>

<P>Point at Llumi to see what she's thinking.

<A HREF="llumipage.html" ONMOUSEOVER=
"document.catpic.src = bigcat.src"
ONMOUSEOUT = "document.catpic.src =
```

Figure 17.14 *This JavaScript script comes from Figure 18.9 on page 305. It preloads the images into cache to ensure speedy rollovers.*

Figure 17.15 *By commenting out the script, it is hidden from old browsers like this one. (Hey, it may not handle scripts, but this old version of Mosaic displays normal pages without trouble and runs on less than 1Mb of RAM.)*

Hiding Scripts from Older Browsers

Older browsers don't always understand the SCRIPT tag. If they don't, they'll just ignore it and display your script as if it were part of the body of the HTML document. To keep that from happening, it's a good idea to use commenting to hide scripts from older browsers.

To hide scripts from older browsers:

1. After the initial SCRIPT tag, type **<!--**.

2. Write the script as usual.

3. Right before the final SCRIPT tag, type your scripting language's comments symbol. For JavaScript, type **//**. For VBScript, type **'** (a single quotation mark). For TCL, type **#**.

4. If desired, add text to remind yourself why you're typing all these funny characters. Something like **end comments to hide scripts** will work just fine.

5. Type **-->**.

✔ Tips

■ The code in step 1 and in step 5 is for hiding the script from the browsers. The code in step 3 is for keeping the final **-->** from being processed as part of the script, and thus must be specific to the particular scripting language you're using.

■ I have to admit I had a hard time finding a browser old enough not to understand scripts. Hiding scripts is recommended, but I'm not sure it's essential.

Adding Alternate Information

If you give your visitors access to information through scripts, you may want to provide an alternate method of getting that data if your visitor uses a browser that can't run the scripts.

To add alternate information for older browsers:

1. Type **<NOSCRIPT>**.

2. Type the alternate information.

3. Type **</NOSCRIPT>**.

✔ Tips

■ If a browser doesn't understand the SCRIPT tag, what hope is there that it will understand NOSCRIPT? Actually it won't. It will completely ignore it and treat its contents as regular text—which is what you want. Only the browsers that understand SCRIPT (and thus can run the script) will understand NOSCRIPT as well. And they'll *ignore* the contents of the NOSCRIPT tag—which is also what you want. Clever, indeed.

■ Netscape allows your visitors to disable JavaScript. The NOSCRIPT tag is perfect for telling those visitors what they're missing **(Figure 17.18)**.

■ The NOSCRIPT tag will not help if the browser doesn't support the scripting language or if there is a problem with the script.

```
code.html
<HTML><HEAD><TITLE>Llumi's big cat
dreams</TITLE>

<SCRIPT LANGUAGE="JavaScript">

<!--

    littlecat = new Image(143,83)
    littlecat.src = "real.jpg"
    bigcat = new Image(143,83)
    bigcat.src = "dream.jpg"

// end comments to hide scripts -->

</SCRIPT>

<NOSCRIPT>

Your browser isn't running scripts, so you can't
see what Llumi's thinking.

</NOSCRIPT>

</HEAD><BODY>

<P>Point at Llumi to see what she's thinking.
```

Figure 17.16 *The NOSCRIPT tag helps you take care of visitors who use really old browsers.*

Figure 17.17 *If your visitor uses a browser that doesn't support scripts (like Mosaic, shown here), they'll get a message explaining what's missing.*

Figure 17.18 *Or if your visitor has turned off JavaScript support (in Communicator here), the NOSCRIPT text will clue them in to the problem.*

Adding Alternate Information

```
                    code.html
<HTML><HEAD>

<TITLE>Setting the default scripting
language</TITLE>

<META HTTP-EQUIV="Content-Script-Type"
CONTENT="text/javascript">

</HEAD><BODY>

<SCRIPT>

document.write("Visca Catalunya! -- which
means Long Live Catalonia!")

</SCRIPT>

<P>Here's the rest of the page.

</BODY></HTML>
```

Figure 17.19 *The META tag is always placed in the HEAD section of your HTML document. Notice that it is no longer necessary to specify the scripting language within the SCRIPT tag.*

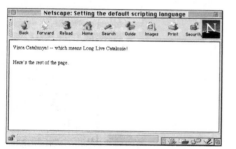

Figure 17.20 *Specifying the scripting language in the META tag saves time and reduces the possibility for errors. The result, though, is not changed.*

Setting the Default Scripting Language

According to the HTML 4 specifications, if you don't say what language you're using, your Web page is "incorrect". If you're including several scripts on a page, you can set the default scripting language for all of them in one fell swoop.

To set the default scripting language:

1. In the HEAD section of your HTML document, type **<META HTTP-EQUIV= "Content-Script-Type"**.

2. Then type **CONTENT="type"**, where *type* indicates the default format and language for your scripts. Use **text/javascript** for JavaScript, **text/vbscript** for VBScript, and **text/tcl** for TCL.

3. Type **>**.

✔ Tip

■ The scripting language indicated with the TYPE attribute in the SCRIPT tag *(see page 292)* overrides the META tag specification. That means you can set the default scripting language, but still use scripts written in other languages, if desired.

Setting the Default Scripting Language

JavaScript Essentials

Many of the most popular effects created on Web pages these days have little or nothing to do with HTML and everything to do with *JavaScript*, a scripting language originally developed by Netscape Communications and now supported by all major browsers. There are entire books—and lots of them!—that go into JavaScript in full detail. This is not one of them.

This chapter, in contrast with the rest of this book, is not even meant to teach you Java-Script. Instead, I want to give you some simple scripts that you can easily paste into your pages in order to create a few cool effects. Please note that there are probably much more elegant methods of achieving these effects that make the script more flexible and more powerful. But that would require a level of JavaScript that would not fit in a book about HTML. If you'd like to find out more about what you can do with Java-Script, you might try *JavaScript for the World Wide Web, 3rd Edition: Visual QuickStart Guide*, by Tom Negrino and Dori Smith.

There are a couple of things to keep in mind while writing JavaScript. You should be very careful with spaces, returns, and all the funny punctuation. If you have trouble typing the scripts in yourself, feel free to download these examples from the Web site *(see page 20)*. I've tested these scripts—and they work fine—on Explorer 4.5 for Mac, Explorer 5 for Windows, and Netscape 4.6 for both Mac and Windows.

Adding the Current Date and Time

Nothing makes your page seem more current than adding the date and the time. While they're a bit more complicated to format in a particular way, just adding them is not difficult at all.

To add the current date and time to your page:

1. Place the cursor where you'd like the time to appear.

2. Type **<SCRIPT LANGUAGE="javascript">** to begin your script.

3. Type **<!--** to hide the script from older browsers.

4. On the next line, type **document.write(**

5. If desired, type **"<TAG>"+**, where *TAG* is the HTML formatting you'd like to apply to the date.

6. **Date()**

7. If you've added formatting in step 5, type **+"<\/TAG>"**, where *TAG* is the corresponding closing tag. Notice the extra backslash.

8. Type **)** to finish the *document.write* function.

9. On the next line, type **// -->** to finish hiding the script.

10. Type **</SCRIPT>**.

✔ Tip

■ When you know more JavaScript, you can format the date, add the full name of the week and month, and change the order of the elements to better suit the situation at hand.

```
code.html

<HTML><HEAD><TITLE>What time is
it?</TITLE></HEAD><BODY>

<SCRIPT LANGUAGE="javascript">

<!--

    document.write("<P ALIGN=right><I>" +
        Date() + "<\/I><\/P>")

// -->

</SCRIPT>

<H1>The Big Ben Home Page</H1>

<IMG SRC="bigben.gif" ALT="A very
rudimentary picture of Big Ben" WIDTH=75
HEIGHT=133 ALIGN=left>

<BR><BR><BR><BR><P>On this page, you'll
find out all the details about your favorite time
keeper, Big Ben. Situated just across the way
from Westminster Abbey and Parliament in the
heart of the City, Big Ben is a popular landmark
and tourist attraction.

</BODY></HTML>
```

Figure 18.1 *Note that there is no return in the JavaScript line. It should all be on one line. (It wraps here in order to fit in this narrow width column.)*

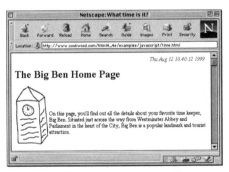

Figure 18.2 *The illustration is amateurish but the time in the upper right-hand corner makes up for everything.*

```
┌─────────────────────────────────┐
│▐         code.html          ▐│
├─────────────────────────────────┤
│ <HTML><HEAD><TITLE>Status bar labels │
│ </TITLE></HEAD><BODY>           │
│                                 │
│ <IMG SRC="../images/Noho.GIF" ALT="Main │
│ Street, Northampton" ALIGN=LEFT │
│ WIDTH="384" HEIGHT="256" BORDER="0" │
│ HSPACE="5" VSPACE="0"           │
│ ONMOUSEOVER="window.status='Main │
│ Street, Northampton'; return true"> │
│                                 │
│ <A HREF="noho.html"             │
│ ONMOUSEOVER="window.status='Click here │
│ for more information about Northampton\'s │
│ sites'; return true">Northampton</A> is a great │
│ place to visit.                 │
│                                 │
│ </BODY></HTML>                  │
└─────────────────────────────────┘
```

Figure 18.3 *Note that the highlighted lines above are all on one line with no returns.*

Figure 18.4 *Adding the ONMOUSEOVER line to links gives visitors extra information before they actually click the link.*

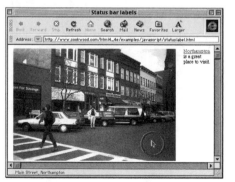

Figure 18.5 *Internet Explorer also supports the ONMOUSEOVER event in image tags. (Netscape currently doesn't.)*

Changing a Link's Status Label

When a visitor points to a link, usually the link's URL appears in the status area of the browser window. If you want something else to appear there, you can use this easy technique to add your own status label.

To change a link's status label:

1. Create the link as usual. For more details, consult Chapter 7, *Links*.

2. In the link tag, type **ONMOUSEOVER ="window.status='**. (First double quotes, then a single one.)

3. Type the text that you want to appear in the status area of the browser window when the visitor points at the link.

4. Type **'; return true"**. (That's a *single quote, semicolon,* and then the rest.)

✔ Tips

■ If there are quotation marks or apostrophes, single or double, in the text entered in step 3, you must precede them with a backslash **(Figure 18.3)**. Otherwise, the browser will probably confuse them with the quotation marks that delimit the script itself (in steps 2 and 4).

■ Make sure you don't add any returns to the status label text. They'll break the script.

■ Internet Explorer also supports the use of the ONMOUSEOVER attribute to add labels to images. Simply add the line to the IMG tag **(Figure 18.5)**. For some reason, Communicator doesn't allow it.

■ You can also make text move through the status area, but the code is a bit involved to go into here.

Changing Multiple Frames with One Link

When you've set up a frameset, it's often nice to change the contents of more than one frame at a time.

To change multiple frames with just one link:

1. First, set up your frameset as described in Chapter 10, *Frames*. Make sure each of the frames has a name *(see step 7 on page 168)*.

2. Type **<A HREF="** to begin the link.

3. Type **javascript:location='url.html'**, where *url.html* is the page that you want to appear in the frame that contains the link. (If you don't want this frame to change, use the URL of the page that is currently in the frame.)

4. Type **;** (a semicolon) to separate this first statement from the next.

5. Type **parent.framename.location= 'new-page.html'**, where *framename* is the name of the frame that will contain the page specified by *newpage.html*.

6. Repeat steps 4 and 5 for each additional frame whose contents you wish to change.

7. Type **">** to complete the link tag.

8. Type the clickable text.

9. Type **</A>**.

✔ Tip

■ If you don't feel like messing with JavaScript, you can get this effect by creating a special frameset that holds the right-hand frames and then set the link to open that frameset. (It's not as fast, but it works — see *http://www.cookwood.com*.)

```
code.html
<HTML><HEAD><TITLE>Table of Contents
</TITLE></HEAD><BODY>

<H1>Wild Animals</H1>

<BR><A HREF="javascript:location='toc.html';
parent.topright.location='birdbuttons.html';
parent.bottomright.location='parrots.html'">
Birds</A>

<BR><A HREF= "javascript:location='toc.html';
parent.topright.location='catbuttons.html';
parent.bottomright.location='tiger.html'">
Cats</A>
```

Figure 18.6 *There are no spaces or returns in the JavaScript lines. The file shown here is called "toc.html" and is referenced in the first part of the script so that when the visitor clicks the link, this TOC remains visible in the left frame (while the two right hand frames are updated).*

Figure 18.7 *When the visitor clicks the Cats link in the left-hand frame...*

Figure 18.8 *...both the top-right and bottom-right frames are updated while the left-hand frame remains constant.*

```
code.html
<HTML><HEAD><TITLE>Llumi's big cat
dreams</TITLE>

<SCRIPT LANGUAGE="javascript">

<!--

    littlecat = new Image(143,83)
    littlecat.src = "real.jpg"
    bigcat = new Image(143,83)
    bigcat.src = "dream.jpg"

// -->

</SCRIPT>

</HEAD><BODY>

Point at Llumi to see what she's thinking.

<A HREF="llumipage.html" ONMOUSEOVER =
"document.catpic.src = bigcat.src"
ONMOUSEOUT = "document.catpic.src =
littlecat.src">

<IMG SRC="real.jpg"  NAME="catpic"
WIDTH=143 HEIGHT=83>

</A>
</BODY></HTML>
```

Figure 18.9 *You can preload as many images as you'd like. There should be two lines for each image—one to create the image space and one to fill it with the appropriate URL. (The lower part of this HTML page is described in detail on page 306.)*

Loading Images into Cache

You can use JavaScript to load all of the images into your browser's cache as the page is initially displayed on the screen. One benefit is that rollovers *(see page 306)* are instantaneous.

To load images into cache:

1. In the HEAD section of your document, type **<SCRIPT LANGUAGE="javascript">**.

2. On the next line type **<!--** to hide the script from older browsers.

3. On the next line, type **label=**, where *label* is a word that identifies the image.

4. Type **new Image(h,w)**, where *h* and *w* are the image's height and width, in pixels.

5. On the next line, type **label**, where *label* matches the label used in step 3.

6. Directly following the name in step 5 (i.e. with no extra spaces), type **.src="image.url"**, where *image.url* is the location of the image on the server.

7. Repeat steps 3–6 for each image you wish to load into cache.

8. Type **// -->** to end hiding the script. (That's two forward slashes, a space, two hyphens, and a greater-than symbol!)

9. Type **</SCRIPT>** to complete the script.

Changing an Image When a Visitor Points

You can make an image change when the visitor points at it. This is commonly called a "rollover".

To change an image when the visitor points at it:

1. Type **<A HREF="page.html"**, where *page.html* is the page that will be displayed if the visitor actually clicks the link (as opposed to just pointing at it).

2. Type **ONMOUSEOVER="document. imgname.src=**, where *imgname* is the value of the NAME attribute in the IMG tag (see step 11, below).

3. Type **'image-in.jpg'**, where *image-in.jpg* is the name and extension of the image file that should be displayed when the visitor *points at* the image.

   Or, if you've preloaded the images into cache, type **label.src**, where *label* matches the label used in step 3 on page 305.

4. Type **"** to complete the attribute.

5. Type **ONMOUSEOUT="document. imgname.src=**, where *imgname* is the value of the NAME attribute in the IMG tag (see step 11, below).

6. Type **'image-out.jpg'**, where *image-out.jpg* is the name and extension of the image file that should be displayed when the visitor points *away from* the image.

   Or, if you've preloaded the images into cache, type **label2.src**, where *label2* matches the label used in step 3 on page 305.

7. Type **"** to complete the attribute.

```
code.html

<HTML><HEAD><TITLE>Llumi's big cat
dreams</TITLE>

<SCRIPT LANGUAGE="javascript">

<!--

    littlecat = new Image(143,83)
    littlecat.src = "real.jpg"
    bigcat = new Image(143,83)
    bigcat.src = "dream.jpg"

// -->

</SCRIPT>

</HEAD><BODY>

Point at Llumi to see what she's thinking.

<A HREF="llumipage.html" ONMOUSEOVER =
"document.catpic.src = bigcat.src"
ONMOUSEOUT = "document.catpic.src =
littlecat.src">

<IMG SRC="real.jpg"  NAME="catpic"
WIDTH=143 HEIGHT=83>

</A>

</BODY></HTML>
```

Figure 18.10 *If you preload the images as shown here (and explained on page 305), you can then reference the label names. Or, if you prefer to keep it simpler, you can reference the image directly as in* document.catpic.src='image.url'.

Figure 18.11 *The image that appears initially is the one specified by the IMG tag.*

Figure 18.12 *When the visitor passes the mouse over the image (which is also a link—notice the status bar), the image referenced by the ONMOUSEOVER attribute is revealed.*

Figure 18.13 *When the visitor points the mouse away from the image, the image referenced by the ONMOUSEOUT attribute is displayed (in this case, it's the same as the original image specified by the IMG tag).*

8. Add other link attributes as desired *(see Chapter 7, Links)*.

9. Type **>** to finish the link.

10. Type **<IMG SRC="initialimage.jpg"**, where *initialimage.jpg* is the file name for the image that should appear before the visitor even picks up their mouse.

11. Type **NAME="imgname"**, where *imgname* identifies this space for the images that will be loaded.

12. Type **WIDTH=w HEIGHT=h**, where *w* and *h* represent the width and height of the images, respectively.

13. Add other attributes to the IMG tag as desired *(see Chapter 5, Using Images)*.

14. Type **>** to complete the IMG tag.

15. Type **</A>** to complete the link tag.

✔ Tips

- The images should be the same size. If they're not, the second one will be shoehorned in to fit.

- If you don't want the image to be part of the link, after step 9, type some clickable text, then do step 15 before completing steps 10–14.

Changing an Image When a Visitor Points

Controlling a New Window's Size

In Chapter 7, you learned how to open a link in a new window. JavaScript lets you control how big that window should be.

To control the size of a new window:

1. Type **<A HREF="javascript:location= 'current.html';**, where *current.html* is the URL of the page that contains the link.

2. Type **window.open('nextpage.html',**, where *nextpage.html* is the URL of the page to be opened in the new window.

3. Type **'label',**, where *label* is the name of the new window.

4. Type **'HEIGHT=h,WIDTH=w**, where *h* and *w* are the desired height and width for the new window. (No spaces!)

5. If desired, type **,windowpart=yes**, where *windowpart* is scrollbars, toolbar, status, menubar, location, or resizable.

6. If desired, type a **,** (comma) and repeat step 5 as desired. Each window part should be separated from the previous one with a comma but no spaces.

7. Type **'** (a straight apostrophe)—whether or not you've set the window parts.

8. Type **)"** to finish the JavaScript code.

9. Type **>clickable text</A>**.

✔ Tip

- To open a new window automatically as the main page loads (with no link at all), within the BODY tag of your main page's HTML code, type **ONLOAD="javascript:** and then follow steps 2–8 above. Then open other links in the new window by using **TARGET="label"**, where *label* matches step 3. For details, see page 122.

```
code.html
<HTML><HEAD><TITLE>American Writers of
the 19th Century</TITLE></HEAD><BODY>

<H1>Nathaniel Hawthorne</H1>

Nathaniel Hawthorne was one of the most
important writers of 19th century America. His
most famous character is <A
HREF="javascript:location='hawthorne.html';
window.open('hester.html','characters',
'HEIGHT=150,WIDTH=150,scrollbars=yes')">H
ester Prynne</A>, a woman living in Puritan
New England. Another famous object of
```

Figure 18.14 *The file name of the document shown here is "hawthorne.html". The first part of the JavaScript statement says "keep displaying the hawthorne.html document right where it is". The second part of the JavaScript code says "and then open a window labeled* characters *that's 150 pixels by 150 pixels, with scrollbars, and display the hester.html file in it".*

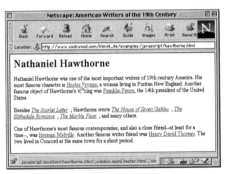

Figure 18.15 *When the visitor clicks a link...*

Figure 18.16 *...the link is displayed in the new window. Contrast this example with the one shown in Figure 7.13 on page 122.*

Extras

In this chapter, you'll find a collection of special touches you can give your Web pages to set them apart from the crowd (or to make them fit in better by following the latest trends).

Perhaps the best advice included in this chapter *(see page 310)* is to take a gander around the Web and see what other people are up to. Every day, innovative Web designers create exciting new effects on their pages to help generate interest, illustrate their content, and foster community throughout the Web. Let them inspire you.

Next, don't take anything at face value. Tables are a perfect example. In the printed world, they're perfect for conveying rows and columns of numbers. In the Web world, they can do so much more. Many other HTML tags can also be stretched beyond their original use. Be creative! Hopefully, this chapter will give you a good start.

The Inspiration of Others

One of the easiest ways to expand your HTML fluency is by looking at how other page designers have created *their* pages. Luckily, HTML code is easy to view and learn from. However, text content, graphics, sounds, video, and other external files may be copyrighted. As a general rule, use other designers' pages for inspiration with your HTML, and then create your own contents.

To view other designers' HTML code:

1. Open their page with any browser.

2. Choose View Source (in the View menu in Netscape), or View (in the View menu in Internet Explorer).

3. The browser will open the helper application you have specified for text files and show you the HTML code for the given page.

4. If you wish, save the file with the text editor for further study.

✔ Tips

- ▪ You can also save the source code by selecting File > Save As and then HTML Source in the Format pop-up menu in the dialog box that appears.

- ▪ If you find something out there on the Web that you can't figure out, drop me an e-mail (how@cookwood.com) and make sure you enclose the URL of the amazing page. I'll see if I can decipher it for you.

- ▪ You can browse through an incredible range of interesting and inspiring pages, including the one in Figure 19.1— all created by readers of various editions of this book—in my readers' gallery: *www.cookwood.com/html4_4e/gallery/*. You all make me very proud. Really!

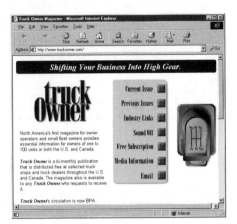

Figure 19.1 *This Web site, cleverly designed by Brian Foster for* Truck Owner Magazine, *is full of inspiring ideas. My favorite is the gear shaft that moves up and down when a visitor points at the different buttons in the list. You can find this page at* www.truckowner.com.

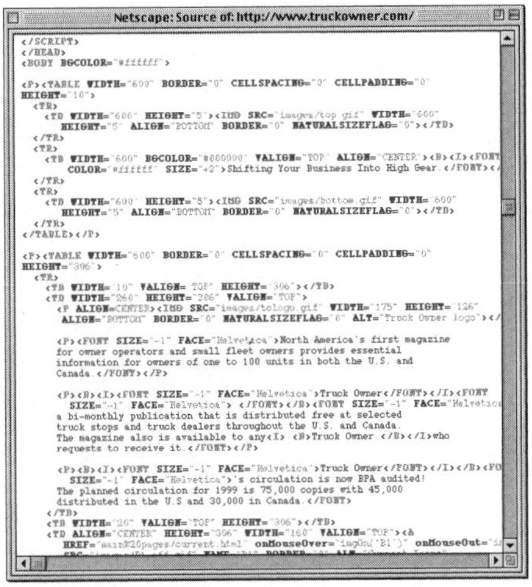

Figure 19.2 *Here's a bit of the code Brian wrote to create the page in Figure 19.1. You can see that much of his layout is structured with tables.*

The Inspiration of Others

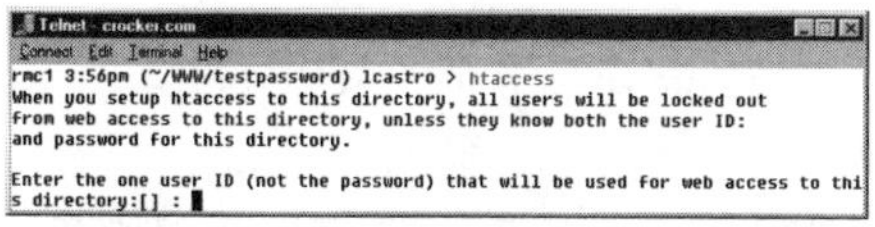

Figure 19.3 *Telnet to your Unix server, navigate to the directory that you want to protect, and type* htaccess.

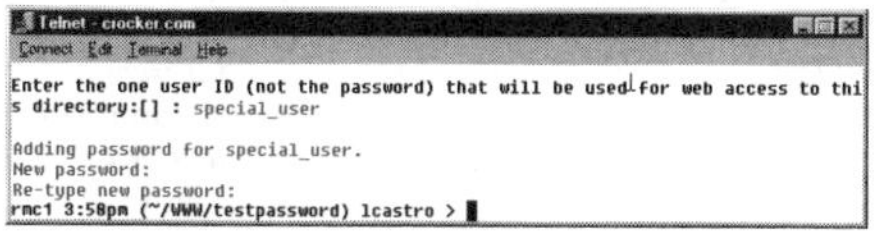

Figure 19.4 *You'll be prompted to type the user name (here I've typed "special_user") and then the password. Be careful, the password is case sensitive.*

Figure 19.5 *When a visitor attempts to view any page in the protected directory, they'll see this dialog box (or one like it). You can try it yourself. Go to www.cookwood.com/testpassword/password.html. And the password? Shhhh. It's "HTML".*

Password Protecting Your Page

Don't like the idea of just anyone visiting your page? Certainly the easiest way to keep people out is to not tell them the page exists. However, most servers also let you protect directories (but not individual pages) with a password. Then you can limit access to the pages within those directories by limiting who you give the password to. To create a separate password for each person, you need a CGI script, but I'm afraid that's a bit beyond the scope of this book—even in the Extras chapter. The other limitation of this method is that it only works on certain servers. If it doesn't work for you, consult your ISP!

To password protect your page:

1. Telnet to your server.

2. Navigate to the directory that you wish to protect with a password.

3. Type **htaccess**.

4. Type the user name at the prompt.

5. Type the password at the next prompt. Then type it again to confirm.

✔ Tips

■ You can use Microsoft Telnet for Windows (it's in your Windows directory) or the free and excellent BetterTelnet for Macintosh, *(www.cstone.net/~rbraun/mac/telnet).*

■ This is only for Unix servers. If this technique doesn't work for you, ask your ISP.

■ You can only use this technique to protect an entire directory and all of the pages that it contains.

Password Protecting Your Page

Creating a Counter

It's nice to know that folks have been stopping by to see your masterpiece, once it's up and running. Many people use a special CGI script called a *counter* to tally each visit. Although CGI scripts are a bit beyond the scope of this book, I can point you in the right direction.

To create a counter:

1. First, contact your ISP. Ask them if they allow counters. If they do, they'll probably have a FAQ page that explains how to add one to your site.

2. If your ISP allows CGI scripts but doesn't have a ready-made counter, you can write your own. If you don't program, try The CGI-Resources Web Site: *www.cgi-resources.com/* (the hyphen is part of the address).

3. Finally, you can use a public counter. Like other "free" services, you pay for this type of counter by including advertising on your site. You might try a service like Pagecount *(www.pagecount.com)* or do a search on AltaVista for other "free" counters.

✔ Tips

- You can usually set the initial value for a counter. Keep that in mind when you marvel at the incredible numbers other sites seem to be attracting.

- Many ISPs offer more sophisticated visit analysis that goes way beyond a simple number. They'll tell you where visitors came from, what time they came, where they went on your site, and much more.

- You can also use search engines like AltaVista to find free guestbooks, e-mail, and even Web hosting.

<p> You are visitor number: <IMG SRC =

"/cgi-bin/Count.cgi?dd=E | df=user4/ lcastro/WWW/data/index.dat" > since March 7, 1996.

Figure 19.6 *This is what the code looks like to create the counter on my ISP. Notice that there is an image tag that calls a CGI script. I've also added some explanatory text so that people know what the counter references. (Of course, this script won't work for you unless you have the same ISP that I have.)*

Figure 19.7 *The counter is created at the bottom of the page and is updated automatically each time the page is loaded. Don't forget though, that* loaded *is not the same as* visited. *If I reload this page five times, the counter will go up, but I'll still only have visited it once.*

Creating a Counter

```
code.html

<HTML><HEAD>

<TITLE>Souped up mailto links</TITLE>

</HEAD><BODY>

Write me a <A HREF=
"mailto:me@cookwood.com?subject=Your
cats">letter</A> about my cats!

</BODY>

</HTML>
```

Figure 19.8 *Notice that there is no space between the end of the e-mail address and the question mark that begins the extra information. Further, spaces are allowed in the subject line but quotation marks are not.*

Figure 19.9 *The souped up mailto tag looks like a regular link.*

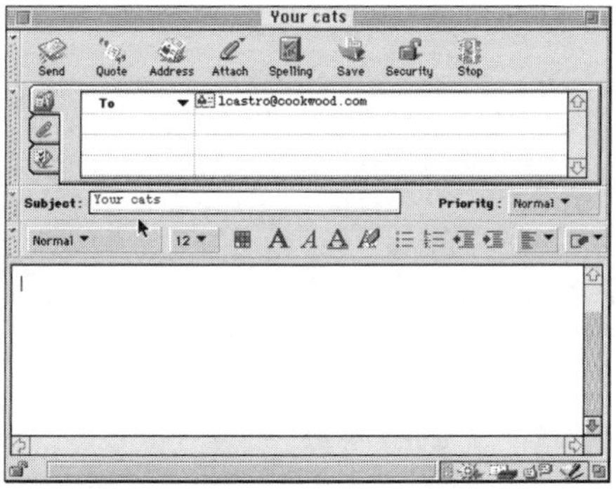

Figure 19.10 *But when you click it, the Subject line is automatically filled out.*

Souping Up Mailto Links

When a visitor clicks a mailto link, the browser switches to a mail client and opens a new message window, pre-addressed with the recipient as defined in the mailto link *(see page 124)*. You can add information to the mailto link to automatically set the subject, cc, and bcc lines as well.

To soup up mailto links:

1. Type **<A HREF="mailto:joe@site.com**, as usual.

2. Type **?subject=topic**, where *topic* is the text you want to appear in the subject line.

   Or type **?cc=person@site.com**, where *person@site.com* is the e-mail address of the person you want to be cc'd automatically.

   Or type **?bcc=person@site.com**, where *person@site.com* is the e-mail address of the person you want to be bcc'd automatically.

3. Finally, type the closing **">**.

4. Type the clickable text.

5. And then type **</A>** to complete the link.

✔ Tips

■ This is not standard HTML, nor does any browser claim to support it. Nevertheless, it does work with Explorer and Communicator on both Macs and Windows.

■ Keep in mind that the visitor can change the subject, cc, or bcc lines as they wish. This technique only starts them off as you want them.

■ Explorer can handle all the variables at once. Communicator only allows one at a time.

Slicing Images into Pieces

In your travels around the Web, you've probably noticed how the top section of many professional-looking sites appear in bits and pieces. There are several good reasons for slicing an image into smaller chunks. By separating out the blocks that appear in multiple places on your site, you can take advantage of the fact that once an image has been viewed on one page, it is viewed much more quickly on the next. Next, if you divide the computer-generated sections of the image with lots of the same color from the photographic elements, the former can be compressed more efficiently with GIF while the latter will take up less space when saved as JPEG. Finally, you can designate particular pieces of the image to hold frequently updated material. That way you don't have to change the entire image every time you want to add something to it.

Many image editing programs have special slicing features that automate both the division of the image and the creation of the table afterwards. If you don't have such a program, you can use these steps outlined below.

To slice an image:

1. First decide how to divide the image. Separate photographic sections from computer-generated ones (for better compression) and sections that will remain the same from ones that will change.

2. Open the RGB image in Photoshop **(Figure 19.11)**.

3. Choose View > Show Rulers **(Figures 19.12 and 19.13)**.

4. Make sure you've selected View > Show Guides and View > Snap To Guides.

Figure 19.11 *Here's the composite image. I'm going to slice it into bits to separate out the photograph (the tiger) for better compression, and the buttons for better flexibility.*

Figure 19.12 *Choose View > Show Rulers.*

Figure 19.13 *Once the rulers are showing, you can drag the guides out from them.*

Figure 19.14 *Use the guides to separate the image into future slices.*

Figure 19.15 *Use the guides to help you select each slice. As long as you have the Snap To Guides option checked in the View menu, the selection rectangle will follow the guides—to the pixel.*

Slicing Images into Pieces

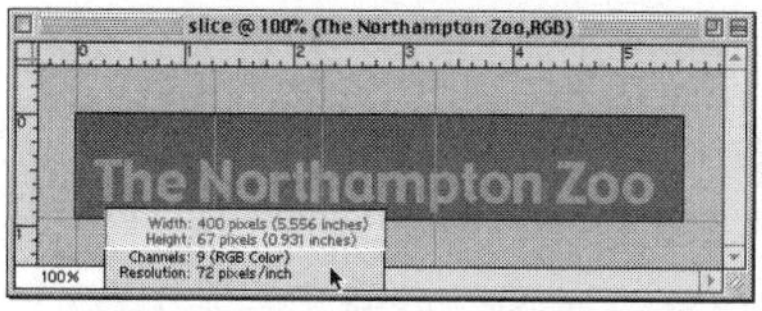

Figure 19.16 *Once the slice is cropped, take a moment to Option-click in the status area and jot down the dimensions (especially the width).*

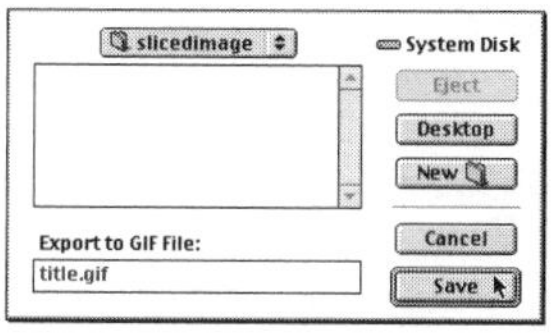

Figure 19.17 *Be sure to give the slice a unique name—you don't want to overwrite the composite image.*

Figure 19.18 *The final step is to choose File > Revert to restore your composite image to its original size.*

```
code.html
<TABLE WIDTH=500 BORDER=0
CELLPADDING=0 CELLSPACING=0>

<TR><TD ROWSPAN=2 WIDTH=100><IMG
SRC="tiger.jpeg" ALT="tiger"></TD>
<TD COLSPAN=4 WIDTH=400>
<IMG SRC="title.gif" ALT="The Northampton
Zoo"></TD></TR>

<TR><TD WIDTH=92><IMG
SRC="members.gif" ALT="Members"></TD>
<TD WIDTH=71><IMG SRC="events.gif"
ALT="Events"></TD>
<TD WIDTH=75><IMG SRC="exhibits.gif"
ALT="Exhibits"></TD>
<TD WIDTH=162><IMG SRC="january.gif"
ALT="January"></TD></TR>

</TABLE>
```

Figure 19.19 *Be sure to specify both the width of the entire table as well as that of each individual cell.*

5. Drag a guide from the ruler to the place in the image where you want to slice it. You make both horizontal and vertical guides **(Figure 19.14)**.

6. Once you have the entire image divided into pieces, use the Rectangular Marquee to select one of the slices **(Fig. 19.15)**.

7. Choose Image > Crop.

8. Option-click in the status area and write down the slice's dimensions **(Fig. 19.16)**.

9. For computer generated slices with large areas of a single color, choose File > Export > GIF89a Export. Then give the file a unique name with the GIF extension **(Figure 19.17)**.

   For photographic slices, choose File > Save a Copy. Then give the slice a unique name, and choose JPEG in the Formats pop-up menu.

10. Finally, choose File > Revert to restore the composite image to its original size **(Figure 19.18)**.

11. Repeat steps 6–10 for each slice of the image.

12. Create a table for the image, using one cell for each slice. Be sure to specify the width of the entire table and of each individual cell **(Figure 19.19)**.

✔ Tips

■ Another great use for sliced images is when you want to create a rollover *(see page 306)* of just a piece of the image. In this example, I could create highlighted buttons that would be swapped with the individual slices. Swapping the entire composite image would be much slower.

■ Work on a copy of the composite image if cropping and reverting make you nervous.

Slicing Images into Pieces

Creating Buttons with Tables

Buttons made out of images sometimes take a maddening amount of time to appear on the screen. If your user has images turned off, they may never appear at all. One solution is to create navigational buttons with tables. The technique is simple: create a table and change the background color of each cell, that is, button.

To create buttons with tables:

1. Create a table as described in Chapter 9, *Tables*.

2. The button cells might look like this:
   <TD BGCOLOR=red ALIGN=middle>
   <A HREF="link.html"><FONT SIZE="+3"
   COLOR=black>Click me</FONT>
   </A></TD>.

✔ Tips

■ Make sure the text that should appear in the cell is large enough to stand out. For more information, consult *Changing the Text Size* on page 48.

■ Use contrasting colors for both the background and the text that appears in the cell. For more information, consult *Changing the Text Color* on page 51 and *Changing a Cell's Color* on page 158.

■ Use a different colored background or image for each cell.

```
code.html
<HTML><HEAD><TITLE>Buttons</TITLE>
</HEAD>

<BODY BGCOLOR=#fce503>

<TABLE CELLPADDING=5 CELLSPACING=0
WIDTH=100%>

<TR>

<TD BGCOLOR="#F3D7E3" NOWRAP><A
HREF="openingpage.html">City Tour</A>

<TD BGCOLOR="#F6D5C3" NOWRAP><A
HREF="market1.html">Market</A>

<TD BGCOLOR="#D8E9D6" NOWRAP><A
HREF="arch1.html">Architecture</A>

<TD BGCOLOR="#D1C9DF" NOWRAP><A
HREF="sports1.html">Sports</A>

<TD BGCOLOR="#D4EBF9" NOWRAP><A
HREF="natlism1.html">Nationalism</A>

<TD BGCOLOR="#CECDB4" NOWRAP><A
HREF="language1.html">Language</A>

</TR>

</TABLE>
```

Figure 19.20 *In this example, all the text is black, but each cell/button is a different color.*

Figure 19.21 *The cells of the one-row table, when colored differently, look just like little buttons—but they load much more quickly than images. This page is used in the examples described in Chapter 10, Frames.*

Figure 19.22 *This is the image I used for the background. It measures 60 pixels wide by 45 pixels high.*

```
code.html

<TABLE BORDER=0 CELLSPACING=0
CELLPADDING=0>

<TR><TD HEIGHT=45 COLSPAN=3
BACKGROUND="butterflyborder.jpg"> <
/TD></TR>

<TR><TD WIDTH=60
BACKGROUND="butterflyborder.jpg"> 
</TD>

<TD><IMG SRC="butterfly.jpg" ALT="Monarch
Butterfly"><BR>This is a monarch
butterfly.</TD>

<TD WIDTH=60
BACKGROUND="butterflyborder.jpg"> 
</TD></TR>

<TR><TD HEIGHT=45 COLSPAN=3
BACKGROUND="butterflyborder.jpg"> <
/TD></TR>

</TABLE>
```

Figure 19.23 *If you set the height and width attributes to match the height and width of the background image, the border will repeat the entire image along the border. Otherwise, it'll just use a portion of the image and repeat that.*

Figure 19.24 *The background image frames the contents of the table.*

Using Images for Table Borders

This technique is very similar to my example of frames in rows and columns described on page 171. Basically it consists of creating empty rows and columns where the image will show through around a central cell that will contain the table's content.

To use an image as a table border:

1. Type **<TABLE BORDER=0 CELLSPAC-ING=0 CELLPADDING =0>** to begin.

2. Type **<TR><TD COLSPAN=3 HEIGHT=n**, where *n* is the thickness of the top border.

3. Type **BACKGROUND="image.gif"**, where *image.gif* is the image that you want to use for the table border.

4. Type **> </TD></TR>** to complete the cell and row and fill it with a non-breaking space to ensure it appears.

5. Type **<TR>**.

6. Type **<TD WIDTH=n**, where *n* is the thickness of the left border.

7. Type **BACKGROUND="image.gif"> </TD>** using the same image as in step 3.

8. Type **<TD>content</TD>**, where *content* is what you'd like to display in the table. It can be anything—even another table.

9. Repeat steps 6–7.

10. Type **</TR>**.

11. Repeat steps 2–4.

12. Type **</TABLE>**.

✔ Tip

- Those non-breaking spaces in step 4 and step 7 ensure the otherwise empty cell appears at all.

Using Images for Table Borders

Creating Drop Caps

Some of the best tricks are the simplest. Since you can't always be sure which fonts your visitors have installed, you can create an image file of the capital letter, make it transparent, and insert it before the rest of the paragraph.

To create a drop cap:

1. In an image editing program, create the capital letter for your drop cap in the desired font. Save it in GIF format and make it transparent *(see pages 64 and 70)*.

2. In your HTML document where you want the drop cap to appear, type **<IMG SRC="dropcap.gif"** where *dropcap.gif* is the location on the server of the image created in step 1.

3. Type **ALIGN=left** so that the text that follows wraps around the drop cap.

4. Type the final **>** to finish the IMG definition.

5. Type the text that should appear next to the drop cap. Generally, next to a drop cap, it is a good idea to type the first few words in all caps.

```
code.html
<HTML><HEAD><TITLE>Here's a drop
cap</TITLE></HEAD>

<BODY>

<IMG SRC=dropcap.gif ALIGN=left>LONG,
LONG TIME AGO, in the middle of a large forest
in Western Massachusetts, there lived a little girl
who was about 14 years old and who loved
baseball.  She thought that if she had grown up
in the Midwest where there were hardly any
trees, she would have been one of the best
baseball players ever, but since she lived in the
middle of a forest, there was no way for her to
```

Figure 19.25 *Use the ALIGN=left attribute to wrap the text around the drop cap.*

Figure 19.26 *Drop caps are ideal for books or stories.*

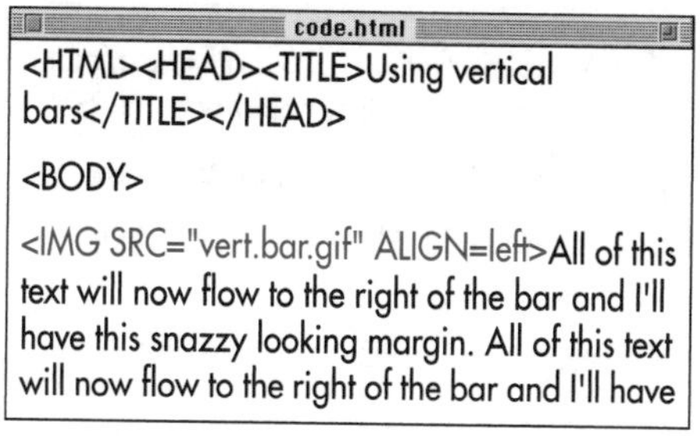

```
┌─────────────── code.html ───────────────┐
<HTML><HEAD><TITLE>Using vertical
bars</TITLE></HEAD>

<BODY>

<IMG SRC="vert.bar.gif" ALIGN=left>All of this
text will now flow to the right of the bar and I'll
have this snazzy looking margin. All of this text
will now flow to the right of the bar and I'll have
```

Figure 19.27 *You can create a vertical bar on the left side of the page by inserting an image and using the ALIGN=left attribute.*

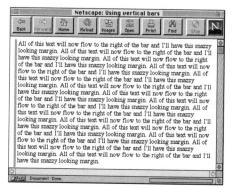

Figure 19.28 *It doesn't really matter if the vertical bar is longer than the text. It will simply continue down the page.*

Using Vertical Rules

It's easy to create horizontal rules in an HTML document. Creating vertical rules, along the left or right margin, for example, is only slightly more complicated.

To create a vertical rule:

1. In Photoshop, or other image editing program, create a bar of the desired color and width, and about 500 pixels high.

2. In the HTML document, place the cursor above the text that should be alongside the vertical bar.

3. Type **<IMG SRC="verticalbar.gif"** where *verticalbar.gif* is the location on the server of the vertical bar created in step 1.

4. *Either* type **ALIGN=left** to place the vertical bar along the left margin *or* type **ALIGN=right** to place it along the right margin.

5. Type the final **>** to complete the IMG definition.

6. Type the text that should appear alongside the vertical rule.

✔ Tips

- You can create a narrow column of text by inserting a transparent vertical rule on either side of the body of your page. You can also use transparent GIFs to adjust the spacing between paragraphs, and even between words.

- Another easy way to make a vertical rule is to create a two-column table and then specify a background color for the left column.

Using Vertical Rules

Labeling Elements in a Web Page

You can use the little-known TITLE attribute to add a tool tip label to practically every part of your Web site. It's particularly helpful for giving clues to what's needed in form elements, but you can use it to label just about anything. Unfortunately, despite being part of the standard HTML 4 specifications, it's only currently supported by Internet Explorer 5 for Windows.

To label elements in a Web page:

In the HTML tag for the item you want to label, add TITLE="label", where label is the text that should appear in the tool tip when a visitor points at the element.

✔ Tip

■ The TITLE attribute overrides the ALT attribute in images.

```
code.html
<FORM METHOD=POST ENCTYPE="text/plain"
ACTION="mailto:lcastro@cookwood.com">

Name: <INPUT TYPE="text" NAME="name">

Address: <INPUT TYPE="text" NAME="address"
SIZE=30>

<P>City: <INPUT TYPE="text" NAME="city">

State: <INPUT TYPE="text" NAME="state"
SIZE=2 MAXLENGTH=2>

Zipcode: <INPUT TYPE="text" NAME="zip"
SIZE=5 MAXLENGTH=5 TITLE="Just the five digit
Zip, please">

Customer Code: <INPUT TYPE="password"
NAME="code" SIZE=8>

<HR>
```

Figure 19.29 *You can add a tool tip to any HTML element by adding the TITLE attribute to its tag.*

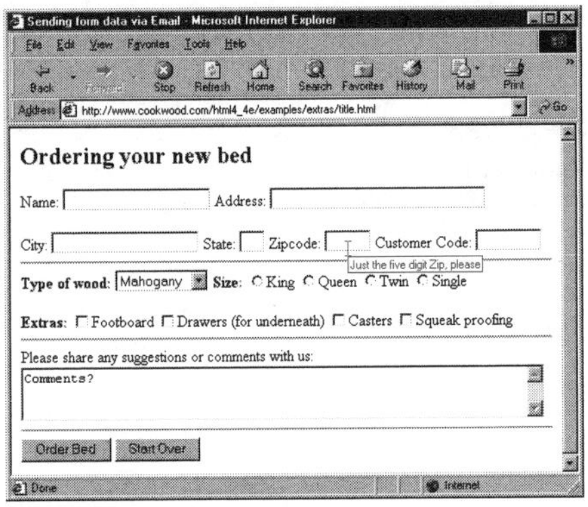

Figure 19.30 *When the visitor points at the titled item, a tool tip appears with the TITLE attribute's contents.*

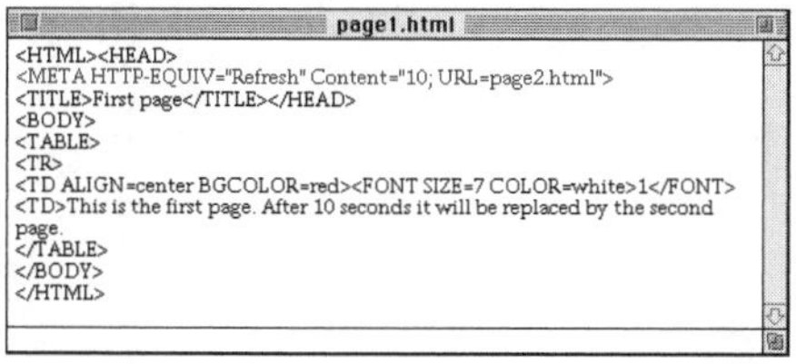

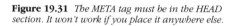

```
page1.html
<HTML><HEAD>
<META HTTP-EQUIV="Refresh" Content="10; URL=page2.html">
<TITLE>First page</TITLE></HEAD>
<BODY>
<TABLE>
<TR>
<TD ALIGN=center BGCOLOR=red><FONT SIZE=7 COLOR=white>1</FONT>
<TD>This is the first page. After 10 seconds it will be replaced by the second
page.
</TABLE>
</BODY>
</HTML>
```

Figure 19.31 *The META tag must be in the HEAD section. It won't work if you place it anywhere else.*

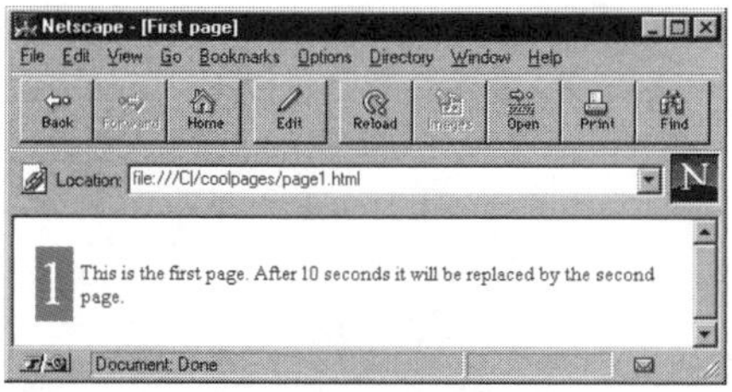

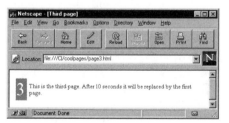

Figure 19.32 *The first page loads as usual. But wait ten seconds, and...*

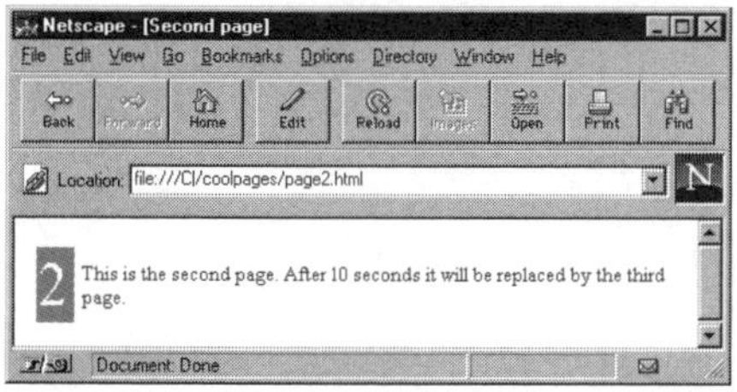

Figure 19.33 *...the second page loads automatically. Wait ten more seconds and...*

Figure 19.34 *...the third page loads automatically. If you wait ten more seconds, it'll go back to page 1 (Figure 19.32) and start the whole process all over again. Of course, if you don't want it to, just leave the META tag out of the last page.*

Creating an Automatic Slide Show

This isn't really an extra, but it's so unusual, I didn't know quite where else to put it. You can use a special feature of the META attribute, within the HEAD section, to automatically move the reader from one page to another. If you set up a series of pages in this way, you create a Web slide show.

To create an automatic slide show:

1. In the first page, within the HEAD section, type **<META HTTP-EQUIV= "Refresh"**. (That's a regular hyphen between *HTTP* and *EQUIV*.)

2. Type **CONTENT="n;** where *n* is the number of seconds the current page should display on the screen.

3. Type **URL=nextpage.html">** where *nextpage.html* is the URL of the next page that you want the visitor to jump to automatically.

4. Repeat these steps for each page in the series.

✔ Tips

- Omit the META tag in the last page of the series if you don't want to cycle around again to the beginning.

- Make sure you use a display time long enough for all of your pages to appear on screen.

- This is a great way to show a portfolio or other series of images without having to create a lot of links and buttons.

- Be careful with the quotation marks. Notice that there is one set before CONTENT and the closing set after the URL.

Creating an Automatic Slide Show

Help!
My Page Doesn't Work!

Figure 20.1 *That text to the right of the image isn't supposed to be so big. What's the problem?*

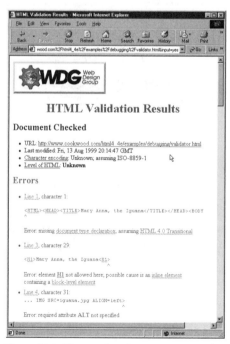

Figure 20.2 *The error found on Line 3 seems to be the problem—instead of a closing </H1> tag, I've put in another opening <H1> tag by mistake.*

So, you've written up a spanking new page and you fire up your browser only to find that it doesn't look anything like you expected. Or it doesn't display at all. This chapter will alert you to some common HTML errors, and will also help you weed out your own home-grown variety.

Checking Your Code

First off, make sure your code is correct. The number one problem with most HTML pages is spelling. Did you type *SCR* or *SRC*? (SRC is correct, it's an abbreviation of *source*.)

If you've gone through the page a few times and can't find your error, you might try using an HTML validator. While the W3C offers one, I personally prefer the one offered (free!) by the Web Design Group. It's called the WDG HTML Validator and you can find it at: *www.htmlhelp.org/tools/validator/*. You can either point it at the page in question, upload the file, or type it in. Regardless, the validator will display all the errors it has found in your page (or pages if you give it more than one).

Note: This might be one reason to use the !DOCTYPE tag I decided not to discuss in the beginning of the book *(see page 35)*. A validator judges your page according to the version of HTML that you say you're using via the !DOCTYPE tag. If you want to validate your documents with something other than HTML 4.0 Transitional, you'll want to check my Web site (or some other source) for information on how to use the !DOCTYPE tag.

The Browser Displays the Code

Although you may be proud of your HTML coding, when you view your file with a browser, you want that code converted into a beautiful Web page, not displayed for all to see.

When the browser displays the code instead of the page:

1. Have you saved the file in Text Only (sometimes called "Text Document") format? Sometimes, if you've saved the file previously as a, say, Word document, saving it as Text Only isn't enough. You have to create a brand new document, copy and paste the code to that new document, and then save it as Text Only.

2. Have you saved the file with an .htm or .html extension? You must.

3. Have you begun the page with the <HTML> tag? You should.

4. Do you shun Word's (or some other word processor's) "Save as HTML" command? That command is only for converting regular text into Word's idea of a Web page. If you're writing your own code, this command will "code your code". Instead, choose Save As and then save the file as Text Document with the .htm or .html extension.

5. Is Windows adding .txt extensions to the files you save as "page.html", creating something like "page.html.txt"? Find out by viewing file extensions in the folder **(Figure 20.3)**. To avoid it, enclose the file name in double quotation marks in the Save As dialog box **(Figure 20.5)**.

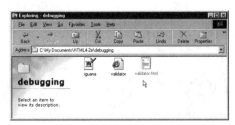

Figure 20.3 *If you set Windows to "hide file extensions for known file types" (choose View > Folder Options > View), the file on the right looks like an html file even though it's really a text file (with the full name of "validator.html.txt". And where did that extra ".txt" extension come from? In Windows, some programs think they know better and add it for you automatically. To avoid such things, enclose the file name in double quotation marks.*

Figure 20.4 *If the extension is .txt, the browser will display it as a pure text file, code and all.*

Figure 20.5 *When you save your HTML file, regardless of the program you use, make sure to save it in Text Only (aka Text Document) format with the .htm or .html extension. To keep Windows from tacking on the .txt extension to your files, enclose the entire file name in double quotation marks.*

```
┌─────────────────────────────────────┐
│ ▦▦▦          code.html           ▦▦ │
├─────────────────────────────────────┤
│ <HTML><HEAD><TITLE>Mary Anna, the   │
│ Iguana</TITLE></HEAD><BODY>         │
│                                     │
│ <TABLE BORDER=0>                    │
│                                     │
│ <TR><TH COLSPAN=2><H1>Mary Anna, the│
│ Iguana</H1>                         │
│                                     │
│ <TR><TD><IMG SRC=iguana.jpg ALIGN=left>│
│ <TD>There once was an iguana        │
│ <BR>whose name was Mary Anna        │
│ <BR>her skin was so dry             │
│ <BR>that she'd have to cry          │
│ <BR>Here's some cream: would you please put it│
│ onna?                               │
└─────────────────────────────────────┘
```

Figure 20.6 *There is no closing </TABLE> tag.*

Figure 20.7 *Explorer doesn't blink an eye if you leave off a closing </TABLE> (or </FRAMESET) tag.*

Figure 20.8 *Netscape, on the other hand, can't deal. The entire table (or frameset) disappears from view.*

Great in Explorer, Nothing in Netscape

You're up all night coding this complicated page, with tables or frames. You upload it to the server, view it with Explorer, smile smugly at your prowess, and go to sleep only to be awakened by your Netscape-using client who wants to know why the page is completely (or mostly) blank. What's gone wrong?

When the page looks great in Explorer, but doesn't appear in Netscape:

1. If you're using tables, you must be sure to create a closing </TABLE> tag to match each and every opening one. Explorer doesn't care, but Netscape does.

2. If your page is set up with several framesets *(see page 172)*, make sure you insert a closing </FRAMESET> tag for each and every opening one. I think this one is easy to miss because you've got all those <FRAME> tags that don't require a closing tag. Remember that the <FRAMESET> tag *does* require a closing tag, and Netscape won't forgive you if you leave it out.

3. If the problem is that the page looks great in Explorer but cruddy in Netscape (as opposed to *nothing* in Netscape), check *Great in One Browser, Ugly in the Other* on page 326.

Great in One Browser, Ugly in the Other

This one's not your fault. Unfortunately, no major browser supports the standard specifications 100 percent. While most support the better part of the HTML 4 specs, Netscape 4.x, in particular, is miles behind Explorer 4 and 5 with respect to Cascading Style Sheets *(see page 243).*

When your page looks great in one browser but ugly in the other:

1. Test your page on as many browsers and platforms as you can. While (according to Statmark, *www.statmark.com*) some 75% of Web surfers use Explorer, that means a full 25% use Netscape, and that's a lot of people to leave behind.

2. If you're relying on Cascading Style Sheets, limit yourself to the tags that both major browsers support. Point your browser at my set of CSS tester pages *(www.cookwood.com/browser_tests/)* to see if it's you or the browser who's at fault.

3. Cater your page to your desired audience. Web designers can be expected to have all the latest plug-ins, members of the American Iguana Club might not.

✔ Tip

■ Check out The Web Standards Project page *(www.webstandards.org)* for more information on what you can do to promote the adoption of standards by the major Web browser manufacturers (as well as by any newcomers to the game).

```
code.html
<HTML><HEAD><TITLE>Mary Anna, the
Iguana</TITLE>
<STYLE>
    IMG {border:thick double red}
    DIV.yellowback {background:yellow}
</STYLE>
</HEAD><BODY><TABLE BORDER=0>
<TR><TH COLSPAN=2><H1>Mary Anna, the
Iguana</H1>
<TR><TD><IMG SRC=iguana.jpg ALIGN=left>
<TD><DIV CLASS=yellowback>There once was
an iguana
<BR>whose name was Mary Anna
<BR>her skin was so dry
<BR>that she'd have to cry
<BR>Here's some cream: would you please put it
onna?</DIV></TABLE></BODY></HTML>
```

Figure 20.9 *While the DIV and IMG tags are supported by both major browsers, the border property is not supported by Netscape and the background property is applied differently by each browser.*

Figure 20.10 *You may question my esthetics (and my poetry) but at least it looks the way I meant it to.*

Figure 20.11 *Netscape does not yet support style sheets very well.*

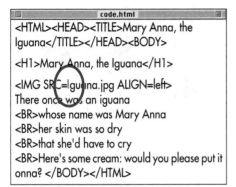

```
code.html
<HTML><HEAD><TITLE>Mary Anna, the
Iguana</TITLE></HEAD><BODY>
<H1>Mary Anna, the Iguana</H1>
<IMG SRC=Iguana.jpg ALIGN=left>
There once was an iguana
<BR>whose name was Mary Anna
<BR>her skin was so dry
<BR>that she'd have to cry
<BR>Here's some cream: would you please put it
onna? </BODY></HTML>
```

Figure 20.12 *The file name for the image is*
iguana.jpg *but here it is incorrectly referenced as*
Iguana.jpg, *with a capital* I.

Figure 20.13 *On your computer, the page looks fine
because your computer doesn't care about upper-
and lowercase letters.*

Figure 20.14 *Once published to the server, which is
case sensitive, Explorer (top) and Netscape have different icons to show missing images.*

Images Don't Appear

Explorer shows you the annoying little red
x's, Netscape gives you either a little image
icon with a question mark in it or a broken
image icon. Regardless, it's a drag if what you
really wanted was a picture of an iguana.

When images don't appear:

1. First, check that the file name of the
    image on the server matches the name
    you've referenced in the IMG tag *exactly*,
    including upper- and lowercase letters,
    the extension, and the whole bit. For
    more information, consult *File Names* on
    page 26.

2. Next, make sure the path to the image on
    the server is reflected in the path that
    you've got in the IMG tag. One easy test
    is to put an image in the same directory
    as the HTML page. That means you'll just
    need the proper file name referenced in
    the IMG tag (but no path information). If
    it shows up, you can be pretty sure that
    the problem with your image is the path.
    For more information about paths, con-
    sult *URLs* on page 27.

3. Have you saved the image as GIF or JPG?
    I've seen Windows users create images in
    BMP format (which Internet Explorer for
    Windows has no trouble with) and then
    not understand when Netscape (on Win-
    dows *or* Mac) displays a broken image
    icon instead of the graphic. For more
    information, see Chapter 4, *Creating Web
    Images.*

Still Stuck?

If you've gotten to this page, you're probably frustrated. Don't think I'm being patronizing when I suggest you go take a break. Sometimes the best thing you can do for a problem is leave it alone for a minute. When you come back, the answer may be staring you in the face. If it's not, let me offer you these additional suggestions.

1. Check again for typos. If you have an HTML validator *(see page 323)*, use it.

2. Check the easy pieces first. I don't know how many times I've spent hours fiddling with an exciting new tag that just wouldn't work only to find that the problem was a typo in some tag that I'd used a thousand times before. Familiarity breeds contempt—check the stuff you think you know really well before you harass the newcomers.

3. Simplify the problem. Go back to the most recent version of your page that worked properly (which might be a blank page in some cases). Then test the page after adding each new element.

4. Read through this chapter again.

5. Check one final time for typos.

6. Post the piece of code that doesn't work on my Question and Answer board *(www.cookwood.com/html4_4e/qanda/)*. Be sure to include the relevant code (or a URL), a description of what is happening and a description of what you think should be happening.

7. If you're at the end of your rope, write me directly at *helphtml@cookwood.com*. But please note that I get a lot of e-mail and while I have the best intentions, I'm sometimes too swamped to answer promptly. I'm much more inclined to try if you assure me you've tried everything else first.

Figure 20.15 *If you get really stuck, try posting a question to my Question and Answer board (http://www.cookwood.com/cookwood/html4_qanda/indexqa.html)*

Publishing Your Page on the Web

Once you've finished your masterpiece and are ready to present it to the public, you have to transfer your pages to your Web host server so that people can get to them.

You may also want to contact your Web host (or Internet Service Provider) to ask them about the best way to upload your files.

Testing Your Page

Many Web page editors offer an automatic or manual way to check your HTML syntax. Although it's a good idea to take advantage of such features, you should always test your HTML pages in at least one browser, and preferably four (Netscape and Explorer for Macintosh and Windows).

Inevitably you will have to make adjustments to your HTML code. You only need to forget one angle bracket for your page to look completely different from what you expected. Other times what you thought might look OK looks awful.

To test your HTML pages:

1. Open the HTML document in your text editor and check for spelling and other errors **(Figure 21.1)**.

2. Open a browser, and choose File > Open File **(Figure 21.2)**.

3. Find the Web page on your hard disk that you want to test and click Open. The page appears in the browser.

4. Go through the whole page and make sure it looks exactly the way you want it **(Figure 21.3)**. For example:

   Is the formatting like you wanted?

   Does each of your URLs point to the proper document? (You can check the URLs by clicking them if the destination files are located in the same relative position on the local computer.)

   Are your images aligned properly?

   Have you included your name and e-mail address (preferably in a mailto URL) so that your users can contact you with comments and suggestions?

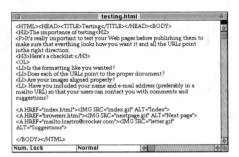

Figure 21.1 *Check your document for typographical errors, missing angle brackets, and other mistakes.*

Figure 21.2 *Choose File > Open File (the name may be slightly different depending on the browser and platform you use) in order to open the page and test it.*

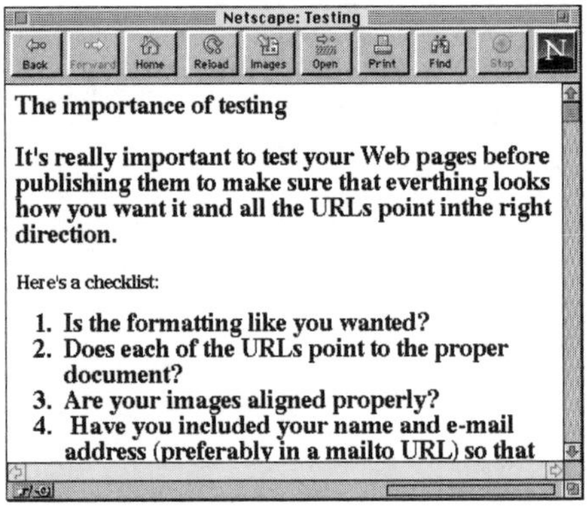

Figure 21.3 *Can you tell what's making this page look so bad?*

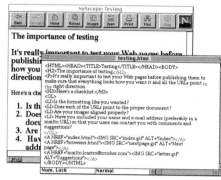

Figure 21.4 *As long as you have enough memory, you can keep the browser and the text editor open at the same time so that you can see what effects your changes are having.*

Figure 21.5 *You must save the changes to your HTML document before reloading, or else the changes will not appear in the browser.*

Figure 21.6 *Select Reload (in the View menu), or click the Reload button on the toolbar in order to show the changes.*

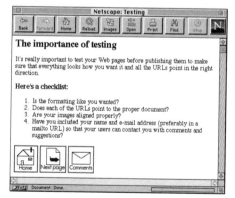

Figure 21.7 *After reloading the fixed HTML document, everything appears as it should—artistic deficiencies aside.*

5. Without closing the page in the browser, open the HTML document with a text or HTML editor. You should be able to simultaneously edit the HTML document with one program and view it with another **(Figure 21.4)**.

6. Save the changes **(Figure 21.5)**.

7. Switch back to the browser and choose Reload to see the changes **(Figures 21.6 and 21.7)**.

8. Repeat steps 1–7 until you are satisfied with your Web page. Don't get discouraged if it takes several tries.

9. Transfer the files to the server and change the permissions, if you haven't done so already *(see page 334)*.

10. Return to the browser and choose File > Open Location.

11. Type your page's URL and click Open. The page will appear in the browser.

12. With your page on the server, go through your page again to make sure everything is all right.

✔ Tips

■ If you can, test your HTML documents in several browsers on various platforms. You never know what browser (or computer) your visitors will use. The major browsers are discussed on pages 13–14.

■ If you're having a particular problem with your page, be sure to consult Chapter 20, *Help! My Page Doesn't Work!*.

■ Sometimes it's not your fault—especially with styles. To see whether a browser supports a particular feature, point it at my tester pages: *www.cookwood.com/ browser_tests/ (see page 20)*.

Testing Your Page

Finding a Host for Your Site

Unless you have your own server, you'll probably have to pay someone to host your site. There are hundreds, maybe thousands of companies that provide Web site hosting. Most charge a monthly fee that depends on the services they offer. Some offer free Web hosting in exchange for advertising from your site. Although you can search on the Internet for a Web host, I recommend talking to friends or looking in your local yellow pages.

When considering a host, there are a number of things—besides price—to keep in mind.

- How much disk space will they let you have for your Web site? Don't pay for more than you need. Remember that HTML files take up very little space while images, sounds, and videos take up successively larger quantities.

- Do they offer technical support? If so, is it by telephone or by e-mail? How long will it take them to get back to you?

- Will they register a domain name *(see page 333)* for you? How much will they charge?

- How fast is their connection to the Internet? This will determine how fast your pages are served to your visitors. Do they have multiple connections in case one of them should become inoperable?

- Do they include dial-up access to the Internet? (They don't usually.) Will they if you need it?

- Will they let you run custom CGI scripts, Server Side Includes, FrontPage extensions, RealAudio, and other advanced features? Is there an extra charge?

- Do they offer a Web hit statistics service to let you know how many people have been visiting your site?

Figure 21.8 *You can go to Network Solutions' site to see if the domain name you want is still available.*

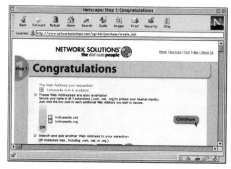

Figure 21.9 *If the name is available, you can either register it through Network Solutions or call your Web host and get them to do it for you. (Now you know: the very useful* www.hotnewsite.com *domain can be yours!)*

Getting Your Own Domain Name

Generally a Web page's address or URL is made up of the name of the server along with the path to the file on that server. When you use a Web hosting service, they rent you a piece of their server and your Web pages take the name of that Web host, by default. For example, in my case, my Web host's server name is *www.crocker.com* and thus the URL for my pages would look something like *www.crocker.com/~lcastro*.

However, if you don't want your Web host's server name to appear in your Web page's URL, you can register your own domain name (for a fee, always for a fee) and then ask your Web hosting company to create a *virtual domain* on their server with your domain name. In my case, while my pages are still on Crocker's server, they *look like* they're on my own server: *www.cookwood.com*. Even if your visitors don't know about servers and where the files actually reside, having your own domain name makes your URLs simpler and easier to type, and thus easier to visit.

They also have one very important advantage. If you ever decide to change your Web host (or if they go out of business), you can move your domain to another server and all of the links will continue to work.

To get your own domain name:

1. Point your browser at *www.network-solutions.com* (no hyphen) and check to see if the domain you want is available.

2. Once you've found a domain name, ask your Web hosting service to set it up for you. They should charge you the standard $70 fee (at press time) for two years plus minimal set-up charges (my host charges $25). Renewal is $35 per year.

Getting Your Own Domain Name

Transferring Files to the Server

In order for other people on the Internet to see your pages, you have to upload them to your Web host's server. One easy way to do that is with an FTP program, like WS_FTP for Windows *(see below)*, or Fetch for Macintosh *(see page 336)*. Many Web page editors offer publishing features as well. For details on publishing files to AOL, see page 338.

To set up WS_FTP to transfer HTML files as text (in ASCII mode):

1. Open WS_FTP.

2. Click Options at the bottom of the window.

3. Click the Extensions tab in the WS_FTP Pro Properties dialog box that appears.

4. In the text box, type .htm and click the Add button. Then type .html and click the Add button again **(Figure 21.10)**. This ensures that all your HTML files will be transferred in ASCII mode.

To define a new FTP site's properties:

1. In the WS_FTP window, click Connect.

2. Click New in the WS_FTP Sites window. In the New Site/Folder Wizard, fill in the boxes and click Next until you've completed all the information **(Fig. 21.11)**.

3. Back in the WS_FTP Sites window, select the profile you've just created and click Properties.

4. In the Site Properties dialog box, click the Session tab and then click Auto Detect at the bottom of the box **(Figure 21.12)**. This ensures that all your files *except* those listed in the Extensions tab *(see Figure 21.10)*, will be transferred in Binary mode.

5. Click OK to save the changes.

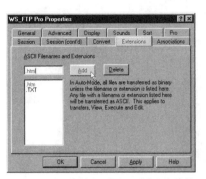

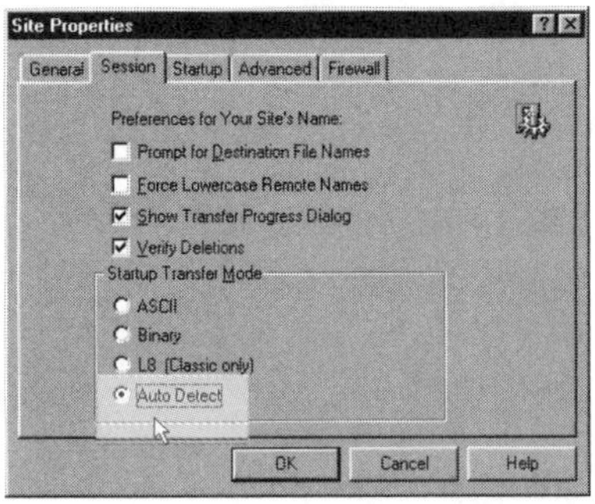

Figure 21.10 *Add the .htm and .html extensions to the list so that HTML files will be transferred in ASCII mode. (Images and other multimedia files should be transferred as Binary.)*

Figure 21.11 *It doesn't matter what you name the site. You enter the proper FTP name in the Host Name/Address field (which appears after you click Next).*

Figure 21.12 *The Auto Detect function means that all files (except those listed in the Extensions tab— Figure 21.10) will be automatically transferred in Binary format. And that's the way it should be.*

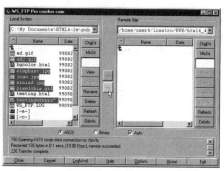

Figure 21.13 *In the left-hand frame, select the files from your hard disk that you want to upload. In the right-hand frame, select the destination directory on the server. Then click the right pointing arrow to transfer the files.*

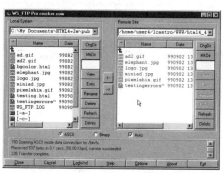

Figure 21.14 *The newly transferred files appear in the right-hand frame. Notice the status messages in the lower left-hand portion of the window.*

To transfer files to the server with WS_FTP (for Windows):

1. Connect to the Internet, if necessary, and then open WS_FTP.

2. Click the Connect button in the lower left-hand corner of the WS_FTP window.

3. Choose your site in the list and click Connect. The server is accessed.

4. On the right side of the window, navigate to the directory on the server to which you want to upload files **(Figure 21.13)**.

5. On the left hand side of the window, navigate to the directory on your hard disk that has the files you want to upload.

6. Select the desired files in the left hand frame and click the right-pointing arrow in the middle of the screen. The files are transferred **(Figure 21.14)**.

7. Click Close to close the connection to the server.

✔ Tips

- HTML files should be transferred in ASCII mode. All other files, including images, sounds, and videos should be transferred in Binary mode. The Auto button means that any file with an extension *not listed* in the Extensions tab will be transferred in Binary mode.

- You can create a new directory by clicking the MkDir button.

- You can find WS_FTP's home page at *www.ipswitch.com/products/ws_ftp/*.

- There are many other file transfer programs for Windows besides WS_FTP. Do a search at CNET's shareware site *(www.shareware.com)* if you'd prefer to use some other program.

Transferring Files to the Server

To transfer HTML files to the server with Fetch (for the Mac):

1. Open your Internet connection.

2. Open Fetch or other FTP program.

3. Choose Preferences in the Customize menu **(Figure 21.15)**, click the Upload tab in the Preferences box that appears, and make sure the Add .txt suffix to text files option is *not* checked **(Fig. 21.16)**.

4. Also make sure the Default text format is Text and the Default non-text format is Raw Data.

5. Click OK.

6. Choose File > New Connection **(Figure 21.17)**.

7. In the Open Connection window, enter the server name in the Host text box, your user name in the User ID box, your password in the Password box, and the path to the directory where you plan to save the Web pages in the Directory box **(Figure 21.18)**.

8. Click OK to open the connection. Fetch will make the connection to the server you requested and open the designated directory.

9. Make sure the correct directory where you wish to place your set of HTML files is showing in the main Fetch window **(Figure 21.19)**.

10. Choose Remote > Put Folders and Files **(Figure 21.20)**.

11. In the dialog box that appears, choose the files that you wish to transfer to the server and click Add. The files will appear at the bottom of the dialog box. When you have selected all the files you wish to transfer, click Done **(Figure 21.21)**.

Figure 21.15 *Choose Preferences in Fetch's Customize menu to open the Preferences dialog box.*

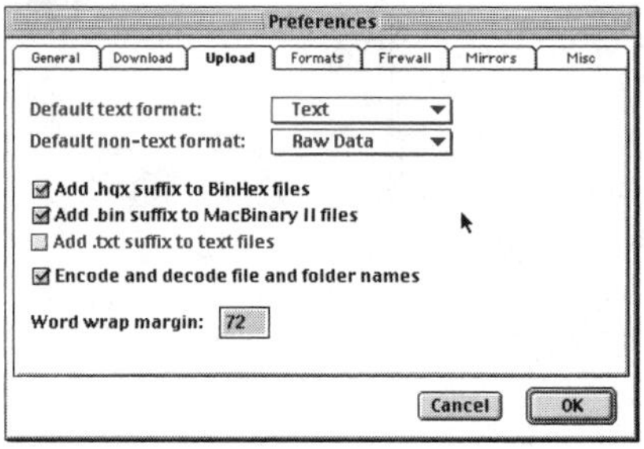

Figure 21.16 *Click the Upload tab and then choose the proper formats for text and non-text uploading. Be sure to uncheck the Add .txt suffix option.*

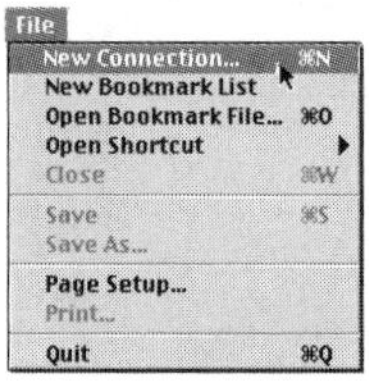

Figure 21.17 *Choose File > New Connection in order to display the Open Connection window.*

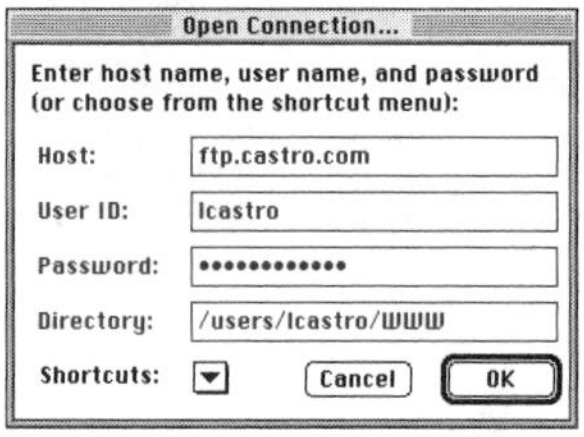

Figure 21.18 *In the Open Connection window, type the server name (Host), your User ID and password, and the directory where you want to transfer the files.*

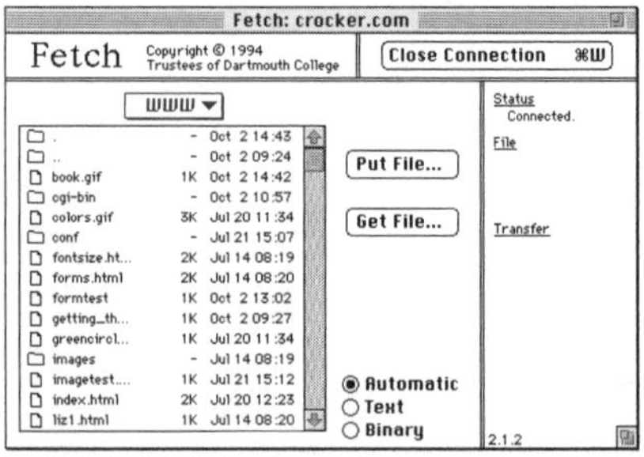

Figure 21.19 *Make sure the proper directory on the server (where you want to transfer the files) is showing in the Fetch window before transferring the files (in this case, WWW).*

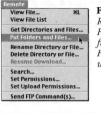

Figure 21.20 *Choose Remote > Put Folders and Files. (To transfer just one file, you can click the Put File button in the main Fetch window.)*

Figure 21.21 *Select each folder or file that you wish to transfer to the server and click Add. When you've finished choosing folders and files, click Done.*

Figure 21.22 *Confirm the Text format for Text Files and the Raw Data format for Other Files.*

Figure 21.23 *The transferred files maintain the same hierarchy that they had on the Mac. Click Close Connection to close the connection to the server.*

12. In the Choose formats dialog box that appears, confirm the appropriate formats for the files. Use Text for HTML and other text documents and Raw Data for other kinds of files **(Figure 21.22)**.

13. Click OK. The files will be transferred to the server and will maintain the hierarchy that they had on the local system **(Figure 21.23)**.

14. Click Close Connection to close the connection to the server.

✔ Tips

- HTML files should always be transferred as Text Files (in ASCII mode). Any other file, including images, sound, and video, should be transferred as Raw Data.

- Fetch's home page is *www.dartmouth. edu/pages/softdev/fetch.html*.

- You can resize the main window so that it shows more files at one time. Just click and drag the bottom-right corner.

- If you have used relative URLs *(see page 29)*, these will be maintained when you transfer the entire folder or directory from your computer to the server. If you have used absolute URLs *(see page 28)*, you will have to change them to reflect the files' new locations.

Transferring Files to the Server

Transferring Files to AOL

Even if you are a member of AOL you can still use the techniques described in this book to create your Web page. The only difference is how to transfer your files to the server.

To transfer files to AOL:

1. Go to keyword **myplace** (or **myftpspace**).

2. In the window that appears, click the See my FTP Space button **(Figure 21.24)**.

3. Create any desired directories and then navigate to where you want to upload the file **(Figure 21.25)**.

4. Click the Upload button.

5. Type the exact file name, and its extension (but not the path). Click ASCII for text documents and Binary for everything else. Then click Continue **(Figure 21.26)**.

6. In the Upload File dialog box that appears, click Select File, and then choose the corresponding file from your hard disk and click OK.

7. Click Send to upload the file **(Figure 21.27)**.

✔ Tips

■ The URL of your pages on AOL is *http://members.aol.com/screenname/file-name*. You can publish up to 2Mb *per screenname* (for a total of 10Mb).

■ It seems incredibly laborious to me, but you can only upload one file at a time.

■ You can create additional directories as needed by clicking the Utilities button.

■ To delete a home page or (empty) folder, select it, click the Utilities button, and then click Delete in the dialog box that appears.

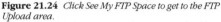

Figure 21.24 *Click See My FTP Space to get to the FTP Upload area.*

Figure 21.25 *Navigate to the desired directory, if necessary, and then click the Upload button at the bottom of the screen.*

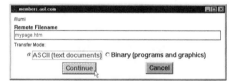

Figure 21.26 *Type the file name and extension (but not the directory), choose ASCII or Binary, depending on the nature of the file, and then click Continue.*

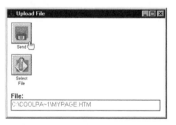

Figure 21.27 *Click Select File to choose the file that you want to upload from your hard disk. Its name appears in the File box at the bottom of the screen. Then click Send to upload the file to AOL.*

Getting People to Visit

With almost one billion Web pages in existence and thousands more being created every day, you may have to shout a little to get your page noticed. This chapter explains the HTML tags you can use to identify your page to search engines like AltaVista and Yahoo as well as a few strategies you can use to get noticed by these portals to the Web.

A number of ideas in this chapter, principally the use of a crawler page and the judicious use of META tags, came from an excellent article on improving a page's rankings on search engines, written by Paul Boutin for WebMonkey. You can find the original at *www.hotwired.com/webmonkey/99/31/index1a.html*

Helping Visitors Find Your Page

In the early days of the Web, surfing was rather arbitrary. You jumped to one site, found an interesting link, and jumped on. Today, surfers most often use search engines to find a page that deals with a particular topic. You can tell search engines exactly what your page is about so that if a visitor searches for that topic, there's a better chance they'll find *your* page.

To help visitors find your page:

1. In the HEAD section of your page, type **<META NAME="keywords" CONTENT="**.

2. Type a few words that concisely describe the topic discussed on your page. Separate each word with a comma and a space.

3. Type **">** to complete the META tag.

✔ Tips

■ Use a combination of very unique and more general words to describe the contents of your page. *Chihuahua* is unique, but *dog* may also net you some visitors who didn't realize they were interested in Chihuahuas (or couldn't spell it).

■ Actually, adding misspelled keywords (in *addition* to correctly spelled ones) is not such a bad idea. You might also offer several alternative spellings for foreign words.

■ More words is not necessarily better. According to Paul Boutin *(see page 339)*, the closer you match what a prospective visitor types (with no extra words), the higher up you'll get listed in the results.

■ Most search engines offer specific tips on using the META tag to describe your site. Check out *altavista.digital.com/av/ content/addurl_meta.htm.*

Figure 22.1 *Here is a page that gives a lot of information about Alpacas.*

```
code.html
<HTML><HEAD><TITLE>Chase Tavern Farm
Alpacas</TITLE>

<META NAME="keywords" CONTENT=
"Alpaca, alpacas, wool, lama, llama">

<META NAME="description"
CONTENT="Chase Tavern Farm Alpacas,
Breeding Australian, Peruvian and Chilean
Alpacas since 1993.">
```

Figure 22.2 *The site designer of the Chase Tavern Farm Alpacas page offered several key words, in addition to Alpaca, to help visitors find the site. Notice that they offer both* lama *and* llama, *just in case someone doesn't know how to spell it.*

Helping Visitors Find Your Page

```
code.html
<HTML><HEAD><TITLE>Chase Tavern Farm
Alpacas</TITLE>

<META NAME="keywords" CONTENT=
"Alpaca, alpacas, wool, lama, llama">

<META NAME="description" CONTENT=
"Chase Tavern Farm Alpacas, Breeding
Australian, Peruvian and Chilean Alpacas since
1993.">
```

Figure 22.3 *Make sure to enclose the description in double quotes.*

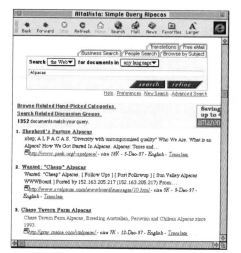

Figure 22.4 *Notice the three descriptions shown here. The first two—a lot of gobbledygook—have obviously been generated automatically from the contents at the top of the HTML document. The third—a lucid, descriptive, complete sentence about the site, was created by the site designer (see Figure 22.3).*

Controlling Your Page's Summary

When a prospective visitor does a search at AltaVista (or wherever), a list of matches appears, each with a little summary of the page's contents. By default, the search engine uses the first few words on your page, but you can choose exactly what appears—and hopefully persuade more visitors to come to your site.

To control your page's summary:

1. In the HEAD section of your page, type **<META NAME="description" CONTENT="**.

2. Type a concise sentence or two that describes your page and hopefully persuades folks to click through.

3. Type **">** to complete the META tag.

✔ Tips

- AltaVista limits the length of the description to 1024 characters.

- For more information on getting noticed by search engines, and indeed by the Web public in general, consult *Getting Hits: The Definitive Guide to Promoting your Website*, by Don Sellers (Peachpit Press).

Controlling Your Page's Summary

Controlling Other Information

You can also add information to your page about who wrote it, what program was used (if any) to generate the HTML code, and if it is copyrighted. Note, however, that search engines do not currently use this information (though they may some day), and browsers don't display it.

To control other information about your page:

1. In the HEAD section of your page, type **<META NAME="author" CONTENT="name">**, where *name* is the person who wrote the HTML page.

2. In the HEAD section of your page, type **<META NAME="generator" CONTENT="program">**, where *program* is the name of the software that created (or started) the HTML page.

3. In the HEAD section of your Web page, type **<META NAME="copyright" CONTENT="© year holder">**, where *year* is the calendar year of the copyright, and *holder* is the name of the person or entity who holds the copyright to the page.

✔ Tips

■ The generator is created automatically by most Web page editors. Feel free to delete it if you prefer not to give them credit.

■ If you browse a page with Internet Explorer 5 for Windows and then save the source to your hard disk, Explorer will actually add META information to the file, claiming to be its generator. (For more information on saving the source code from a page on the Web, consult *The Inspiration of Others* on page 310.)

```
code.html
<HTML><HEAD>
<TITLE>Identifying ownership</TITLE>
<META NAME="generator"
CONTENT="BBEdit 4.5">
<META NAME="author"
CONTENT="Liz Castro">
<META NAME="copyright"
CONTENT="&copy; 1998 Liz Castro">
</HEAD>
<BODY>
This is my page!
</BODY></HTML>
```

Figure 22.5 *You can use as many META tags as you need.*

Figure 22.6 *The META information is always invisible in the browser.*

```
code.html
<HTML><HEAD>

<TITLE>Identifying ownership</TITLE>

<META NAME="generator"
CONTENT="BBEdit 4.5">

<META NAME="author"
CONTENT="Liz Castro">

<META NAME="copyright" CONTENT="&copy;
1998 Liz Castro">

<META NAME="robots"
CONTENT="NOINDEX, NOFOLLOW">

</HEAD><BODY>

This is my personal page! Here is a personal <A
HREF="personal.html">link</A>.
```

Figure 22.7 *When a search engine's robot encounters this page, it will ignore both the page and the page's links.*

Keeping Visitors Away

Search engines employ little programs called *robots* or *spiders* to hang out on the Web and look for new pages to add to the engine's index. But sometimes, you don't want search engines to know your page exists. Perhaps it's a personal page designed only for your family or an internal page for your company. You can add information to the page so that most search engine robots will stay out.

To keep search engine robots out:

1. In the HEAD section of your page, type **<META NAME="robots" CONTENT="**.

2. If desired, type **NOINDEX** to keep the robot from adding the page to its index.

3. If desired, type **NOFOLLOW** to keep the robot from following the links on the page and indexing those pages.

4. Type **">** to complete the META tag.

✔ Tips

■ Separate multiple values with a comma and a space.

■ With about one billion Web pages in existence, the easiest way to keep people away from your page is to never create any link *to* that page from any other page on your or anyone else's site (and, obviously, don't submit it to a search engine).

■ If a page has already been indexed, you'll have to go to the search engine's Web site and use the Remove URL page.

■ You can use the values ALL and INDEX to have robots add the current page (and its links) to the search engine's index. However, these are the default values and so leaving them out is the same as specifying them (but faster).

Creating a Crawler Page

Most search engines, like AltaVista or Yahoo, ask that you submit just one URL and promise that they will follow all the links and find the rest of the pages on your site. But why make it difficult for them? You can create a page with links to all of the most important sections of your site and then submit that to the search engine, thus ensuring that the proper pages will be noticed.

To create a crawler page in Explorer:

1. Choose Favorites > Organize Favorites.

2. In the dialog box that appears, click Create Folder **(Figure 22.8)**.

3. Type the name of the crawler page (it appears in the right hand box).

4. Close the dialog box.

5. Navigate to the important pages on your site that you want to be sure the search engine finds.

6. Choose Favorites > Add to Favorites **(Figure 22.9)**.

7. Select your crawler page folder from the list and then click OK. If your folder doesn't appear, click the Create in button to see the list of folders.

8. Click OK.

9. When you've added all the desired pages, choose File > Import and Export.

10. Use the Wizard to create an HTML file of your crawler page favorites folder **(Figure 22.10)**.

11. Upload the page to your server *(see page 334)*.

12. And then don't forget to submit it to the desired search engines *(see page 346)*.

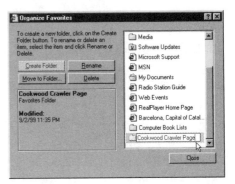

Figure 22.8 *In the Organize Favorites dialog box, click Create Folder and give the new folder a name. Then click Close.*

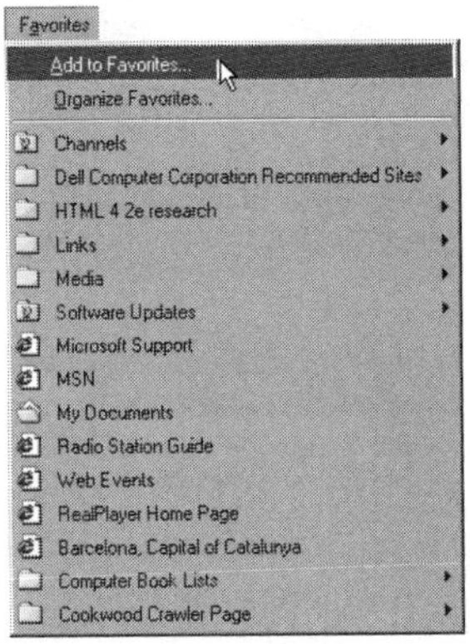

Figure 22.9 *Navigate to the important pages on your site and then choose Favorite > Add to Favorites.*

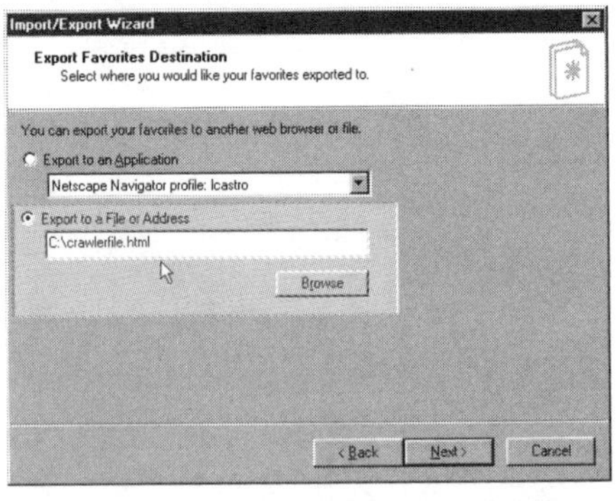

Figure 22.10 *In the Import/Export Wizard, be sure to choose the Export to a File or Address option and then choose a simple name for your crawler file.*

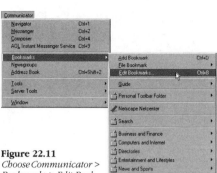

Figure 22.11
Choose Communicator > Bookmarks > Edit Bookmarks to display the Bookmarks window.

Figure 22.12 *Once the Bookmarks window is open and active, choose File > New Folder.*

Figure 22.13 *Once you've created bookmarks for all the important pages on your site, choose File > Save As to save the bookmarks file as an HTML document.*

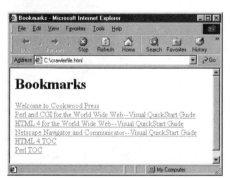

Figure 22.14 *A crawler page should contain links to all of the pages on a site that you want indexed by a search engine.*

To create a crawler page with Netscape:

1. Choose Communicator > Bookmarks > Edit Bookmarks **(Figure 22.11)**.

2. Choose File > New Folder in the Bookmarks window to create a new folder to hold the bookmarks for your most important pages **(Figure 22.12)**.

3. Select the folder in the Bookmarks window and choose View > Set as New Bookmarks Folder so that all new bookmarks will be automatically added to this folder.

4. Close the Bookmarks window.

5. Navigate to the important pages on your site that you want to be sure the search engine finds.

6. Choose Communicator > Bookmarks > Add Bookmark (Ctrl/Command+D) to add the page to your crawler page bookmarks folder.

7. When you've added all the desired pages, choose Communicator > Bookmarks > Edit Bookmarks to open the Bookmarks window.

8. Choose File > Save As to save the bookmarks as an HTML file **(Figure 22.13)**. Unfortunately, you can't choose a particular folder of bookmarks to save.

9. Open the bookmarks file and delete everything except the links to the important pages on your site.

10. Continue with step 11 on page 344.

✔ Credit

■ I got the idea of using a crawler page from Paul Boutin *(see page 339)*.

Creating a Crawler Page

Submitting Your Site to a Search Engine

Once you have added META tags to all of the desired pages on your site and perhaps created a crawler page as described on page 344 that lists those pages, you'll want to invite a search engine to visit your site in order to add your pages to its database.

To submit your site to a search engine:

1. Connect to the search engine of your choice **(Figure 22.15)**.

2. Find their Add URL page.

AltaVista's is at: *altavista.digital.com/av/content/addurl.htm* **(Figure 22.16)**.

Yahoo's is at *www.yahoo.com/docs/info/include.html*.

Lycos' is at *www.lycos.com/addasite.html*

3. Type your (crawler) page's URL in the appropriate text box and click the Submit button.

4. Go back to the search engine in two weeks and search for your site. If it doesn't appear, submit it again.

✔ Tips

■ The most popular general search engines are AltaVista, Yahoo, Lycos, Excite, Go, and HotBot.

■ You might also want to register your site with a search engine that specializes in a particular topic. For example, if your page is about Star Trek, you'd want to register it with the James Kirk Search Engine: *www.webwombat.com.au/trek/*. Yahoo has a very complete list of specific topic search engines.

Figure 22.15 *Go to the search engine's home page and click the Add URL link. This is AltaVista. Its Add URL link is at the bottom of its home page.*

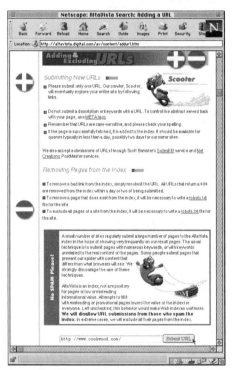

Figure 22.16 *Follow the directions in the Add URL page. In AltaVista, type the URL of your home (or crawler) page and then click Submit URL (at the bottom of the page).*

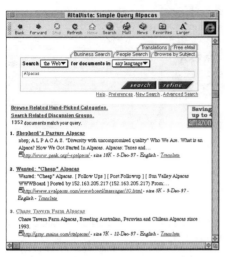

Figure 22.17 *Chase Tavern Farm's use of META tags (see Figure 22.2 on page 340) surely helped them appear close to the top of the list of 1352 documents when I searched for Alpacas on AltaVista.*

Appearing at the Top of the Search Results

Even if your page is indexed by all the major search engines, it won't get hits unless it appears somewhere near the top of the list. There are several ways to improve your prospects, most of them having to do with *The Price is Right* technique: get as close as possible to what a prospective visitor might search for, without going over—no extra words!

To appear at the top of a search:

1. Create a title for your page *(see page 37)*. The closer it matches what a prospective visitor types, the higher your page will appear on the list.

2. Use keywords judiciously *(see page 340)*. Again, the closer you match what a prospective visitor types—with no extra words—the higher you'll rate.

3. Plan your description *(see page 341)* carefully to both give descriptive information about your site and to attract that visitor's click.

4. Keep your page short and the words that might match a search as close to the top of the page as possible.

5. Create several copies of important pages with different sets of keywords and descriptions in order to match different search criteria.

6. Don't forget to submit your page to a search engine *(see page 346)*.

✔ Credit

■ Most of these ideas came from an excellent article written by Paul Boutin in WebMonkey *(see page 339)*.

Chapter 22

Other Techniques for Publicizing Your Site

Although getting your site to appear at the top of the list when a prospective visitor looks for related topics at AltaVista is a laudable goal, there are several additional ways to let people know your page exists.

- Add your URL to your signature so that it will be included in all outgoing e-mail.

- Answer questions or post information on a related newsgroup and make sure your URL is prominently included in your signature.

- Post a note in the moderated newsgroup *comp.infosystems.www.announce* or the in the unmoderated *comp.internet.net-happenings*. (The hyphen is part of the address.)

- Join a Web ring. A Web ring is a group of related Web sites that have links that go from one site to the next. Web rings encourage visitors from one site to explore related ones. You can search for pertinent Web rings at Yahoo.

- Even simpler than a Web ring is to exchange links with other sites that have similar content.

- Add your page to my readers' gallery: *www.cookwood.com/html4_4e/gallery/* **(Figure 22.18)**.

- And of course, you can always pay someone to advertise your page for you.

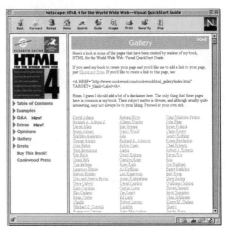

Figure 22.18 *Adding your page to my gallery is just one of a number of techniques you can use to get people to come visit your site.*

HTML Tools

The lists on the following pages are by no means exhaustive. There are literally hundreds of programs, some commercial, some shareware, and some freeware, of varying quality, that you can use as you design and create your Web pages. If you don't find what you're looking for on these pages, jump to any search service on the Web (e.g., *http:// altavista.digital. com*) and look for *Web tools, Web graphics*, or whatever it is you need.

HTML Editors

You can use *any* text editor to write HTML, including SimpleText or TeachText on the Macintosh, WordPad for Windows, or vi in Unix systems. The HTML code produced with these simpler programs is no different from the HTML produced by more complex HTML editors.

A simple text editor is like the most basic SLR 35 mm camera. You have to set your f-stop and aperture manually, and then focus before shooting. The dedicated HTML editors are point-and-shoot cameras: just aim and fire, for a price. They are more expensive, and generally less flexible.

What HTML editors offer	Disadvantages of HTML editors
Dedicated HTML editors offer the following advantages over simple text editors (of course, not every HTML editor has every feature): • they insert opening and closing tags with a single click • they check and verify syntax in your HTML and typos in your text • they allow you to add attributes by clicking buttons instead of typing words in a certain order in a certain place in the document • they offer varying degrees of WYSIWYG display of your Web page • they correct mistakes in existing HTML pages • they make it easy to use special characters	These extra features come at a price, however. Some things that may annoy you about HTML editors is that • they don't all recognize new or non-standard HTML codes • they don't all support forms, frames, and tables • they are more difficult to learn, and less intuitive than they promise • they cost money (all simple text editors are included free with the respective system software) • they use up more space on disk and more memory • some add proprietary information (like *their* name, for example), and tags to the HTML document • some eliminate tags that they don't understand—even if the tags are part of the standard HTML specifications

HTML Editors

High-end		
Dreamweaver (M, W)	$300. Macromedia. Probably the most popular editor among Web professionals.	http://www.macromedia.com/ software/dreamweaver; *demo available*
Adobe GoLive (M,W)	$300. Formerly GoLive CyberStudio. Dreamweaver's main competition.	http://www.adobe.com/ prodindex/golive/main.html; *demo available*
NetObjects Fusion (M, W)	$300. NetObjects WYSIWYG editor for professional Web masters.	http://www.netobjects.com/ products/html/nof.html; *demo available*
Middle-to-low end		
FileMaker Home Page (M, W)	$100, WYSIWYG Editor from FileMaker, Inc. (formerly Claris Corp.).	http://www.filemaker.com/ products/homepage3.html; *demo available*
Microsoft FrontPage (M, W)	$130. WYSIWYG Editor from Microsoft Corporation.	http://www.microsoft.com/ frontpage/. *(FrontPage Express included with Office; demo also available)*
Adobe PageMill (M, W)	$100. An aging pioneer.	http://www.adobe.com/ prodindex/pagemill/
Netscape Composer	Mediocre editor included free with Netscape Communicator.	http://home.netscape.com/
SoftQuad HoTMetaL (M, W)	$100, WYSIWYG editor that creates standard, universal HTML. SiteMaker also available.	http://www.sq.com/products/ hotmetal/ *demo available*
Text Based		
BBEdit (M)	$120. Excellent HTML editor from Bare Bones Software. The most popular non-WYSIWYG HTML editor.	http://www.barebones.com *demo available*
HotDog Professional (W)	$130, Sausage Software. "Express" version also available	http://www.sausage.com/
Allaire HomeSite (W)	$100. Popular text-based HTML editor for Windows.	http://www.allaire.com/ products/homesite/
Shareware		
World Wide Web Weaver (M, W)	$60, Miracle Software.	http://www.miracleinc.com/ Products/W4
ANT_HTML (W)	$40, Jill Swift; template for use with Microsoft Word (several versions and platforms).	http://telacommunications.com/ ant/index.htm

HTML Editors

Free-use Images for Your Pages

Name	Description	URL
Yahoo	List of sites with graphics	http://dir.yahoo.com/Arts/ Design_Arts/Graphic_Design/ Web_Page_Design_and_Layout/ Graphics/
Lycos Picture Gallery	Searchable database of images and sounds	http://www.lycos.com/picturethis/
AltaVista	Site that searches the Web for images that fit your criteria	http://www.altavista.com (and click the Images button)

Graphics Tools

Name	Description	URL
Adobe Photoshop (M, W)	$600. Excellent, all-purpose image editing program. Version 5.5 includes ImageReady, Adobe's Web graphics program	http://www.adobe.com/prodindex/ photoshop/main.html. *demo available*
Macromedia Fireworks	$200. A specialized graphics program for creating Web images	http://www.macromedia.com/ software/fireworks/ *demo available*
Macromedia Flash	$300. Designed for creating Web animations.	http://www.macromedia.com/ software/flash/ *demo available*
Paint Shop Pro (W)	$100. JASC Software. Powerful image editing program for Windows. Commercial and shareware versions available. Supports JPEG, PNG, GIF.	http://www.jasc.com/psp.html; *download:* http://www.jasc.com/ pspdl.html
GraphicConverter (M)	$35. Thorsten Lemke's image editor for Macintosh. Reads and writes an incredible array of graphics formats, including Progressive JPEG, GIF89a (Animated), etc.	http://www.lemkesoft.de/ us_gcabout.html
LView Pro (W)	$40. Popular shareware graphics program.	http://www.lview.com

Image Map Tools

Name	Description	URL
Mapedit (M, W)	$25. Thomas Boutell. Useful for both client-side and server-side image maps.	http://www.boutell.com/mapedit

Special Symbols

You can type any letter of the English alphabet or any number into your HTML document and be confident that every other computer system will interpret it correctly. However, if your Web page contains any accents, foreign characters, or special symbols, you may have to use a special code to make sure they appear correctly on the page.

The ISO Latin-1 character set is the standard for the World Wide Web. It assigns a number to each character, number, or symbol in the set. In addition, some characters, especially the accented letters, have special names.

However, some computer systems, especially Macintosh and DOS, do not use the standard character set. That means that you could type an *é* in your HTML document and have it appear as a | (a straight vertical line) on your Web page.

To make sure accented characters and special characters appear correctly, no matter what system you write on, use the steps described on page 354 to enter them into your HTML document.

Using Special Symbols

The symbols numbered 32 to 126—which include all the letters in the English alphabet, the numbers, and many common symbols—can be typed directly from the keyboard of any system. The symbols numbered 127 to 255 should be entered as described below.

To use special symbols:

1. Place the cursor where you wish the special character to appear.

2. Type **&**.

3. *Either* type **#n** where *n* is the number that corresponds to the desired symbol *or* type **name** where *name* is the code that corresponds to the desired symbol *(see pages 355 and 356).*

4. Type **;**.

5. Continue with your HTML document.

✔ Tips

■ To create curly or smart quotes ("") on your Web page, use **“** and **”**.

■ All characters have a corresponding number. Not all characters have a corresponding name. It doesn't matter which one you use.

■ The character names are case sensitive. Type them exactly as they appear in the tables.

■ Although this system is supposed to eliminate differences across platforms, the tables illustrate that it is not 100% effective.

■ The easiest way to add foreign symbols that don't appear on the following pages is by creating a GIF image and inserting it on your page.

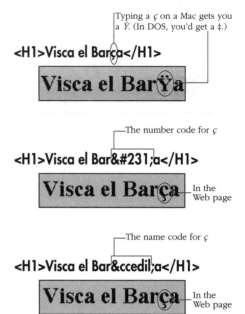

Figure B.1 *To display a ç properly, you must use either its number or name. It looks awful in your HTML document, but on the Web page, where it counts, it's beautiful—on any platform.*

Table I: Characters

To get this...	...type this...	...or this.	To get this...	...type this...	...or this.
à	&#224;	&agrave;	ò	&#242;	&ograve;
á	&#225;	&aacute;	ó	&#243;	&oacute;
â	&#226;	&acirc;	ô	&#244;	&ocirc;
ã	&#227;	&atilde;	õ	&#245;	&otilde;
ä	&#228;	&auml;	ö	&#246;	&ouml;
å	&#229;	&aring;	ø	&#248;	&oslash;
æ	&#230;	&aelig;	œ	&#156;	*
À	&#192;	&Agrave;	Ò	&#210;	&Ograve;
Á	&#193;	&Aacute;	Ó	&#211;	&Oacute;
Â	&#194;	&Acirc;	Ô	&#212;	&Ocirc;
Ã	&#195;	&Atilde;	Õ	&#213;	&Otilde;
Ä	&#196;	&Auml;	Ö	&#214;	&Ouml;
Å	&#197;	&Aring;	Ø	&#216;	&Oslash;
Æ	&#198;	&AElig;	Œ	&#;	*
è	&#232;	&egrave;	ù	&#249;	&ugrave;
é	&#233;	&eacute;	ú	&#250;	&uacute;
ê	&#234;	&ecirc;	û	&#251;	&ucirc;
ë	&#235;	&euml;	ü	&#252;	&uuml;
È	&#200;	&Egrave;	Ù	&#217;	&Ugrave;
É	&#201;	&Eacute;	Ú	&#218;	&Uacute;
Ê	&#202;	&Ecirc;	Û	&#219;	&Ucirc;
Ë	&#203;	&Euml;	Ü	&#220;	&Uuml;
ì	&#236;	&igrave;	ÿ	&#255;	&yuml;
í	&#237;	&iacute;	Ÿ	&#159;	*
î	&#238;	&icirc;	ç	&#231;	&ccedil;
ï	&#239;	&iuml;	Ç	&#199;	&Ccedil;
Ì	&#204;	&Igrave;	ß	&#223;	&szlig;
Í	&#205;	&Iacute;	ñ	&#241;	&ntilde;
Î	&#206;	&Icirc;	Ñ	&#209;	&Ntilde;
Ï	&#207;	&Iuml;			

* These characters don't have a name code.

Table II: Symbols

To get this...	...type this...	...or this.
"	&#34;	&quot;
"	&#147;	*
"	&#148;	*
«	&#171;	&laquo;
»	&#187;	&raquo;
#	&#35;	*
&	&#38;	&amp;
<	&#60;	&lt;
>	&#62;	&gt;
¬	&#172;	&not;
±	&#177;	&plusmn;
÷	&#247;	&divide;
µ	&#181;	&micro;
$\frac{1}{4}$	&#188;	¼[1]
$\frac{1}{2}$	&#189;	½[1]
$\frac{3}{4}$	&#190;	¾[1]
‾	&#175;	&hibar;
%	&#37;	*
‰	&#137;	*
¢	&#162;	&cent;
$	&#36;	*
£	&#163;	&pound;
¥	&#165;	&yen;
™	&#153;	*
©	&#169;	*
®	&#174;	*
@	&#64;	*
...	&#133;	*

To get this...	...type this...	...or this.
¡	&#161;	&iexcl;
¿	&#191;	&iquest;
¦	&#166;	&brkbar;[2]
•	&#149;	*
°	&186;	&deg;
§	&#167;	*
¶	&#182;	*
º	&#186;	*
ª	&#170;	*
1	&#185;	¹[3]
2	&#178;	²[3]
3	&#179;	³[3]
soft hyphen	&#173;	­[4]
non-break space		

* These characters don't have a name code.

[1] These fractions only appear in Windows. For Macs, you'll have to construct them with super- and subscripted numerals.

[2] The break bar is solid on a Mac (but doesn't appear in Netscape) and dashed on Windows machines.

[3] These superscripted numbers don't display at all in Netscape for Mac, and display as regular numbers in Explorer for Mac. I recommend using SUB and SUP (see page 52).

[4] The soft hyphen is not supported by all browsers.

Colors in Hex

You can choose the color for the background of your page as well as for the text and links. Both Netscape and Internet Explorer understand sixteen predefined color names: Silver, Gray, White, Black, Maroon, Red, Green, Lime, Purple, Fuchsia, Olive, Yellow, Navy, Blue, Teal, and Aqua. Some browsers also recognize Magenta (same as Fuchsia) and Cyan (same as Aqua). Consult the inside back cover for a look at these colors.

You can also specify any color by giving its red, green, and blue components—in the form of a number between 0 and 255. To make things really complicated, you must specify these components with the hexadecimal equivalent of that number. The table on page 359 gives the corresponding hexadecimal number for each possible value of red, green, or blue.

Check the inside back cover for a full-color table of many common colors, together with their hexadecimal codes. Note that they are not browser safe colors. Since browser safe colors are based on the RGB color system, it's kind of pointless to try to print them. They end up looking all the same.

Since only 10% of the Web surfing public is still on 256 color monitors, using non-safe colors is not as much of a problem as it used to be. Nevertheless, if you'd still like to limit yourself to browser safe colors, I've created a complete table of browser safe colors on my site: *www.cookwood.com/html4_4e/colors/*.

Finding a Color's RGB Components—in Hex

The inside back cover contains a full-color table of many common colors and their hexadecimal equivalents. If you don't see the color you want, you can use Photoshop (or other image editing program) to display the red, green, and blue components of the colors you want to use on your page. Then consult the table on page 359 for the hexadecimal equivalents of those components.

To find a color's RGB components:

1. In Photoshop, click one of the color boxes in the toolbox **(Figure 3.1)**.

2. In the Color Picker dialog box that appears, choose the desired color.

3. Write down the numbers that appear in the R, G, and B text boxes. These numbers represent the R, G, and B components of the color **(Figure 3.2)**.

4. Use the table on the next page to find the hexadecimal equivalents of the numbers found in step 3.

5. Assemble the hexadecimal numbers in the form *#rrggbb* where *rr* is the hexadecimal equivalent for the red component, *gg* is the hexadecimal equivalent for the green component, and *bb* is the hexadecimal equivalent of the blue component.

✔ Tips

- You can find instructions for specifying the background color on page 98, for specifying the text color on pages 50 and 51, and for specifying the links' color on page 133.

- You can also use styles to format color (*see pages 256, 265, 266, 285, and 286*).

Figure 3.1 *In Photoshop, click on one of the color boxes in the toolbox to make the Color Picker dialog box appear.*

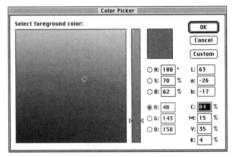

Figure 3.2 *Choose the desired color and then jot down the values shown in the R, G, and B text boxes. This color, a teal blue, has an R of 48 (hex=30), a G of 143 (hex=8F), and a B of 158 (hex=9E). Therefore, the hexadecimal equivalent of this color would be #308F9E.*

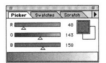

Figure 3.3 *You can also use the Picker palette to choose colors and see their RGB components.*

Hexadecimal Equivalents

#	Hex.	#	Hex.	#	Hex.	#	Hex.	#	Hex.	#	Hex.	#	Hex.	#	Hex.
0	00	32	20	64	40	96	60	128	80	160	A0	192	C0	224	E0
1	01	33	21	65	41	97	61	129	81	161	A1	193	C1	225	E1
2	02	34	22	66	42	98	62	130	82	162	A2	194	C2	226	E2
3	03	35	23	67	43	99	63	131	83	163	A3	195	C3	227	E3
4	04	36	24	68	44	100	64	132	84	164	A4	196	C4	228	E4
5	05	37	25	69	45	101	65	133	85	165	A5	197	C5	229	E5
6	06	38	26	70	46	102	66	134	86	166	A6	198	C6	230	E6
7	07	39	27	71	47	103	67	135	87	167	A7	199	C7	231	E7
8	08	40	28	72	48	104	68	136	88	168	A8	200	C8	232	E8
9	09	41	29	73	49	105	69	137	89	169	A9	201	C9	233	E9
10	0A	42	2A	74	4A	106	6A	138	8A	170	AA	202	CA	234	EA
11	0B	43	2B	75	4B	107	6B	139	8B	171	AB	203	CB	235	EB
12	0C	44	2C	76	4C	108	6C	140	8C	172	AC	204	CC	236	EC
13	0D	45	2D	77	4D	109	6D	141	8D	173	AD	205	CD	237	ED
14	0E	46	2E	78	4E	110	6E	142	8E	174	AE	206	CE	238	EE
15	0F	47	2F	79	4F	111	6F	143	8F	175	AF	207	CF	239	EF
16	10	48	30	80	50	112	70	144	90	176	B0	208	D0	240	F0
17	11	49	31	81	51	113	71	145	91	177	B1	209	D1	241	F1
18	12	50	32	82	52	114	72	146	92	178	B2	210	D2	242	F2
19	13	51	33	83	53	115	73	147	93	179	B3	211	D3	243	F3
20	14	52	34	84	54	116	74	148	94	180	B4	212	D4	244	F4
21	15	53	35	85	55	117	75	149	95	181	B5	213	D5	245	F5
22	16	54	36	86	56	118	76	150	96	182	B6	214	D6	246	F6
23	17	55	37	87	57	119	77	151	97	183	B7	215	D7	247	F7
24	18	56	38	88	58	120	78	152	98	184	B8	216	D8	248	F8
25	19	57	39	89	59	121	79	153	99	185	B9	217	D9	249	F9
26	1A	58	3A	90	5A	122	7A	154	9A	186	BA	218	DA	250	FA
27	1B	59	3B	91	5B	123	7B	155	9B	187	BB	219	DB	251	FB
28	1C	60	3C	92	5C	124	7C	156	9C	188	BC	220	DC	252	FC
29	1D	61	3D	93	5D	125	7D	157	9D	189	BD	221	DD	253	FD
30	1E	62	3E	94	5E	126	7E	158	9E	190	BE	222	DE	254	FE
31	1F	63	3F	95	5F	127	7F	159	9F	191	BF	223	DF	255	FF

The Hexadecimal system

"Regular" numbers are based on the base 10 system, that is, there are ten symbols (what we call numbers): 0, 1, 2, 3, 4, 5, 6, 7, 8, and 9. To represent numbers greater than 9, we use a combination of these symbols where the first digit specifies how many *ones*, the second digit (to the left) specifies how many *tens*, and so on.

In the hexadecimal system, which is base 16, there are sixteen symbols: 0, 1, 2, 3, 4, 5, 6, 7, 8, 9, a, b, c, d, e, and f. To represent numbers greater than *f* (which in base 10 we understand as *15*), we again use a combination of symbols. This time the first digit specifies how many ones, but the second digit (again, to the left) specifies how many sixteens. Thus, 10 is one *sixteen* and no *ones*, or simply *16* (as represented in base 10).

In addition to colors, you can use hexadecimal numbers to represent special symbols in URLs. Find the corresponding number in the table on pages 355–356, convert it to hexadecimal with the above table and precede it with a percent sign (%). Thus, the space, which is number 32, and has a hexadecimal equivalent of 20, can be represented as %20.

HTML and Compatibility

Like many of the pages you'll find out on the Web, HTML is a language under construction. There are three main driving forces that determine what HTML will look like tomorrow: the World Wide Web Consortium (W3C), Netscape Communications, and Microsoft.

Theoretically, both Netscape and Microsoft have agreed to abide by the decisions of the W3C (of which they are members) in an attempt to maintain HTML's universality. However, the reality is a bit different. These two companies are in a heated battle to determine whose browser is used by the Web-surfing public. If a new extension to HTML will tip the balance in their favor, their agreement with the W3C may be at least momentarily forgotten.

On the following pages, you'll find a list of the HTML tags and attributes described in this book. In the "Vers." or *version* column, I've indicated if the tag or attribute belongs to HTML 4, or if it is only recognized by Netscape (N), by Internet Explorer (IE), or by both (N+IE). That way, you can decide if a given tag is "universal enough" for your page. If a tag is part of standard HTML, it is *probably* supported by both browsers (or will be soon), but you should always test to be sure.

Deprecated tags are marked with a *D* in the Vers. column. Although the W3C doesn't recommend their use, browsers are expected to continue to support these tags for some time.

A special section at the end is devoted to intrinsic events and the HTML elements they can be associated with *(see page 368).*

HTML Tags

TAG/ATTRIBUTE	DESCRIPTION	VERS.
--MOST TAGS--	The following attributes may be used with most HTML tags	
CLASS	For identifying a set of tags in order to apply styles (p. 249)	4
EVENT	For triggering a script (p. 294)	4
ID	For identifying particular tags for JavaScript functions and styles (p. 250)	4
STYLE	For adding local style sheet information (p. 248)	4
TITLE	For labeling elements with tooltips (p. 320)	4
!--	For inserting invisible comments (p. 56)	4
!DOCTYPE	Theoretically required. For indicating version of HTML used (p. 35)	4
A	For creating links and anchors (p. 118)	4
ACCESSKEY	For adding a keyboard shortcut to a link (p. 126)	4
EVENT	For triggering a script (p. 294)	4
HREF	For specifying URL of page or name of anchor that link goes to	4
NAME	For marking a specific area of page that a link might jump to (p. 120)	4
TABORDER	For defining the order in which the Tab key takes the visitor through links and form elements (p. 127)	4
TARGET	For specifying a particular window or frame for a link (pp. 122, 123)	4
ADDRESS	For formatting the e-mail address of the Web page designer (p. 46)	4
APPLET	For inserting applets (p. 237)	4D
CODE	For specifying the URL of the applet's code	4D
WIDTH, HEIGHT	For specifying width and height of an applet	4D
AREA	For specifying coordinates of image maps (p. 130)	4
ACCESSKEY	For adding a keyboard shortcut to a particular region of the map	4
COORDS	For giving coordinates of area in image map	4
HREF	For specifying destination URL of link in area in image map	4
NOHREF	For making a click in image map have no effect	4
SHAPE	For specifying shape of area in image map	4
TARGET	For specifying window or frame that link should be displayed in	4
B	For displaying text in boldface (p. 46)	4
BASE		4
HREF	For specifying the URL to be used to generate relative URLs (p. 123)	4
TARGET	For specifying the default target for the links on the page (p. 123)	4
BASEFONT	For specifying default font specifications throughout page (p. 47)	4D
COLOR	For specifying the default color for text	4D
FACE	For specifying the default font for text	4D
SIZE	For specifying the default size for text	4D
BGSOUND	For inserting background sound for page (p. 225)	IE
LOOP	For specifying how many times sound should play	IE
SRC	For specifying URL of sound	IE
BIG	For making text bigger than surrounding text (p. 49)	4
BLINK	For making text disappear and reappear (p. 55)	N
BLOCKQUOTE	For setting off block of text on page (p. 110)	4

Page numbers are omitted for those attributes discussed on the same page as the tag to which they belong.

HTML Tags

TAG/ATTRIBUTE	DESCRIPTION	VERS.
BODY	For enclosing main section of page (p. 36)	4
ALINK, LINK, VLINK	For specifying color of active links, new links, and visited links (p. 133)	4D
BACKGROUND	For specifying a background image (p. 99)	4D
BGCOLOR	For specifying the background color (p. 98)	4D
LEFTMARGIN, TOPMARGIN	For specifying left and top margins (p. 101)	IE
TEXT	For specifying color of text (p. 50)	4D
BR	For creating a line break (p. 102)	4
CLEAR	For stopping text wrap (pp. 90, 150)	4D
BUTTON	For creating buttons (pp. 207, 209, 296)	4
ACCESSKEY	For adding a keyboard shortcut to a button	4
EVENT	For associating the button with a script	4
NAME	For identifying buttons (perhaps for a JavaScript function)	4
VALUE	For specifying what kind of button to create	4
CAPTION	For creating a caption for a table (p. 145)	4
ALIGN	For placing caption above or below table	4D
CENTER	For centering text, images, or other elements (p. 100)	4D
CITE	For marking text as a citation (p. 46)	4
CODE	For marking text as computer code (p. 54)	4
COL	For joining columns in a table into a non-structural group (p. 160)	4
ALIGN	For specifying alignment of columns in column group	4
SPAN	For specifying number of columns in column group	4
COLGROUP	For joining columns in a table into a structural column group (p. 160)	4
ALIGN	For specifying alignment of columns in column group	4
SPAN	For specifying number of columns in column group	4
DD	For marking a definition in a list (p. 140)	4
DEL	To mark deleted text by striking it out (p. 53)	4
DIV	For dividing a page into logical sections (p. 253)	4
ALIGN	For aligning a given section to left, right, or center	4D
CLASS	For giving a name to each class of divisions	4
ID	For giving a unique name to a particular division	4
DL	For creating a definition list (p. 140)	4
DT	For marking a term to be defined in a list (p. 140)	4
EM	For emphasizing text, usually with italics (p. 46)	4
EMBED	For adding multimedia (and others) to pages (pp. 222, 234)	N+IE
ALIGN	For aligning controls	N+IE
AUTOSTART	For making multimedia event begin automatically	N+IE
CONTROLS	For displaying play, pause, rewind buttons	N+IE
LOOP	For determining if multimedia event should play more than once	N+IE
SRC	For specifying URL of multimedia file	N+IE
WIDTH, HEIGHT	For specifying size of controls	N+IE
FIELDSET	For grouping a set of form elements together (p. 211)	4

Page numbers are omitted for those attributes discussed on the same page as the tag to which they belong.

HTML Tags

Find extra tips, the source code for examples, and more at www.cookwood.com

TAG/ATTRIBUTE	DESCRIPTION	VERS.
FONT	For changing the size, face, and color of individual letters or words	4D
COLOR	For changing text color (p. 51)	4D
FACE	For changing text font (p. 45)	4D
SIZE	For changing text size (p. 48)	4D
FORM	For creating fill-in forms (p. 193)	4
ACTION	For giving URL of CGI script for form	4
METHOD	For determining how form should be processed	4
FRAME	For creating frames (p. 168)	4
BORDER	For determining thickness of frame borders (p. 178)	N+IE
BORDERCOLOR	For determining color of frame borders (p. 177)	N+IE
FRAMEBORDER	For displaying or hiding frame borders (p. 179)	4
FRAMESPACING	For adding space between frames (p. 178)	IE
NAME	For naming frame so it can be used as target (p. 168)	4
NORESIZE	For keeping users from resizing a frame (p. 180)	4
MARGINWIDTH, MARGINHEIGHT	For specifying a frame's left and right, and top and bottom margins (p. 175)	4
SCROLLING	For displaying or hiding a frame's scrollbars (p. 176)	4
SRC	For specifying initial URL to be displayed in frame (p. 168)	4
TARGET	For specifying which frame a link should be opened in (pp. 181, 182)	4
FRAMESET	For defining a frameset (p. 168)	4
BORDER	For determining thickness of frame borders (p. 178)	N+IE
BORDERCOLOR	For determining color of frame borders (p. 177)	N+IE
COLS	For determining number and size of frames (pp. 170, 171)	4
FRAMEBORDER	For displaying or hiding frame borders (p. 179)	4
FRAMESPACING	For adding space between frames (p. 178)	IE
ROWS	For determining number and size of frames (pp. 170, 171)	4
H*n*	For creating headers (p. 38)	4
ALIGN	For aligning headers	4D
HEAD	For creating head section of page (p. 36)	4
HR	For creating horizontal rules (p. 95)	4
ALIGN	For aligning horizontal rules	4D
NOSHADE	For displaying horizontal rules without shading	4D
SIZE	For specifying height of horizontal rule	4D
WIDTH	For specifying width of horizontal rule	4D
HTML	For identifying a text document as an HTML document (p. 35)	4
I	For displaying text in italics (p. 46)	4
IFRAME	For creating floating frames (p. 174)	4
ALIGN	For aligning floating frames	4D
FRAMEBORDER	For displaying or hiding frame borders (p. 179)	4
NAME	For specifying the name of the floating frame, to be used as a target	4
WIDTH, HEIGHT	For specifying size of floating frame	4
SCROLLING	For displaying or hiding scrollbars (p. 176)	4
SRC	For specifying the URL of the initial page	4

Page numbers are omitted for those attributes discussed on the same page as the tag to which they belong.

HTML Tags

TAG/ATTRIBUTE	DESCRIPTION	VERS.
IMG	For inserting images on a page (p. 82)	4
ALIGN	For aligning images (p. 93) and for wrapping text around images (pp. 88, 89)	4D
ALT	For offering alternate text that is displayed if image is not (p. 83)	4
BORDER	For specifying the thickness of the border, if any (pp. 82, 128)	4D
CONTROLS	For displaying or hiding video controls (p. 235)	IE
DYNSRC	For specifying URL of video file (p. 235)	IE
HSPACE, VSPACE	For specifying amount of space above and below, and to the sides of an image (p. 91)	4D
LOOP	For specifying number of repeats of video file (p. 235)	IE
LOWSRC	For specifying URL of low resolution version of image (p. 87)	N+IE
SRC	For specifying URL of image (p. 82)	4
START	For determining when video should begin (p. 235)	IE
USEMAP	For specifying the image map that should be used with the referenced image (p. 130)	4
WIDTH, HEIGHT	For specifying size of image so that page is loaded more quickly, or for scaling (pp. 84, 92)	4
INPUT	For creating form elements (pp. 196, 197, 199, 200, 203, 205, 206, 208)	4
ACCESSKEY	For adding a keyboard shortcut to a form element (p. 214)	4
CHECKED	For marking a radio button or check box by default (pp. 199, 200)	4
DISABLED	For disabling form elements (p. 215)	4
EVENT	For triggering a script with an event like ONFOCUS, ONBLUR, etc.	4
MAXLENGTH	For determining maximum amount of characters that can be entered in form element (pp. 196, 197)	4
NAME	For identifying data collected by this element	4
SIZE	For specifying width of text or password box (pp. 196, 197)	4
SRC	For specifying URL of active image (p. 210)	4
READONLY	For keeping visitors from changing certain form elements (p. 216)	4
TABORDER	For specifying the order in which the Tab key should take a visitor through the links and form elements (p. 213)	4
TYPE	For determining type of form element	4
VALUE	For specifying initial value of form element	4
INS	For marking inserted text with an underline (p. 53)	4
KBD	For marking keyboard text (p. 54)	4
LABEL	For labeling form elements (p. 212)	4
FOR	For specifying which form element the label belongs to	4
LAYER	For positioning elements (p. 114)	N
LEGEND	For labeling fieldsets (p. 211)	4
LI	For creating a list item (p. 136)	4
TYPE	For determining which symbols should begin the list item	4D
VALUE	For determining the initial value of the first list item	4D
LINK	For using an external style sheet (p. 247)	4
MAP	For creating a client-side image map (p. 130)	4
NAME	For naming map so it can be referenced later	4

Page numbers are omitted for those attributes discussed on the same page as the tag to which they belong.

HTML Tags

HTML Tags *(side tab)*

TAG/ATTRIBUTE	DESCRIPTION	VERS.
MARQUEE	For creating moving text (p. 236)	IE
BEHAVIOR	For controlling how the text should move (scroll, slide, alternate)	IE
DIRECTION	For controlling if the text moves from left to right or right to left	IE
LOOP	For specifying how many times the text should come across the screen	IE
SCORLLAMOUNT	For specifying amount of space between each marquee repetition	IE
SCROLLDELAY	For specifying amount of time between each marquee repetition	IE
META		4
HTTP-EQUIV	For creating automatic jumps to other pages (p. 321) and setting the default scripting language (p. 299)	4
NAME	For adding extra information to the Web page (pp. 340, 341, 342, 343)	4
NOBR	For keeping all the enclosed elements on one line (p. 103)	N+IE
NOFRAMES	For providing alternatives to frames (p. 185)	4
NOSCRIPT	For providing alternatives to scripts (p. 298)	4
OBJECT	The W3C would like this tag to eventually replace the IMG and APPLET tags. It is not currently supported very well.	4
OL	For creating ordered lists (p. 136)	4
TYPE	For specifying the symbols that should begin each list item	4D
START	For specifying the initial value of the first list item	4D
OPTGROUP	For dividing a menu into submenus (p. 202)	4
OPTION	For creating the individual options in a form menu (p. 201)	4
SELECTED	For making a menu option be selected by default in a blank form	4
VALUE	For specifying the initial value of a menu option	4
P	For creating new paragraphs (p. 39)	4
ALIGN	For aligning paragraphs	4D
PRE	For displaying text exactly as it appears in HTML document (p. 113)	4
Q	For quoting short passages of text (p. 111)	4
S	(Same as STRIKE) For displaying text with a line through it (p. 53)	4D
SAMP	For displaying sample text—in a monospaced font (p. 54)	4
SCRIPT	For adding "automatic" scripts to a page (p. 292)	4
CHARSET	For specifying the character set an external script is written in (p. 293)	4
LANGUAGE	For specifying the scripting language the script is written in	4D
SRC	For referencing an external script (p. 293)	4
TYPE	For specifying the scripting language the script is written in	4
SELECT	For creating menus in forms (p. 201)	4
NAME	For identifying the data collected by the menu	4
MULTIPLE	For allowing users to choose more than one option in the menu	4
SIZE	For specifying the number of items initially visible in the menu	4
SMALL	For decreasing the size of text (p. 49)	4
SPAN	For creating custom character styles (p. 255)	4
CLASS	For naming individual custom character styles	4
ID	For identifying particular HTML elements	4
STRIKE	(Same as S) For displaying text with a line through it (p. 53)	4D

Page numbers are omitted for those attributes discussed on the same page as the tag to which they belong.

TAG/ATTRIBUTE	DESCRIPTION	VERS.
STRONG	For emphasizing text logically, usually in boldface (p. 46)	4
STYLE	For adding style sheet information to a page (p. 244)	4
SUB	For creating subscripts (p. 52)	4
SUP	For creating superscripts (p. 52)	4
TABLE	For creating tables (p. 145)	4
BGCOLOR	For specifying the background color of the table (p. 158)	4D
BORDER	For specifying the thickness, if any, of the border (p. 146)	4
BORDERCOLOR	For specifying a solid color for the border (p. 146)	IE
BORDERCOLORDARK	For specifying the darker (shaded) color of the border (p. 146)	IE
BORDERCOLORLIGHT	For specifying the lighter (highlighted) color of the border (p. 146)	IE
CELLPADDING	For specifying the amount of space between a cell's contents and its borders (p. 155)	4
CELLSPACING	For specifying the amount of space between cells (p. 155)	4
FRAME	For displaying external borders (p. 163)	4
HEIGHT	For specifying the height of the table (p. 148)	N+IE
RULES	For displaying internal borders (p. 164)	4
WIDTH	For specifying the size of the table (p. 148)	4
TBODY	For identifying the body of the table (p. 162)	4
TD; TH	For creating regular and header cells, respectively, in a table (p. 145)	4
ALIGN, VALIGN	For aligning a cell's contents horizontally or vertically (p. 154)	4
BGCOLOR	For changing the background color of a cell (p. 158)	4D
COLSPAN	For spanning a cell across more than one column (p. 152)	4
NOWRAP	For keeping a cell's contents on one line (p. 165)	4D
ROWSPAN	For spanning a cell across more than one row (p. 153)	4
WIDTH, HEIGHT	For specifying the size of the cell (p. 148)	4D
TEXTAREA	For creating text block entry areas in a form (p. 198)	4
ACCESSKEY	For adding a keyboard shortcut to a text area	4
NAME	For identifying the data that is gathered with the text block	4
ROWS, COLS	For specifying the number of rows and columns in the text block	4
TFOOT, THEAD	For identifying the footer and header area of a table (p. 162)	4
ALIGN	For aligning the footer or header cells (p. 154)	4
TITLE	Required. For creating the title of the page in title bar area (p. 37)	4
TR	For creating rows in a table (p. 145)	4
ALIGN, VALIGN	For aligning contents of row horizontally or vertically (p. 154)	4D
BGCOLOR	For changing color of entire row (p. 158)	4D
TT	For displaying text in monospaced font (p. 54)	4
U	For displaying text with line underneath it (p. 53)	4D
UL	For creating unordered lists (p. 138)	4
TYPE	For specifying the type of symbols that should precede each list item	4D
WBR	For creating discretional line breaks in text enclosed in NOBR tags (p. 104)	N+IE

Page numbers are omitted for those attributes discussed on the same page as the tag to which they belong.

Intrinsic Events

An intrinsic event determines when an associated script will run. However, not every intrinsic event works with every HTML element. This table illustrates which events and tags work together. For more information on associating a script with an intrinsic event, consult *Triggering a Script* on page 294.

EVENT	WORKS WITH	WHEN
ONBLUR	A, AREA, BUTTON, INPUT , LABEL, SELECT, TEXTAREA	the visitor leaves an element that was previously in focus (see ONFOCUS below)
ONCHANGE	INPUT, SELECT, TEXTAREA	the visitor modifies the value or contents of the element
ONCLICK	All elements *except* APPLET, BASE, BASEFONT, BR, FONT, FRAME, FRAMESET, HEAD, HTML, IFRAME, META, PARAM, SCRIPT, STYLE, TITLE	the visitor clicks on the specified area
ONDBLCLICK	Same as ONCLICK	the visitor double clicks the specified area
ONFOCUS	A, AREA, BUTTON, INPUT, LABEL, SELECT, TEXTAREA	the visitor selects, clicks, or tabs to the specified element
ONKEYDOWN	INPUT (of type NAME or PASSWORD), TEXTAREA	the visitor types something in the specified element
ONKEYPRESS	INPUT (of type NAME or PASSWORD), TEXTAREA	the visitor types something in the specified element
ONKEYUP	INPUT (of type NAME or PASSWORD), TEXTAREA	the visitor lets go of the key after typing in the specified element
ONLOAD	BODY, FRAMESET	the page is loaded in the browser
ONMOUSEDOWN	Same as ONCLICK	the visitor presses the mouse button down over the element
ONMOUSEMOVE	Same as ONCLICK	the visitor moves the mouse over the specified element after having pointed at it
ONMOUSEOUT	Same as ONCLICK	the visitor moves the mouse away from the specified element after having been over it
ONMOUSEOVER	Same as ONCLICK	the visitor points the mouse at the element
ONMOUSEUP	Same as ONCLICK	the visitor lets the mouse button go after having clicked on the element
ONRESET	FORM (*not* INPUT of type RESET)	the visitor clicks the form's reset button
ONSELECT	INPUT (of type NAME or PASSWORD), TEXTAREA	the visitor selects one or more characters or words in the element
ONSUBMIT	FORM (*not* INPUT of type SUBMIT)	the visitor clicks the form's submit button
ONUNLOAD	BODY, FRAMESET	the browser loads a different page after the specified page had been loaded

Index

Index

Colophon:

I wrote and laid out this book entirely in Adobe FrameMaker 5.5. I could never have done any of the cross references, figure numbering, and especially the index without it. If you're curious about Frame (or indexing), drop me a line. I'm geeky enough to like to talk about it.

I took screen captures with Paint Shop Pro (Windows) and Flash-It (Macintosh) and then cleaned them up with Adobe Photoshop 5. I used Adobe Illustrator (version 6!) to create the line drawings. The font faces in this book are various weights of Garamond and Futura. The handwriting (like in Figure 9.2 on page 144) is created with a font called Notepad.

Except for the ones in other people's Web sites (obviously), and for the wild animals—which come from the Adobe Image Library (Animal Life)—the photos and drawings in this book are of my own creation, though I'm sometimes embarrased to admit it.

Index

WWB chat!

Whether you're a Web design professional or just putting together a personal Web site, you won't want to miss **HTML with Elizabeth Castro**, a monthly chat from Peachpit Press and World Without Borders, the premier browser-based chat community.

Liz will be there to answer all your tough questions, from creating images and links, to working with tables, frames, forms and more.

Join
LIZ CASTRO
**1st Tuesday
of every month**

**7pm Pacific,
10pm Eastern**

To join the chat
point your browser to
http://www.worldwithoutborders.com
and click CHAT NOW!

Want more great Peachpit authors? Join us every Wednesday at 6pm Pacific, 9pm Eastern for the World Without Borders *Author! Author!* chat series. Each week a different Peachpit author is featured, answering questions and offering expert advice on a specific area. To see what's coming up, go to **http://www.peachpit.com/news/index.html**.

HTTP://WORLDWITHOUTBORDERS.COM